'To be successful in my sport I don't just have ~~ ~~~~ ~~~~. ~ need to make sure I get enough rest and eat good healthy food. This book will help you find the perfect "recipe" to reach your peak performance. Be a complete athlete and don't leave anything to chance.'

Susie O'Neill, Olympic gold medalist (Atlanta 1996) and World Champion in the 200 metres butterfly (Perth 1998)

'With the ever-increasing demands of professional Rugby, it is even more important for players to have an awareness of nutrition and performance. Having a balanced high-carbohydrate diet not only fuels athletes for competition, it also helps the most important aspect of our game—recovery. This is the rule of thumb that I've used throughout my career.'

George Gregan, Australian Wallaby half-back, 1994–

'Peak Performance is a refreshing and challenging mix of the theory of sports scientists, the practicality of coaches, and the dedication of athletes. This combination, most importantly, provides strategies for improvement that will benefit both athletes and coaches in assisting them to achieve their peak performance.'

Paul Thompson, coach of 1995 World Champion women's rowing pair and 1996 Olympic gold medallists, Megan Still and Kate Slater

Dr John Hawley is Associate Professor in the Department of Physiology at the University of Cape Town Medical School, and the Director of the High Performance Laboratory at the Sports Science Institute of South Africa. **Dr Louise Burke** is the Head of the Department of Sports Nutrition at the Australian Institute of Sport, was on the medical team for the Australian athletes at the 1996 Atlanta Olympics, and is the author of *The complete Guide to Food for Sports Performance*. Both authors have participated in elite-level sport themselves, having competed internationally in middle-distance running and triathlon respectively, and are now both well known in sports science research. Between them, they have over 30 years' experience working with elite sportspeople, and in putting together this book they have also called on the contributions of many respected sports scientists, leading coaches and athletes who share the secrets to their success.

Other books by these authors

Clinical Sports Nutrition edited by L.M. Burke and V. Deakin
The Complete Guide to Food for Sports Performance Louise M. Burke

Peak Performance

Training and nutritional strategies for sport

John Hawley and Louise Burke

ALLEN & UNWIN

To our year in Cape Town,
and to the future

First published in 1998 by
Allen & Unwin
9 Atchison Street, St Leonards NSW 1590 Australia
Phone: (61 2) 8425 0100
Fax: (61 2) 9906 2218
E-mail: frontdesk@allen-unwin.com.au
Web: http://www.allen-unwin.com.au

National Library of Australia
Cataloguing-in-Publication entry:

Hawley, John, 1957– .
  Peak performance: training and nutritional strategies for sport.

  Includes index.
  ISBN 1 86448 469 1.

  1. Athletes—Nutrition. 2. Physical education and training.
  3. Sports—Physiological aspects. I. Burke, Louise. II. Title.

613.2024796

Set in 10/12 pt Plantin Light by DOCUPRO, Sydney
Printed and bound by South Wind Production Services, Singapore

10 9 8 7 6 5 4 3 2

Foreword

Professor Tim Noakes

The origins of modern coaching are to be found, it seems, in an unlikely source, for it was from the practitioners of cock fighting and horseracing, perhaps the most popular British sports of the first half of this millenium, that the original sports coaches emerged. Their coaching wisdom, acquired over generations, incorporated four essential components, all considered of equal importance—purging with a popular concoction known as Glauber's salts, sweating by exercising and sleeping in heavy clothing, a liberal diet of stale bread, beer and underdone meat, and finally exercise, especially walking. When boxing and running emerged as the first professional sports for humans, it was natural that these original trainers of animals should become the first trainers of men.

The knowledge of these pioneers was conveyed to successive generations through the spoken word. By the end of the 19th century, this spoken wisdom began to be written and more widely distributed. Yet its content remained the experience of those original coaches, modified perhaps by more widespread exposure.

The strength of this practical wisdom is that it must contain a core of truth—that which does not work seldom survives the harsh scrutiny of competitive sport. But a certain weakness is that its veracity was not validated independently—the scientific method. Furthermore, an alternate truth cannot emerge if all coaches practise a common method.

Two events ensured that blind devotion to a common coaching dogma would not survive forever. The more important was the growing importance of international sporting success, initiated perhaps by the watershed event—the 1968 Mexico City Olympic Games. The initial breach of that final bastion of sporting amateurism began after those Games. The inexorable march of professionalism ensured that future success in Olympic and other sporting competition would no longer be the birthright of the amateur. This development also provided scientific opportunity, for it became conceivable that scientific investigation of coaching techniques and training methods might uncover new paths to success.

It was predictable that a clash loomed between those who practised an honourable profession according to an ancestral wisdom, and those who grasped the challenge of this new opportunity—the sports scientists of the post-1968 Mexico City era. These mavericks, interested in hypothesis, refutation and measurement honed in the confined, yet also confining, enclave of the research laboratory, brought a new inquisitiveness to sport, for they wished to discover the core of the ancestral wisdom that was correct. If purging and sweating were to be advised to modern athletes, then the scientists needed to know that these techniques were, at least, better than doing nothing. In future, athletes would be advised according to information that had the stamp of scientific approval.

But just as part of the historical wisdom is likely to be flawed, so too can be the results of an unrestrained interference by scientists, wise only in the ways of the laboratory. Too few scientists have an adequate understanding of the complexity of international sport, of the human face of training and competition, and of the contribution to success of factors beyond the narrow understanding of laboratory science. Then there are those who consider the study of human sporting excellence to be an undignified luxury, unworthy of those with a grander ambition.

So how is the remaining divide between a historical wisdom and a scientific approach to be traversed? Two ingredients would seem essential—intellect and innovation; the result is coaches who are prepared to interact with those inquisitive scientists who understand both the strengths and limitations of their craft especially when it is applied to the study of complex human biology.

Fortunately, there are some rare individuals who combine the detached analytical mind of the scientist with the practical experiences and insights of the athlete and coach. When they commit that information to text, the results are likely to be revolutionary. Such is this book, which is co-authored by two teachers who have practised the theories of the training turf and locker room, who have experienced the anguish of competition, and who have learned the reason of the laboratory.

John Hawley is Associate Profesor of Physiology at the University of Cape Town Medical School, and the Scientific Director of the High Performance Laboratory at the Sports Science Institute of South Africa. In both these roles, he combines his practical experience as a competitive athlete and consultant to a broad range of elite athletes in both individual and team sports, with a compulsion to study the practical issues that daily confront superior athletes. Indeed his doctoral studies of fuel metabolism during exercise have identified the optimum type and amount of carbohydrate necessary for ingestion during prolonged exercise, information of substantial practical value. He is also one of few modern scientists to analyse systematically how different training programs can optimise racing performance and the physiological changes that result. This work has established the value of adding a few bouts of high intensity training to the more standard diet of high volume training.

Louise Burke is an essential cog in one of the most remarkable phenomena in modern sport, the rise of Australia as perhaps currently the most successful sporting nation, particularly in Olympic competition. Louise makes her contribution through her position as Head of the Department of Nutrition at the Australian Institute of Sport, the core ingredient for the Australian success. Her sporting apprenticeship was served in the cauldron that is the Hawaiian Ironman triathlon, which she has completed seven times. Her practical expertise has been gained over seventeen seasons working with elite and recreational athletes from numerous codes, culminating in her appointment in 1996 as the first sports dietician to travel with an Australian Olympic team. Her scientific training has produced a range of important practical contributions including two international best-selling books on sport nutrition.

Their combined wisdom and experience has produced a compelling and up-to-date evaluation of how science views that which is currently believed and practised by the world's best athletes in a variety of sports. It promotes the global view that a host of factors both within and outside the athlete's body influence his or her performance. It provides the scientific understanding of the technical and physiological requirements for success in a variety of sports. It details the physiological, biochemical and performance changes that are produced by different training methods, by rest and by dietary factors, and how these may be influenced by the athlete's unique individual characteristics. No popular belief or popular training practice has escaped the authors' cold logic and meticulous evaluation. The result is this definitive, practical, one-stop-guide for any serious athlete, coach or researcher wishing to discover what science currently believes about any of the common sporting theories and practices.

This book has defined the field. The sporting future belongs to its owners.

May their (more) scientific training begin!

Professor Tim Noakes
University of Cape Town
December 1997

Contents

Figures

Tables

Boxes

Preface

Many of the 'magic moments' in our lives are provided by sport. We are inspired and uplifted as we watch the achievements of the world's best. For at least two weeks every four years, our emotions are captured by their triumphs and tragedies. Between times we are drawn to our own sporting interests as competitor and spectator.

Hopefully among the readers of this book will be a few athletes who are rewarded for their efforts with fame, financial reward, and even a place in history. But for the most part, sport is undertaken for more personal reasons—to enjoy the camaraderie, the good health and the thrill of reaching within yourself to find the best. It is for these last reasons that this book has been written.

Whether your goal is to achieve an Olympic gold medal, to win the final in a local competition, or just to finish an endurance event with a smile on your face, there is a shared bottom line. All athletes strive to improve from a starting point and to reach the limits of their potential. Their tools are effective training, a sound nutrition plan, the right outlook, and suitable equipment. You cannot plan the genetic potential that your parents bestowed on you. But you can certainly plan strategies to rise to this level. This book focuses on optimal training and nutrition strategies.

The book starts with a look at the contributions certain legendary coaches have made to training. This trial-and-error approach has produced some great sports performances, but it is a slow and costly way to achieve results. We offer the alternative of a scientific approach to training and nutrition.

Throughout the book we develop a summary of state-of-the-art knowledge and practice from sports scientists around the world. A new understanding of the principles of training and of the body's power systems allows us to develop separate training strategies for endurance, team and power sports. Getting it right on the day requires a number of special fine-tuning practices.

Nutrition for the athlete encompasses strategies to keep the athlete in shape, healthy and on the right side of the fine line of fatigue. Creative practices before, during and after the event will help to optimise performance in all training and competition sessions. Recovery is the buzz word in both situations and requires a practical approach. Supplements are of great interest to athletes. We examine which ones are worth considering and how best to use them. We also provide some guidelines to help athletes understand when to believe the claims made for new products and training strategies.

Finally, we have invited prominent sports scientists and coaches to help us take a look into the future. How will performance improve in a number of sports? What will it take to be stonger, swifter and higher in the next decade?

We hope this book will help you to achieve these goals in your sport.

Acknowledgements

During the past eight years we have both had the privilege of working (hard) alongside some of the best sports scientists, athletes and coaches in our respective countries. In South Africa, Professor Tim Noakes, athlete, academic, author, philosopher and mentor, has readily shared his vast knowledge and provided the most stimulating environment any scientist could hope to work in. In addition, Tim found time to write the foreword for this book, for which we are very grateful. The establishment of the Sports Science Institute of South Africa, as an extension of the the Bioenergetics of Exercise Reseach Unit of the University of Cape Town, has allowed the opportunity to put theory into practice. The staff of the High Performance Laboratory, in particular Justin Durandt and Nicola Scales, have been instrumental in undertaking physiological testing of many of South Africas national teams, and we thank them for making some of their data available for this book.

The Australian Institute of Sport is now world renowned as a centre of coaching and scientific excellence. To work 'at the coal face' and in the company of such a wonderful team has been a privilege. It is not hard to thrive in the motivating atmosphere of the Sports Science and Sports Medicine building, and with the example set by Dr Allan Hahn in the Department of Physiology and Applied Nutrition, and Professor Peter Fricker in the Department of Sports Medicine. The support of the members (past and present) of the Department of Sports Nutrition is also gratefully acknowledged. We are grateful for the generosity of these work places in allowing us to undertake a sabbatical exchange program. This provided an opportunity to take stock of our present knowledge and experience, learn from a new environment, and recharge our batteries towards future goals. From a more practical viewpoint, it allowed us to be on the same continent (in Cape Town) to write this book together.

We thank our publishers, Allen & Unwin, for the opportunity to write the book; particularly Patrick Gallagher for his confidence that we would deliver a manuscript of appropriate length in the stipulated time frame, and our editor Lynne Frolich who transformed the manuscript into a book. We also thank Glenda Gouws and Elske Schabort for their unpaid administrative help and reliability.

We gratefully acknowledge the following sports scientists who contributed their knowledge and experience in special panels throughout the book: Sherryle Calder, Dr Will Hopkins, Dr David Martin, Dr Mike McCoy, Dr David Pyne, Dr Richard Stretch and Doug Tumilty

In addition, the following coaches were generous and brave enough to commit their insights and predictions of future performances in their respective sports to paper: Peter Keen, Professor Dick Telford, Daniel Topolski and Gennadi Tourestski.

Finally we pay tribute to the many athletes, coaches, fellow scientists and graduate students whose commitment and achievements continue to provide motivation and inspiration. Sport and sports science are both founded on blood, sweat and tears!

Part I

LEARNING FROM THE PAST: WHAT THE GREAT COACHES HAVE TAUGHT US

1

The evolution of training: The trial-and-error method

'Training is principally an act of faith.'

> Franz Stamfl, British coach of Roger Bannister, first man to break four minutes for the mile

'The training of athletes for strenuous physical activity today is much an art and less of a science.'

> Forbes Carlile, legendary Australian swimming coach whose swimmers included Terry Gathercole and Shane Gould

'For years I ran many kilometres trying to find the correct balance for my conditioning training. I knew you could both under-train and overtrain in both mileage and effort. I ran from extremes of 80 to 500 kilometres a week at close to my best aerobic effort.'

> Arthur Lydiard, New Zealand distance running coach, commenting on his trial-and-error methods

'The early competitions revealed serious flaws in his methods of attaining fitness, so he continued changing patterns and gradually evolved his basic theory. A need to perfect his system drove him to further refinements.'

> Garth Gilmour, sports writer, commenting on Arthur Lydiard's training methods

'Training methods, being dependent on more factors than it is possible at present to analyse, are likely to remain empirical.'

> Sir Roger Bannister

'The most important factor in coaching is to be yourself. A lot of coaches try to copy other coaches or other programs. There's a lot of discussion on whether a coach should be scientific or whether one should coach as if it's an art. Every coach should find a personal way of coaching . . . the way that is best for oneself, because, first of all, coaching is the art of communication.'

> Gennadi Touretski, coach of Alexandre Popov, 1992 and 1996 Olympic champion for 50 and 100 metres freestyle, and Michael Klim, 1998 World Champion for 100 metres butterfly and 200 metres freestyle

During the past century a select group of coaches has consistently produced successful athletes or teams. In turn, these coaches have been credited with developing certain training systems, many of which have had an important and long-lasting impact on our current view of the physical preparation of athletes for competitive sport.

While the successes of these coaches are inspiring, nevertheless, they rely heavily on a trial-and-error approach. An element inherent in this technique is a risk-taking personality, often to the point of flamboyance and eccentricity. Such coaches must have the vision and conviction in their beliefs to tread unknown paths. The disadvantage is that often there is error in this technique: more 'miss' than 'hit'. Indeed, it may take many years to refine and perfect a certain technique before the rewards are evident. And sometimes, athletes and opportunities are lost forever when an experiment fails or a novel technique is imperfect.

The other disadvantage of the trial-and-error method is that it can be likened to a 'shotgun approach' wherein a number of factors are continually being changed, often at the same time, in an attempt to determine the 'right mix'. If performance *does* improve, it is often difficult to identify the precise reason why. A coach may just have been lucky enough to stumble across an athlete of exceptional genetic talent. No matter *how* that athlete was trained, they would have improved! But the fact remains that the empirical, field-based observations of coaches have had, by far, the greatest impact on the training practices of today's athletes. Here we acknowledge the contribution that a handful of great coaches have made to sport science over the years.

EMIL ZATOPEK (Czechoslovakia)

As an athlete, Emil Zatopek had few peers. He broke eighteen world records and won five Olympic medals, four of them gold. But as his own coach, he was an innovator and leader, going where no-one else had dared.

He was fascinated by human physiology. To Zatopek the body was like traffic moving in a city, controlled in a system. Where there was a block, some help was needed. He reasoned that the more you learned, the better you would be. Soon after starting to run seriously, he abandoned other coaches and their methods and started thinking for himself, training his own way. And this training was longer and harder than any other coach or athlete thought possible. He ran every day, often three times. Others tried to run with him, but usually quit long before he finished. But he did not train hard all the time, and he knew the importance of rest while preparing for big races.

The basis of Zatopek's training for long-distance running was speed and stamina. He extended the interval training systems pioneered by German coach Woldemar Gerschler. But his methods were somewhat unorthodox. He developed speed by running short distances, such as 100 metres. This was crazy, other runners told him: he wasn't a sprinter. He developed stamina by running these short distances many times, with short recoveries. Stamina through speed. These training methods paid dividends. In the 1948 Olympics he won the 10,000 metres and was second in the 5000 metres.

By 1951 Zatopek had modified his training to include many repetitions over longer distances. He constantly experimented with different workouts, always trying to think of new ways to train. He ran on the spot, pumping his knees almost to chin height; he ran in the snow with heavy boots on his feet and he practised holding his breath until he collapsed. One winter he decided to experiment with weight training. This included several hours of riding a stationary bike with weights on each foot, followed by hundreds of repetitions of knee bends with weights on his shoulders. He abandoned these training techniques after running poorly the next season.

His best known and most publicised workout leading up to the 1952 Olympics was twenty times 200 metres, followed by forty times 400 metres, then another twenty 200 metres, all with just a 200 metre jog between runs. It is difficult to know just how fast these training sessions were, because

Zatopek never timed himself. But the results were phenomenal. At the 1952 Helsinki Olympic Games he won both the 5000 metres and the 10,000 metres. Three days later he defeated then world-record holder, Britain's Jim Peters in the marathon.

Sadly, Zatopek's running and lifestyle were largely controlled by the communist regime under which he lived in Czechoslovakia. With the fall of the Iron Curtain he virtually disappeared from world view. Although he coached his wife, Dana, to the javelin gold medal in the 1952 Olympics, he never really had a formal opportunity to pursue his passion for the sport which shaped his life. Nevertheless, Zatopek's innovative methods, incorporating huge volumes of running combined with plenty of interval training, were followed by athletes for the next quarter-century. Singlehandedly, he changed the notion of how much training a runner could handle.

Major coaching highlights

1948 Olympic Games, London
Emil Zatopek, gold medal (10,000 metres) silver medal (5000 metres)
1952 Olympic Games, Helsinki
Emil Zatopek, gold medal (5000 metres)
Emil Zatopek, gold medal (10,000 metres)
Emil Zatopek, gold medal (marathon)
World records
Eighteen throughout his career
1952 Olympic Games, Helsinki
Dana Zatopek, gold medal (javelin)

Summing up

'Why should I practise running slow? I already know how to run slow. I must learn how to run fast.'

'You must be fast enough. You must have endurance. So you run fast for speed and repeat it many times for endurance.'

PERCY CERUTTY (Australia)

Born in the working-class suburb of Prahran in Melbourne in 1895, Percy Cerutty was a weak, sickly, underprivileged child who overcame lack of opportunities and a frail physique to eventually become a better than average athlete. A perfectionist who demanded total commitment from everyone he met, Cerutty became one of the most outspoken and dynamic coaches of all time. His approach to training and racing mirrored his philosophy on life: it wasn't good enough just to win; you had to win well, dynamically and aggressively. More than anything else, Cerutty demanded character and strength in an athlete. He believed that only the self-disciplined could demand genuine respect. It was an outlook on life that made good sense to him, even though it was often extreme.

At the age of 44, Cerutty was given six months' sick-leave from work to try and restore his failing health. He was, he said, 'at death's door'. During his enforced rest, Cerutty had time to read and think. On his long walks along the banks of the River Yarra he evolved a new approach to life, an approach he believed would either kill or cure him. Driven by an iron willpower and never-say-die attitude, he began his rehabilitation program by running on the sand-dunes and later lifting weights. He became so fit that he decided to start a career in athletics and became one of Australia's outstanding long-distance runners. At the age of 51 he covered 101 miles (162 kilometres) in under 24 hours, and set records at several other distances. But just as important, he knew he had discovered conditioning methods that could help athletes reach new levels of performance. He quit his job and started coaching full-time.

Cerutty's training methods were considered brutal. They included frequent weekend training camps near his beach-side home in Portsea. Here Cerutty and his athletes ate only uncooked, natural foods and lived the spartan lifestyle he espoused. The camps included exhaustive interval sessions up steep sand-dunes, fartlek running on the beach, long runs of two hours or more, and extensive weight training. One of his teachings was that the upper body was equally as important as the lower body in running. Indeed, Cerutty believed that all athletes should be strong and powerful. In particular, he spent many hours working on the basic techniques of running and lifting. He recommended that athletes from all sports spend at least a third of their time either weight training or participating in activities which were unrelated to their sport.

The emphasis on speed through power and strength was his unique contribution to the modern-day concept of training.

Cerutty's first protégé was John Landy, who broke Roger Bannister's world mile record in 1954 (3:57.9). But his most famous pupil was Herb Elliot, world-record holder (3:54.5) and Olympic 1500 metre champion (3:35.6), who retired undefeated at the age of 22 after 36 mile races and nine 1500 metre races. Elliot, the athlete, epitomised everything Cerutty, the coach, stood for. He didn't just win races, he annihilated all opposition in the process!

Major coaching highlights

1960 Empire Games, Cardiff
Herb Elliot, gold medal (mile)
1960 Olympic Games, Rome
Herb Elliot, gold medal and world record (1500 metres)
World records
John Landy, mile (3:57.9), 1954
Herb Elliot, 1500 metres (3:36.0), 1958
Herb Elliot, mile (3:54.4), 1958
Elliot ran—and won—36 mile races and nine 1500 metre races between 1957 and 1961.
1954 Empire Games, Vancouver
John Landy, silver medal (mile)
1956 Olympic Games, Melbourne
John Landy, bronze medal (1500 metres)

Summing up

'Never curb your emotion. Put the whole of yourself into everything that you do. Only then will you find a great champion.'

ARTHUR LYDIARD (New Zealand)

It is doubtful whether any coach will have more impact on the training practices of endurance athletes than this New Zealander. Arthur Lydiard revolutionised training with regard to the volume of work he thought athletes should perform in their conditioning phase. His programs were simple, based on a consistent, thorough and direct application of hard work. Lots of it.

A soccer player originally, Lydiard was amazed at the haphazard and casual way in which most team players prepared for their sport. Realising he was nowhere near fit for his sport, he began experimenting, running a wide range of distances—sometimes up to 500 kilometres a week—in an attempt to find the correct stimulus for his conditioning phase of training.

Lydiard's trial-and-error approach to training was not without its shortcomings, however. His early methods exposed serious flaws, and only gradually did he evolve his basic theory. A need to perfect his system drove him to many refinements, but eventually he became New Zealand's top marathon runner. Lydiard believed that most athletes should run up to 160 kilometres a week at their *best maximum steady-state pace*, a philosophy that was to become the cornerstone of his training methods. No matter whether the event was the mile or the marathon, building stamina through volume was an essential prerequisite to the specialised training that followed. Lydiard claimed that athletes who undertook aerobic marathon training improved their condition faster and better than athletes using anaerobic interval training. Indeed, he saw staleness as a physiological reaction caused by too much anaerobic training. His system of aerobic base training has been applied to the conditioning of team players, squash players, canoeists and many other sportspeople.

Unfortunately, many athletes and coaches have misinterpreted Lydiard's conditioning phase as being merely 160 kilometres a week of long slow distance running. This was not his strategy. Neither was it a rigid requirement. His athletes were regularly running 160 km a week at their *best aerobic effort* but, in addition, were supplementing their training with easier morning and evening sessions, often totalling up to 250 km a week. Lydiard advocated running year-round, and pointed out that an athlete training six days a week could not hope to beat one who trained every day. He reasoned that anyone who lost 52 days of training a year would not have optimum results.

But perhaps just as important a contribution to athletic training was Lydiard's concept of periodisation. He knew that an athlete could not train hard and perform well simultaneously. As such, he mixed the different types of conditioning—long mileage, hill work, speed work, sharpening and freshening—so that his runners arrived at the start line at their peak.

But it wasn't all plain sailing. Although his success led to a number of overseas coaching appointments, including spells in Venezuela, Mexico and Scandinavia, Lydiard was initially ignored in his native New Zealand. And during his stay in Scandinavia he was continually at odds with the Swedish sports scientists (considered at the time to be the best in the world) about his methods of training. But his record speaks for itself. Among his most famous athletes were Peter Snell, Murray Halberg, Barry Magee and John Davies, who between them won four Olympic gold and two bronze medals.

Major coaching highlights

1960 Olympic Games, Rome
Peter Snell, gold medal (1500 metres)
Murray Halberg, gold medal (5000 metres)
Barry Magee, bronze medal (marathon)
1964 Olympic Games, Tokyo
Peter Snell, gold medal (800 metres)
Peter Snell, gold medal (1500 metres)
John Davies, bronze medal (1500 metres)
World records
Peter Snell, 800 metres (1:44.3), 1962
Peter Snell, 1000 metres (2:16.6), 1964
Peter Snell, mile (3:54.4), 1962
Peter Snell, mile (3:54.1), 1964

Summing up

'Long even-paced running at strong speed increases strength and endurance, even when it is continued close to the point of collapse.'

'Successful training is intelligent training. Intelligent training is knowing the why of an exercise, as well as the what and how.'

PETER COE (United Kingdom)

Peter Coe devoted almost two decades to full-time coaching, an effort that resulted in twelve world records and four Olympic medals for his son, Sebastian. It is highly unlikely that there will ever be such a sustained coach–athlete partnership in athletics again. Nor such a successful one.

Peter Coe was a self-taught coach. Early in his career he read widely on exercise physiology and talked to many international experts on the different methods of training available at the time. He also attended numerous conferences on the physical preparation of athletes given by many of the world's leading sports scientists. He quickly realised that the scientists did not have the answers to most of his questions and he began to devise his own long-term training objectives for his young son, who he realised had the potential to become one of the fastest runners of all time. Coe also knew that in order to fully realise this potential, traditional coaching techniques had to be modified in order to suit his athlete.

The trial-and-error approach was not for Peter Coe. Instead, he opted for specialised event analysis, the scientific formulation of training programs based on frequent physiological testing and monitoring of his athlete, event-specific strength training, and a long-term outlook on racing. He was not an advocate of high mileage, believing that the 800 metres was mostly a 'sustained sprint'. He estimated the proportion of anaerobic and aerobic energy production for the half-mile to be 70–30, and not the 55–45 proposed by sports scientists and other coaches. He continually adapted existing training principles to the needs and specialities of his own athlete.

Sebastian Coe was very small and light for a middle-distance runner, so Peter had him develop speed through resistance training and quality hill workouts. At the time, resistance and circuit training for middle-distance runners was virtually unheard of, but Peter Coe recruited coach and biomechanist George Gandy, from Loughborough University, to assist with these specialised components of winter training. He also sought help from Dr Dave Martin, a leading American exercise physiologist who, at the time, worked with a number of America's top middle- and long-distance runners. Based on the results of many physiological tests, training was evaluated, fine-tuned and then reassessed.

But it was for his long-term planning, and the conviction that he was doing things right for his athlete, that Peter Coe will best be remembered. When Sebastian Coe came back from serious illness and injury and won his second Olympic gold medal for the 1500 metres in the 1984 Los Angeles Olympic Games, no-one could doubt Peter Coe's coaching ability.

Major coaching highlights

1980 Olympic Games, Moscow
Sebastian Coe, gold medal (1500 metres)
Sebastian Coe, silver medal (800 metres)
1984 Olympic Games, Los Angeles
Sebastian Coe, gold medal (1500 metres)
Sebastian Coe, silver medal (800 metres)
1982 European Championships, Athens
Sebastian Coe, silver medal (800 metres)
1986 European Championships, Stuttgart
Sebastian Coe, gold medal (800 metres)
Sebastian Coe, silver medal (1500 metres)
World records
Sebastian Coe, 800 metres (1:42.33), 1979
Sebastian Coe, 800 metres (1:41.73), 1981
Sebastian Coe, 1000 metres (2:13.40), 1980
Sebastian Coe, 1000 metres (2:12.18), 1981
Sebastian Coe, 1500 metres (3:32.03), 1979
Sebastian Coe, mile (3:48.95), 1979
Sebastian Coe, mile (3:48.53), 1981
Sebastian Coe, mile (3:47.33), 1981

Summing up

'At fourteen I knew he was good. At sixteen I felt a strange kind of certainty that if I was patient I had a world beater.'

'Think like a good modern industrial manager: identify your short-term and long-term objectives, marshall your resources and coordinate your help. Above all, think first, and only then act with conviction.'

Part II

LEARNING FROM SCIENCE

'I couldn't believe that so many athletes were working without a training plan, and simply by instinct, which typically was to do too much.'

Dave Martin, exercise physiologist and adviser to Sebastian Coe

'So much coaching is hit and miss, coaches giving you sessions without knowing why. Everything should have a reason, a scientific base. Every time I went out the door, the session had a purpose, a means to an end. That is where so many get it wrong.'

Wendy Sly, 1983 Olympic 3000 metre silver medallist

'We are all our own sports scientists in a way. We have got to experiment, we have got to listen and try new ideas. No matter how long you have been doing a sport, there is always something more you can learn.'

Linford Christie, Olympic 100 metre track champion, 1992

Our current knowledge of training techniques has evolved largely as a result of the trial-and-error observations of a few innovative coaches and the outstanding performances of their athletes. For the most part, sports science has played an 'after-the-fact' role, explaining the mechanisms of why certain training practices work. Up until the past few years there have been few breakthroughs from sports scientists arising from laboratory-based investigations with top performers. This is

15

because most coaches are very reluctant to change or even modify their training recommendations, many of which have been nurtured and perfected over many decades and are firmly entrenched as coaching lore. Persuading successful athletes to experiment with their training programs for the purpose of scientific inquiry has had limited success.

Nowadays it is acknowledged that sports science is making valid contributions to assist coaches in the preparation of their athletes. With recent advances in athlete testing and monitoring of fitness, nutrition and ergogenic aids, equipment and technology, science is assuming a more prospective and proactive role in the preparation of athletes from a growing number of sports. At various locations throughout the world, such as the Australian Institute of Sport in Canberra, the Sports Science Institute of South Africa in Cape Town, and the United States Olympic Training Centre at Colorado Springs, sports scientists and coaches have been working together in order to prepare athletes in their quest for new levels of performance. Indeed, it is highly likely that any future innovations in training techniques and the subsequent improvements in athletic performance will have been accomplished as a result of this closer working relationship between coach, athlete and those sports scientists who possess a comprehensive and practically based knowledge of the physiology of specialised athletic events.

2

Scientific principles of physical training

'It was not on the rugby field but in the sports laboratory that our secret lay. The secret to our success (if there was one) was the scientifically based program of physical preparation which we began implementing among Australia's elite players in late 1989.'

> Bob Dwyer, former coach of the Australian Wallabies, who won the 1991 Rugby World Cup, and currently coach of the Leicester Tigers

'The thinking must be done first, before training begins.'

> Peter Coe, coach and father of Sebastian Coe

'Training must be systematic, which means it must be thorough, regular and organised.'

> Connie Carpenter, 1984 Olympic cycling road race champion

'A systematic approach to training is one of the key factors in becoming a successful athlete. It is not enough to know how to do something, you must know why you're doing it.'

> Greg LeMond, three-time winner of the Tour de France

'It's not always the best athletes who win the big ones: it's the best-prepared ones, those who are completely ready on the vital day.'

> Arthur Lydiard, New Zealand distance running coach

Improvements in performance in any sport require:

- careful systematic planning;
- the application of appropriate training and nutritional programs;
- an injury-free build-up to a competitive peak;
- sound tactical strategies;
- optimal environmental conditions; and
- on the day of a competition, a fair measure of luck!

Success is much more likely if an athlete or team has trained hard and maintained a careful program based on scientific training principles, than if they have adopted a haphazard, hit-or-miss approach to their physical preparation.

The final outcome of any planned training program is the athlete's or team's performance on a specified day in a given competitive situation. Most sports lend themselves well to objective scientific analysis because measures of success, such as winning or losing, or improving a personal best performance, are easily observed and quantified. During training and subsequent competitive efforts, the sports scientist and the coach should determine the most important factor(s) which are likely to affect an athlete's performance and then, if practical, systematically manipulate these variables in an attempt to improve performance. The challenge for the coach is first to isolate and change a single important component of performance, and then to observe the effect on competition success. In practice, however, this is not easy. Hence, the physical preparation of athletes for competition will never be a total science, and nor is it the intent of this book to portray it as such.

Nevertheless, the performances of some of the great athletes and successful teams of the past and present suggest that the human body responds in a relatively predictable and uniform manner to daily training and that these responses can be measured with a high degree of precision. As such, several widely accepted training principles have evolved which are common to most sports and have been studied extensively by sports scientists. When these basic principles are combined with the practical, field-based observations of many coaches, they can provide a framework on which to base more precise and comprehensive sports-specific training recommendations.

PROGRESSIVE OVERLOAD

'Nature has given the human body a wonderful engine management system. It actually responds to stress by adapting to cope with it better.'

> Peter Keen, exercise physiologist and coach of Chris Boardman, world champion British cyclist

'Traditionally you get three choices: train hard, train hard, or train harder.'

> Richard Dale and Colin Cameron, in *The contenders*

The overload principle states that habitually overloading a physiological system will cause it to respond and adapt to that stressor—in this case, physical training. The principle of progressive overload states that once an athlete has adapted to a certain training load, the subsequent training stimulus must be progressively increased in order to achieve a further and improved adaptation. Overload can be quantified according to the volume of training (how much), the intensity, load or perceived effort of training (how hard), and the frequency of training (how often). The magnitude of adaptation of any training program is dependent on the interaction between these variables, as well as on the initial level of fitness of the athlete.

Volume overload: How much?

'It's a foolish idea that if you do a little more, faster, then you'll get better than the rest. It ignores the fact that you must train at your optimal level, not your maximum level.'

> Rob de Castella, Australian champion marathon runner (2:08:18)

'If you want to run your ideal marathon, ask yourself what you think would be the maximum, absolute top mileage that you could run. Then chop twenty per cent off that!'

> Alberto Salazar, 2:08:13 marathoner and Comrades ultra-marathon winner

'I don't think we are doing the right type of training and the right volume of training. One of the trends in world swimming through the eighties has been towards a more sprint-oriented, high-intensity,

low-volume program, particularly coming out of North America. I think this certainly has set distance swimming back.'

> Dr David Pyne, swimming physiologist at the Australian Institute of Sport

'Provided you watch the degree of effort, you can't really do too much.'

> Arthur Lydiard, New Zealand distance running coach

'He or she who trains the most does not necessarily improve the most or perform the best.'

> Connie Carpenter, twelve-time US champion cyclist

'The first week's training program included a total of nine outings on the water. The morning outings were scheduled for one-and-a-half hours, whilst afternoon rowing was scheduled from 1.30–5.00 p.m. On top of the rowing they were scheduled to complete three sessions in the gym, each two hours long, with track running to finish, one timed run, and a sixteen-minute workout on the ergometer to be completed in the rowers' spare time. This program was just the beginning: it was customary to start the season slowly and build up the amount of time and the intensity of training.'

> Alison Gill, international rower, describing the training program set by Oxford University rowing coach, Dan Topolski

'It was hard to envisage spending any more time training!'

> Oxford University rower

It is assumed by many coaches and athletes that improvements in performance are directly related to the amount of work performed during training, and that an athlete can only reach their full potential by undertaking extremely long and arduous training. Although the volume of exercise is one of the key variables known to determine the degree of adaptation to training, there is obviously some limit beyond which further increases in training volume are not beneficial for athletic performance. The phenomenon of adding more and more units of input (training) which result in a progressively smaller output (improvement in performance) has been termed 'the law of diminishing returns' by economists. Simply restated, more is not always better, and there are many cases where athletes subjected to excess volume overload have reported an increased number of injuries, a higher rate of infectious illnesses due to a continually suppressed immune system and, in extreme cases, psychological disturbances.

Fortunately, there is now some scientific evidence, at least for swimmers, that such severe training may not necessarily lead to enhanced performances. Professor Dave Costill at Ball State University, Indiana, has evaluated the influence of volume overload on the performances of well-trained college swimmers. During one season Costill—himself a world age-group record holder in the pool—persuaded the head swim coach, Bob Thomas, to divide his 24-member male squad into two groups. One group trained for two sessions each day (approximately three hours' pool time), covering a distance of approximately 10,000 m. The other group swam only once each day, for a total distance of approximately 5000 m. These different training regimens were maintained for six weeks, at which time swimming performances over a wide range of distances were determined. As might be expected, the group that trained massive over-distance (two sessions per day) improved over the longest distance (3000 yds) by 2.9%. However, this group swam 1.0–1.5% slower in the shorter sprint events (50 and 100 yds). In contrast, the performances of the group who trained only once each day remained the same for the sprint events but showed a similar improvement (2.5%) as that for the twice-a-day group in the longer (3000 yds) distance. Thus, evidence from this study does not support the concept that such extensive over-distance training is required to maximise conditioning and enhance swimming performance.

Although it is tempting to recommend that all swimmers confine their training to less than 5000 m per day, it is difficult to extrapolate the results of this study to swimmers of vastly different levels of ability, or to take into consideration the effect a taper might have had on these swimmers' performances. Nevertheless, the fact that increasing the volume of training twofold impaired sprint swim speed, while also failing to improve performance over the longer distances to a greater degree than that achieved by the swimmers training only once each day, leads to the assumption that such volume overload may not be necessary for optimal swimming performance.

Although other studies with athletes from a variety of

sports need to be conducted to confirm these results, it is clear that volume overload may not be the most important determinant of successful performance.

Intensity overload: How hard?

'Quality running rather than quantity is what will make you a better runner, no matter what your level of ability.'

> Grete Waitz, nine-time winner of the New York City marathon

'The idea that the harder you work the better you're going to be is just garbage. The greatest improvement is made by the man who works most intelligently.'

> Bill Bowerman, running coach at the University of Oregon

'Train smarter, not harder.'

> Rob de Castella, world marathon champion, 1983

'I learned years ago when I was training about 24 kilometres a day that if I shifted the daily balance to 32 kilometres one day and 16 the next, I got better reactions without increasing the total distance I was running.'

> Arthur Lydiard, marathon runner and coach

There is currently much debate among coaches of endurance athletes centring around the question of whether 'quality' (intensity overload) or 'quantity' (volume overload) produces the best training effect and subsequent performance. Yet, paradoxically, this aspect of the overload principle, which is probably the most critical to successful performance, is the least well studied by sports scientists.

Intensity overload refers to the relative severity of a training stimulus. This can be accurately quantified in most training sessions according to either the speed of movement (for sports such as running, swimming or cycling), the mass lifted (during weight training), or the power generated by an athlete (on a stationary ergometer). With the advent of portable, accurate heart-rate monitors, it is now possible to measure the exact intensity of a training session according to the physiological load it places on the athlete's cardiovascular system (see Chapter 8). Regardless of how it is quantified, the greater the intensity overload, the more prolonged is the resultant fatigue and the longer the period of recovery needed before the same load can be performed again. Recovery might refer to the rest period needed between successive work bouts performed in the same training session (referred to as an interval), or the time required for an athlete to recover between intense training sessions undertaken on different days.

In an attempt to investigate the effect of intensity overload on performance, Dr Inigo Mujika and colleagues at Jean Monnet University in France studied eighteen experienced national- and international-level sprint swimmers (100 metre and 200 metre specialists) during the course of a competitive season. All workouts over the season were timed for each swimmer and the mean intensity of the training sessions categorised from intensity level I (easy) to intensity level IV (maximal intensity sprinting). In addition to their normal water training, all swimmers undertook supervised dry-land workouts. The major finding of this study was that a positive relationship was observed between improvements in seasonal swim performances and the mean intensity of the swimmers' training sessions. On the other hand, there was no relationship between either training frequency or volume, and the subsequent improvements in performance. These results suggest that for swimmers whose event lasts less than two minutes, intensity overload, rather than volume or frequency overload, was the key factor in producing a training effect, leading to improvements in performance (also see Chapter 5).

But athletes cannot train intensely every workout. Nor, indeed, should they attempt to. In organising a weekly training schedule for his runners, Bill Bowerman, a track coach at the University of Oregon for more than a quarter of a century, observed that in order to achieve the desired training impulse (volume × intensity × frequency) he needed to adopt a 'hard-day/easy-day' training pattern for his athletes. Such an approach involved alternating very intense days of running (intensity overload) with one or more easier days of less intense, but more prolonged runs (volume overload). This systematic approach to the structure of a training program is based on the physiological premise that any adaptation to a training stimulus requires a period of recovery or restoration before further training-induced responses are possible. Indeed, recovery is an integral part of any well-structured training program. Bowerman's hard/easy system of training was very successful. Among his most famous athletes were the late Steve Prefontaine, who once held every American record on the track from 3000 metres up to 10,000 metres; Alberto Salazar, whose best marathon performance was 2:08:13; and Mary Decker, former world mile record holder who ran in her fourth Olympic Games in Atlanta in 1996 at the age of 37.

Frequency overload: How often?

'Train little, hard, and often.'

> Jim Peters, first man to run under 2:20 for the marathon

'If time allows, it is advisable to train two or three times a day, provided there is no imbalance between aerobic and anaerobic efforts.'

> Arthur Lydiard, New Zealand distance running coach

The principle of frequency overload refers to either the number of successive work bouts performed by an athlete during a single training session, or the number of training sessions undertaken by an athlete in a given period of time. Since the mid-1980s there has been a tendency towards more frequent training sessions by competitors in almost all sports. This trend has generally been aimed at increasing the total training volume. However, it is not known whether increasing the frequency of training sessions while maintaining the same volume has a positive effect on performance. For example, is it better to run 10 km as one training session in the afternoon, or to do two runs of 5 km, one in the morning and the other in the evening? Surprisingly, this aspect of frequency overload has not been studied systematically by exercise scientists, and the answers to such questions must be addressed by future research.

Recovery

'The hardest thing for an athlete to do is not to train. You can't sit still. You feel you should be out there working.'

> Graham Obree, world champion cyclist

'The bottom line is that the body does not get fitter through exercise; it gets fitter through recovering from exercise.'

> Peter Keen, coach of Chris Boardman

'Recovery. That's the name of the game in cycling. Whoever recovers the fastest does the best.'

Lance Armstrong, professional road cyclist

'I have had many outstanding races after a forced rest. This illustrates the critical role rest and recovery play in getting the most from training.'

Emil Zatopek, five-time Olympic medal-winning runner, holder of eighteen world records

'There is a time to train and there is a time to rest. It is the true test of the runner to get them both right.'

Noel Carroll, Irish Olympian and running coach

'I take a nap almost every day. I couldn't do without my nap.'

Scott Molina, world-class triathlete

'Resting is easy. It's the training that is hard.'

Arturo Barrios, ex-world record holder for 10,000 metres (27:08.23)

An often neglected principle of training is rest and recovery. Indeed, athletes and coaches often need to be reminded that adaptations to the stresses of daily workouts only occur when an athlete is *not* training!

Obviously the purpose of any training session is to place a specific stress on a physiological system so that the resulting response will produce a positive adaptation in that system and a subsequent improvement in training capacity or performance. It follows, then, that a training session is beneficial only if it forces the body to adapt to the stress of the physical workload. If that stress is inadequate to overload a physiological system, then no adaptation will occur. Conversely, if the workload is too great—that is, applied too quickly—or performed too often without adequate rest, then fatigue follows, and the resultant performance will be impaired. The effectiveness of a stressor in creating an adaptive response is specific to each athlete and depends on a variety of factors, such as current state of fitness, the time elapsed since the last workout, environmental conditions and a multitude of other subtle influences. It is the role of the coach to ensure that training programs are structured such that the athlete attains the maximal possible physiological adaptations while reducing the risk of residual fatigue, which may result in illness or injury.

TRAINING SPECIFICITY

'Running is, without question, the best exercise for runners.'

Arthur Lydiard, New Zealand distance running coach

'All that cycling one hundred miles a day would make me good at is cycling one hundred miles a day. The more specific your training is, the better.'

Graham Obree, world 4000 metres pursuit cycling champion

'Long slow distance makes long slow runners.'

Jim Bush, head track coach at the University of California

'On the first day I watched her train I was shocked. Why did they spend two hours going through the same pattern of lengths? Why did the coach start the sprint work after a couple of hours of going up and down in the same ritual? It didn't make sense.'

Erik de Bruin, coach of Michelle Smith, triple Olympic medal-winning swimmer

'We would warm up by running around the field as much as 14 times. I can never remember running a lap of the field during a match.'

Andy Haden, New Zealand All Black Rugby Union player

It has been repeatedly observed that training for a particular sport or action has little effect on the performance of another (different) activity. Any training-induced adaptations that accrue to an individual are specific to the type of exercise mode performed. Simply stated, an athlete cannot expect to excel in one sport while vigorously training for another! Therefore, the closer the training routine is to the requirements of competition, the better will be the performance outcome. For this reason, the core of any training program should reflect the desired training adaptation. Specificity of training is an important consideration in those sports where the acquisition of skilful, coordinated movements is essential to superior performance: sports-specific training produces improvements in the recruitment of those muscle groups primarily involved in the execution of the primary action.

The principle of training specificity should also operate with regard to the intensity or speed at which athletes train. For example, competitive swimmers often train twice a day, for four to five hours, covering up to 18,000 m. Since the majority of competitive swimming events last less than five minutes, the question arises of how training at such non-specific speeds, which are obviously far slower than planned race pace, can possibly prepare the swimmer optimally for the maximal efforts of competition?

INDIVIDUALITY AND THE GENETIC CEILING

'Everyone is an athlete. The only difference is that some of us are training, and some are not.'

> Dr George Sheehan, cardiologist, runner and philosopher

'In our business, son, we have a saying: "You can't put in what God left out!"'

> Sam Mussabini, coach of Harold Abrahams in the film 'Chariots of Fire'

'God determines how fast you are going to run. I can help only with the mechanics.'

> Bill Bowerman, running coach at the University of Oregon

'It's a series of concepts, it's about developing, it's about consistency. The schedule is just a little bit of it—you have to have got it right, but it can be different for every individual.'

> Chris Wardlaw, Olympic marathoner and coach of Steve Moneghetti, on 'The System'

'Every athlete is unique. I have never coached two runners who have reacted the same way to training. There is no recipe for

success—only sound physiological principles which must be adhered to.'

> Dick Quax, ex-world-record holder for 5000 metres (13:12.8) and running coach

'Whereas an accident of birth can give you an advantage, that alone isn't enough: winners may be born but they are not born winning.'

> Richard Dale and Colin Cameron, in *The contenders*

The general principles of physical training can be applied to athletes of all abilities because the physiological responses to particular stimuli are largely predictable. However, the precise response of one athlete to a training program might vary considerably from that of another athlete. There is now strong scientific evidence to support the concept that for non-technical, low-skill sports such as endurance running, performance is ultimately determined by hereditary factors. Results of research undertaken by Dr Claude Bouchard and colleagues at the University of Laval in Quebec reveal that as much as 70–80% of endurance performance and the ability to adapt to training is predetermined by genetic factors. Of equal significance is that these researchers identified approximately 5% of the population who do not, and cannot, improve their performance with physical exercise, regardless of their adherence to a balanced, systematic training program. Obviously those athletes who are capable of superior performances are not only genetically endowed with the necessary physical attributes for success, but also are fortunate enough to have the potential to optimise these factors to the greatest possible extent with training.

The practical ramification of the principle of individuality is that the same training program will not equally benefit all those who undertake it. Therefore, the coach must assess the physiological status of each athlete and apply training techniques that are consistent with that athlete's requirements and limitations. Training benefits are more likely to be optimised when training programs reflect individual athletes' needs and capacities. Unfortunately, when all is said and done, the situation may well be beyond our control. As the renowned Swedish exercise physiologist Professor Per Olaf Astrand once said, 'If you want to be an Olympic champion, you must choose your parents wisely.'

REVERSIBILITY AND LOSS OF TRAINING-INDUCED ADAPTATIONS: DETRAINING

'When I take a vacation in the winter I worry about eating too much and getting fat. I feel I should run or do something active. Everybody thinks you race from February to October and then have the whole winter free. It isn't true. There's an underlying pressure to always be in shape because that's what it takes to stay on top.'

> Greg LeMond, three-time winner of the Tour de France

'Use it or lose it.'

> Popular athletics aphorism

Quite simply, reversibility is the principle of detraining, or loss of training-induced adaptations. Whereas regular training elicits a variety of adaptations which enhance performance, periods of sustained rest, or even severe reductions in training, diminish this response and lead to performance decrements.

Most teams and serious recreational athletes participate in a year-round training program with just a few weeks' complete break in training at the end of a season. These 'active' breaks in training during the off-season are considered to be a necessary component of both physical and mental recuperation for players. However, unless properly structured, such breaks may result in a significant loss of fitness. The crucial question for coaches and athletes is: how much training is necessary to maintain a reasonable level of fitness during non-competitive periods, or during an enforced lay-off caused by injury or illness?

Several scientific studies have examined the effects of either a reduction in or a short-term cessation of training in both endurance athletes (runners and swimmers) and individuals participating in strength/power events. Dr Joe Houmard of the University of East Carolina examined the effects of training cessation in well-trained distance runners. He found that after fourteen days of complete inactivity, the length of time the athletes could continue to run on a laboratory treadmill decreased by 9%, indicating a significant drop in endurance capacity. Accompanying this fall-off in running time to exhaustion, the subjects' maximal aerobic power ($\dot{V}O_{2max}$), often considered the laboratory gold standard by which endurance capabilities are assessed, also fell by 5%. The findings from this study demonstrate that even previously well-trained runners experience significant losses of training adaptation with as little as fourteen days of complete inactivity.

In another investigation, Australian researcher Dr Glenn McConell persuaded a group of well-trained runners to reduce their weekly training volume from 81 to 24 km, the frequency of training from six to five days per week, and the intensity of their running from 70–80% of $\dot{V}O_{2max}$ (or around 85% of the athletes' maximal heart rate) to less than 70% of $\dot{V}O_{2max}$ (about 75% of maximal heart rate). Despite two weeks of this reduced training stimulus, 5 km running performance and the athletes' laboratory measure for $\dot{V}O_{2max}$ were maintained. However, when training was reduced for a whole month and the exercise intensity was not well maintained, the runners' 5 km performance time was considerably slower despite the fact that there was no change in their $\dot{V}O_{2max}$.

Two conclusions seem warranted from the results of these studies. First, reductions in training volume by up to two-thirds for three weeks are sufficient to maintain most cardiorespiratory measures of fitness in previously well-trained runners. However, there are likely to be measurable drop-offs in endurance capacity and performance after a month of reduced training. Secondly, it seems clear that some laboratory tests such as the determination of an athlete's $\dot{V}O_{2max}$ may not always mirror actual changes in athletic performance. Hence, both exercise physiologist and coach alike should be aware that if laboratory tests are to be utilised to monitor an athlete's state of training, they should not be used in isolation.

Unlike most of the adaptations that accrue from prolonged endurance training, and which are relatively well maintained even in the face of several weeks of reduced training, there is some evidence to indicate that maximal strength gains are lost quite rapidly with training cessation. After only ten days of inactivity, there is an 8% drop in maximal strength; with twelve weeks of rest this decline is as high as 70% of the trained value. Although maximal muscular strength drops dramatically with the complete termination of training, the good news is that it is possible to maintain some degree of muscle power for several weeks when training is reduced from three to two sessions per week. The key here is to ensure that the intensity of training is well sustained. Thus, it appears that for strength-trained athletes, training intensity is a more important stimulus for the retention of adaptation than the frequency of training. It also seems that muscular strength is better preserved during detraining if such training includes eccentric as well as concentric contractions.

Finally, the magnitude of loss of strength during detraining has been shown to be higher for individuals participating in free weights, rather than in either isometric or isokinetic exercise. The reason for this observation remains unclear, but it may be related to the fact that during free weights, technique and synchronous muscle recruitment play a more important role in the execution of a lift when compared to a similar movement utilising a machine. These 'neural' adaptations to strength training appear to be lost at a rather rapid rate.

CROSS-TRAINING: A MISNOMER OF TERMINOLOGY

Cross-training is when an athlete undertakes training in a discipline other than their main sport for the sole purpose of enhancing performance in their primary event. This form of training became popular in the 1980s with the emergence of the sport of triathlon (swimming, running and cycling), and has been widely recommended in recent years as a technique for retaining training adaptations and even improving performance. Some world-class athletes, such as Mark Allen, six-time winner of the Hawaii Ironman, believe that a heavy cycling program improves distance running performance, and point out that elite triathletes seldom run more than 100 km a week in preparation for a marathon. Paradoxically, the available scientific data generally suggest that the training effects gained in running are more likely to transfer to cycling than vice versa!

Since both running and cycling utilise the major muscle groups in the lower extremities, it seems logical to speculate that transfer of training effects is likely to occur due to some 'overlap' of the use of the same muscles. However, a closer examination of the two disciplines shows that while the quadriceps muscle group of the upper leg is used extensively in cycling, the smaller plantar flexors of the lower leg are preferentially recruited in running. This observation is supported by the finding that the muscle enzyme activities of the quadriceps muscles of competitive cyclists are always far higher than those found in endurance-trained runners.

Based solely on the principle of the specificity of training adaptations, the performance benefits to athletes who participle in cross-training must be seriously questioned. To date, however, there have been only a few scientific studies which have examined the effects of combined cross-training on endurance performance.

In possibly the first attempt to investigate the benefits of cross-training, Dr Russell Pate of the University of South Carolina examined the effects of either arm-training only or leg-training only on the retention of training effects originally induced by leg exercise (cycling). After four weeks of cross-training, the leg-trained athletes had retained or actually increased their cycling capacity. However, those individuals who trained the upper body had simply detrained. The results of this study imply that pure cross-training (that is, training another body part from that which is used in the athlete's primary activity or event) is useless as a means of retaining training effects.

In the most recent and perhaps well controlled study, Deborah Hutton and colleagues at California State University investigated the effects of five weeks of high-intensity cross-training (a combination of cycling and running) versus an equal-intensity running-only training program on one mile and 5000 metres run performance, as well as on the laboratory measurement of $\dot{V}O_{2max}$. Twelve moderately fit men who had been running up to 30 km per week for two months prior to the study acted as subjects. After five weeks of training, there were improvements in both the run-only and the cross-trained athletes for one mile time (21 seconds versus 18 seconds), 5000 metre performance (1.7 minutes for both groups) and maximal aerobic power (5.2% versus 5.9%). However, there were no differences in any of the performance measures between the two groups. These scientists concluded that their results 'support the use of "cross training" as an alternative to increasing performance'. However, as the effects of cross-training on performance never exceeded those induced by a specific training regimen, it is difficult to see how such a conclusion is warranted. In addition, the principles of the specificity of training are likely to have greater significance for well-conditioned competitive athletes than for the moderately-trained recreational subjects who participated in this study.

Both scientific evidence and anecdotal reports overwhelmingly indicate that the best way to retain a training effect and improve subsequent performance is to continue using the primary mode of activity in which the athlete wants to participate—or, at the very worst, an exercise which is very similar in terms of neuromuscular recruitment. Observation of the world's top athletes shows clearly that the best marathon runners do not undertake any of their training in the swimming pool, and conversely, the best swimmers certainly wouldn't be advised to take to the road and start serious running! Thus, the term 'cross-training' is somewhat of a misnomer, and for the serious single-event athlete is something best left to those multi-event sports (such as the triathlon) that require competitors to be proficient in more than one discipline.

A common but slightly different example of cross-training is where swimmers undertake dry-land training, usually cycling or running, in addition to their already huge swimming load in an attempt to control their body fat levels. Whether this is of benefit to energy balance has not been studied systematically. However, the additional fatigue or increased risk of injury associated with the extra training makes it a risky practice.

Perhaps the only advantage of so-called cross-training is when an athlete has been forced to stop training for their primary activity (usually because of injury), and there is a need to maintain general fitness. In this case, the injured runner, for example, may choose to substitute cycling or 'water running' with a flotation vest in place of their habitual activity. If an athlete has to revert to training by undertaking activity in another discipline, then the closer the range of motion of the substitute training to the primary activity, the better will be the retention of training adaptation. However, if the intent of training is simply to maintain or increase general cardiorespiratory fitness, then any aerobic exercise may be appropriate.

Finally, a possible advantage of cross-training might be that an individual is able to undertake a greater total volume of training without the risks of over-training or injury from a single sport.

So why do athletes cross-train?

- It is better than doing nothing.
- It provides a variety of training stimuli.
- It increases overall fitness.
- It *may* help prevent injury.
- It is trendy and there are specially designed cross-training shoes to work out in!
- All of the above.

TRAINING FOR PEAK PERFORMANCE: A SUMMARY

'Even if you train hard for long periods, your potential will not develop unless you train systematically and intelligently.'

Arthur Lydiard, New Zealand distance running coach

With the principles of training in mind, a practical definition of training begins to emerge. It should be clear that the successful athlete or team has a pre-planned, methodical approach to their physical preparation. Such preparation should be based upon sound scientific principles, such as progressive overload and the specificity of training. The response to any training program should, ultimately, be quantified in a competition situation to assess its effectiveness. A definition of training for the serious athlete could be 'a systematic, planned program of physical preparation based upon sound scientific principles for the sole purpose of improving sports performance'.

It is important that the aims of improving athletic performance should not be confused with the objectives of a health and fitness program. While both are worthy causes, the athlete strives to extend the barriers of human capability through severe, fatigue-inducing training sessions. Competitive athletes are performance-oriented and are only marginally concerned with any health benefits that might accrue due to their participation in rigorous physical training for sport. On the other hand, most, if not all, of the health-related benefits of regular exercise can be realised by most individuals through a more moderate approach to physical activity. Indeed, the man credited with starting the exercise boom in North America, Dr Kenneth Cooper, once said that if a person runs in excess of fifteen miles a week, they are doing so for other than health-related reasons. Thus, while being on the same continuum, peak fitness for competitive sport, and health and fitness for well-being, are probably not as close as one might have imagined.

Finally, training is not, and will never be, a purely scientific endeavour. Current knowledge of training practices has evolved mainly through the experiences of coaches and their charges and not usually because of scientific breakthroughs arising from laboratory-based investigations by sports scientists with top athletes. Future innovations in training techniques, improvements in athletic performance and breakthroughs in applied exercise science will only be accomplished as a result of closer working relationships between athletes, coaches and sports scientists who possess a comprehensive and practically-based knowledge of specialised events.

3

Fuels for the fire: The body's power systems

'Performance utlimately depends on the capacity to produce power for the duration of an event, and on the efficiency with which that energy is translated into movement.'

Peter Snell, exercise physiologist and triple Olympic gold medal winner

'The more a player knows about his body the better he trains. And the better he trains, the fitter he becomes.'

Bob Dwyer, coach of the 1991 Australian World Rugby Union champions

The purpose of this chapter is to provide a general overview of the different ways in which the body meets the demands of exercise of varying intensity and duration. It is not intended to be a comprehensive description of muscle contraction and muscle biochemistry during exercise. Previous books have dealt with these topics in great detail. (See the selected reading list at the back of the book.) Although some readers might be tempted to skip this chapter and concentrate on those dealing with the nuts and bolts of peak performance, a basic under-standing of the power systems which fuel exercise will provide a firm base on which more advanced concepts of training and nutrition can be built.

POWER SYSTEMS VERSUS ENERGY SYSTEMS

When describing the physiological entities that produce the energy required to sustain all cellular processes, including muscular contraction, most exercise physiology texts and coaching manuals use the term 'energy systems'. However, as the primary function of such systems is to produce *power* for exercise, such terminology seems inappropriate. It would seem conceptually more correct to call them *power systems*. The distinction between *energy* systems and *power* systems is not merely semantic. The output of a physiological system should be quantified as the power that can be *produced*, and not merely as the amount of energy *potentially available* for muscular work. Obese individuals, for example, have vast reserves of energy stored in the form of fat but are not renowned for their ability to sustain high-power outputs! This book will use the term 'power system' rather than 'energy system', since it provides a more accurate description of the processes which occur during exercise.

Athletic events can be classified into four main categories:

1   power events;
2   speed events;
3   endurance events; or
4   ultra-endurance events.

The body has four distinct power systems it can use to supply energy for these different types of events:

1   the (ATP–CP) phosphagen system;
2   the anaerobic or oxygen-independent glycolytic (carbohydrate) system;
3   the aerobic glycolytic system; and
4   the aerobic lipolytic (fat) system.

These names are really just descriptive summaries of how each system produces power for exercise. They are considered distinct by exercise scientists because:

• they have substantially different biochemical pathways;
• their relative contributions to the power required for

exercise depend on the intensity (speed) and duration of an event; and

• these contributions can be modified by appropriate training and dietary interventions.

For the coach, a knowledge of the contribution of the power systems used during exercise is essential. They need to be able to assess whether their current training programs provide the physiological stimuli necessary for superior performance. An athlete's performance is dependent on their being able to maximise the delivery of power from the various systems involved in their event. Clearly, then, training must target these systems selectively in order to enhance their function. A 'systematic' training program involves a mix-and-match of workouts aimed at stressing the key power systems called upon by the specific demands of competition. Logically, this mix varies between sports, and even between individuals in the same sport but in different playing positions or events. The notion of specialised training sessions to optimise each of the major power systems used during an event is in agreement with many of the principles of training outlined in Chapter 2. The later chapters on nutrition summarise dietary manipulations and ergogenic aids that also may enhance the capacity of the various power systems.

The ATP–CP (phosphagen) system

The phosphagen system uses adenosine triphosphate (ATP) and creatine phosphate (CP) stored within the muscle fibres to provide energy for maximal bouts of strength and speed that last for up to six seconds. ATP and CP are stored at the contractile site of the muscle, making this anaerobic power system the most readily available during high-intensity exercise. The amount of ATP and CP stored within skeletal muscle is, however, quite small. Only 60–70 grams of ATP are found in the muscles of a trained athlete. As a result, the phosphagen system can only power bursts of maximal exercise for very short periods. Indeed, after only a few seconds of exhaustive work, the power produced by the ATP–CP system drops dramatically, so that after six seconds it provides only half of the total energy requirements of exercise. The ATP–CP system powers the initial seconds of sprint events, as well as other movements where maximal force is needed, such as near-maximum lifts in the gym.

The anaerobic (oxygen-independent) glycolytic system

This system derives its name from the biochemical pathway that produces energy from the breakdown of carbohydrates *without the use of oxygen*. Strictly speaking, this system should be termed 'oxygen-independent', but most coaches and athletes are more familiar with the term 'anaerobic'. For ease of understanding, the term 'anaerobic' will be used throughout this book.

The anaerobic glycolytic system is rapidly activated at the onset of intense work, so that even during a six-second maximal sprint, the contribution to the total energy requirements of exercise from the breakdown of muscle glycogen reaches almost 50%. In an event lasting approximately 30 seconds, the contribution from anaerobic glycolysis to the total energy requirements of exercise increases to 60%. The longer the exercise duration, or, conversely, the slower the speed, the smaller is the contribution to muscle metabolism from the anaerobic glycolytic power system. Thus, after a maximal effort lasting one minute, anaerobic energy release has decreased to 50% of overall metabolism, and after two minutes of high-intensity work, to around 35%. The anaerobic release of energy from carbohydrate is associated with the production of lactate by the working muscles and its release into the blood.

LACTATE: IT'S NOT ALL BAD NEWS

Coaches and athletes often blame lactate for the 'burning' feeling that accompanies fatigue and exhaustion during or just after maximal exercise. Strictly speaking, this is not the case. It is the production of hydrogen ions and the rise in muscle acidity which interferes with muscle contractility and inhibits further high-intensity exercise. But lactate is not just a useless by-product of anaerobic metabolism. In 1985, Professor George Brooks of the University of California, Berkeley, proposed the 'lactate shuttle' to explain how lactate production in the muscles and its removal from the blood were finely balanced. This theory holds that lactate produced at the active muscle site where glycogen is broken down has two possible fates. The first is to be transported into the capillaries surrounding the muscle fibre where it is carried into the bloodstream. From here it is taken up by the liver and converted and stored as glycogen, a process called gluconeogenesis (the formation of new glucose). The second option is that lactate formed in the active muscle during exercise can be 'shuttled' to adjacent muscle fibres where it can then be used as a fuel to sustain further contractions. The practical significance of this theory is that the lactate produced *during* exercise cannot be responsible for the muscle soreness and stiffness experienced by athletes *after* exercise. Within fifteen minutes of finishing the most strenuous training session, lactate in both the muscle and blood is back to near resting levels. Muscle damage is much more likely than lactate to cause stiff muscles after a strenuous exercise bout. Although Professor Brooks's hypothesis was considered very controversial at the time it was proposed, it is now widely accepted by exercise physiologists.

The aerobic glycolytic and aerobic lipolytic power systems

The two aerobic systems are named for the fact that they generate power for muscle contraction from the breakdown of carbohydrate and fats *in the presence of oxygen*. High-intensity exercise lasting longer than two minutes and up to three hours is powered predominantly by the aerobic glycolytic (carbohydrate) system. For longer and, by necessity, less intense ultra-endurance events, the oxidation of fat via the aerobic lipolytic (fat) system provides most of the energy for muscle metabolism. Note that fat can only be used in the presence of oxygen. During prolonged exercise the use of fat relative to carbohydrate varies according to a number of factors. The most important of these factors are the current fitness level of the athlete, the intensity and duration of the exercise, and the athlete's diet. The duration of maximal exercise for which equal contributions to energy metabolism are made by the aerobic glycolytic and aerobic lipolytic power systems is around four to five hours.

FUELS FOR THE FIRE: HOW THE BODY STORES ENERGY

The human body utilises carbohydrate, lipid (fat) and, to a small extent, protein as fuels for muscular exercise. These fuels are contained in the athlete's muscles, liver and adipose tissue. The amounts of these fuels stored in the body differ. Compared to carbohydrate, fat is stored in vast quantities. The average individual will store 10–12 kilograms of lipid, mostly in adipose tissue, with only 300–400 grams contained within the fibres of those muscles that are active in training.

On the other hand, carbohydrate stored as glycogen in the muscles and liver amounts to only 500 grams. Not only is fat found in plentiful quantities, but it is also a more compact form of stored energy compared to carbohydrate. Each gram of stored fat yields 37 kilojoules (9 kilocalories) of energy, compared to 17 kilojoules (4 kilocalories) for a gram of carbohydrate. Additionally, whereas fat is stored neatly in lipid droplets, glycogen is packed with approximately 2 grams of water, making the total fuel store bulkier and less energy dense.

Figure 3.1 shows the body's various energy storage depots and the amount of fuels located at each site. Given such huge amounts of endogenous energy, it seems inconceivable that in all but very long events, the athlete could run out of fuel for the exercising muscles. But this does sometimes happen.

FIGURE 3.1

The amount of energy stored in the human body*

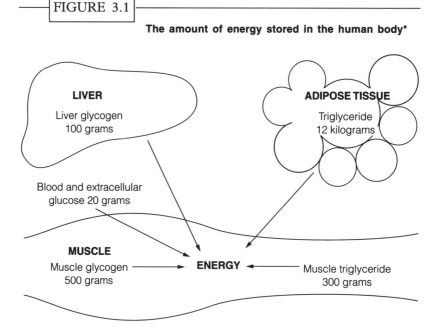

LIVER
Liver glycogen
100 grams

ADIPOSE TISSUE
Triglyceride
12 kilograms

Blood and extracellular
glucose 20 grams

MUSCLE
Muscle glycogen
500 grams

ENERGY

Muscle triglyceride
300 grams

* These amounts are those typically stored by a 70–75 kilogram athlete.

THE LIMITATIONS TO PERFORMANCE: WHEN THE POWER RUNS OUT

Figure 3.2 plots the speed of men's running world records against the time taken to complete them (duration of the event). The shortest sprint, the 50 metres, is on the extreme

FIGURE 3.2

The speed of men's world running records versus the event duration

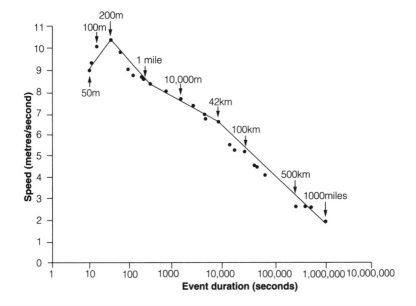

left of the graph, while the longest event, the record for 1000 miles, is on the extreme right. The general slope of the line is down. This indicates that as the distance of a race increases, the average running speed decreases. The exceptions to this rule are the first four points on the graph, namely the records for the 50, 60, 100 and 200 metres. Here the *average* running speed actually increases from 50 metres up to the 200 metres. The reason for this apparent anomaly is simple. The slowest part of any race is the start. As the total race time gets shorter, the proportion of this time taken up by the start gets correspondingly longer. So during a 200 metre race, the *average* speed is actually faster than the average speed for the 100 metres. Athletes like 200 metres world-record holder Michael Johnson get a rolling start for the last half of their race, making it possible to run at a pace that is faster than the existing world record for the 100 metres in an event twice as long!

The four distinct components (or slopes) of the graph provide strong evidence for the existence of the four power systems discussed earlier. Traditionally, exercise physiology textbooks have referred to only three power systems. The failure to identify the fourth power system can be explained by the omission of athletic events lasting longer than about two-and-a-half hours. The existence of four power systems provides scientists with a tool for explaining the different mechanisms of fatigue associated with events of different duration. Fatigue, as defined by sports scientists, is an inability to sustain a given power output or speed. Basically it is a mismatch between the demand for energy by the working muscles and the supply of energy in the form of ATP (derived from the breakdown of carbohydrate and fat). Sprinters complain of fatigue and start to slow down after only a few seconds of running. On the other hand, long-distance runners and cyclists cover many miles before they are fatigued. Interestingly, both these types of athletes think they have run out of energy. But this is not always the case.

During high-intensity sprint events there is a rapid activation of both the ATP–CP and anaerobic glycolytic power systems. ATP and CP can provide power for only five or six seconds, but theoretically there is enough muscle glycogen to sprint for about 75 seconds. So why do even the best sprinters start to slow down after about 150 metres? The simple answer is that the demand for ATP by the sprinter's muscles exceeds the *readily available* supply. Although, hypothetically, there is enough glycogen to supply the needs of the working muscles, there is a subtle control mechanism at work which prevents the athlete from totally exhausting their energy stores. This protective device ensures that the athlete's muscle fibres never deplete their energy content to such an extent that the muscle cells are in danger of being irreversibly damaged. The bottom line is that maximum speeds and power outputs are sustainable for only very brief periods of time. They are associated with extremely high rates of breakdown of stored energy and a rapid onset of fatigue. But the athlete can recover reasonably quickly and, after several hours' rest, can perform at almost the same intensity again.

In events lasting longer than 30 seconds and up to about 30 minutes, fatigue is caused by a different mechanism. Here the likely scenario responsible for a reduction in speed or power output is a mismatch between lactate production in the working muscles and its removal by the blood. During intense exercise lasting up to half-an-hour there is a gradual increase in muscle acidity which reduces the ability of the exercising muscles to maintain intense contractions. This acidity ultimately results in a decrease in the force of muscle contraction, which makes the athlete reduce their speed. With plenty of glycogen still available in the working muscles, they are able to switch to the more efficient aerobic glycolytic power system to sustain exercise, albeit at a slower pace.

It is probably only during maximal events lasting longer than two hours that depletion of the muscles' energy stores is the main factor responsible for fatigue. Carbohydrate stores are particularly vulnerable, since they are in short supply compared to the body's fat depots. But since the aerobic glycolytic power system is capable of sustaining a higher absolute exercise intensity than the aerobic lipolytic system, the athlete should aim to sustain the fastest possible pace which gets them to the end of a race with almost no muscle glycogen left. Indeed, if a marathoner crosses the finish line with a substantial amount of glycogen left in their leg muscles, they should have run faster!

In the case of ultra-endurance events lasting five hours or longer, reduced speeds are caused by two factors. The first is related to the extremely low levels of muscle glycogen. Once this fuel has been used, the body has to switch to the aerobic lipolytic power system to sustain race pace. And herein lies the second problem. Although lipid is a very concentrated form of energy, it cannot be supplied to the muscles at a rate fast enough to support their requirements. So, in the face of ample stores of bodily energy, the athlete is forced to reduce their pace. Again, this is due to the mismatch between demand (by the working muscles) and supply (from the lipid stores). At those (slower) speeds at which there is a match between energy demand and energy supply (from fat), it should be theoretically possible to continue exercising for many hours, if not days. It is likely that acute muscle damage, and fatigue due to lack of sleep, are the main factors limiting the maximal speed an athlete is capable of attaining.

CONTRIBUTIONS OF THE POWER SYSTEMS TO ATHLETIC EVENTS OF DIFFERENT DURATION

The contributions of the power systems to the requirements of exercise have generally been studied in laboratory situations in which athletes have been asked to generate as much power as possible in a given time. This is analogous to athletic competitions such as running, swimming, cycling, speed-skating or rowing, where the winner is basically the athlete who produces the most power over the duration of an event. Figure 3.3 summarises the results of these studies.

Perhaps the most surprising feature of Figure 3.3 is the contribution to total power production from aerobic sources, even when the exercise duration is as short as one minute. Obviously as the distance of an event increases beyond two minutes, and the intensity of exercise decreases, the contribution from aerobic pathways must be even higher. Indeed, for a maximal effort lasting five minutes, the contribution from the aerobic glycolytic power system is as high as 75%. By the time the event duration is one hour, the aerobic glycolytic power system is contributing approximately 92% of the total energy requirements, with the aerobic lipolytic power system covering the rest. It is estimated that the aerobic glycolytic and lipolytic power systems contribute in equal proportions to maximal events lasting four hours.

Does this mean that if your event lasts 30 seconds you should be spending 40% of your time training the aerobic glycolytic power system and 60% training the anaerobic glycolytic system? Certainly not. Such a simplistic approach implies that the different power systems respond to a training stimulus in the same manner. Clearly this is not the case. It takes much longer to establish the endurance and fatigue resistance necessary to compete in long-distance races than it does to fine-tune an athlete's anaerobic capacity. Nevertheless, it does highlight the need to base training programs on a precise analysis of an athlete's event, and then to organise programs that will optimise those power systems necessary for optimal performance in that event.

AEROBIC POWER PRODUCTION: IT ALL ADDS UP

Figure 3.3 provides a time-course of the contribution of the various power systems to maximal bouts of exercise lasting from a few seconds up to several hours. This is a somewhat simplistic approach to event analysis. It assumes that the contribution to the entire event is the same from start to finish. Although the *average* contributions of the different power systems to events of varying duration are the same as those shown in the figure, the relative contributions to power production during exercise lasting longer than three to five seconds change throughout the exercise period.

FIGURE 3.3

The contributions of different power systems to the requirements of high-intensity competition

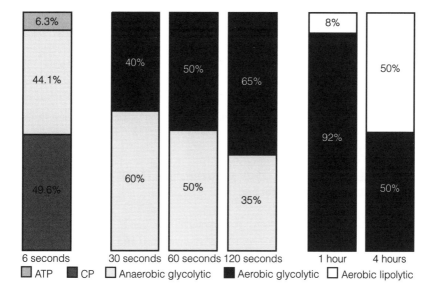

| 6 seconds | 30 seconds | 60 seconds | 120 seconds | 1 hour | 4 hours |

☐ ATP   ■ CP   ☐ Anaerobic glycolytic   ■ Aerobic glycolytic   ☐ Aerobic lipolytic

Dr Jens Bangsbo of the August Krogh Institute in Copenhagen has studied the energy demands of athletes participating in high-intensity exercise. He found that the contribution to power production from anaerobic sources falls off rapidly as the exercise duration increases. For example, when an athlete performs a maximal work bout lasting 120 seconds, 35% of the total power comes from anaerobic glycolysis with the remaining 65% being provided by aerobic glycolysis (see Figure 3.3). However, these numbers represent the *average* contributions of the two power systems over the *whole* exercise bout. When Bangsbo made simultaneous measurements of power production from both anaerobic and aerobic sources, he found that they changed significantly throughout exercise. Table 3.1 shows how the contributions to power production from anaerobic and aerobic power systems vary depending on which segment of the exercise bout is analysed.

| TABLE 3.1 |

The progressive change in the contributions of aerobic and anaerobic power systems to maximal exercise lasting two minutes

Time period	Anaerobic (%)	Aerobic (%)
First 30 seconds	80	20
Second 30 seconds	60	40
Third 30 seconds	42	58
Last 30 seconds	33	66

Source: Adapted from Bangsbo et al. 'Anaerobic energy production and O_2 deficit–debt relationship during exhaustive exercise in humans' *Journal of Physiology* 422: 539–59, 1990

A SUMMARY OF THE POWER SYSTEMS AND HOW BEST TO TRAIN THEM

Table 3.2 provides an overview of the major power systems utilised during events of varying duration and the corresponding type of workout that best trains those systems. Most events in which an athlete has to cover a given distance in the fastest time possible require the contribution of two major power systems. As a result, training for a sprint or endurance event is relatively straightforward. These events represent extremes on a continuum. At one end are the explosive events powered exclusively by oxygen-independent anaerobic processes (see Chapter 5). At the other end are endurance events powered exclusively by oxygen-dependent aerobic processes (see Chapter 6).

But what about team sports such as soccer, rugby, field-hockey and Australian Football? These activities require players to be able to sustain 80 to 100 minutes of non-stop running, much of it at close to top speed, with little recovery between work bouts. Clearly these players depend on both anaerobic and aerobic power systems during the course of a match. Table 3.3 highlights the major physiological differences between intermittent exercise and endurance events.

Given such diverse activity profiles, it is not surprising that the physiological requirements for success in team sports are vastly different to those needed to reach the top in endurance events. Neither should it be difficult to understand why team sports require distinct training and nutritional strategies for success. A comprehensive discussion of these

TABLE 3.2

The major power systems used during exercise of varying duration, and the best type of workouts to train them

Event duration	Major power system	Principal fuels	Training objective and best type of workouts
6 seconds or less	Phosphagen	ATP and CP	*Development of explosive power* sprint starts maximal sprints (< 6 seconds) with complete recovery (3–5 minutes) power/resistance training (3 sets of 3–5 repetitions @ 95% of 1 RM)
30 seconds or less	Phosphagen Anaerobic glycolytic	ATP and CP Muscle glycogen	*Lactate tolerance* sprint repetitions (< 30 seconds) with long (3–5 minutes) rest intervals power/resistance training (3 sets of 8–10 repetitions @ 85% of 1 RM)
15 minutes or less	Anaerobic glycolytic Aerobic glycolytic	Muscle glycogen Blood glucose	*Development of maximal aerobic power* maximal steady-state repetitions (5–10 minutes) with short (1 minute) recovery
15–60 minutes	Aerobic glycolytic	Muscle glycogen Blood glucose	*Lactate threshold* maximal steady-state repetitions (as above) sustained exercise at best aerobic pace
60–90 minutes	Aerobic glycolytic	Muscle glycogen Blood glucose Intra-muscular triglycerides	*Development of fatigue resistance* sustained moderate- to high-intensity exercise
Longer than 90 minutes	Aerobic glycolytic Aerobic lipolytic	Muscle glycogen Blood glucose Intra- and extra-muscular triglycerides	*Development of endurance* prolonged low- to moderate-intensity exercise

Note: RM = repetition maximum.

three distinct types of sporting activities will be provided in future chapters (Chapters 5–7).

TABLE 3.3

A physiological and nutritional profile of the demands of intermittent versus endurance exercise

Profile	Intermittent exercise (team sports)	Endurance exercise
Major power system	ATP–CP Anaerobic glycolytic Aerobic glycolytic	Aerobic glycolytic Aerobic lipolytic
Major fuel	Intra-muscular	Intra-muscular Extra-muscular
Activity profile	High-intensity Stochastic Repetitive	Moderate intensity Prolonged, continuous
Physiological requirements	High maximum speed Moderate to high aerobic power Skill/technique	High aerobic power Resistance to fatigue
Nutritional strategy	High-carbohydrate diet in training, pre-event and prior to event Carbohydrate and fluid replacement during event	High-carbohydrate diet in training, pre-event and prior to event Carbohydrate loading Carbohydrate and fluid replacement during event *Ultra-endurance* Adaptation to a high-fat diet? Medium-chain triglyceride ingestion?

4

Physiological testing for athletes: What the numbers mean

SPORTS SCIENCE FOR 2000 AND BEYOND

'It was not on the rugby field but in the sports laboratory that our secret lay.'

> Bob Dwyer, coach of the 1991 Australian World Rugby champions

'You learn by doing physiological analysis. We were into longitudinal testing of the same athlete over a period of time—using each athlete as their own control, fine-tuning their training so as to give the optimum gain from the best (training) strategy.'

> Dave Martin, exercise physiologist and adviser to elite US distance runners

The superior performances of the modern-day athlete are the product of a complex interaction of physiological, biomechanical, nutritional and psychological factors. Coaches now recognise that the most consistently effective methods of preparing their athletes for the demands of top competition are those based on proven scientific principles rather than on trial and error. Therefore, it has become commonplace to seek input from qualified sports scientists in order that athletes might reach their full potential.

During the past two decades several countries, most notably the former East Germany, Australia and the United States, have committed substantial financial and human resources to identifying and developing their sporting talent.

A key feature of the sporting infrastructures in these countries has been the establishment of national or regional sports institutes where athletes undergo sophisticated physiological and medical testing and receive the most up-to-date sports-specific scientific feedback to aid the coach to optimise training programs. Although some of the methods employed by the coaches from several Eastern bloc countries remain of dubious scientific credibility, there is no question that the establishment of centres of sporting excellence in other countries has been associated with improved athletic success. Since the establishment of the Australian Institute of Sport (AIS) in 1981 the performances of Australia's athletes has improved quite remarkably. Whereas in the 1976 Olympic Games in Montreal the Australian medal tally was five, with no golds, at the 1992 Barcelona Olympics they won 27 medals, including seven golds. In the 1996 Atlanta Games, Australia won a total of 41 medals, of which nine were gold. For the Sydney 2000 games a target of 60 medals has been set—twenty of these, gold.

According to former director of the Australian Institute of Sport, Robert de Castella, 'the job of the AIS is to seek out the raw talent that ultimately is the limiting factor in any nation's sporting accomplishments'. Indeed, a strong case could be put forward that those countries which are not competitive in the sports sciences will ultimately become uncompetitive in those international sports identified for scientific study by other leading nations. A country's future success in any sport at the highest level is likely to be determined by the ability of its sports scientists to identify individuals with special sporting talents and to initiate the appropriate research programs to foster the specific human factors that determine success in that sport.

THE AIMS OF PHYSIOLOGICAL TESTING PROGRAMS

Laboratory testing of athletes to try and identify sporting potential and predict performance is not a new phenomenon. Scientific interest in the physiological factors that determine athletic success dates back to the turn of the century when researchers from Scandinavia and Germany measured oxygen uptake in runners and swimmers. Since then a multitude of tests have been developed to evaluate the fitness of athletes from a wide variety of sports. But what is the value of testing the athlete in the laboratory, other than to provide sports scientists with standardised conditions in which to collect reliable descriptive information about an athlete? Until recently this question was largely academic because only a small number of elite athletes had access to laboratory facilities, and the tests they underwent did not usually allow sports scientists to make particularly accurate predictions of their athletic performance in the field. However, during the last twenty years, more sophisticated laboratory and field tests have been developed that provide the sports scientist and coach with more precise information about an athlete's potential.

THE BENEFITS OF LABORATORY TESTING

The primary benefits of a laboratory-based exercise testing program are:

- to aid in talent identification;
- to determine the physiological and health status of an athlete;
- to construct a sports-specific physiological profile of an individual athlete or team;
- to act as a motivational and educational process whereby the athlete and coach better understand the physiological components of their sport;
- to provide baseline data for individual training program prescription and to identify each athlete's or player's strengths and weaknesses relevant to their sport; and
- to provide feedback to coaches so that they can evaluate the success of their training interventions.

Most coaches would probably feel that the last two benefits are the most valuable. If the primary purpose of testing is to monitor the effectiveness of a particular training program or other intervention (such as dietary modification, injury rehabilitation or psychological counselling), it is obvious that the tests should be repeated at regular intervals, ideally before and after each phase of training. It is important that the results of tests are interpreted directly to the coach and athlete and that the sports scientist advises the coach of the most suitable and practical methods of implementing specific training interventions. The test protocols described in this chapter have been chosen because:

- they have been reported in the sports science literature;

- they are valid—that is, they measure what they claim to measure;
- they are reliable—that is, they are consistent and reproducible;
- they are sports-specific;
- they are sufficiently sensitive to detect small changes in the athlete's state of fitness and performance; and
- they cover a wide range of sporting disciplines.

VALIDITY VERSUS RELIABILITY

Scientists use these terms. Students often get them mixed up. Athletes and coaches just get confused. So what do they mean, and why are they important? *Validity* means a test is measuring what it says it is measuring. *Reliability*, on the other hand, refers to the reproducibility of a test or measure. Can the same test be repeated again with the same or a very similar result? This is important if the athlete wishes to detect changes that occur due to, say, a training intervention. Clearly, a test needs to be reliable if real changes are to be distinguished from the variability that arises simply from repeating a test.

However, a test can be reliable—that is, reproducible over and over again—without being valid. For example, an athlete might be training on a running track which he assumes measures the standard 400 metres. However, the groundsman has marked the track out incorrectly. Instead of being 400 metres, it measures only 380 metres. The athlete is able to reproduce his split times on the track with remarkable consistency. His reliability is good. Unfortunately, unbeknown to him, the validity of his training times and distances is lousy. In fact, they are totally incorrect. All laboratory and field tests should be *both* valid *and* reliable. This is a function of choosing tests well, and then standardising the conditions and equipment for testing. In real life most tests carry some small error of validity or reliability, or both. It is part of the expertise of the sports scientist to recognise and take account of this when interpreting the results of tests to the coach and athlete.

For some sports it may be preferable to assess athletes by field tests rather than by laboratory-based protocols. Indeed, undertaking testing in the field under the specific conditions of training and competition is a useful exercise to bridge the gap between sports scientists and the athlete and coach. In the end, any results obtained from either laboratory or field testing should complement the observations of the coach, and neither should ever be considered a replacement for the other.

FROM LAB TO FIELD . . . AND BACK

Physiological testing is often used to predict athletic performance in the field. And historically, the most frequently used laboratory apparatus for assessing the physiological status of endurance subjects has been the cycle ergometer. However, competitive cyclists often complain that the position they are forced to adopt on such ergometers is not the same as the normal riding position on their own bike. As such, it is difficult for the sports scientist to determine if the test results obtained under such conditions in the laboratory are a true reflection of a cyclist's potential.

In the 1990s, several cycle-simulators have become available which allow the cyclist to ride their own bike in the laboratory. Such systems can be used for physiological testing, as well as for training. After removal of the front wheel, the bike is attached to an ergometry system by the front forks, with additional support being provided from an adjustable pillar under the bottom bracket. From the output of a photo-electric cell mounted on a flywheel and linked to a computer, it is possible to determine the power a cyclist is generating and the speed at which they would be travelling on level terrain in the field. But are these ergometry systems reliable or valid?

Garry Palmer and his colleagues at the University of Cape Town, South Africa, assessed the test to re-test reproducibility of an air-braked cycle ergometry system (Kingcycle™) and compared performances measured in the laboratory to actual races in the field. During a two-week testing period, they had ten highly-trained competitive cyclists ride three 20 km and three 40 km time-trials on the Kingcycle ergometer. Then they persuaded eight of the cyclists to compete in two 40 km races. One of these races was the state championships, held on a flat course in favourable conditions. When they rode on the Kingcycle ergometer, the variability of the cyclists' performance over the three 20 and 40 km time-trials was only 1%. This indicates that the cyclists' performances were very reproducible and that the Kingcycle ergometry system was very reliable. Further, they found an excellent ($r = 0.98$) relationship between the average 40 km time recorded in the lab and in the 40 km road race times. But of practical significance to the coach and athlete was the finding that the times recorded during the 40 km laboratory time-trial were, on average, 8% faster than the road performances. The faster laboratory performances compared to road race performances could be due to a number of factors, including environmental conditions (wind speed) and road surface (drag), both of which would cause the field times to be slower. The results of this study indicate that the Kingcycle ergometry system can be used by sports scientists as a reliable and valid method for assessing short-term (30–60 minutes) endurance performance.

STANDARDISED TESTING PROCEDURES

Consistency is crucial if the results of various physiological tests undertaken at different stages of the athlete's preparation are to be comparable. Testing should be conducted under the following standardised conditions.

The laboratory environment and equipment

- Select a dedicated quiet area which is free from other influences or disturbances.
- Conduct tests in a well-ventilated area, with the laboratory temperature at 20–22°C and the relative humidity at less than 60%.
- Conduct the test procedures without peripheral personnel who may influence the performance.
- Ensure that the same practitioner is employed in subsequent testing.
- Ensure that all laboratory equipment is calibrated before testing according to the procedures and instructions for that specific apparatus.

The athlete

- Check that the athlete is not suffering from any condition which may adversely affect performance, such as a cold or an injury. An athlete with a viral infection should not be allowed to perform any test, no matter how mild the condition may be considered.
- Ensure that the athlete has not undertaken any intensive training or competition for 48 hours prior to a test, nor performed a similar test within the previous 72 hours.
- Ensure that the athlete has not eaten for two hours before a maximal test. Allow fluids such as carbohydrate–electrolyte solutions or water to be taken without restriction in the hours before the test. Note that some individuals are susceptible to reactive hypoglycaemia if they ingest beverages with a high sugar content in the 30–60 minutes before strenuous exercise. In these athletes this practice should be avoided.
- Prior to any test procedure, allow the athlete to perform their own warm-up routine, which must then be standardised for subsequent tests.
- Ensure that the athlete uses the same equipment they utilise during training and competition, such as racing shoes, clothing and other specialised gear.

Test procedures

- Ensure that the athlete is familiar with all the test equipment before starting any tests.
- Explain, in detail, all test procedures to the athlete, particularly those with which the athlete is unfamiliar.
- Ideally, allow the athlete to become habituated to all test procedures. It usually takes two or three performances of the criterion test before the results reflect true performance.
- For the most valid and reliable results, schedule physiological tests during the mid-to-late afternoon or early evening period, when strength and endurance are optimal.

TESTS TO MEASURE AEROBIC CAPACITY

There are both direct and indirect tests to measure maximal oxygen uptake (VO_{2max}).

Laboratory determination of VO_{2max}

The test for VO_{2max} is perhaps the single most commonly employed laboratory procedure in exercise physiology. This measurement determines an athlete's ability to take in, transport and utilise oxygen and is probably the best assessment of the athlete's endurance capabilities. Studies conducted in the 1920s established that when expressed relative to body weight, VO_{2max} was highest in the best endurance athletes. This led to a popular belief that VO_{2max} would be a good predictor of athletic potential in *all* endurance events. However, although VO_{2max} is a good predictor of endurance potential when a group of athletes with vastly different performance capabilities is studied, it is a relatively poor predictor when athletes of similar ability are evaluated.

Part of the reason that the VO_{2max} of an athlete is not the single best predictor of athletic potential is because it is only one of many physiological variables positively related to successful endurance performance (see Chapter 6). Recently, sports scientists have shown that the maximal speed or power output that an athlete attains during the maximal test is also an important predictor of athletic performance. For example, in runners, the peak treadmill speed attained during a progressive exercise test has been shown to be as good a predictor of running performance over races 10 km or longer as any physiological variable currently measured in the laboratory. For cyclists, the peak power output (PPO) attained during an exhaustive test is a good predictor of 20 and 40 km time-trial

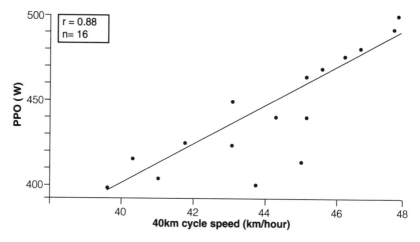

FIGURE 4.1

The relationship between the peak sustained power output (PPO) a cyclist can attain during a maximal test and their 40 km time-trial speed

r = 0.88
n= 16

PPO (W)

40km cycle speed (km/hour)

Source: Adapted from Lindsay et al. 'Improved athletic performance in highly trained cyclists after interval training' *Medicine and Science in Sports and Exercise* 28: 1427–34, 1996.

performance (see Figure 4.1). Thus, although VO_{2max} still remains the test of choice for assessing the upper limit of aerobic exercise capacity, the highest workrate that the athlete reaches during such a test should also be determined for predictive purposes and to monitor the maximal sustained workrate the athlete is capable of attaining.

The most frequently employed laboratory protocols for assessing an athlete's VO_{2max} are progressive, incremental exercise tests to exhaustion on either a cycle ergometer or a motor-driven treadmill. Although testing protocols will vary between different sports science laboratories, an athlete will usually be required to exercise for seven to ten minutes while the exercise intensity (either the speed of movement or the power output) is progressively increased until the athlete is exhausted. For rowers, the Concept II rowing ergometer is utilised; but instead of a progressive maximal test, VO_{2max} values are measured during a simulated competitive effort over 2000 metres. Oxygen uptake (VO_2) values determined during simulated maximal efforts are typically 6–7% higher than those recorded during a standard rowing ergometer test of increasing intensity. As such, this value is often referred to as the athlete's peak oxygen consumption (VO_{2peak}).

Throughout a maximal test the athlete wears a noseclip, while their expired air is collected through a mouthpiece and instantly analysed by a computer for volume, as well as oxygen and carbon dioxide content. The ratio of the athlete's carbon dioxide production to their oxygen consumption, called the respiratory exchange ratio (or RER), allows an estimate of the type of fuel being used during exercise to be determined. The sports scientist has both objective and subjective criteria for determining whether or not the athlete has produced a true maximal effort. Such criteria include:

- severe fatigue, or exhaustion resulting in the inability of the athlete to maintain exercise at the desired workrate;
- a subjective rating by the athlete that their perception of effort is maximal;
- a plateau in the athlete's heart rate for several minutes despite an increase in the workrate; and
- an RER value greater than 1.15.

$\dot{V}O_{2max}$: IT'S ALL RELATIVE

When an athlete's $\dot{V}O_{2max}$ is determined in the laboratory, it can be expressed either in *absolute* or *relative* terms. The maximum volume of oxygen collected during a maximal test (measured in litres per minute) is what exercise physiologists call the *absolute* $\dot{V}O_{2max}$. But the bigger the athlete, the larger the absolute $\dot{V}O_{2max}$ value will be. To compare athletes from either the same sport or different sports, $\dot{V}O_{2max}$ values can be expressed relative to an athlete's body weight. For example, a 75 kg cyclist with an absolute $\dot{V}O_{2max}$ of 5.0 litres per minute would have a *relative* value of 66.6 ml/kg/min (absolute $\dot{V}O_{2max}$ [litres per minute] divided by body weight [kg], multiplied by 1000 [1000 millilitres = 1 litre]).

A word of caution. In some sports the athlete's *absolute* rather than *relative* $\dot{V}O_2$ may be more important for predicting performance. In situations where the athlete's weight is supported, such as track cycling or rowing, there is little need to express $\dot{V}O_2$ relative to body weight, as the athlete does not have to transport their mass over the ground (as in running). For example, in US Olympic rowers, absolute $\dot{V}O_2$ values in excess of seven litres per minute have been recorded for four elite heavyweight oarsmen, with the highest being 7.5 litres per minute. Three female rowers had a $\dot{V}O_2$ greater than 5.5 litres per minute. But when these values are expressed relative to the rower's body weight, they look a little less impressive (see Table 4.1).

TABLE 4.1		

Maximal oxygen uptake values of athletes from several endurance sports and of players from a variety of team sports

Sport	n^*	$\dot{V}O_{2max}$ (ml/kg/min)
Cross-country skiing		
Olympic/World Champions (males)	5	83.8
Cycling		
Australian National team (male)	17	68.4
US National team (male)	23	74.0
Running		
Elite female middle-distance (<5000 m)	6	68.0
Elite female long-distance (>10,000 m)	9	66.4
Elite male US middle-distance runners	11	78.8
Elite male US distance runners	20	76.9
Rowing		
Australian 'highly-ranked' (male)	8	63.5
Australian 'highly-ranked' (female)	12	53.3
1992 US Olympic team (females)	25	58.6
1992 US Olympic team (males)	35	70.9
Swimming		
US Collegiate (male)	12	56.2
Triathlon		
Elite male	10	75.4
Elite female	10	65.6
Cricket		
South African squad (pre-season)	17	60.5
English county batsmen	12	54.0
English county bowlers	13	51.7
Field-hockey		
Australian state level (females)	6	50.1
Australian state level (males)	14	60.7
UK National team (males)	20	62.2
Soccer		
Danish professionals	8	60.4
English First Division team (in season)	10	66.0
English First and Second Division (pre-season)	122	60.4

Note: n^* refers to the number of athletes or players tested.

Table 4.1 shows the *relative* $\dot{V}O_{2max}$ values of endurance-trained athletes from a variety of events, as well as values

TABLE 4.2		

Peak sustained power outputs (PPO) attained during maximal tests for various sports

Sport	n^*	PPO (W)
Cycling		
US Elite National class (male)	9	407
US state class (male)	6	390
US state class (female)	6	258
US National road team (male)	10	470
US National road team (female)	10	333
US National mountain-bike (male)	10	420
US National mountain-bike (female)	10	313
Australian road squad (male)	17	406
Australian track squad (male)	14	411
Rowing		
Australian 'highly-ranked' (male)	8	381
Australian 'highly-ranked' (female)	12	244
1992 US Olympic squad (male)	35	467
1992 US Olympic squad (female)	25	310
Triathlon		
Highly-trained (male, cycling)	10	405

Note: n^* refers to the number of athletes or players tested.

obtained from players from several team sports. For a comparison, the healthy but untrained 25-year-old has a $\dot{V}O_{2max}$ of around 40 ml/kg/min which, with appropriate training, can be increased by up to 25%, giving an absolute value of around 50 ml/kg/min. Table 4.2 shows typical peak power outputs that would be attained during a maximal test for athletes from different sports.

Clearly these values, which were measured in elite individuals, represent the upper end of the range required for success in the various sporting disciplines. They emphasise once more that no matter how good the athlete's training program may be, the ultimate limit to their performance is likely to be governed by genetic factors. However, for those athletes interested in assessing their distance running potential, Dr Dave Costill in his book *Inside running* has provided an estimate of 10 kilometre potential based upon an individual's $\dot{V}O_{2max}$ (Table 4.3).

TABLE 4.3

The range of potential 10 km run times as predicted from an athlete's maximal oxygen uptake ($\dot{V}O_{2max}$)

Maximal oxygen uptake ($\dot{V}O_{2max}$) (ml/kg/min)	Potential 10 km run time (minutes:seconds)
Less than 39.0	53:10 or slower
40.0 to 44.0	52:30 to 49:50
45.0 to 49.0	49:15 to 46:40
50.0 to 54.0	46:00 to 43:25
55.0 to 59.0	42:45 to 40:10
60.0 to 64.0	39:30 to 36:50
65.0 to 69.0	36:15 to 33:40
Above 70.0	33:00 or faster

Source: Costill D.L. *Inside Running: Basics of Sports Physiology*, Benchmark Press Inc., Indianapolis, p. 16, 1986.

THE LIMITS TO HUMAN MUSCLE POWER

What events do the most powerful athletes compete in? The shot-put, weightlifting, judo? Does an athlete's size and strength mean they are also powerful? Surprisingly not. Power is not a measure of how big an athlete is or how much weight they can lift; it is the *rate* or speed at which they can complete a given amount of exercise or work. Ever since records of human power have been documented, people have been interested in feats requiring enormous strength. In early times, the horse was viewed as the most powerful of animals, and it is no coincidence that records of human power were compared to those attainable by this great beast. Today, the international unit of power is the watt (abbreviated W) and 745.7W equals one horsepower.

The easiest method of assessing the net mechanical power of an athlete is during a maximal effort on a cycle ergometer (see 'Laboratory measurement of anaerobic power, speed and agility' later in this chapter). While the maximum power output of any athlete depends on a number of factors, including their body size, bigger is not always better.

The highest power output reported in the scientific literature for any athlete is 1644W for five seconds. This was measured in an Italian sprint cyclist Renzo Sarti. Power outputs of 1500W for six seconds have been reported for several sprint-cyclists. Players from team sports are also able to generate high power outputs for brief periods of time. This is not surprising, since explosive power is required during short sprints or to accelerate from a stationary position. For example, professional Rugby Union players can sustain power outputs of 1300–1400W for several seconds. Certainly such high outputs are impressive. However, just as important in some sports is the capacity to maintain high power outputs over prolonged periods. Champion Belgian cyclist Eddie Merckx sustained a power output of 455W when he set a world one-hour record of 49.432 kilometres in the 1980s. Although the current world one-hour cycling record, held by Britain's Chris Boardman, stands at 56.375 kilometres, such an improvement in speed is largely due to advances in equipment (disc wheels, and aerodynamic bikes and clothing) rather than to an increase in sustainable power. Indeed, using a SRM power-meter system, coach Peter Keen has estimated that Boardman's average power output during his record-breaking ride was 442W. Power outputs of 211W have been maintained for five-and-a-half hours by endurance-trained cyclists. In comparison, trained recreational cyclists can only maintain power outputs of 400W for a minute or two, while healthy but untrained individuals can sustain 150W for an hour.

POWER TO WEIGHT RATIOS: APPLES AND ORANGES

All things being equal, a heavier athlete will be able to generate more power than a smaller one, due to their greater muscle mass. And for this reason, males are generally more powerful than females—even when they are matched for weight. So will a 'good big one' always beat a 'good little one'? Not necessarily. Although a heavier, more powerful athlete may have an advantage in a sport like rowing, in cycling, another weight-bearing sport, the answer is not as simple. Compared to their smaller competitors, large cyclists are at a considerable advantage in terms of power output/body weight while cycling on the flat. This is because when they adopt a low-profile racing position, their frontal surface area is not much different to a much smaller, lighter rider. But they can produce more power, so they ride faster. However, when the same two cyclists hit the mountains, the picture changes. In this situation the riders must carry their body weight up an incline, even though it is supported by the bike. This means the heavier cyclist has to do more work. And here the cyclist with the best power to weight ratio will be the most successful. Still want to be a successful rider? Make sure you have a *minimum* sustainable power to weight ratio of 5.5W per kilogram of body mass.

TABLE 4.4

Training intensity for cycling based on $\dot{V}O_{2max}$, heart rate and power output

% of $\dot{V}O_{2max}$	% of maximal heart rate	% of PPO*
40	55	30
50	65	40
60	70	50
70	80	63
80	90	70
90	95	80
100	100	100

Note: PPO* refers to the cyclist's peak sustained power output in watts.

Training with $\dot{V}O_{2max}$ —from lab to field

Many athletes have the opportunity to undertake some form of testing in a sports science laboratory. Numbers are generated—VO_{2max}, maximum heart rate, peak power output, maximal running speed. How can laboratory data be used in the field to help the athlete train more effectively?

Ultimately a coach will want their athlete to undertake a certain training session at a specific intensity or effort. For the endurance athlete, this intensity is expressed as a percentage of their VO_{2max}. However, this laboratory measure requires the use of sophisticated equipment. In the field, the athlete needs a simpler method of determining how hard they are working which relates to VO_{2max}. In cycling this is easy, since there is a good relationship between an athlete's VO_{2max}, heart rate and power output. Heart rates can be accurately measured by portable monitors (see Chapter 8), while devices such as SRM cranks can quantify the cyclist's instantaneous power. Therefore, the cyclist is able to follow laboratory-based training prescription in the field.

Table 4.4 summarises the relationship between the laboratory-based measure of VO_{2max} and the cyclist's heart rate and power output in the field. Unfortunately, it is not possible to provide an estimate of the relationship between an athlete's running speed and their percentage of VO_{2max} or maximal heart rate because of the differences in running economy or efficiency between athletes.

WHEN AVERAGE IS BETTER THAN MAXIMAL

In many endurance events the $\dot{V}O_{2max}$ is still considered by some exercise physiologists to set the ultimate limit to performance. However, in many sports, including middle-distance running, speed skating, rowing and time-trial cycling, the *average* $\dot{V}O_2$ an athlete can sustain during a race or simulated competitive effort is a much better predictor of performance than the $\dot{V}O_{2max}$ This is because one of the physiological attributes of the successful endurance athlete is their ability to race at a high percentage of $\dot{V}O_{2max}$ and maintain high absolute power outputs or speeds (see Chapter 6).

British coach and sports scientist Peter Keen has estimated that Chris Boardman was able to sustain more than 90% of his $\dot{V}O_{2max}$ (more than 95% of his maximum heart rate) throughout his world one-hour cycling record (see Chapter 18). This equates to an average $\dot{V}O_2$ of around 5.1 litres per minute or 73.8 ml/kg/min for the entire ride!

In rowing, there is a much better relationship between the average $\dot{V}O_2$ measured during a simulated competitive effort and competitive performance than there is between a rower's peak $\dot{V}O_{2max}$ and on-water performance. Rowing physiologist Dr Fredrick Hagerman has reported that during a 2000 metre simulated effort, elite oarsmen sustain average power outputs of 467W and a $\dot{V}O_2$ of 6.3 litres per minute (70.9 ml/kg/min). It may well be that the single most impressive physiological attribute of elite endurance athletes is this ability to sustain an extremely high percentage of peak power or oxygen uptake for the duration of their event.

The practical implication of these observations is that, for some sports, the *average* $\dot{V}O_2$ measured during a simulated competitive effort is far more important than either $\dot{V}O_{2max}$ or $\dot{V}O_{2peak}$ when selecting potentially successful competitors.

Indirect methods for estimating $\dot{V}O_{2max}$

The direct determination of an athlete's $\dot{V}O_{2max}$ in the laboratory provides the most accurate assessment of aerobic power. However, such a measurement requires expensive equipment and trained personnel. Consequently, sports scientists have developed several field tests which can provide an estimate of an athlete's VO_{2max} with a high degree of accuracy. While the results from field tests can never be as *reliable* as those conducted in the laboratory, under standardised controlled conditions, they may often be more *valid* because the athlete can use their own equipment in a familiar environment.

The 15-minute run

A good estimation of an athlete's $\dot{V}O_{2max}$ can be made from a 15-minute all-out run on a standard 400 metre running track, as described below.

1   The athlete runs as far as possible in 15 minutes.
2   The total distance run (in metres) is divided by 15 in order to determine the athlete's running speed in metres per minute.
3   Subtract 133 from the athlete's running speed.
4   Multiply this new figure by 0.172.
5   To the number calculated above, add 33.3.
6   This figure is the athlete's $\dot{V}O_{2max}$ in ml/kg/min.

EXAMPLE OF CALCULATION OF $\dot{V}O_{2max}$ FROM THE 15-MINUTE RUN

An athlete covers 4000 m in 15 minutes. This is equivalent to a running speed of 266.6 m per minute (4000 divided by 15).

- $266.6 - 113 = 133.6$
- $133.6 \times 0.172 = 22.9$
- $22.9 + 33.3 = 56.3$

$\Rightarrow$ The estimated $\dot{V}O_{2max}$ of this athlete is 56.3 ml/kg/min.

Although there is a strong relationship between the $\dot{V}O_{2max}$ predicted from the 15-minute run and an athlete's actual $\dot{V}O_{2max}$ measured in the laboratory, many athletes find it difficult to pace themselves to run at their best steady-state pace for 15 minutes continuously. Often athletes will start the run too quickly, lacking good pace judgment, and consequently experience fatigue prematurely during the later stages of the test. If this occurs, it is likely that the athlete's true aerobic capacity will be underestimated. In addition, there are many sports in which players are required to have a moderate to high oxygen uptake, but whose discipline does not require participants to either run (uphill) on a treadmill, or run for 15 minutes without stopping. Both laboratory and sustained running tests of $\dot{V}O_{2max}$ are unsuitable for assessing the aerobic power of these athletes.

Soccer, rugby (union and league) and field-hockey are all sports which demand a high level of aerobic fitness, with players covering many kilometres during the course of a game (see Chapter 7). However, in these sports players frequently change both the pace and direction of running, and have to accelerate from a standing start many times during a match. For this reason, the multi-stage shuttle run test for aerobic fitness was developed as a more appropriate test for players from a variety of team sports.

The multi-stage shuttle run test

The maximal multi-stage shuttle run test was designed by Dr Luc Leger and colleagues from the University of Montreal, Quebec, and first published in the scientific literature in 1988. Since then, the original protocol has been modified slightly by Professor Clyde Williams and co-workers from Loughborough University, England. However, there are only small differences between the predicted $\dot{V}O_{2max}$ values found in the two studies, and the data from the original investigation have been reported here.

For the multi-stage shuttle run test, players are required to run back and forth for a distance of 20 m on a playing field or gymnasium floor at a pace determined by a sound signal emitted from a prerecorded audio-tape. The frequency of the sound signal gets progressively faster so that the running speed is increased by 0.5 km per hour for each minute of running. The starting speed is 8.5 km per hour, and, for fit players, the first few minutes of the test act as a good warm-up and allow them to get used to accelerating from a stationary position, decelerating, turning and then accelerating once more. Each stage of the shuttle lasts exactly one minute, and as the speed of each successive shuttle is increased, so too are the number of runs (called levels) within that time. The test is terminated when the player is no longer able to reach a 20 m line at the prescribed time despite two verbal warnings. The last completed stage is defined as the maximal shuttle run speed. A player's $\dot{V}O_{2max}$ can then be obtained immediately upon termination of the test from Table 4.5.

In the 1990s the multi-stage shuttle run has become an integral part of aerobic fitness testing and training for many team sports. Indeed, it is now widely accepted as the best test for the determination of aerobic fitness in players from team sports. This is because, compared with either the 15-minute run or a laboratory measurement of a player's $\dot{V}O_{2max}$, the shuttle run:

- is sports-specific;
- is portable and can be conducted on any playing surface;
- is simple to administer;
- does not require expensive equipment or highly qualified personnel;
- allows many players to be tested at once, in a competitive setting; and
- allows the same protocol to be used for players from a variety of sports and of varying ages.

TABLE 4.5

Prediction of maximal oxygen uptake ($\dot{V}O_{2max}$) from the multi-stage shuttle run test

Final stage completed (minutes run)	Maximal shuttle (Level–Shuttle)	Predicted $\dot{V}O_{2max}$ (ml O_2/kg/min)
1	L1–S7	23.6
2	L2–S8	26.6
3	L3–S8	29.6
4	L4–S9	32.6
5	L5–S9	35.6
6	L6–S10	38.6
7	L7–S10	41.6
8	L8–S11	44.6
9	L9–S11	47.6
10	L10–S11	50.6
11	L11–S12	53.6
12	L12–S12	56.6
13	L13–S13	59.6
14	L14–S13	62.6
15	L15–S13	65.6
16	L16–S14	68.6
17	L17–S14	71.6
18	L18–S15	74.6
19	L19–S15	77.6
20	L20–S16	80.6

Source: Leger, L.A., Mercier, D., Gadoury, C., Lambert, J. 'The multistage 20-metre shuttle run test for aerobic fitness', *Journal of Sports Sciences* 6: 93–101, 1988.

Table 4.6 displays the maximal shuttle run stage and level, along with the predicted $\dot{V}O_{2max}$ values of players from a number of different team sports and playing positions. It is clear that the $\dot{V}O_{2max}$ varies between players from different sports and also between players from the same sport. The

TABLE 4.6

Estimated values for maximal oxygen uptake from the multi-stage shuttle run

Sport	n*	Maximal shuttle	$\dot{V}O_{2max}$ (ml/kg/min)
Rugby Union			
New Zealand 'A' (pre-season)			
Forwards	50	L12–S3	54.6
Backs	43	L13–S9	58.6
New Zealand 'B' (pre-season)			
Forwards	19	L12–S8	55.6
Backs	19	L12–S9	55.6
New Zealand Under 19			
Forwards	29	L11–S6	52.6
Backs	24	L11–S11	54.6
South African squad (pre-season)			
Props and locks	6	L11–S2	51.1
Loose-forwards	5	L12–S6	55.5
Flyhalves and centres	4	L12–S6	55.5
Fullbacks and wings	4	L12–S8	56.0
English National squad (end season)			
Forwards	9	L12–S10	58.0
Backs	9	L13–S13	59.6
South African Under 19 (pre-season)			
Props and locks	10	L11–S9	53.3
Loose-forwards	13	L13–S2	57.5
Flyhalves and centres	4	L12–S11	56.9
Fullbacks and wings	6	L12–S8	56.1
Soccer			
South African squad (early season)	13	L13–S4	58.0

Note: n* refers to the number of players tested.

implication of this finding is that training programs for team players must be individualised to the specific fitness requirements of each playing position (see Chapter 7).

TESTS TO MEASURE ANAEROBIC POWER, SPEED AND AGILITY

There are both laboratory and field tests for measuring anaerobic power.

Laboratory determination of anaerobic power

Because it is very difficult to sprint on a motorised treadmill at speeds faster than 25 km per hour, and because most treadmills do not go much faster anyway, the most widely used laboratory test to measure anaerobic power is undertaken on a cycle ergometer. Developed in Israel at the Wingate Research Institute, the Wingate anaerobic power test (WAT) consists of 30 seconds of exhaustive cycling against a supra-maximal workload proportional to the body mass and training status of the athlete. The workload is such that the athlete is completely fatigued at the end of the 30-second test. Most laboratories interface their cycle ergometer to a computer system which can sample the athlete's power output at very regular time intervals, usually every half a second. At the end of the test, three parameters can be determined from the WAT:

1   the athlete's peak power;
2   the athlete's average power; and
3   the athlete's fatigue index.

The athlete's peak power is the highest power output they sustain for any five-second period of the test, which is always the first five seconds of the ride. The peak power gives an estimate of the capacity of the athlete's ATP–CP, or phos-phagen power system (see Chapter 3). The average power is the total work performed by the athlete throughout the entire test and gives an estimation of the maximum power of the anaerobic glycolytic power system. A fatigue index measures the decay in power during the test, or simply, the rate at which the athlete slows down. Most scientific studies tend to report only an individual's peak and mean power output from the WAT. Such values should be expressed relative to an athlete's body mass to allow comparisons between individuals from different sports, and also between individuals within the same sport or playing position. Table 4.7 displays a summary of the results of several scientific investigations which have measured anaerobic power in individuals from both endurance and team sports.

Although the WAT is the most commonly used laboratory procedure for estimating an athlete's anaerobic power, most individuals will not have access to facilities to undertake such a test. In addition, a strong case could be made that a cycling test is not the most appropriate manner in which to evaluate the physiology of athletes from sports other than cycling (see Chapter 2). As a result, several field tests have been developed which allow the coach to better assess the speed, agility and fatigue resistance of their players under more sports-specific conditions.

TABLE 4.7

Anaerobic performances of individuals from a variety of sports, as assessed by the Wingate anaerobic test

Sport	n*	Peak power (W)	Peak power (W/kg)	Mean power (W)	Mean power (W/kg)
Cycling					
US National road (male)	7	994	13.9	804	11.2
US National road (females)	6	784	12.2	615	9.6
Swimming					
Age-group (males, upper body)	12	266	4.9	204	3.7
Age-group (females, upper body)	10	205	3.7	159	2.8
Age-group (males)	12	585	10.8	449	8.3
Age-group (females)	10	534	9.5	370	6.6
Soccer					
English first and second division	122	1123	14.6	748	9.7
Rugby League					
Forwards	13	1111	12.1		
Backs	12	1114	13.9		
Rugby Union					
International (props)	5	1342	13.1	992	9.7
International (back row)	6	1388	13.8	1144	11.3
International (backs)	5	1336	15.7	1013	11.9

Note: n* refers to the number of athletes or players tested.

Field tests of speed, agility and repeated sprint ability

Maximum running speed and acceleration

A high maximal aerobic power is now a prerequisite for most players participating in team sports at a high level. Additionally, all outfield players are required to sprint at maximum speed and to accelerate from stationary positions throughout the duration of a game. Therefore, any test battery for evaluating the physiological status of players involved in team sports should include a measure of maximum sprint speed and acceleration.

For these tests, which can be conducted on a level field or in a gymnasium, an electronic sprint timer with photo-electric sensors is set at chest height and placed at 10, 20, 30 and 40 m intervals from a start line. After a thorough warm-up and some acceleration runs of increasing speed, the player is instructed to position himself, in a standing start position, close to the start line without breaking the beam of the start sensor. Upon an auditory count-down signal, the player sprints maximally for 40 m, passing through the sensors. The player completes two flat-out runs separated by a five-minute recovery period. The instantaneous times at 10, 20 and 40 m are recorded for each run, as well as the fastest split and total time attained during either run (see Table 4.8). Some coaches also like to determine the speed of their players over a short distance from a moving or rolling start. Such a test negates

---

TABLE 4.8

Sprint–run times (seconds) from stationary starts for players from a variety of team sports

Sport	n*	10 m	30 m	40 m
Soccer				
German professionals	20	1.79	4.19	
German amateurs	19	1.88	4.33	
South African squad (early season)				
Defenders	2	1.77	4.13	5.30
Midfield	5	1.79	4.16	5.34
Forwards	4	1.72	4.09	5.20
Rugby League				
Elite British (end of season)				
Forwards	13			5.61
Backs	12			5.30
Rugby Union				
English National squad (off-season)				
Forwards	9		4.4	
Backs	9		4.1	
English National squad (in-season)				
Forwards	9		4.3	
Backs	9		3.9	
New Zealand 'A' (pre-season)				
Forwards	45		4.5	
Backs	37		4.3	
New Zealand 'B' (pre-season)				
Forwards	12		4.8	
Backs	12		4.5	
New Zealand Under 19 (pre-season)				
Forwards	29		4.6	
Backs	24		4.4	
South African squad (pre-season)				
Props and locks	6	1.83		5.52
Loose-forwards and scrum-halves	5	1.86		5.53
Flyhalves and centres	4	1.80		5.21
Fullbacks and wings	4	1.81		5.19

Note: n* refers to the number of players tested.

some of the disadvantage that the heavier players have when commencing the sprint run from a stationary position. The start is always the slowest segment of any sporting movement.

Agility test (T-drill)

The purpose of this test is to measure the player's acceleration, speed and agility. The test is set up as shown below:

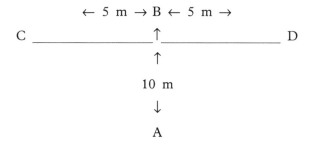

The player commences the test at point A. Upon an auditory signal the player sprints to point B and touches the base of the cone with the right hand. The player then moves laterally to point C and touches the base of the cone with the left hand; then moves laterally to the right to point D and touches the base of the cone with the right hand. The player then moves laterally back to point B and touches the base of the cone with the left hand and then runs backwards past point A. While moving laterally the player must face the front and must not cross feet. The player completes two timed trials separated by a five-minute recovery period, with the fastest time being recorded as the player's best effort.

Sports scientists Justin Durandt and Nicola Scales, working at the High Performance Laboratory at the Sports Science Institute of South Africa, have tested several National teams using the agility run. These data are shown in Table 4.9.

Repeated shuttle run

The ability to attain a high maximal running speed over a short distance is obviously a necessary attribute in athletes participating in explosive running events and in most playing positions in a variety of team sports. However, just as important for team sport players is the ability to perform repeated sprints over varying distances throughout the duration of a match. Thus, a measure of repeated sprint ability should always be included in a test battery for evaluating team sport players, or indeed any event which requires participants to

TABLE 4.9

Agility test scores for players from various team sports

Sport	n*	Time (seconds)
Soccer		
South African National squad (early season)	13	10.70
Goalkeepers	2	10.53
Defenders	2	10.64
Midfield	5	11.09
Forwards	4	10.38
Rugby Union		
South African National squad (pre-season)		
Props and locks	6	11.75
Loose-forwards	5	11.27
Flyhalves and centres	4	10.80
Fullbacks and wings	3	10.74
South African Provincial (pre-season)		
Props	5	12.50
Locks	6	11.96
Loose-forwards	10	11.03
Flyhalves and centres	6	10.89
Fullbacks and wings	7	10.60
South African Under 19 (pre-season)		
Props	2	12.15
Loose-forwards	4	10.90
Flyhalves and centres	5	11.23
Fullbacks and wings	1	11.19

Note: n* refers to the number of players tested.

exercise at or near maximal speed for short durations with minimal recovery between work bouts. For this test, six cones are placed 5 metres apart in a straight line on a level surface, as shown below.

A ↔ B ↔ C ↔ D ↔ E ↔ F
← 5m →

Players commence the test at point A and, upon an auditory signal, sprint to cone B, touch the base of the cone, turn, return to point A, reach down to touch the base, and then sprint to point C. The player continues in this manner, sprinting to the remaining cones (D, E and F), making sure to return to the start (A) between each outward shuttle. If a very fit player can run the entire shuttle (A to F and back) in under 30 seconds, then they commence the cycle again. An auditory signal after 30 seconds of the test indicates the end of that stage of the shuttle run. The number of stages is recorded while the player takes a 35-second rest, during which they make their way back to the start point (A). After 35 seconds they begin the run again. The test is repeated six times and the distance covered during each run is recorded. The variables determined from this test are:

- the total distance covered by a player during the six shuttle runs; and
- a fatigue index, determined from the difference between the maximum distance covered by the player during any single shuttle run minus the shortest distance covered during a run, usually the last shuttle.

As the total distance covered by a player during the entire test is a combined measure of their anaerobic and aerobic power systems, most laboratories tend only to report this value and disregard any measure of fatigue. To execute this test effectively, a maximum of five players should perform the test simultaneously. This is because each player will require one dedicated tester to accurately record the distance covered in each run. Interestingly, of all the tests prescribed for team sport players, the repeated shuttle run is the one considered the most difficult, and as such is feared by almost all players regardless of ability! To cover a total distance in excess of 750 m requires good basic speed, the ability to turn at pace and accelerate, and an excellent aerobic system for a rapid recovery between the runs (see Table 4.10).

PHYSIOLOGICAL TESTING: HOW OFTEN AND WHEN?

One of the questions most frequently asked by coaches is how often should their athletes or teams undergo physiological testing? The simple answer is 'as frequently as practically possible', bearing in mind the constraints of regular training and competition. Since each athlete will differ in their responses to training (see Chapter 2), it is important that their physiological status be regularly evaluated so that exercise prescription can be individually modified and optimised.

With endurance-trained athletes it is suggested that a full battery of physiological tests be undertaken a *minimum* of twice a year. The first testing session should take place at the end

---

TABLE 4.10

Distance run during the repeated shuttle run for players from various team sports

Sport	n*	Distance (metres)
Rugby Union		
South African National squad (pre-season)		
Props and locks	4	702
Loose-forwards and scrumhalves	4	743
Flyhalves and centres	2	757
Fullbacks and wings	3	741
South African Provincial (pre-season)		
Props	4	642
Locks	6	672
Loose-forwards	7	720
Flyhalves and centres	4	745
Fullbacks and wings	6	737
South African Under 19 (pre-season)		
Props	2	688
Loose-forwards	7	735
Flyhalves and centres	5	731
Soccer		
South African National squad		
Defenders	2	735
Midfield	5	748
Forwards	3	749

Note: n* refers to the number of players tested.

of the athlete's pre-season. The results of such tests provide the coach with baseline data on which subsequent, more intense training programs are based. If the athlete can undertake only two testing sessions per year, then the subsequent evaluation should be undertaken immediately prior to, or during, the athlete's competition phase. The results of these tests provide the coach with laboratory data which can be related to actual performances in the field. Ideally, the results should be close to the best the athlete is capable of attaining during that particular season.

For players involved in team sports such as rugby, cricket or soccer, it is more difficult to prescribe the frequency at which physiological testing should be undertaken. Although players need to be assessed regularly, the competition schedule is often demanding. The modern-day team player is expected to participate in a greater number of games with each passing season. This sometimes means that their off-season can be as short as four to six weeks. In such cases, it is recommended that physiological testing be incorporated into the early season fitness training of players. This approach to testing has the advantage of being time effective for both players and coaching staff, as well as providing the coach with on-the-spot feedback as to the current fitness status of their squad.

The issue of whether or not sports scientists should be recommending minimum fitness standards for team sport players is controversial. Match analysis of most field games reveals that contemporary players cover more distance during a game, at a higher intensity and with less time for recovery, than their counterparts from just several years ago. As such, the physiological demands of the game have changed, and today's players need to be fitter, faster and stronger than ever before. Resistance to implementing minimum fitness standards for team sport players comes mostly from the players themselves! They believe that while fitness is vital for success at the top level, there will always be those talented individuals who score badly during physiological test sessions, but who are natural choices for a place in the team on match day. Such players have vision, tactical acumen and possess abilities which cannot be measured during routine physical tests. At first, such an argument appears convincing. However, from a scientific point of view, it is hard to see how these players would not perform even better were they not even fitter!

A DISCLAIMER: WHAT LABORATORY TESTING WILL NOT DO

'An ergometer test is only a test of how people perform on that machine. It does not tell you how well a man can perform in a moving boat, rolling around on difficult water, how well he works within a team, how well he follows his crew, and above all the size of the fight within him when the chips are down in a race.'
Dan Topolski, Oxford University rowing coach, 1976–87

'Put an ergometer on the water and it sinks.'
Fran Reininger, Oxford University rower

As physiological testing has become more accessible and popular for both competitive and recreational athletes, a certain mystique has evolved in the athletic community regarding the benefits of such tests. For example, judging by the frequency with which some endurance athletes discuss their $\dot{V}O_{2max}$ values it would appear that they steadfastly believe this laboratory-derived measure is the single best predictor of their athletic potential. If this were the case, then why turn up to race at all? Why not just have competitors report to the lab, exercise to exhaustion, draw up a rankings list and give out medals based solely on the results of these tests? Fortunately, such a scenario is never likely to become a reality. Accordingly, athletes, coaches and sports scientists should be aware of some of the limitations of scientific testing.

Laboratory testing is not a magical tool for predicting future gold medallists. Indeed, many tests have severe limitations when it comes to predicting actual performance in the field. This is hardly surprising, as the ultimate performance of any athlete or team is the result of several interdependent factors, only one of which is physiological function. With regard to identifying athletic talent, sports scientists still do not know how to accurately forecast an athlete's ultimate performance, their so-called genetic ceiling. That is, they cannot predict with accuracy how much an athlete might improve their strength, speed or aerobic capacity; merely, that with the appropriate training program, they will improve! Finally, there are athletes capable of producing superb laboratory test results, but who consistently fail to perform to their physiological potential under the extreme pressures of competition.

5

Training for speed and power

THE EVOLUTION OF SPRINT RUNNING

Sprinting is the simplest form of athletic competition known to mankind. From a fixed starting position, athletes attempt to get from one point to another as quickly as possible. The winner is the person who crosses the finishing line first. The shortest event on the program in the Olympics of 776 BC was the stade, won by Koroibos of Elis. Sprinters ran the full length of the stadium, a distance of approximately 192 metres. There were only two other races in the ancient Games, the equivalent of the 400 metres (two stades) and the 5000 metres (24 stades). Other sports were not added until the advent of the modern Olympic movement. In these early Games, race times were not considered important by either athletes or officials. The reason for this was simple: the length of the stade varied considerably even in and around the athletic stadiums of Greece!

The keeping of records for standard sprint distances is a relatively modern phenomenon, becoming possible when reliable forms of time-keeping became widespread. A major landmark in the history of sprint records was in 1968 when electronic timing was first used at the Olympic Games. New technology, combined with the thin air of Mexico City, resulted in a large number of world-best performances in many sprint events.

Considering the long and detailed history of sprinting, it is somewhat surprising to find that sports scientists have virtually ignored this area of research. Indeed, compared to the vast literature on a multitude of endurance events, the scarcity of information is remarkable. There are several reasons for this.

For many years it was accepted that sprinters were 'born and not made'. As a result, the pursuit of any serious training was frowned upon. When British sprinter Harold Abrahams employed a professional coach, Sam Mussabini, to help him prepare 'scientifically' for the 100 metres at the 1924 Olympic Games, he was branded a professional cheat!

It was not until the emergence of athletes from the Eastern bloc nations in the late 1970s that sports scientists began to focus their attention on scientific methods to improve sprint performances. Unfortunately, this period of intense scientific inquiry undertaken by many full-time professional coaches and scientists benefited only a select few. The training theory created and implemented by the communist sports system remained, for the most part, a state secret. Not even their scientists were at liberty to share the results of potentially valuable data with fellow professionals throughout the Western world. To what extent the athletic success of Eastern bloc nations, particularly their women, was drug-assisted, as opposed to training-induced, remains a mystery.

Finally, sports scientists have found it difficult to study the physiology and mechanics of sprinting in the laboratory setting. Conventional equipment lacks the sophistication and accuracy to determine the small difference in performance between a good and average sprinter. In addition, the majority of available data relate to sprinters of mediocre ability. Generalising the results of studies undertaken on these subjects to elite performers is not a valid scientific exercise, nor of much practical relevance to the coach or athlete. Nevertheless, despite these limitations, there are certain physical characteristics that allow sports scientists and coaches to distinguish successful sprinters from athletes from other events or sports.

PHYSIOLOGICAL REQUIREMENTS FOR SUCCESSFUL SPRINTERS

The most striking feature of elite sprinters is their muscular development, which allows them to generate high absolute power outputs for short periods of time. Sprinters are heavier and taller than athletes who compete in races of longer duration. But more important than height is the length of the limbs involved in propulsion. Top-class sprint swimmers have a significantly greater arm span than moderately-trained swimmers or swimmers who compete in longer races. In running, leg length influences both stride length and stride rate. Taller sprinters have longer leg lengths, and correspondingly slower stride frequencies, than shorter sprinters. However, even when matched for height and leg length, women still run about one second slower for 100 metres than men. Although this has been attributed to a slower stride frequency, it is likely that the lower muscle mass of a female of the same height and body mass does not allow the generation of the large propulsive forces necessary for high absolute speeds.

Although there is only limited data, studies conducted in the early 1970s suggest that the best sprinters have a higher proportion of 'fast twitch' fibres in their leg muscles than the general population. But just as important as the quality of the muscle is the number of fast twitch fibres that can be recruited during maximal exercise. An adaptation to heavy resistance training is that the highly-trained sprinter is able to use a greater proportion of their fast twitch fibres compared to less well-trained athletes. To what extent reaction time is genetically predetermined as opposed to trainable is not known (see Chapter 9). Sprinters generate peak force faster and have quicker transit reaction times (the time taken to react to a stimulus). Some sports scientists have taken this to mean that there are differences in the functional organisation of the neural system. But this issue remains contentious.

From the results of scientific investigations of elite sprinters, the minimum physiological requirements for any individual wishing to compete at a high level in high-intensity events lasting less than 30 seconds are:

- a high degree of muscularity;
- long lever lengths of the limbs involved in propulsion;
- a high proportion of fast twitch fibres in the muscles involved in the activity;

- the ability to maximally recruit a large proportion of these fibres;
- a fast reaction time;
- the ability to generate and sustain high power outputs or speeds of movement for up to 30 seconds; and
- a moderate aerobic power.

FIBRE TYPING: HELP OR HINDRANCE?

In the 1970s it was very popular for sports scientists to biopsy small portions of an athlete's muscle and classify the athlete according to their fibre type. It emerged that the outstanding performers at each end of the athletic spectrum possessed totally different fibres in the muscles involved in their sport. Sprinters had a predominance of 'fast twitch' fibres, while the muscles of athletes who excelled in endurance events were found to contain mostly 'slow twitch' fibres.

These differences in fibre type were presumed to be genetically determined. The practical implication of this idea is that athletic performance is largely governed by factors outside an athlete's control—namely, their 'choice' of parents. Athletes today still believe it is important to know their 'fibre type'. In fact, when volunteer subjects undergo a muscle biopsy as part of a scientific study (see Chapter 14), they invariably ask if they can have their fibre type determined.

A closer analysis of the results of some of the classic investigations conducted over twenty years ago reveals that although *on average* the endurance-trained athletes studied possessed a higher percentage of slow twitch fibres, the *range* of values for fibre type was large and varied, even for athletes who were successful in the same event. For example, in one famous study of elite runners, two athletes with best performance times for the marathon of 2:18:06 and 2:17:00 had 50% versus 98% slow twitch muscle fibres, respectively! Clearly a high percentage of slow twitch fibres is not the only requirement for success in endurance sports.

A recent study conducted by Dr Pieter Coetzer and colleagues from the University of Cape Town, South Africa, suggests that the preoccupation of both athletes and sports scientists with muscle fibre type and event suitability may have been overstated. They studied the top black distance runners from that country and found that fast twitch fibres made up 40–60% of all their leg muscles. This fibre profile would be typical of a middle-distance rather than a long-distance runner. So even if muscle fibre composition is largely an inherited characteristic, it may not set the ultimate limit to performance.

Here is a useful method for determining your fibre type: jump! If your vertical jump height from a two-footed take-off is less than 25 cm, chances are your muscles are mostly slow twitch. On the other hand, if you can jump over 120 cm, you likely possess a high number of fast twitch muscle fibres, and might want to give the Chicago Bulls basketball team a call!

COMPONENTS OF A SPRINT

'I really get anxious on the blocks. That is the moment of truth. All the training is done, all the head games have been played. Now all you can do is run the best you can.'

Carl Lewis, multiple Olympic gold medal winner

The start

Any sprint can be broken down into several distinct phases (Figure 5.1). The start, which is made up of an athlete's reaction time and movement time, is of paramount importance for sprinters in events which last less than 30 seconds. This is because as the duration of the event decreases, the proportion of the race that comprises the start increases. As a result, reaction times and movement times get slower as the distance of the event gets longer. Although reaction time was thought to be limited by genetic factors, there is some evidence that this can (and should) be trained.

FIGURE 5.1

The components of sprinting

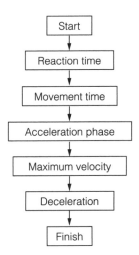

IMPROVING THAT START

'The hundred is a split-second thing. You win or lose by split-seconds. If I make a mistake in the start I will know in the first step. And by five metres I know whether I'm going to run a fabulous race, a medium race, or a lousy race.'

Carl Lewis, Olympic 100 metre champion, 1984 and 1988

If you want to improve the first 10 m of your race, and thus your total race time, then you might have to modify your starting position and employ the latest biomechanical feedback techniques to improve starting technique.

A recent investigation conducted by Drs Luis Mendoza and Wolfgang Schollhorn from the Institute of Sport in Frankfurt suggests that reaction time and movement time over short distances can be improved by giving an athlete immediate feedback relating to their start position. Eight male sprinters with best 100 metre times ranging from 10.4 to 10.8 seconds were studied, using portable equipment which allowed for the simultaneous measurement of the athletes' reaction times, movement times, force generated on the starting blocks and certain biomechanical information. They then modified the athletes' starts by altering either the distance of the starting blocks from the start line, the knee angle of the front leg, or the proportion of the runner's weight falling on their hands in the start position. Immediately after a sprint start, the athletes were given biomechanical feedback and, if necessary, their start position was modified. Seven of the eight sprinters had a significantly faster start after modifying the position of their blocks. The average improvement in starting performance was 0.03 seconds. Sprinters were also able to improve their 10 metre times by maintaining a lower horizontal velocity at take-off. They also found that the horizontal power developed during the starting action was highly related to the athletes' times over 10 m.

The results of this study suggest that an individual's sprint start can be optimised using biomechanical feedback, providing the feedback is given to the athlete immediately after a sprint start has been completed. Such an approach allows the coach to individualise an athlete's starting position and monitor the effects of small changes in body position on performance.

The ground reaction forces generated during sprint starts are very high. The mean power output during the push-off phase can easily exceed 1500W, with instantaneous peak power outputs for very brief periods as high as 3000W. A male sprinter weighing approximately 80 kg and who attains a peak velocity of 11.5 metres per second generates about 1300W for several seconds to accelerate his body mass to reach this speed. Obviously, minimising the time taken for the start is one of the principal concerns for the optimisation of performance in sprinting. In speed skating events, for example, Dr Jos de Koning of the Free University, Amsterdam, found a good correlation ($r = 0.72$) between the mean acceleration during the very first *second* of the start phase and final race time for competitors at the 1988 Winter Olympics. This means that even in a group of elite speed skaters, about 50% of the differences in their final times for 500 metres could be explained by the differences in the initial acceleration phase of the race. Such a finding highlights the need for a short-as-possible start and acceleration phase.

Improving start-times in events like cycling would appear to be a simple matter. Maximal speed is not limited by the requirement to move body segments, an energy costly process, but by friction due to air resistance and the contact between bike and the track surface. The drag coefficients for cyclists, for example, are still quite high compared to other streamlined bodies. For the 1000 and 4000 metres pursuit, which both commence from a stationary start, the development of a better gearing system would allow the cyclist to generate far higher power outputs and speeds than are currently possible. A gear system that automatically adapts itself to the instantaneous velocity of the rider would allow massive improvements in sprint cycle records.

WEIGHT TRAINING FOR KAYAKING: VELOCITY-SPECIFIC

The ability to accelerate from a stationary start is crucial to success in kayaking, particularly the K1 and K2 classes. As such, kayakers preparing for such events commonly include weight training in their training programs. However, the effectiveness of the different types of weight training on sprint performance is unclear. In an attempt to determine which type of strength training is best for kayakers, David Liow and Dr Will Hopkins from the University of Otago, New Zealand, investigated the effect of slow and explosive heavy weight training on kayak sprint performance.

They recruited 39 experienced male and female sprint kayakers who were matched for gender, sprint time and training volume, and then randomly allocated to either a slow weight training group, an explosive weight training group or a control group. The weight training consisted of two sessions per week for a six-week period. In each session the athletes completed three to five sets of six to ten repetitions for two sport-specific exercises, bench press and bilateral dumbbell prone row. The load was equivalent to 80% of their maximum single lift, called 'repetition max' or RM. The two training programs were performed with identical movement patterns and training loads, and differed only in the velocity of the concentric phase of lifting. Athletes from all three groups continued with their usual training and did not participate in any form of additional weight training during the study period.

Both forms of weight training were effective in improving strength, as measured by a 1-RM. The bench press improved by 13.4% for the 'fast' group versus 10.4% for the 'slow' group. Those kayakers who did no weight training but acted as control subjects improved by only 3.0%. For the 1-RM prone-row test the fast group improved by 14.8% and the slow group by 7.9%, while the control group decreased by 2.6%.

In order to determine the effects of the different weight-training programs on sprint acceleration and peak kayaking speed, the kayakers performed sprints over 15 m before and after the training period. An electronic timing system provided split times at 3.75 m, 7.5 m and upon completion of the 15 m. Over the first 3.75 m, the improvement in the slow group (6.9%) was greater than that of the fast group (3.2%) and the control group (1.4%). Over the last 7.5 m the fast group showed a greater improvement (3.0%) than the slow group (2.1%) and the control group (who actually got slower by 0.8%).

The results of this study show that slow weight training was more effective for the acceleration phase of sprinting, when movement is slow. On the other hand, fast or explosive weight training was more effective in enhancing peak sprint speed. To enhance sprint kayaking performance it appears that kayakers should select weight-training velocities that closely match the velocities of the movements specific to their sport.

The acceleration and deceleration phases

'Everybody decelerates toward the end of a 100 metre race. It is impossible to keep accelerating. When I win it is because I run smoother than anyone else and do not decelerate as much as my opponents do.'

Carl Lewis, former world-record holder for the 100 metres

The second part of any sprint is the time taken to accelerate and reach maximum velocity, which varies considerably even between elite sprinters (Table 5.1). There are also significant differences between male and female sprinters in this phase of a race. Males have a longer acceleration phase and reach top speed later in a race than females. However, when they reach their maximal velocity, males are able to sustain that speed longer than females.

| TABLE 5.1 |

Range of times for the different components of a 100 metre sprint for top-level runners

Race component	Men (seconds)	Women (seconds)
Reaction time	0.10–0.30	0.10–0.30
Drive from blocks	0.30–0.40	0.30–0.40
Acceleration phase	5.50–7.00	5.00–6.00
Maximum speed	1.50–3.00	1.50–2.50
Deceleration	1.00–1.50	1.50–2.50

Note: Data are based on a 100 metre time of 10 seconds for males and 11 seconds for females.

Source: Adapted from Radford, P.F. in *Physiology of Sports* Reilly, T., Secher, N., Snell, P., and Williams, C. (eds) E. & F. Spon, London, pp. 71–99, 1990.

| TABLE 5.2 |

An analysis of sprinting at the highest level—a breakdown of the men's 100 metres final at the 1991 World Athletics Championships

Variable	Carl Lewis (USA)	Leroy Burrell (USA)	Dennis Mitchell (USA)
Reaction time (m/sec)	140	120	90
10 metre speed (m/sec)	5.31	5.46	5.56
20 metre speed (m/sec)	9.26	9.43	9.35
30 metre speed (m/sec)	10.87	10.99	10.75
40 metre speed (m/sec)	11.24	11.36	11.36
50 metre speed (m/sec)	11.90	11.49	11.49
60 metre speed (m/sec)	11.76	11.63	11.49
70 metre speed (m/sec)	11.90	11.49	11.63
80 metre speed (m/sec)	12.05	11.90	11.63
90 metre speed (m/sec)	11.49	11.24	11.36
Finishing speed (m/sec)	11.63	11.49	11.24
Finishing time (seconds)	9.86	9.88	9.91
Stride length (metres)	2.37	2.41	2.25
Stride rate (strides/sec)	4.51	4.40	4.70

Source: Ae, M., Ito, A. and Suzuki, M. 'The men's 100 metres.' *New Studies in Athletics* 7: 47–52, 1992.

For swimming, running, rowing and some other sports the equation is simple. An athlete's maximal speed is the product of the distance covered with each stroke or stride multiplied by the frequency of those movements. Change one, and the other is altered automatically. For example, during the 100 metre sprint both males and females take between 45 and 50 strides. But because males are generally taller and have longer leg length, their stride length is correspondingly greater. As a result, they go faster.

At the 1991 World Athletics Championships the International Amateur Athletics Federation (IAAF) allowed sports scientists to collect comprehensive data on selected track events. One of these was the men's and women's 100 metres. Table 5.2 shows a breakdown of the main components of the sprint for the medal winners in the men's final. This race was remarkable in that the first four runners did not reach top speed until after 70 or even 80 metres. This is much later than traditionally thought. Even more unusual was that Lewis and Burrell actually accelerated from 90 metres until the finish. Most coaches have previously contended that it was impossible for *any* runner to accelerate over the final 40 metres of a 100 metre sprint, let alone the last 10 metres of a race. Runners only *appeared* to be accelerating because they were slowing down less than their opponents. Clearly, this paradigm is in need of revision. Today's elite sprinters reach maximal speed during the latter stages of a race and sustain high velocities for significantly longer than was formerly believed. This scientific finding has practical implications for the physical preparation of athletes in the shortest sprint events.

MICHAEL JOHNSON: NOW YOU SEE HIM, NOW YOU DON'T

Why is Michael Johnson, winner of the 200 and 400 metres at the 1996 Atlanta Olympics, so fast? What allows him to run the second 100 metres of a 200 metre race faster than the world record for the individual 100 metres? Especially as he looks like a road runner, with a low knee lift and a short, choppy stride.

His coach, Clyde Hart of Baylor University, Houston, Texas, explains that Johnson is only 1.83 m tall—much shorter than most of today's elite sprinters. This gives him relatively short legs and a correspondingly short stride length compared with many of his rivals. To compensate, Johnson's stride frequency *has* to be higher. But coach Hart believes that Johnson's foot placement is the real key to his speed. Many athletes place their foot slightly ahead of their centre of gravity on foot-strike. In effect, that's like braking every step. But Johnson's feet hit the track under his centre of gravity. As a result, he appears never to stop moving.

High-speed cinematographical analysis of Johnson's technique confirms coach Hart's observations. Johnson's feet stay in contact with the ground for just 0.08 of a second. Other world-class sprinters stay planted on the ground for 0.09 of a second, compared to good sprinters, who are comparatively landlocked at 0.10 of a second.

Not only is the generation of high forces essential for the sprinter, but when they reach maximum speeds they must only have the briefest contact with the track. Coach Hart says, 'There were times when I thought we should do drills to lengthen his stride. Make him reach out. Then I realised it's not broke, so don't fix it!'

TRAINING FOR SPEED

Speed and power are critical to most team sports (see Chapter 7) and to all athletic events lasting less than a few minutes. Yet, training for speed is one of the most poorly addressed areas of sports science: sprint-training methods have been left almost entirely to the empirical knowledge of the coaching fraternity. However, there is some consensus on the main features which characterise the core components of physical preparation for sprinting. They include:

- the establishment of a moderate base of aerobic conditioning and non-specific general fitness during the athlete's off-season;
- considerable attention to technique and specific drills during the pre-season training period;
- extensive, year-round resistance and circuit training;
- use of plyometrics and other forms of high-velocity resistance training to improve muscle power;
- stretching and mobility exercises performed before and after most hard training sessions; and
- periodisation of the training and racing program.

Loughborough University track and field coach George Gandy has developed a broad framework on which a program for an athlete preparing for sprint events can be organised. Gandy splits the program up into three distinct phases during which the athlete focuses on attaining different goals for that particular period. The phases are:

1   general preparatory phase;
2   competition preparation; and
3   competitive season.

During each of these phases of training, primary emphasis is given to the development of one or more of the specific physiological objectives detailed above.

General preparatory (non-competitive) phase

The period of general preparation is undertaken so that an athlete can establish a foundation of non-specific general fitness during which subsequent, more intense event-specific training can be based. This phase should last between 12 and 16 weeks, during which time the sprinter gradually eases into a full training routine. During the general preparatory period, which is always undertaken during the athlete's non-competitive period, the athlete commences a 'total-body' resistance training program, as well as commencing circuit training. Several aerobic running sessions of 3–5 km are undertaken

TABLE 5.3

Performance tests and minimum standards for 100 metre sprinters of different abilities

Skill	100 m (10.70)	100 m (10.50)	100 m (10.20)	100 m (10.00)
Sprint 30 metres from a crouch start (seconds)	4.1–4.2	4.0–4.1	3.8–3.9	3.7–3.8
Sprint 30 metres from a rolling start (seconds)	2.9–3.0	2.8–2.9	2.8	2.7
Maximum sprint velocity (metres/second)	10.86	11.11	11.62	11.90
Sprint 150 metres (seconds)	15.7	15.2	14.8	14.7
Sprint 300 metres (seconds)	35.2–36.2	34.0–35.0	32.4–33.2	32.0–32.4
Standing long jump (metres)	2.85–2.90	2.90–3.00	3.00–3.10	3.00–3.10
Standing triple jump (metres)	8.60–8.80	8.90–9.20	9.30–10.0	9.30–10.0
10 hops from a standing start (metres)	33–34	34–35	35–36	35–36

Source: Williams, C. and Gandy, G. 'Physiology and nutrition for sprinting', in *Perspectives in Exercise Science and Sports Medicine* vol 7, *Physiology and Nutrition for Competitive Sport*, Lamb, D.R. Knuttgen, H.G. and Murray, R., (eds) Cooper Publishing Group, Carmel, Indiana, p. 91, 1994.

each week. In addition, after four to six weeks, some sprint-run technique work should be introduced. This takes the form of relaxed striding, with short jog–walk rest intervals (see box below).

Stretching is included at the end of most workouts.

Competition preparation

During the second phase of a sprinter's training program, the main emphasis shifts to more specific conditioning. The aerobic conditioning of the general preparatory phase gives way to speed–endurance training, with the introduction of some timed runs and associated performance tests (see Table 5.3). There is more emphasis on power, and speed drills and starting practice are introduced. The competition preparation should be undertaken for four to six weeks.

Competition phase

During the competitive period, the athlete should plan to compete in about a dozen races, of which the first few may be over-distance. The aim of this phase is to produce personal best performances in selected important competitions. Training is therefore scheduled around competition dates. The emphasis of such training should be the maintenance of speed and power, and high-quality speedwork. Recovery intervals between work bouts must be sufficient to allow for high technical quality. The volume of weight training should be reduced, but the intensity should be maintained or even slightly increased.

WEEKLY TRAINING PLAN FOR SPRINTERS: GENERAL PREPARATION PHASE

(To be undertaken for 12–16 weeks)

Monday	a.m.	Weight training Three sets of 10–15 repetitions at 80% of 1 RM of leg press, bench press, hamstring curls, biceps curls, knee extensions, dips, cleans and snatches or squats.
	p.m.	Easy run (3–5 kilometres)
Tuesday	a.m.	Track session Warm-up jog (1 kilometre), 6 × 60 metres relaxed

strides, then: 2–4 sets of 100 metre jog, 100 metre stride, 100 metre jog, 300 metre stride, 100 metre jog, 200 metre stride

Rest 2–3 minutes between sets. Strides @ 80% effort, emphasis on form and technique. Warm-down jog (800 metres).

Wednesday	a.m.	Easy run (3–5 kilometres)
	p.m.	Circuit training
Thursday	p.m.	Track session (same as Tuesday)
Friday	a.m.	Weight training (same as Monday)
Saturday	a.m.	Track session

Warm-up jog (1 kilometre), 6 × 60 metres relaxed strides, then: 2 × 6 × 200 metres @ 80% effort with 200 metres jog-recovery between repetitions and 3–5 minutes' rest between sets. Warm-down jog (800 metres).

Sunday	a.m.	Easy run (6 kilometres)

Note that these are the sessions an athlete should be completing at the *end* of the specified training period. Build up to them gradually. Supplementary stretching and the inclusion of other training methods (water running, yoga, etc.) is optional.

WEEKLY TRAINING PLAN FOR SPRINTERS: COMPETITION PREPARATION

(To be undertaken for 4–6 weeks)

Monday	a.m.	Weight training

Three sets of 4–6 repetitions at 90% of 1 RM of leg press, bench press, hamstring curls, biceps curls, knee extensions, cleans and snatches or squats.

	p.m.	Fartlek run (3 kilometres)
Tuesday	a.m.	Track session

Warm-up jog (1 kilometre), 6 × 60 metres relaxed strides, then: 3 × 3 × 100 metres @ 90% effort, rolling starts, building up speed. Walk-back recovery between repetitions, and 3–5 minutes' rest between sets. Warm-down jog (800 metres).

Wednesday	a.m.	Technique/drills (one of the following sessions): *Starting practice*: 6–8 × 40 metres with 2–3 minutes' recovery. *Hill sprints*: 6–8 × 60 metres hill sprints, emphasising knee lift and form, with 2–3 minutes' recovery. *Downhill sprinting*: 6–8 × 100 metres, emphasising leg speed.
	p.m.	Circuit training
Thursday	p.m.	Track session (same as Tuesday)
Friday	a.m.	Weight training (same as Monday)
Saturday	a.m.	Track session/performance tests/timed runs Warm-up jog (1 kilometre), 6 × 60 metres relaxed strides, then: timed runs over 60, 150, 300 metres. Performance tests (see Table 5.4). Up and down the clock session: 2 × 60, 90, 120, 150, 120, 90 and 60 metres, with walk-back recovery between runs and 5–7 minutes' rest between sets. Warm-down jog (800 metres).
Sunday	a.m.	Technique/drills (one of the following sessions): *Starting practice*: 6–8 × 40 metres with 2–3 minutes' recovery. *Hill sprints*: 6–8 × 60 metres hill sprints, emphasising knee lift and form, with 2–3 minutes' recovery. *Downhill sprinting*: 6–8 × 100 metres, emphasising leg speed.

Source: Williams, C. and Gandy, E. 'Physiology and nutrition for sprinting' in *Perspectives in Exercise Science and Sports Medicine*, vol. 7, *Physiology and Nutrition for Competitive Sport*, Lamb, D.R., Knuttgen, H.G., and Murray, R. (eds), Cooper Publishing Group, Carmel, Indiana, 1994, pp. 88–90.

> TRAINING WITH THE CHAMPIONS:
> CARL LEWIS'S BUILD-UP TO THE
> 1996 ATLANTA OLYMPICS

The following program was typical of the training that Carl Lewis was undertaking in January 1996, some seven months before the Atlanta Olympics. From January until May the program changed, with the number of days spent running gradually being increased from three to five. It should be noted that this schedule was originally aimed at Lewis competing in the 100 and 200 metres, as well as the long jump.

Monday	a.m.	Breakdown session* (track)

Monday   a.m.   Breakdown session* (track)
Warm-up jog and strides, then: 1 × 400 metres (less than 51 seconds), 1 × 300 metres (less than 39 seconds), 1 × 200 metres (less than 25 seconds). Five minutes' rest between runs. Warm-down jog.
Or
6 × 200 metres fast and relaxed (24–25 seconds) with 90 seconds' recovery between repetitions.

Tuesday   a.m.   Weights
          p.m.   Starting practice

Wednesday p.m.   Plyometrics, bounding, stadium steps
                   Long jump practice

Thursday   a.m.   Track session
                   Warm-up jog, strides, then: 6–8 × 150 metres, flying starts, or 8 × 100 metres. Warm-down jog.

Friday   a.m.   Weights
          p.m.   Long jump practice

Saturday   Time trial or race

Sunday   Rest day

* *Breakdown session*: By the end of February the times for the various runs were down to 48 seconds (400 metres), 33 seconds (300 metres) and 21 seconds (200 metres) with the same rest interval.

Source: Lewis, C. and Marx, J. 'One more victory lap', *Athletics International*, Santa Monica, California, 1996, pp. 18–19.

THE TRAINING OF OLYMPIC SPRINT SWIMMER ALEXANDRE POPOV

By Coach Gennadi Touretski and Dr David Pyne
(Australian Institute of Sport)

Alexandre Popov is the champion Russian swimmer who won Olympic gold medals in both the 50 and 100 metres freestyle events at the 1992 Barcelona Games, and then again at the 1996 Atlanta Games. He is also the world-record holder for the 100 metres freestyle in both long-course (48.21 seconds) and short-course (46.70 seconds) pools. He currently resides in Canberra, Australia, where he trains at the Australian Institute of Sport under his long-time coach, Gennadi Touretski.

The philosophy of Popov's training program is based on two main elements. First, swimming is an endurance sport and requires a well-developed aerobic capacity with attention to low-intensity aerobic and anaerobic threshold and maximal oxygen uptake speeds. Secondly, all training, from low-intensity to supra-maximal race speeds, is undertaken with a high degree of technical precision.

The training week presented here is taken from a typical three-week-long endurance training macro-cycle completed early in the season. This endurance training consists of eleven sessions in six days, for a total of approximately 60 km. It contains a blend of training, from dive sprints through the full range of aerobic speeds, and incorporates all four swimming strokes, pull and kick sets, and a range of technique drills. Although Alexandre's training volume can vary from 20 to 80 km a week, the majority is in the region of 40–60 km during any six-day period.

Key to abbreviations: FS, freestyle; BK, backstroke; Fly, butterfly; BR, breaststroke; IM, individual medley; w/p, with paddles; w/up, warm-up; MAX, maximal efforts; 5/5, breathing every five strokes.

Day 1   a.m.   (4,500 m)
                 1,600 m kick–pull–swim
                 1,200 m pull w/p (150 FS + 50 BK)
                 8 × 100 m FS 7/7 on 1:25
                 400 FS
                 8 × 20 FLY MAX on 55 sec
         p.m.   (5,000–9,500 m)
                 600 m w/up
                 3 × 8 × 100 m + 200 drill FLY
                   1. FS–BK on 90 sec
                   2. FS–pull w/p on 1:25
                   3. FS–kick on 1:50
                 9 × 100 IM with 10 sec rest
                 300 m w/down

Day 2   a.m.   (4,800 m)
                 1,200 m FS–IM w/p
                 800 m (150 FS–50 BK) w/p
                 600 FS–IM w/p
                 400 (50 FS + 50 BK) w/p
                 200 IM
                 16 × 50 m on 50 sec (3 FS + 1 FLY)
                 400 m drill

3 × 24 MAX FLY–BK–BR to 600 m
100 m w/down

p.m.   (1,200–6,000 m)
1,200 swim

Day 3   a.m.   (6,100 m)
800 m w/up
8 × 400 FS + BK w/p on 6:00
FS + pull w/p on 5:30
800 m kick drill FLY
18 × 50 IM (25 max + 25) on 55 sec
8 × 50 kick FS on 55 sec

p.m.   (6,000–12,000 m)
600 w/up
2 × 3 × 200 kick on 3:30 FS
3 × 200 pull w/p on 2:30 FS
3 × 200 IM on 3:00
100 swim w/down
8 × 50 on 45 sec (20 FLY MAX + 30 FS)
400 drill
4 × 25 on 2:00
500 pull–kick FS swim down

Day 4   a.m.   (4,000–4,500 m)
8 × 100 FS + BK on 90 sec
4 × 4 × 100 kick FS on 1:45 + 100 on 2:00
1,200 IM kick + drill + 25 MAX

p.m.   Off

Day 5   a.m.   (7,500 m)
1,200 FS + IM
3 × 4 × 100 kick on 1:50 FS
4 × 100 pull on 1:20 FS
400 FS + BK (150 + 50) on 5:30
300 drill BK
3 × 15 MAX BK to 200
10 × 100 FS + BK
5 × 100 pull FS on 1:20 (5/5)
5 × 100 FS on 90 sec
50 drill FLY
150 swim down

p.m.   (7,500–15,000 m)
1,000 FS + BK
2,000 as 100 to 400 on 90 sec (5/5/) FS + BK

400 to 100 pull FS on 1:20
20 × 50 kick FS on 55 sec
20 × 50 pull FS on 60 sec
400 drill IM on 50 sec
6 × 200 IM on 3:20
4 × 25 FS MAX dive to 150
300 swim down

Day 6   a.m.   (7,000 m)
300 w/up
1,500 pull (100 FS + 50 BK)
10 × 50 on 60 sec kick
5 × 300 on 4:15
      1,3,5 as 150 FS + 50 FLY + 100 FS pull
      2,4 as 300 BK
10 × 25 MAX on 55 FLY + BK to 50
3 × (300 pull FS w/p on 4:00/200 IM on 3:00)
5 × 25 MAX on 1:45 to 100 FLY, BK, FS
7 × 100 kicks FS on 1:50

             p.m.   (6,500–13,400 m)
3 × (200 FS + BK, 200 drill–IM, 3 × 15 MAX)
2 × (4 × 100 FS + BK drill on 2:00, 4 × 50 pull)
5 × 200 FS on 2:45
2 × 4 × 50 FLY on 2:00 to 100
200 drill FS + BK + BR
6 × 25 FS to 50 on 90 sec
400 kick swim down

Day 7   Rest!

WHEN IS A SPRINT NOT A SPRINT?

The shortest event on the Olympic swimming program is the 50 metres
'sprint'. The world record for men is 21.81 seconds. The shortest
recognised distance for speed skaters is the 500 metres. Typical race
time, 36–40 seconds. The K1 singles kayak 'sprint' event takes upwards
of 100 seconds. And if you are a rower and want to compete in a
'sprint' event, well, forget it. Even in a coxed eight you can bet on a
minimum of five-and-a-half minutes of racing.

Compare these events to those in track competition. The 50 metres
dash takes under six seconds, the 60 metres just a fraction longer, the
100 metres around 10 seconds, and half a lap of the track, sub 20
seconds. Track cyclists have a match sprint lasting 200 metres, which is

typically covered in approximately 10 seconds. Technically, 'sprint' is used to describe the shortest event in a sport. But when is a sprint *really* a sprint? And should 'sprinters' from one sport really be compared to 'sprinters' from another, completely different, sport?

From a physiologist's perspective, the common point of comparison between sports is the contribution the body's power systems make to the event. In sports in which competitors are required to produce as much power as possible, such as running, swimming, cycling and speed skating, a true sprint would involve a race distance which takes the athletes less than 10 seconds, and certainly no more than 15 seconds, to cover. In such an event, the contribution of the anaerobic power systems would be high (see Chapter 3). But presently, the 'splash-dash' in the pool has a relatively high aerobic component (around 30%), while any event lasting longer than 60 seconds is powered predominantly by aerobic sources.

So, the current nomenclature of classifying the shortest event on a program as a 'sprint' is physiologically inappropriate. More to the point, it should be stressed that in some sports, there really is no true sprint event. At the other end of the continuum, it is common to refer to the longest event on a particular sporting program as a 'marathon'. This is also incorrect.

Of course, the length of a sports event is based on factors such as the physical confines of the arena in which it is held, historical tradition (the distance of 26 miles, 385 yards for the marathon—see Chapter 18), or even 'round' numbers, rather than any physiological criteria. Incorrect terminology is not a major problem if you are a sports commentator. However, if you are a coach it pays to know the physiology of your athlete's event precisely. And then to train the appropriate power systems for the correct physiological challenge.

RESETTING THE SPEED CLOCK: OVERSPEED TRAINING

In recent years, the practice of 'overspeed' training has become popular among many coaches. In particular, top American sprint coach Tom Tellez, who works with Carl Lewis and Leroy Burrell, has advocated the use of 'overspeed' workouts as the final stage of a sprinter's competition preparation.

The purpose of overspeed training, or 'sprint-assisted' training, is to perform the running action at a much faster speed than you would otherwise be able to do without assistance. In theory, such training should also allow the neuromuscular system to initiate much faster rates of contraction than normal. There are several types of overspeed training:

• downhill running;
• high-speed stationary cycling;
• towing; and
• high-speed treadmill running.

Downhill running is perhaps the easiest, most practical form of overspeed training, requiring no specialised equipment. Coach Tellez recommends a 50 metre slope of no more than three degrees on which the athlete builds up to eight to ten repetitions at maximal speed over a four- to five-week period. Such workouts should preferably take place on a soft surface, such as grass, as the rate of lower limb injuries associated with downhill running is high. An alternative and safer, but as yet unproved, method of speed training is high-speed cycling on a stationary ergometer. The basic premise here is that increasing leg speed during *any* movement has a positive effect on running speed. However, the concept of training specificity would predict that there is only minimal 'cross-training' from cycling to running, particularly among well-trained athletes (see Chapter 2).

Towing (a technique where the athlete is literally pulled along and assisted to run faster) and high-speed stationary treadmill running are more likely to improve running speed. But a lot more scientific research needs to be undertaken in highly-trained athletes before any of these techniques should be incorporated into an athlete's training routine.

MUSCLE ACTIONS: SOME WORKING DEFINITIONS

The terminology of resistance training is often confusing for the athlete, coach and sports scientist alike. That is probably because there are so many definitions essentially centred around the same concepts. Here are brief definitions of some of the most frequently used terms.

Muscle actions

Concentric A normal muscle action in which a force is applied, the muscle(s) shorten, and the joint moves. For example, lifting a weight during the first phase of a biceps curl.

Eccentric A muscle action in which a force is applied while a muscle is lengthening. For example, lowering a weight during the second phase of a biceps curl.

Isometric A contraction of the muscle without any change in the length of the muscle. For example, when an athlete pushes or pulls an immovable object.
Isotonic A contraction during which the tension or load on a muscle remains the same during all phases of the movement.
Isokinetic A contraction during which the speed of movement remains constant throughout the entire range of motion.

RESISTANCE TRAINING TO IMPROVE SPEED AND STRENGTH

'The effectiveness of lifting [weights] for runners has been argued for years. Until the 1960s most runners stayed away from too much lifting because they were afraid of becoming "muscle bound" and forfeiting flexibility. But almost all top runners do at least some lifting now.'

Carl Lewis, former world-record holder for the 100 metres

'The one year I did the most lifting, I probably ran the worst.'

Carl Lewis, nine-time Olympic champion

Resistance training techniques have been used by athletes to enhance their performance for centuries. In past years, resistance training was primarily the domain of athletes involved in 'strength events' such as weight lifting or the throwing events in track and field. But during the past decade, resistance training has become a popular training method with athletes from a wide range of sports.

Although most coaches would agree that resistance training is a key element in the preparation of any sprinter or athlete involved in an event which requires bouts of maximal speed, the precise content of the best resistance training program is still a topic of considerable debate. The challenge for any coach is to devise a resistance training program that enhances the athlete's capacity to meet or exceed the physical demands of their event and leads to an improved performance. Development of the optimal program requires a careful consideration of many factors, including:

- the absolute strength requirements of the athlete's event;
- the ability of the athlete to meet these physiological requirements;

- the muscle groups utilised during the athlete's event;
- whether the athlete's event comprises concentric contractions, eccentric contractions, or both (see panel);
- whether resistance training should be isometric, isotonic or isokinetic;
- the intensity (load) and frequency of resistance training; and
- the rate of progression of resistance training.

Although there are a multitude of resistance training methods that can be used to enhance strength and performance, these can be split broadly into three main categories:

1 high-resistance weight training;
2 dynamic resistance training; and
3 plyometrics.

High-resistance weight training

This type of training involves lifting heavy loads (80–90% of 1 RM) a relatively few times (four to six repetitions) and is based on the theory that lifting the heaviest load results in the maximal recruitment of motor units and significant increases in muscle size (hypertrophy) and strength. A typical session would involve three to four sets of four to six repetitions of each exercise, with a long (two to three minutes) recovery between sets. Often serious athletes will 'split' training sessions into upper or lower body parts, working on one or the other on alternate days. This procedure allows for adequate recovery between training sessions of the same musculature.

Dynamic resistance training

In contrast to high-resistance weight training, dynamic resistance training involves lifting lighter weights (30–40% of 1 RM) at very high speeds. This form of resistance training is more 'sports-specific' in that the athlete can perform exercise at velocities which mimic their chosen event. This type of training produces the highest power outputs of the muscles, which has been reported to result in the greatest gains in performance. A typical session might involve four sets of ten to fifteen repetitions of each exercise, with a short (less than 30 seconds) recovery between sets.

FREE WEIGHTS OR MACHINES?

Coaches and athletes agree to disagree when it comes to the benefits of free weights versus machines. But the scientific facts are that both methods of training have their own unique benefits and advantages. Free weights are obviously much less expensive than the majority of resistance machines. They allow multiple joint movements to be performed, and are more effective in developing the smaller synergistic and stabiliser muscles. Compared to most machines, free weights also require greater proprioception, balance and coordinated movement patterns. Coaches feel this aspect is important when teaching a specific weight-lifting technique. But training alone with free weights can be dangerous, as heavy weights can cause injury if movement control or balance is lost. Adjustments of weights between sets or exercises is often time-consuming and tedious.

In the case of machines, no two are alike and most have been designed to fit the average athlete: very tall individuals find it very hard to use many of the current machines on the market. Some resistance training machines limit an athlete to single-joint movement in a fixed plane of movement. But machines do allow the athlete to isolate specific body parts or muscle groups more easily than free weights. Try doing knee extensions with free weights! Recently, machines utilising hydraulic systems or air-braking devices have taken over in many gyms. These machines have been termed 'accommodating resistance devices', since they provide resistance that either increases or decreases according to the force applied. An advantage of these machines is that they allow the athlete to exert maximal force through the entire range of motion. Unfortunately, however, most accommodating resistance devices do not permit eccentric contractions. This might be beneficial during the early stages of a resistance training program because it limits muscle soreness.

The 'space-age' appearance of some 'high-tech' machines can lull the athlete into believing that technology equals maximum strength gains. But in the final analysis, nothing beats hard work. Among experienced weight lifters and strength-trained athletes, the verdict is that 'high tech equals low technique' and that free weights are still the best way to optimise strength.

Plyometrics

'The main objective of plyometric training is to improve an athlete's ability to generate maximum force in the shortest time.'

Coaches Dintiman, Ward and Tellez, in their book *Sports Speed*

Plyometric training utilises the acceleration and deceleration of the athlete's body mass and gravity to overload the muscles. For example, an athlete might jump off a box, storing potential energy in their muscles, and then immediately release that energy in the opposite direction (kinetic energy) upon ground impact. The goal of plyometrics is to enhance the ability of an athlete to exert maximal force during high-speed movements. Activities that require such movements include sprinting and any team sports that involve jumping or changes of pace and/or direction at speed (e.g. basketball, football, diving, volleyball). Typically, plyometric drills involve activities such as jumping or bounding, in which there is a rapid rate of stretch of the muscles involved in the activity. The amazing progress and success of Russian sprinter Valeri Borzov, 1972 Olympic 100 metre champion, is partially attributed to the use of plyometric exercises. During the six years prior to his gold medal victory, Borzov progressed from a 100 metre time of 13.0 seconds at age fourteen to 10.0 seconds by the time he was twenty.

A plyometric movement can be broken down into three distinct components:

1 the eccentric phase;
2 the amortisation phase; and
3 the concentric contraction.

The eccentric phase is the time during which the athlete lands and their working muscles are lengthening in response to the landing or impact forces. The eccentric component of any movement is associated with the production of the largest muscular forces and is therefore associated with the highest potential for injury. The amortisation phase is the time from landing to the initiation of the concentric, or shortening, contraction. And to maximise the training effect of plyometrics, this phase should be accomplished as quickly as possible. As such, it is important to remember that an athlete is capable of producing greater power when the depth of a jump is short and rapid, rather than long and slow. The concentric phase begins with the start of the upward (or counter) movement, usually a jump. In sport, such a movement would be analogous to a basketballer jumping for a rebound. It is important to note that it is the *rate* of stretch (i.e. the speed) rather than the magnitude of the stretch (i.e. the size) which is important in plyometric training.

Like any other aspect of physical preparation for sport, a program of plyometric exercises must comply with the principles of training (see Chapter 2). With regard to frequency, plyometric training should not be performed more than three times a week during any stage of the athlete's conditioning. During the off-season two sessions per week are considered optimal, while dropping to one maintenance session each week during the actual playing season is recommended. For high-impact sports such as rugby, it may not be advisable to carry out any plyometric training in-season.

The volume of plyometric training is typically expressed as the number of foot contacts per workout (when an athlete undertakes jumping exercises), or the total distance covered during a single session (when bounding exercises are performed). For athletes commencing a plyometric training program the number of foot contacts should not exceed 100 per session. For athletes who have previously undertaken plyometric training, 100–120 foot contacts is recommended (see Table 5.4). Athletes with a history of weight training and who have completed several years of plyometrics can perform up to 150 foot contacts per workout. It is difficult to set precise upper limits for the distances to be covered during plyometric training as bounding drills encompass a wide variety of different types of exercise. However, if the intensity or effort of such exercise is high, the volume should be low.

The optimal intensity of plyometric drills can be assessed according to the following factors:

- the direction of a jump (horizontal or vertical);
- the athlete's horizontal or vertical speed;
- the change in the position of an athlete's centre of gravity;
- the nature of the landing surface and whether one or two feet make ground contact; and
- whether or not the athlete is carrying extra weight while performing a drill.

If a drill is vertical (such as a jump), then the ground reaction forces will usually be higher than a horizontal movement (such as a bound). Accordingly, for the same number of repetitions, the intensity will be lower. But the speed of motion is also an important factor in determining the amount of stress placed on an athlete. The higher a jump, or the longer a bound, then the greater the intensity compared to a lower or shorter drill and the higher the risk of injury. The

TABLE 5.4

The recommended volume (number of foot contacts) for plyometric training for athletes of varying abilities

Phase of training	Intensity	Novice	Intermediate	Advanced
Off-season	Low	50–100	100–150	125–175
Pre-season	Moderate	100–150	150–200	150–300
In season	High	50–100	75–100	100

Source: Chu, D. Jumping into Plyometrics, Champaign, Illinois: Human Kinetics, 1992.

recommended height for depth-jumping ranges from 50 cm to one metre. But for heavy athletes who weigh more than 100 kg, it is recommended that depth-jumps should not be performed from a height of greater than about 70 cm.

The type of surface the athlete is training on also has a direct influence on the intensity of any plyometric exercise. Although hard surfaces may result in a shorter amortisation phase and/or greater distances being covered in an exercise, they also produce higher impact forces and increase the probability of soft tissue or joint injury. Conversely, training on soft surfaces reduces the risk of injury, but does not provide the same training stimulus. Landing and taking off from one or two feet also contributes to the impact forces. Bounding exercises using alternate legs result in greater vertical than horizontal displacement of the athlete's centre of gravity than two-footed take-offs. Finally, it is not usually necessary to add extra mass in the form of weight vests or ankle weights. The addition of external weight greatly increases the impact forces, but may also increase the amortisation phase while concomitantly increasing the risk of injury, especially in those athletes who have poor technique.

TRAINING FOR SPEED: HIGH RESISTANCE OR HIGH VELOCITY?

Coaches agree that resistance training is a key element in improving an athlete's speed. Trouble is, they can't reach a consensus on the best *type* of training. Some coaches prescribe high-resistance weight training for their athletes, in the belief that working against the heaviest load possible will result in the biggest increases in maximal strength which, in turn, will translate into improvements in speed. On the other hand, the principle of specificity dictates that the closer the training routine is to the requirements of competition, then the better will be the performance (see Chapter 2). And here some coaches steadfastly believe that high-velocity dynamic resistance training, such as plyometrics, is the only method for enhancing the velocity of a sporting movement. There have been two recent studies which have attempted to determine the optimal training load for developing explosive speed and power for athletes involved in explosive events.

In the first investigation, Dr Greg Wilson and his co-workers from the University of New England, New South Wales, examined the effects of three resistance training methods on a series of athletic activities, including a 30 m sprint, a six-second all-out cycling test, a maximal vertical jump and the athlete's maximal isokinetic strength. They randomly assigned 55 subjects, all with previous strength training experience, to either a high-resistance, high-velocity or plyometric training program. Each subject performed three to six sets of between six and ten repetitions of a single exercise (a squat). However, the load was different in each of the three groups. The high-resistance group trained at a load that enabled them to undertake a maximum of ten reps each set. The high-velocity group performed six to ten squats with low resistance as fast as possible on a hydraulic system. The plyometric training group performed six to ten jumps from a maximal height of 80 cm. The training load for all three groups was progressively increased throughout the study period. Subjects trained twice a week and were tested before and at the end of the 10-week program. After training, the athletes who had participated in the high-resistance program showed the greatest gains in maximal isometric force production. But for all of the dynamic performance tests, the subjects who undertook high-velocity and plyometric training improved most. The investigators of this study concluded that 'the optimal training strategy to enhance strength and dynamic athletic performance is a hybrid between traditional weight training and plyometric training'.

In a more recent investigation, Dr Christophe Delecluse and his colleagues at the University of Leuven, Belgium, compared the effects of two resistance training methods on the different phases of the 100 m sprint. They had 43 physical education students participate in either a high-resistance or a high-velocity training program three times a week for nine weeks. In addition, both resistance training groups participated in a sprint running program. The high-resistance program consisted of both upper and lower body exercises specific to the muscle groups involved in sprint running. The high-velocity program comprised standard plyometric drills, including standing broad jumps, vertical jumps, bounding and hopping. As would be expected, the subjects on the high-resistance program showed a clear increase in strength, as indicated by their 1 RM values pre- and post-training. And their performance over the first 10 metres of the sprint run also improved. However, neither the acceleration phase of the run (from 10 to 40 m) nor the overall sprint performance was improved after the training program. On the other hand, the high-velocity training resulted in an improved initial acceleration, a higher maximum running speed, and a decreased speed endurance (i.e. a faster overall time). These results show that a high-velocity training program resulted in significant improvements in all aspects of a 100 m sprint run and that this program was superior to a high-resistance program for enhancing overall performance. More studies employing highly-trained athletes from a variety of different sports need to be conducted before sports scientists can make definitive recommendations to coaches regarding the optimal methods of enhancing an athlete's speed. Nevertheless, the results of these two well-controlled investigations support the use of high-velocity training techniques.

IF THE SHOE FITS . . . DON'T WEAR IT!

Add nine inches to your vertical jump height. Reduce your 40 yard sprint time by 0.2 of a second. And increase the size of your calf muscles by two inches. Introducing the 'Strength Shoe'. This is no normal item of footwear. With a built-up platform at the front end of the shoe, it is designed to 'cause the calf muscles to support the body weight totally' and 'increase muscle size and explosive power'. At least, according to the manufacturer.

There is only one well-controlled, peer-reviewed report of the effects of training in Strength Shoes in well-trained athletes. Dr Stephen Cook and colleagues from Tulane University, New Orleans, had twelve inter-collegiate track and field athletes participate in an eight-week training program in either their normal footwear or Strength Shoes. The training, which was the same for both groups, was performed according to the recommendations of the manufacturer of Strength Shoes.

During the experimental period, two of the athletes who were training in the Strength Shoe complained of leg pain, and one was forced to quit the study. There were no injuries or drop-outs among the athletes training in their normal footwear. Although calf circumference increased after training in the Strength Shoe compared to normal footwear (2.3% versus 0.2%), none of the performance measures were any different between the two groups. On the contrary.

Athletes who trained in the normal shoe showed a tendency to improve more than those who trained in the Strength Shoe on all performance indices. The 40 yard sprint was faster (8.3% versus 6.9%), vertical jump height was greater (9.2% versus 3.3%), and measures of muscle power were also better (14.5% versus 7.5%). Clearly, it is the manufacturers rather than their shoes that are a little over the top. For now, the most cost-effective way to improve vertical jump height and sprint speed is to train appropriately!

6

Training techniques for successful endurance performance

'There is no coach in the world who can say exactly what an endurance athlete should do as far as number of repetitions, distances, and intervals are concerned. Not even physiologists can tell an athlete that. The important point is that the athlete knows what he is trying to achieve and goes out and works at it until he does.'

Arthur Lydiard, New Zealand distance running coach

'The purpose of training is to improve the energy delivery systems according to the demands of the event, and to improve (running) economy.'

Peter Snell, triple Olympic gold medal winner

'Performance is the difference between fitness and fatigue.'

Dr Hugh Morton, sports scientist and statistician

THE PHYSIOLOGICAL REQUIREMENTS FOR SUCCESSFUL ENDURANCE PERFORMANCE

It has often been said that the phenomenal success of many of the African distance runners in recent years is due to their superior natural talent, exceptional genetics, or even a different body type. Not so, says Martin Keino, son of the great Kipchoge Keino, winner of five Olympic medals, three gold and two silver: 'There is no secret. All there is is hard work, just very hard training. That's how my father did it, and that's how the others are doing it.'

107

Whether or not the accomplishments of several of the African nations in long-distance running are the result of inherited traits or just superior training techniques remains to be established (see panel 'The Kenyans'). One thing is certain—there are many scientific studies which have consistently identified certain physiological variables that distinguish successful endurance athletes from their less talented rivals. For the most part, such investigations have examined the relationship between a number of physical variables and various athletic feats and assumed that the factors most related to superior achievements are the most crucial determinants of performance. While this approach completely ignores the psychological component of any athletic performance, it does provide a basis on which to discuss specific training techniques for improving endurance performance.

OUT OF AFRICA: THE KENYANS

'The Kenyans. There are always new Kenyans.'
Noureddine Morceli, 1996 Olympic 1500 metre champion

'The Kenyans rule the world of distance running. Their dominance is not their fault, it's our fault. What are they supposed to do, go slower? What we have to do is learn how to go faster, how to keep up with them.'
Bob Kennedy, USA, the first white man to run under thirteen minutes for 5000 metres

'The reason the Africans do so well is that they train bloody hard.'
Derek Clayton, Australia, former marathon world-record holder

Running barefoot in the 1960 Tokyo Games, Ethiopia's Abebe Bikila became the first black African Olympic medallist when he won the marathon. Since then, African athletes have dominated international distance running, and one nation's Olympic success is unrivalled. Kenya's medal haul since 1968 is twelve gold, fourteen silver and eight bronze. And they didn't participate in either the 1976 or 1980 games due to political boycotts! At the 1987 World Cross Country Championships, Paul Tergat won his third consecutive title, and his Kenyan team-mates filled four of the top seven places. Before this, John Ngugi won the title an unprecedented five times. The Kenyan Senior men have won the team title for the last twelve years and the Senior women five of the past seven years. Not to be outdone, the Kenyan Junior men have provided the individual champion nine times during the last thirteen years and the Junior women eight of the last nine years. That's a total, for all divisions, of 35 team championships from a possible 49 in which they have competed: a 71% success rate.

In middle- and long-distance track events, the number of male Kenyan runners in the world annual top twenty *Track and Field News* ranking list has risen steadily from two in 1964, to 26 in 1996 (see Table 6.1). Kenyan men currently hold the world records for 3000 metres, 3000 metres steeplechase, two miles, 5000 and 10,000 metres. And 800 metre world champion and record holder, Wilson Kipketer, who now runs for Denmark, was born and raised in Kenya!

TABLE 6.1

The number of Kenyan male runners in the annual world top 20 rankings list, 1964–96

Event	1964	1974	1984	1994	1996
800 metres	1	4	2	8	4
1500 metres	1	2	1	4	4
3000 metres steeplechase	0	2	2	11	9
5000 metres	0	1	2	6	5
10,000 metres	0	2	3	4	4

So what is the reason for such athletic prowess? Genetics? Training at altitude? Lifestyle? Probably all three! Although more than three-quarters of the country's 28 million people live at altitudes of 1600 metres (5000 feet) or higher, the Kenyan runners, with very few exceptions, come from four of the nation's 40 tribes: the Kikuyu, the Kamba, the Kisii (or Gusii) and the Kalenjin. Indeed, about 75% of Kenya's best distance runners come from just one of these tribes—the Kalenjin—who comprise only 10% of the population. In his recent book *Train Hard, Win Easy: The Kenyan Way*, Toby Tanser speculated that Kenya's altitude and the extent of its economic development have provided a fortuitous combination that has helped to produce legions of world-class athletes. Consider that, on average, there is just one TV set for every 106 people and one passenger car for every 180 people (the ratio in the United States is one hundred times greater—one car for every 1.8 people). Taken collectively, this means that Kenyans, especially children, spend many hours running around outdoors. And although stories of youngsters running many kilometres to school and back every day are tired clichés, there is no doubt that all those miles, always covered barefoot, help establish a firm base of general conditioning on which future training programs are grounded.

Finally, one should not underestimate the lure of possible financial reward should a runner be selected to race in Europe. The average annual income in Kenya is about 5% of that in the USA and when one considers that appearance money at a major international track meeting can be anywhere from US$10,000 to US$50,000, it's hardly surprising to find a great willingness to train hard!

And train hard they certainly do. Moses Kiptanui, silver medallist at the 1996 Atlanta Olympic Games and the 1997 World Athletic Championships, as well as the first man ever to break the eight minute barrier for 3000 metre steeplechase (7:59.18 in 1995) often runs three times a day! He does an early morning easy run of about 40 minutes (the Kenyans run for time, not distance), a quality interval session mid-morning, and then sometimes another long easy run in the afternoon. All training is undertaken at altitudes ranging from 1300 to 2700 metres, and all easy running is undertaken on hilly courses, often on gravel or dirt roads. An interesting concept of Kenyan training, notes Tanser, is the employment of two training runs in the morning. A large majority of runners will begin the first session of the day at around 0600 hours and then follow this up with a second (harder) session at 1100 hours. This means that they give their bodies a longer time to recover after the main workout compared with the conventional training strategy of a full-time athlete, who would normally train once in the morning and then again in the evening. Although there is no scientific evidence to demonstrate that either way is superior, it certainly works for the Kenyans!

And strength training? Well, gyms are rare in Kenya. Dumbbells are made out of cement-filled paint cans joined by iron bars. But even these devices are not utilised very much: most Kenyan runners can barely manage ten consecutive press-ups, and score even worse when it comes to pull-ups. They argue that running is the best form of strength training, supplemented with 'light exercises' and stretching. Scientific testing and monitoring of athletes is unheard of.

So what is the reason for their success? Genetics helps, but practice makes perfect. And wearing a Kenyan vest certainly helps!

THE RIGHT STUFF: WHAT IT TAKES TO SUCCEED IN ENDURANCE SPORTS

From a large number of scientific investigations of distance runners, cyclists, rowers, cross-country skiers, swimmers and triathletes, the minimum physiological requirements for any individual wishing to compete at a high level in continuous, moderate-to-high intensity endurance events lasting longer than 30 minutes are:

- a high maximal aerobic power ($\dot{V}O_{2max}$)—greater than 60 ml/kg/min for females; greater than 65 ml/kg/min for males;
- a high power to weight ratio;
- a low level of body fat;
- the ability to train and race at a high percentage of $\dot{V}O_{2max}$ (or a high percentage of maximal heart rate) for sustained periods;
- a high power output or speed at the so-called anaerobic or lactate threshold;
- the ability to maintain high absolute power outputs or speeds and to resist the onset of muscular fatigue;
- an efficient and economical technique; and
- the ability to utilise fat as a fuel during sustained exercise at high workrates and thus 'spare' the body's own carbohydrate reserves.

Although many of the characteristics of the successful endurance athlete can be improved and modified by the implementation of the correct training techniques, it is important to emphasise that many of the physical traits of top performers are ultimately governed by hereditary factors. For the most part, champions are born and not made. Many athletes who turn in mediocre performances train longer and harder than some elite athletes but fail to attain comparable results. The bottom line is that it is often impossible to determine with any degree of precision whether or not a superior performance is the direct result of a specific training program or a better choice of parents! The goal of any training program, therefore, should always be to maximise each individual's unique potential; training should be viewed merely as the vehicle which will ultimately determine how close any individual comes to reaching their own genetic limits (see Chapter 2).

CURRENT TRAINING TECHNIQUES OF TOP ENDURANCE ATHLETES

There is currently considerable spirited debate among athletes, coaches and sports scientists as to which specific training techniques best promote the physiological attributes previously described, and thus constitute the optimal training program for enhancing endurance performance. A principal question usually centres on the issue of 'quantity versus quality', although this topic is hardly a modern phenomenon (see

Chapter 2). Most coaches and athletes steadfastly believe that maximal aerobic fitness can only be achieved through the application of extensive volume overload. And while it is probably true that the highest level of aerobic conditioning is likely to be attained when the volume overload is close to the level that would eventually result in an athlete over-reaching or over-training, the simplistic 'more is better' approach contradicts the scientific principles of training.

Nevertheless, it is possible to characterise the core components of physical preparation on which the training systems utilised by the current generation of top athletes are based. They include:

- year-round training and competition, with only short breaks (two to four weeks) of active recovery;
- periodisation of training into 'micro' and 'macro' cycles, with emphasis on volume overload in the winter or non-competitive season, and intensity overload during the pre-competition and competition phases;
- a consistently high volume overload: during some periods of their build-up, elite long-distance runners may train up to 250 km/week, professional cyclists ride as much as 1000 km/week, and top swimmers cover a staggering 100 km/week; top rowers and cross-country skiers typically train for 25–30 hours per week;
- a 'hard/easy' pattern in the overall organisation of training;
- interval or transition training incorporating prolonged, steady-state bouts of exercise with short recovery;
- speedwork, performed at speeds faster than planned race pace, with maximal recovery;
- resistance training, undertaken in the non-competitive season;
- stretching and mobility exercises, performed after most hard training sessions;
- special dietary preparation and supplementation before and during a major competition;
- peaking or tapering before major competitions; and
- a long-term outlook on training and racing.

CONSTRUCTING A SUCCESSFUL ENDURANCE TRAINING PROGRAM: THE PERIODISATION OF TRAINING

'In constructing an effective training plan, six questions must be answered: What should be done? Why is it being done? When *should it be done? How is it done best? Where should it be done? Who should do it?'*

David Martin and Peter Coe, on a unified training strategy

'Basically you have different types of training. You've got distance . . . you've got fartlek . . . you've got anaerobic training sessions and then you've got the rest phase. You take these phases and you arrange them in the right order.'

Jerome Drayton, winner of the 1977 Boston marathon

During the past decade there have been many texts and coaching manuals written about the periodisation of training for improving endurance performance. Several of these have advocated the use of elaborate 'multi-tier' training systems as a basis for periodisation (the organisation of a training program into distinct phases). Others have presented complicated diagrammatic representations of intricate techniques which utilise the concept of several 'macro' and 'meso' cycles throughout a year or competitive season. Many such programs are open to criticism in that they are far too complex and often include recommendations for which there is no current scientific basis. Perhaps more important, however, is that it is not readily apparent how such elaborate programs can be applied to the current generation of athletes, many of whom compete frequently and all year round.

Intuitively the perfect training program for enhancement of endurance performance should include all of the training techniques currently practised by today's successful performers. However, most of the key facets that constitute the generic core of a year-round training program for the endurance athlete can be divided into just four main phases (Figure 6.1):

1 aerobic base or foundation training;
2 transition ('threshold') training;
3 speed or power training; and
4 a taper phase before a major competitive peak.

During each of these four phases of endurance training, primary emphasis is given to the development of one or more specific physiological objectives.

Base/foundation training

'If you put down a good solid foundation and build one room after another, pretty soon you have a house. You build in your speedwork, your pace and increase your ability gradually.'

Rod Dixon, 1972 Olympic bronze medallist, 1500 metres

'What you do is directly proportional to the amount and quality of your base training. And by quality, I don't mean speed. Rather quality in base training means aerobic work.'

Dave Welch, distance running coach

'I did a lot more base training than in previous years. Sometimes I went up to 100 kilometres a week in the pool, which takes six hours of swimming every day.'

Michelle Smith, triple Olympic gold medal-winning swimmer, Atlanta, 1996

'Long runs are the hardest part of training, and the Sunday long run is the most important part of my training.'

Rob de Castella, champion Australian marathoner

'Of course you need the base, but what you need is quality base. And the quality has to be good quality over-distance. The focus is not on counting the miles, but on counting quality sessions.'

Dave Martin, exercise physiologist and adviser to Sebastian Coe

'Building stamina is best done at just under your maximum steady-state, for approximately 160 kilometres a week of aerobic running.'

Arthur Lydiard, New Zealand distance running coach

Base, or foundation, training should be performed during the winter or the non-competitive period of an athlete's macro-cycle. The primary emphasis of this phase of training is the establishment of a sound endurance foundation on which to base subsequent more intense training. There are many physiological benefits ascribed to base/foundation training, including:

- a more efficient oxygen transport system characterised by an enlarged heart and an enhanced vascular system;
- an expanded blood volume;
- a higher maximal aerobic power;
- an increase in the activity of several muscle enzyme systems, particularly those involved in oxidative metabolism;
- improved fuel utilisation, especially an increase in fat mobilisation and utilisation; and
- adaptation of non-muscular structures such as ligaments, tendons and bones to withstand the stresses of daily training.

During the base/foundation phase of training, the overall training quotient (i.e. the duration × intensity × frequency) is kept just below that threshold that would eventually over-extend the athlete and lead to staleness and fatigue. However, the highest level of aerobic fitness is likely to be gained when the athlete's weekly training quotient is fairly close to the level that would *eventually* over-train the athlete, often termed the over-training threshold.

Base training should be performed at an intensity of 70–75% of VO_{2max}, which corresponds to approximately 80–85% of the athlete's maximum heart rate. Such training should be carried

---

FIGURE 6.1

The main components of a systematic, balanced endurance training program

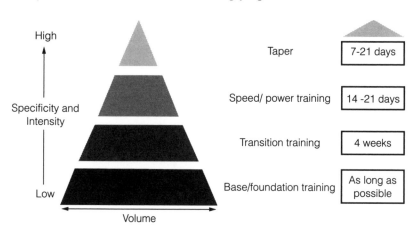

Source: Hawley, J.A., Myburgh, K.H., Noakes, T.D. and Dennis, S.C. 'Training techniques to improve fatigue resistance and enhance endurance performance', *Journal of Sports Sciences*, 15: 325–333, 1997.

out as continuous exercise for a minimum of 30 minutes, up to several hours each day, depending on the athlete's sport. During the base/foundation phase, those athletes participating in non-weight-bearing sports such as cycling, rowing and swimming will be able to spend more *time* training than participants in weight-bearing events, such as runners, without incurring such a high risk of injury.

Depending on the ability level of the athlete, and practical time restraints, the frequency of base/foundation training should be between six and twelve sessions each week. Ideally, the athlete should aim to undertake a minimum of three to four months' base/foundation training, but this time will vary depending on the time lag after the athlete's last competitive phase. It seems reasonable to suggest that endurance athletes should undertake as much base/foundation training, for as long as possible, until such time that performance over their specialised distance fails to improve. Although this hypothesis has not been scientifically validated, it makes intuitive sense. Also, it provides a definitive time point at which the endurance athlete should perhaps shift the focus of their training program to the next phase.

TRAINING WITH THE PROS

Before each European racing season starts, most of the top professional cycling teams hold annual training camps. For the team doctors and physiologists, these camps are 'an opportunity to top up the rider's aerobic engines'. For the team management, they provide a chance to review the riders' personal and team goals. For the riders themselves, the camps offer a chance to meet new team-mates, fine-tune their bike set-ups, and train without distractions.

As preparation for a camp, the Motorola team are given a prescribed training program for the off-season (between mid-October and the beginning of February). Riders are expected to show up for the camp with between 3000 and 3500 km in their legs. One year, American Lance Armstrong logged 7000 km during this period. The riders turn in signed monthly training logs to enable team management to monitor their progress. Then the hard work commences. The following is a typical schedule for the two to three weeks of the camp.

Monday		Rest day or easy ride
Tuesday	a.m.	Medium long ride (3–4 hours) (110 kilometres)
Wednesday	p.m.	Medium long ride (4 hours) (130 kilometres)

Thursday	a.m.	70 kilometres
	p.m.	Interval session (2–3 hours) Warm-up low-gear spinning, then: 2 minutes hard (90% effort) with 2 minutes slow riding recovery.
Friday	a.m.	90 kilometres
Saturday	a.m.	Long ride (170 kilometres)
Sunday		Physiological testing or training in small groups

Source: Abt, S. *A Season in Turmoil*, Velopress, Boulder, Colorado, 1995, pp. 23–28.

WHEN ONE ISN'T ENOUGH: BASE TRAINING FOR TRIATHLETES

Base training is hard enough for a swimmer, cyclist or runner. But what about the triathlete who needs to incorporate all three disciplines into their weekly training schedule? The following program is designed for the competitive triathlete who will be racing over the standard Olympic distance (swim 1500 m, cycle 40 km, run 10 km). The sessions indicated are those the athlete should be attaining by the end of their base phase.

Monday	a.m.	Swim (4000–5000 metres) Warm-up (500 metres freestyle), then: 4 × 400 metres at best steady-state pace with 60 seconds' recovery. Warm-down pull (400 metres).
	p.m.	Easy run (30–45 minutes). On grass, flat.
Tuesday	a.m.	Steady-state run (60–75 minutes) Warm-up jog (15–20 minutes), then: 30–40 minutes at best aerobic effort on undulating surface. Warm-down jog (15 minutes).
	p.m.	Recovery ride (60 minutes). Low-gear spinning, on the flat.
Wednesday	a.m.	Swim (3000–4000 metres) Warm-up (500 metres), then: 20 × 100 metres on 90 seconds. Warm-down pull (400 metres).
	p.m.	Medium-long ride (120–150 minutes). To include some hills.
Thursday	a.m.	Easy run (45 minutes). On grass, flat.
	p.m.	Easy ride (60–75 minutes). Low-gear spinning, on the flat.

Friday	a.m.	Swim (3000 metres) Warm-up (500 metres). Technique drills. Warm-down (500 metres).
	p.m.	Recovery ride (60 minutes)
Saturday	a.m.	Brick session (ride, run) Warm-up spin (15–20 minutes), then: steady-state ride (45 minutes), followed by transition to run: steady-state run (5–8 kilometres). Warm-down jog (10 minutes)
Sunday		Long ride (180 minutes). To include some hills.

TRAINING WITH STEVE MONEGHETTI

Winner of the 1994 Tokyo marathon (2:08:55), gold medal winner 1994 Commonwealth Games, Victoria (2:11:49), runner-up 1995 London marathon (2:08:33), bronze medal winner 1997 World Championships (2:14:16).

The following is a typical week's training during the base phase in the build-up to a marathon.

Monday	a.m.	Easy run (10 kilometres)
	p.m.	Easy run (16 kilometres)
Tuesday	a.m.	Easy run (8 kilometres)
	p.m.	Fartlek Warm-up easy run (6 kilometres), then 6 kilometres fartlek. Warm-down (6 kilometres).
Wednesday	a.m.	Easy run (8 kilometres)
	p.m.	Easy run (24 kilometres) Weights
Thursday	a.m.	Easy run (8 kilometres)
	p.m.	Track session Warm-up (4 kilometres) and strides, then: 8 × 400 metres with 200 metres float between repetitions. Warm-down (4 kilometres).
Friday	a.m.	Easy run (8 kilometres)
	p.m.	Easy run (15 kilometres)
Saturday	a.m.	Hill run

		Warm-up (4 kilometres), then: hill run (hard 7 kilometres). Warm-down (easy 4 kilometres).
	p.m.	Easy run (12 kilometres)
Sunday	a.m.	Long run (35 kilometres, 2 hours 30 minutes)
	p.m.	Easy run (10 kilometres)
		Weights

Fartlek consists of: 2 × 90 seconds, 4 × 60 seconds, 4 × 30 seconds, 4 × 15 seconds repeated so total time approximately 20 minutes. Total weekly distance: 200 kilometres.

Source: Moneghetti, S. and Howley, P. *In the Long Run. The Making of a Marathon Runner.* Penguin Books, Victoria, p. 256, 1996.

Recommendations for an upper limit to volume overload

'Why dost thou run so many mile about?'

William Shakespeare, *Richard III*

'If someone says, "Hey, I ran 100 miles this week. How far did you run?" ignore him. What the hell difference does it make? The magic is in the man, not the 100 miles.'

Bill Bowerman, running coach

'I wondered what would happen if I went beyond my 120–130 miles a week. Would I reach another plane of fitness? I had to find out . . . But I was never really happy. A lot of the time I felt slightly fatigued and towards the end of this increased training stint, I seemed to be doing nothing but changing in and out of running gear.'

Ron Hill, winner of the 1970 Commonwealth Games marathon (2:09:28)

'Well, well. Winning the (Enschede) marathon at the end of a rest period, on an average of only 56 miles a week. And in 2:18:06 on a hot day, and with very little effort. It made me think. Yes, it made me think that 120–130 miles a week weren't absolutely necessary for good marathon performances.'

Ron Hill

'When an athlete has reached a plateau of endurance capability, additional mileage will produce no further improvement, and the

plateau can be maintained on only sixty per cent of the work required to reach it.'

Peter Coe, coach of Sebastian Coe, former
world-record holder for 800 metres (1:41.73)

Although it is difficult to put a precise figure on the maximum training volume that endurance athletes should be undertaking, scientific evidence and the experiences of many coaches and athletes suggest that for running, there is little physiological benefit to be gained by covering more than 130 km/week. For cyclists, this ceiling would correspond to about 500 km/week, while most swimmers should probably not be covering much more than 40 km during any seven-day period.

Naturally, there will be athletes who choose to train more (and less!) than these suggested guidelines. There may even be certain sports in which specific phases of a training cycle necessitate greater volumes. Indeed, it is entirely plausible that extreme and chronic volume overload over many seasons of training might even increase the athlete's efficiency of movement, or induce subtle changes in the function of skeletal muscle or other organs that sports scientists are currently unable to measure. Such changes may, ultimately, lead to significant improvements in performance. However, the balance of probability indicates that the risk to benefit ratio involved when the *majority* of athletes are subjected to such extremes of volume overload is high and does not necessarily guarantee a superior performance.

VOLUME OVERLOAD: THE OTHER SIDE OF THE STORY

You've read the scientific rationale and the suggestions for an upper limit to the amount of endurance training an athlete might reasonably be expected to perform. But to get another perspective, we asked Dr David Pyne, a sports scientist at the Australian Institute of Sport and physiologist to the Australian swimming team, for his views on the mileage mania. Swimming seems to be a sport particularly afflicted with the 'more is better' mindset, so we were especially interested in Dr Pyne's comments, which are given below.

'Hell week! Many of the traditions in a swimming club contain an element of truth but don't always let them get in the way of a good story. Tales of 100 km training weeks, and the coaches who prescribe them, are a major source of tall tales. Like the coach who made swimmers do 10 km in a single session during hell week. Various workout combinations were randomly drawn by individual swimmers from a hat before each training session. This might be ten times one kilometre, or 100 times 100 metres. But one session was "swim 300 metres and go have a shower". Of course, every swimmer wanted to be the lucky one who drew that program.'

Why do swimmers spend all those hours looking at a black line on the bottom of the pool when most competitive swimming events last one or two minutes? The actual practices of endurance athletes from many sports, including cycling, running, rowing, kayaking, triathlon and swimming, seem to suggest that they actually need such large training volumes to prepare adequately for international-level competition. But the training loads undertaken by some athletes are prodigious, so the question of the relevance of this training practice to their performance is a good one. Taking swimming as an example, observers of the sport often consider training between 60 and 100 km per week (20 to 30 hours of pool time) for a 50 m race (lasting approximately 22 seconds) or a 100 m event (lasting up to one minute) an extremely questionable practice! And while there are several research studies that question the benefits of, or even the need for, such high training volumes, the majority of swimming coaches still follow the traditional wisdom of moderate to high mileage. So who is right?

Most of the studies reported in the scientific literature are limited in that they usually employ swimmers whose ability level and training background are vastly different to top international competitors to whom the results are supposedly meant to apply. In addition, the scope of experimental treatments and the length of the intervention periods usually bear little resemblance to the year-round training programs of elite swimmers. A four-week training study on moderately active individuals undertaking a limited training program doesn't exactly capture the attention of the average international-level swimming coach! The majority of scientific research on the specificity and overload of training generally points to low-volume, race pace-specific training, as opposed to the high-volume, aerobic-based training currently practised by most top swimmers. The approach we have adopted in Australia is to be *guided* by these findings, rather than directed by them, for some of the following reasons.

Swimming has several unique features that make it different from most other sports. It is a weight-supported, aquatic-based activity which utilises short, intense intervals rather than long, continuous training. And in comparison to, say, running or cycling, it is a more technique-dependent sport. Swimming also involves a cyclical but discontinuous application of muscular force. And coaches say that aerobic training is essential to support the development and maintenance of a swimmer's sprint abilities.

The scientifically-minded like to cite the relative energy contributions to different events when criticising high-volume swimming training, but recent research by Australian Dr Paul Gastin of the Victorian Institute of Sport indicates that the aerobic contribution for short-duration, high-intensity exercise has probably been grossly underestimated. In fact, the aerobic system may contribute almost 50% to energy supply for events of a minute's duration (see Chapter 3). This figure is at odds with a large number of swimming books and academic texts which say that there is only minimal aerobic contribution to sprint events.

Australia has a strong heritage in swimming. The men's 1500 m event is considered a prize event in competitive swimming and Australia has had several Olympic champions, world long course and short course champions, and world-record holders over the years, including Murray Rose, John Konrads, Glen Housman, Kieren Perkins, Daniel Kowalski and Grant Hackett. This legacy had been built upon a steady diet of quality aerobic work. The key lies in the careful blending of both endurance and speed. It is relatively easy to overload training volume if you have sufficient time. But the right proportions of aerobic, threshold and race-pace training make the difference to the final performance in the end. The question of weekly training distances was raised earlier, and here one senses that often a swimmer's mileage is exaggerated or embellished in order either to psyche out the opposition or to look good. While conversations often reflect on 'hell weeks', where swimmers try to cover over 100 km per week, these are the exception and not the rule, and are very rarely undertaken in modern swimming.

While acknowledging that the high-intensity, low-volume approach adopted by *some* swimmers can still be very successful, most coaches feel that ultimately this will limit a swimmer's potential. Our experience has been that some swimmers can succeed, even at the international level, with such an approach, but that it is difficult to make progress from year to year and to take that final step to major international success. The two greatest sprint swimmers of the modern era, Matt Biondi of the United States and Alexandre Popov of Russia, both had balanced aerobic-based training programs during their peak years.

Finally, the timing of high-volume training is perhaps as critical as the volume itself. Some astute observers of international swimming have noted that many swimmers perform better in the year *after* the Olympic Games or World Championships than in the year of the Games itself. Every swimmer will train harder and further in an Olympic year, but many leave this work until it is too late. The result is that they end up in good shape after the Games and tend to peak in the post-Olympic period. Too many swimmers leave their Olympic build-up to the last six months, when they should begin their final preparation in the year before the Olympics.

Transition training

'After a solid base is built, start introducing speed gradually with transitional workouts such as road, fartlek and hills.'

Steve Spence, 1991 world marathon bronze medallist

The second phase of endurance training is undertaken after the athlete has established a solid endurance base (see Figure 6.1). The prime objective of transition training is to expose the various physiological power systems to sustained exercise at an intensity or effort which corresponds to the athlete's *highest current steady-state pace*. The physiological benefits ascribed to transition training include:

- an increase in an athlete's peak sustained power output, or velocity of movement;
- an increase in VO_{2max};
- an improved specific endurance or resistance to muscular fatigue;
- an enhanced ability of the working muscles to tolerate and 'buffer' lactate; and
- the recruitment and stimulation of the specific muscle fibres that will be needed during a competitive effort.

Transition training should be performed as long bouts (5–10 minutes) of continuous steady-state exercise with short recovery intervals (less than 60 seconds). The intensity of transition training should correspond to approximately 85% of VO_{2max} or 90–95% of the athlete's maximal heart rate, the so-called 'aerobic –anaerobic threshold', or the athlete's *best current race pace* for either 10 km (running), a flat 40 km time-trial (cycling/triathlon) or 1500 m (swimming). Although exercise prescription based on an athlete's blood lactate concentration during training has been a popular practice with swimmers and, more recently, some top European cyclists, there is little scientific evidence to support such practices. More to the point, it is highly impractical for a coach to have to take repeated blood samples from athletes during training in order to monitor the stresses of a particular workout.

---| WHAT'S IN A NAME? |----------------------------------

It has been called the 'anaerobic threshold', the 'lactate threshold', the 'lactate inflection point', OBLA (the onset of blood lactate accumulation), and various other names by coaches and sports scientists. It describes an arbitrary point on a graph where blood lactate levels rise disproportionately to a small increase in exercise intensity. Unfortunately, the 'anaerobic threshold' *per se* gives sports scientists no information about anaerobic metabolism. It merely reflects the balance between lactate entry into the blood from the working muscles and its removal by the liver. Indeed, such a 'threshold' may not even exist. Blood lactate concentration rises continuously during exercise of increasing intensity, rather than suddenly at any one time. But more to the point, there is no scientific evidence that training at a prescribed lactate concentration will lead to improved endurance performance. For example, it is not known whether a runner, cyclist, swimmer or rower should train at a lactate concentration of 4, 5 or 6 mmol/litre in order to race faster. Unfortunately, some sports scientists are making recommendations to athletes about the 'optimal' training intensity based on little or no knowledge about the effect of such an intervention on subsequent athletic performance. The bottom line is that sports scientists do not, at present, have any idea of the most appropriate lactate concentration at which to perform endurance training.

Transition training should be performed up to twice a week for three or four weeks immediately following the base phase. Such a recommendation is in line with the observations of top endurance athletes who, out of a total of the 30 or so hours of total training time a week, focus on achieving a *maximum* of two high-quality sessions. There is also scientific research showing that more than two transition sessions per week results in fatigue and a subsequent decline in performance. During this phase of training, the athlete can replace a transition training session with a time-trial over a distance significantly less than their planned competitive event. As most athletes are reluctant to perform numerous time-trials during their training, all-out timed efforts should be utilised sparingly and only when the athlete and coach need a definitive measure of training status. When time-trials are utilised for training purposes, the athlete should aim to complete them at a pre-planned pace or effort, at close to projected race pace, but not necessarily all-out.

Although interval or transition training has been employed by endurance athletes since the turn of the century, and has been the cornerstone of swim training for many decades, there have been very few scientific studies of the effects of interval training on the performances of well-trained competitive athletes. Indeed, it could be argued that some sports scientists are currently making recommendations about the role of various training regimens in the preparation of athletes without a precise knowledge of the effects of such interventions on performance. To address this, a series of studies were recently conducted at the Sports Science Institute of South Africa using highly-trained competitive cyclists. These investigations specifically examined the effects of transition training on cycling performance and several other laboratory measures. The findings from these studies are likely to be applicable to a number of endurance sports, such as distance running.

In the first investigation, Fiona Lindsay and her co-workers had eight well-trained endurance cyclists who had not performed any interval training for three to four months replace a portion of their 300 km/week base training with transition training. Each transition training session consisted of a warm-up at the cyclist's chosen pace, followed by six to eight five-minute rides at an effort corresponding to 80% of the cyclist's VO_{2max}, or 90% of their maximum heart rates. Cyclists undertook two transition training sessions each week for just three weeks, but kept their total weekly training volume constant. By replacing just 15% (about 50 km) of their 305 km weekly base mileage with six transition training sessions during a three-to-four week period, well-trained cyclists were able to significantly reduce their 40 km time-trial performance times from 56.4 minutes to 54.4 minutes. This two-minute improvement represents an increase in average cycling speed from 42.7 km/hour before to 44.2 km/hour after the transition training program. And this improvement occurred in cyclists who were already well-trained.

Encouraged by these results, Chris Westgarth-Taylor and Scott Rickard then examined whether a longer period of transition training would lead to even greater improvements in endurance cycling performance. Following the same experimental design, these workers had another group of eight well-trained cyclists replace about 15% of their 300 km/week base mileage with transition training, which was undertaken twice a week at the same intensity as was prescribed in the previous study. This time, however, the training period was extended from three to six weeks and cyclists performed a total of twelve transition workouts. These investigators also found that after six transition training sessions, 40 km cycling performance improved by 90–120 seconds, or 1.5–2.0 km/hr. However, increasing the number of sessions from six to twelve for a further three weeks resulted in only a very small additional improvement in 40 km performance. Taken collectively, the results from these studies indicate that in well-trained subjects, improvements in endurance performance for events lasting approximately one hour that result from an increase in training intensity can be accomplished within three to four weeks.

The reason for such improvements in performance after such a short exposure to transition training can be found largely in subtle adaptations occurring in the leg muscles of the cyclists. In a third study, Adele Weston and her co-workers persuaded six of the cyclists to have two muscle biopsies, one before they started transition training, and the other after they had completed four weeks of high-intensity interval training. She found that although the transition training did not alter the activity of several of the muscle enzymes involved in energy production, it did improve the muscle's ability to buffer lactate. Indeed, there was a good correlation between a cyclist's muscle buffering capacity and their subsequent 40 km cycling performance, suggesting that in well-trained athletes, peripheral (skeletal muscle) rather than central (cardiovascular) factors might ultimately limit high-density endurance performance lasting approximately one hour.

THE ORIGINS OF INTERVAL TRAINING: FROM PATIENT TO ATHLETE

Interval training was first employed as a technique for improving physical fitness during the 1930s by a German cardiologist, Dr Heinz Reindell. He prescribed bouts of intense exercise interspersed with short rest periods for his cardiac patients. He recommended that during exercise bouts, heart rate should climb to 170–180 beats/minute. When it had dropped to around 120 beats/minute, the patient was ready to commence the next work bout. This technique was very effective in increasing the patient's maximal oxygen uptake ($\dot{V}O_{2max}$), as well as the size of their heart and the volume of blood ejected by the heart each beat (the stroke volume). It was the famous German coach, Woldemar Gerschler, who introduced interval training into the athletic community in 1935. Gerschler trained many athletes using various interval training techniques ('interval' refers to the rest period and not the work bout). His most famous pupil was Rudolf Harbig who set a world record for 800 m (1:46.6) in 1939, a time which was not broken for sixteen years. Other coaches soon included interval training in their programs, among them Austrian

Franz Stampfl, coach of Roger Bannister, and Hungarian Mihaly Igoli, who coached world-record holders for the 1500, 3000, 5000 and 10,000 metres.

Speed/power training

'It is true that speed kills. It kills anyone who doesn't have it.'

Brooks Johnson, head track coach, Stanford University

'I tend to use some of my races as speedwork.'

John Walker, 1976 Olympic 1500 metre champion

The final phase of endurance training is designed to expose the various physiological power systems to maximal or supramaximal exercise at speeds which are *slightly faster than planned race pace*. Speed/power training entails high-intensity

---
TABLE 6.2

Endurance training at a glance

Phase of training	Typical workout	Comments
Base training	*Duration:* 30 minutes to several hours *Intensity:* 70–75% of $\dot{V}O_{2max}$ 75–80% of maximal heart rate *Frequency:* 7–12 sessions per week	• Undertaken during non-competitive period for as long as possible (3–6 months) • High volume of training • Low to moderate intensity • Prolonged, continuous exercise
Transition training	*Duration:* 30–90 minutes *Intensity:* 85–90% of $\dot{V}O_{2max}$ 90–95% of maximal heart rate *Frequency:* 2–3 sessions per week	• Undertaken 6 weeks prior to competitive season for 3–4 weeks • Moderate volume of training • Maximum steady-state/race pace • Continuous or intermittent exercise
Speed training	*Duration:* 30–60 minutes *Intensity:* Maximal *Frequency:* 2–3 sessions per week	• Undertaken for 2–3 weeks after transition training prior to major competitions • Low volume of training • Faster than race pace Intermittent exercise with long recovery between work bouts

work bouts of short duration with long rest periods. An example of a speed/power session for a runner or cyclist would involve an extended warm-up, consisting of 15–20 minutes of moderate-intensity exercise followed by some stretching and acceleration sprints. This is then followed by six to eight maximal repetitions of *up to* 90 seconds' duration with a complete (5–7 minute) recovery between work bouts. The use of a heart-rate monitor to determine the intensity of speed/power workouts is neither valid nor recommended; often an athlete will attain a higher heart rate *after* the exercise bout.

Speed/power training should be performed two to three times a week during the final 21 days before a major competition. It is important to emphasise that the overall volume of work undertaken during this phase of training is low but of a high quality. See Table 6.2.

TRAINING WITH SEBASTIAN COE

The following week's training took place 16–22 July 1984 in the final build-up to the Los Angeles Olympics, where Coe won the 1500 metres gold medal in an Olympic record of 3:32.53 and a silver medal in the 800 metres (1:43.64).

Monday	a.m.	Warm-up, then: 6 × 800 metres in 2:00 with 3 minutes' recovery. Warm-down (easy jogging).
	p.m.	Easy run (4 miles)
Tuesday	a.m.	Easy run (5 miles)
	p.m.	Warm-up, then: 10 × 100 metres acceleration runs, walk-back recovery. Warm-down (easy jog).
Wednesday	a.m.	Warm-up, then: 6 × 300 metres in 41 seconds with 3 minutes' recovery. Warm-down (easy jog).
	p.m.	Easy run (4 miles)
Thursday	a.m.	Warm-up, then: 20 × 200 metres in 27–28 seconds with jog recovery. Warm-down (easy jog).
	p.m.	Easy run (5 miles)
Friday	a.m.	Warm-up, then relaxed sprints over varying distances from 100 to 200 metres, jog-back recovery. Warm-down (easy jog).
Saturday	a.m.	Endurance run (6–7 miles), including mixed accelerations.
Sunday	a.m.	Recovery run (6 miles)

Taper

'I give notice to members of my team that within a week or so of an international contest, I shall be using the "rest principle" very much more than the "train hard" principle. My experience as coach has convinced me of the great importance of the "rest principle" in making peak performances.'

Forbes Carlile, Australian swimming coach

'I seldom run hard in training leading up to a big race. There is little point in leaving my best work on the training track.'

John Walker, first man to run under 3:50 for the mile

Competitive endurance athletes often focus on optimising performance at just one or two major events during an entire season. As such, they will often 'taper', or reduce the volume of their training preceding such competitions. Indeed, it is now widely accepted that a properly designed taper should be an integral part of any endurance athlete's preparation for a major competitive effort. Most athletes look forward to a taper because it signifies a break from the normal rigours of intense training. On the other hand, many coaches approach the taper period with some trepidation: has the athlete undertaken sufficient training during the season? Has the athlete raced too much or too little? Does the athlete need more rest?

During a taper, several variables can be manipulated in an attempt to maximise subsequent performance. These include the *duration* of the taper, the *frequency* of training sessions, and the exercise *intensity* during the taper. Several scientific studies have been performed with athletes from a variety of sports to determine the optimal taper that will result in the best performance. From these studies several common characteristics emerge as being essential to a successful taper.

First, the training volume is reduced in an incremental or stepwise fashion for 10–14 days so that two to three days immediately before a major competition it is almost zero. Although tapers as long as six weeks have been examined, such extended tapers only maintain, rather than improve, performance. Thus, from the available data, a taper of up to, but no longer than, 21 days seems optimal. A second component of a successful taper is that despite a significant reduction in the overall volume of training, training *intensity* should be maintained, or even slightly increased. Such intense training is probably necessary to preserve some of the training-associated adaptations that may be lost with the marked reduction in training volume. Results from a study undertaken by Dr Bruce Shepley and colleagues at McMaster University in Canada revealed that competitive cross-country runners training 80 km/week improved their performances more when they followed a low-volume, high-intensity taper for seven days, compared to a low-volume (30 km/week) low-intensity regimen or no running at all. The low-volume, high-intensity taper consisted of between three and five 500 m repetitions in 70–75 seconds with 6–7 minutes' recovery between runs, for a total weekly running volume of less than 10 kilometres!

The final characteristic of a successful taper relates to the frequency of training sessions undertaken in the days prior to a major competition. The reduction in training volume necessary for a taper to be most effective should not be achieved at the expense of a drastic decline in the number of training sessions undertaken during this period; hence, the athlete should reduce training frequency by no more than 20–30%. Reducing the total number of exercise sessions by more than this amount usually results in a decrement in performance because the athlete loses their 'feel' for the activity, a complaint often voiced by swimmers if they are forced to miss pool sessions for more than several days.

To summarise, the scientific evidence indicates that most well-trained individuals can expect a performance improvement of up to 3% above their seasonal best time following a taper (Table 6.3). In reality, however, most endurance athletes, particularly long-distance runners and cyclists, do not taper sufficiently prior to competitions. Many of these athletes fear that a one-to-two week reduction in their training schedule will result in a drastic loss of fitness and, ultimately, an inferior performance to that they would have achieved if they had trained hard right up to the event. Such a fear is totally unwarranted.

A 10-DAY TAPER PROGRAM FOR ELITE ROWERS

The following program is a 10-day taper program used by elite US rowers before a world championship event.

Saturday   a.m.   4–6 × 500 metres with 3 minutes' recovery. Maximal effort and stroke rating.

	p.m.	2 × 1000 metres with 5 minutes' recovery, then 1 × 1500 metres. Maximal effort and stroke rating.
Sunday	a.m.	1 × 500 metres, 5 minutes' recovery, 1 × 1000 metres, 5 minutes' recovery, then 1 × 500 metres all-out.
	p.m.	Steady-state row (45 minutes) Stroke rating 20–24/minute
Monday	a.m.	Steady-state row (60 minutes) Stroke rating 20–24/minute
Tuesday	a.m.	Fartlek (30 minutes) 20 seconds on/20 seconds off
	p.m.	Start practice (40 minutes)
Wednesday	a.m.	1 × 1000 metres, 5 minutes' recovery, 1 × 500 metres. Maximal effort and stroke rating.
	p.m.	Steady-state row (45 minutes)
Thursday	a.m.	Easy row (45 minutes) Stroke rating 20–24/minute
Friday	a.m.	Steady-state row (40 minutes) 10 starts
	p.m.	Steady-state row (40 minutes)
Saturday		Regattas
Sunday		Regattas

Source: Hagerman, F.C. 'Physiology and nutrition for rowing', in *Perspectives in Exercise Science and Sports Medicine*, vol. 7, *Physiology and Nutrition for Competitive Sport*, Lamb, D.R., Knuttgen, H.G. and Murray, R. (eds), Cooper Publishing Group, Carmel, Indiana, p. 279, 1994.

RESISTANCE TRAINING AND ENDURANCE PERFORMANCE

'Strength or power measured in non-rowing circumstances often seems to have little value when applied to rowing performance.'

Fredrick Hagerman, rowing physiologist

'Many top road riders do not do weight training, particularly the European professionals. However, this does not mean weight training is not useful.'

Harvey Newton, strength training coach of American cyclists

'I firmly believe in resistance training with heavy weights. So long as I taper sufficiently before a race, I feel they improve my performance.'

Marianne Kriel, 1996 Olympic swimming medallist

Resistance training, also called strength or power training, is commonly undertaken by elite and recreational endurance athletes in the belief that it will improve performance. But in their extreme forms, training for endurance and training for maximal strength and power represent completely different and opposite forms of activity. Endurance training consists of many thousands of submaximal muscle contractions performed at low to moderate workloads, while training for strength and power involves relatively few contractions at maximal or near

──┤ TABLE 6.3 ├──────────────────────────────────

The effects of different taper and reduced-training regimens on the performances of highly-trained endurance athletes

Athletes	Taper regimen	Performance measure	Change (%)
Cross-country runners	5 days high-intensity intervals	Maximal leg extension	⇑ 33.0
Cross-country runners	5 days low-intensity intervals	Maximal leg extension	⇑ 33.0
Cross-country runners	7 days no running	Maximal leg extension	⇑ 37.0
Cross-country runners	5 days high-intensity intervals	Treadmill run time to exhaustion	⇑ 22.0
Cross-country runners	5 days low-intensity intervals	Treadmill run time to exhaustion	⇑ 6.0
Cross-country runners	7 days no running	Treadmill run time to exhaustion	⇓ −3.0
Distance runners	14 days no running	Treadmill run time to exhaustion	⇓ −9.2
College swimmers	14 days reduced volume (53%)	Biokinetic swim bench power	⇑ 17.7
College swimmers	14 days reduced volume (53%)	Maximal swim power	⇑ 24.6
College swimmers	14 days reduced volume (53%)	Swim performance (50–1650 yards)	⇑ 3.1
College swimmers	10–13 days reduced volume (65–76%)	Maximal swim power	⇑ 5.0
College swimmers	10–13 days reduced volume (65–76%)	Swim performance (50–400 yards)	⇑ 2.8

Source: Hawley, J.A. 'The effects of tapering and reduced training on maximal strength and performance', *The New Zealand Coach*, vol. 3, no. 2, pp. 18–19, 1994.

maximal force. From a physiological standpoint, it seems unlikely that muscle would be able to adapt to two seemingly incompatible training stimuli when they are undertaken simultaneously. Surprisingly, few good scientific studies have been conducted using well-trained athletes to determine if the improvements in muscular strength gained from resistance training result in enhanced endurance performance.

Resistance training and swimmers

Swimming is one sport where the majority of competitors practise some form of resistance training. Although most competitive swimming distances might not be considered true endurance events, there is no question that elite swimmers perform huge volumes of over-distance training. To determine whether adding resistance training to pool training might improve sprint-swim performance, Professor Dave Costill and colleagues from Ball State University, Muncie, Indiana, studied 24 experienced swimmers during fourteen weeks of their competitive season. The swimmers were divided into two groups of twelve swimmers and matched for stroke specialities and performance. The two groups performed all swim training sessions together for the duration of the season, but in addition to the pool training, one group performed resistance training three days a week, on alternate days for eight weeks. The resistance training program was intended to simulate the muscles employed in front crawl swimming and utilised weight-lifting machines, as well as free weights. Swimmers performed three sets of eight to twelve repetitions of the following exercises: lat pull-downs, elbow extensions, bent-arm flys, dips and chin-ups. In order to maximise the resistance training effect, weights were progressively increased over the duration of the training period. Following the resistance training program both groups tapered for approximately two weeks prior to their major competition.

The most important finding of Costill's study was that resistance training did not improve sprint-swim performance, despite the fact that those swimmers who combined resistance and swim training increased their strength by 25–35%. Neither did the extra strength gained from the resistance training program result in improved stroke mechanics: stroke length, an index of swimming technique, was the same for both groups of swimmers during a 400 yard swim. These investigators concluded that 'the lack of positive transfer between dry-land strength gains and swimming propulsive force may be due to the specificity of training'.

Resistance training and rowers

In rowing, supplementary resistance training programs are still advocated by most coaches. In the early 1970s it was common to employ a program of high-resistance, low-repetition training during the pre-season period, followed by a gradual transition to lower-resistance, high-repetition endurance work nearer the competitive season. But during the past decade emphasis has shifted to a greater volume of local muscle endurance work during the pre-season, with more widespread use of exercises that simulate the rowing action being employed as the competitive period nears.

In an effort to determine the efficacy of this new approach, Dr Gordon Bell and his co-workers from the University of Alberta, Edmonton, studied eighteen varsity oarsmen who undertook three different resistance training programs during their winter training. In addition to their normal rowing, one group performed 18–22 high-velocity, low-resistance repetitions (HVLR), while another group did low-velocity, high-resistance (LVHR) repetitions (6–8 reps). All exercises were rowing-specific and performed on variable-resistance hydraulic equipment four times a week for five weeks. A third group did no resistance training. After training, the HVLR group performed better in high-velocity movements, while the LVHR group did better at low-velocity actions. But when tested on a row ergometer, there was no difference between any group for peak power output or peak lactate levels. These investigators concluded that the training effects were specific to the resistance training mode and did not transfer to the more complex action of rowing. Further, they suggested that resistance training programs may actually restrict the volume of 'beneficial, sports specific training that can be achieved because of the level of fatigue that results from their execution'.

Resistance training and cross-country skiers

Although cross-country skiing is one sport where most elite competitors do not regularly undertake strength training, one study has determined the effects of dynamic resistance training on maximal isometric strength and aerobic power. In that investigation, Dr Leena Paavolainen and colleagues from the

University of Jyvaskyla in Finland studied fifteen national class cross-country skiers during six weeks of their pre-season training period. Seven of the skiers supplemented their normal aerobic workouts with 'explosive' strength sessions. These sessions consisted of various plyometric jumping exercises and heavy-resistance (80% of 1 RM) squats and contributed about a third of the total training load. The other eight skiers performed the same aerobic training, but during the last three weeks of the study added 'endurance strength-training' which comprised many repetitions of various 'specific' leg and arm exercises. Jumping height and time to reach maximal isometric force production improved significantly in the explosive strength trained group. There were no differences in these measures before or after the six-week training period for the endurance trained group. But neither were there any differences in VO_{2max} or measures of the aerobic and anaerobic 'thresholds' between the two groups after the different training regimens.

Paavolainen and co-workers concluded that 'endurance athletes can undertake explosive strength training programs without a concomitant reduction in aerobic capacity'. But even though such a conclusion is valid, and supported by their data, it is difficult to see why an athlete would wish to follow this advice. The only effect of the explosive strength training was to improve jump height and time to reach maximal force production. Both these measures are totally unrelated to the demands of competitive cross-country skiing. In the first instance, cross-country skiers certainly do not need to be able to jump great heights during their event. Neither are they required to produce low numbers of maximal contractions; cross-country races typically last from 15 to 120 minutes, the forces involved are quite low, and the number of repetitions very high. The most important determinant of success in this sport is a skier's VO_{2max}, and this did not improve with either strength training regimen!

Resistance training and endurance cyclists

Another group of athletes who do *not* regularly undertake resistance training are endurance cyclists. They believe that such training will result in extra muscle bulk and added weight, which will reduce their endurance capacity. To investigate this possibility, James Home and co-workers at the University of Cape Town recently examined the effects of a six-week progressive resistance training program on 40 km cycling performance. Seven endurance-trained cyclists who were riding approximately 200 km per week added three resistance training sessions to their normal cycling workouts. These sessions consisted of three sets of six to eight maximal repetitions of leg press, quadriceps extensions and hamstring curls, all exercises which recruit those muscles used in cycling.

The resistance training program resulted in substantial maximal strength gains of about 25%. Such improvements, however, did not transfer into superior cycling performances. On the contrary, 40 km times slowed from 58.8 minutes to 61.9 minutes after resistance training. Additionally, cyclists complained of feeling 'tired and heavy' while riding and were forced to reduce their weekly training distance by about 20% during the study. Although it is impossible to determine whether the resistance training *alone*, or a combination of resistance training *and* the reduced endurance training volume, caused the impaired performance, it is clear that there was certainly no positive effect from undertaking the two different training modes concurrently.

Resistance training and well-trained endurance athletes

The evidence against *well-trained* endurance athletes incorporating resistance training into their normal workouts to improve their endurance performance appears to be strong. Nevertheless, there are several scientific studies that report a beneficial effect of resistance training on both short- and long-term endurance capacity. Possibly the most frequently cited investigation supporting the use of strength training to improve endurance was that conducted by Dr Robert Hickson and colleagues at the University of Illinois in 1988. They found that a three-times-a-week strength training program undertaken for ten weeks did not change the VO_{2max} of *moderately-trained* runners and cyclists. However, a short-term (four to eight minutes) endurance test was improved by 12% for both running and cycling, while long-term endurance improved from 70 to 85 minutes for cycling. These workers concluded that 'some types of endurance events can be improved by the addition of strength training'.

A study undertaken by Dr Ed Marcinik and colleagues at the University of Maryland also showed that strength training had positive effects on endurance cycling capacity. They recruited eighteen healthy male volunteers and subjected them to twelve weeks of 'strength' training three times a week. The 'strength' training consisted of 8–12 repetitions of upper body exercises (bench press, push-ups, lat pull-downs, arm curls) and 15–20 repetitions of lower body exercises (knee extensions, hip flexions, parallel squats) with a 30-second rest between exercises. The strength training program had no effect on the subjects' $\dot{V}O_{2max}$ (44–45 ml/kg/min before and after training). However, 1 RM for knee extension and hip flexion improved by 30% and 52% respectively. More importantly, cycle time to exhaustion at 75% of $\dot{V}O_{2max}$ improved by a massive 33% from 26.3 minutes before 'strength' training to 35.1 minutes after training. These workers concluded that 'strength training improves cycle endurance performance independently of changes in $\dot{V}O_{2max}$ . . . and that this improvement appears to be related to increase in leg strength'.

The results of the investigations by Drs Hickson and Marcinik *appear* to contradict the previously described studies undertaken on well-trained swimmers, rowers, cross-country skiers and cyclists. But there is a good reason which explains why some individuals improve their endurance capabilities with strength training while others don't. It appears that there is a *minimal* amount of muscle strength required to perform in any endurance event. This general principle applies to athletes of all abilities, but is especially important for those individuals who are new to a sport and therefore only moderately-trained in that discipline. These novice athletes will benefit from *any* increase in general fitness, be it an improvement in strength or endurance. This explains why the greater muscle power seen after short-term strength training programs increases endurance capacity in these individuals. In all likelihood, *any* training stimulus which overloads the working muscles would have improved their performance. The large improvements in muscle power seen after strength training merely compensate for their poor technique or efficiency of movement. This is especially true in sports such as swimming and rowing, where stroke mechanics and technical proficiency are perfected only after many years of training and hours on the water.

But for highly-trained athletes who are already capable of generating high power outputs in their chosen discipline, further improvements in strength are a less important factor in enhanced endurance performance. At the highest level of competition, increases in strength and power *per se* are not as critical to successful performance as the development of correct technique. For these athletes, the concept of specificity rules! The bottom line is that modern training studies do not support the use of resistance training programs for improving the performances of highly-trained athletes.

MODELLING TRAINING: A MATHEMATICAL APPROACH

Pharmaceutical companies have been using the modelling technique for years in order to study the dose-response characteristics of certain drugs. But only recently have sports scientists begun to apply the same approach to athletics. Dr Hugh Morton of Massey University, New Zealand, has undertaken complex mathematical modelling in an attempt to better understand the relationship between training (the dose) and subsequent performance (the response). The basic assumption in his model is that it is possible to accurately measure a given input dosage and then examine the effects of changing this dose on a measured output response. Input dosages in this case include an athlete's training, diet or psychological state. Output responses comprise weather, track surface and the nature of the competition, all of which combine to affect the final performance. As Morton points out, not all inputs are under the control of scientists or coaches. Nevertheless, the whole purpose of the modelling technique is to help the coach better understand techniques to maximise fitness and minimise fatigue, not accurately predict a certain performance. Indeed, in the final analysis, an athlete's performance at any given time is simply the difference between their fitness (which is good for performance) and fatigue (which is bad for performance). If fatigue is high and fitness is low, a poor performance is predicted, and vice versa.

Some of the results of Morton's mathematical modelling suggest the following:

- Immediately after the onset of a new training load, an athlete will suffer a performance decline before any improvement is evident.
- After about five months of a given training dose, little or no improvement in performance is possible unless the dose is increased.
- When training ceases or is significantly reduced, the decay in fatigue is more rapid than the decay in fitness: this period of taper should be exploited for maximising performance.
- Training undertaken in the last 12–14 days before a major competition has a net overall negative effect.
- Training undertaken in the 12–14 weeks before a major competition has the largest influence on subsequent performance.
- The heaviest training inputs should be performed about six weeks before an important event.

- Athletes should train at a high intensity on alternate days for a short (five-month) season and then take a complete rest.

In some cases, the theory agrees reasonably well with the current practices of top athletes. But some recommendations are diametrically opposite to normal training routines. Imagine an athlete being told by their coach not to train hard at all in the 12–14 days before a major event? Imagine only training hard every second day? It would take a brave coach and a faithful athlete to implement these strategies. The advantages of Morton's theoretical model is that, unlike an athlete, it doesn't worry about what the opposition is doing! It just takes the data and makes quantitative assumptions about the dose-response effects of training and other interventions on fitness and fatigue. But the major limitation with this approach is that it depends on being able to measure *all* the inputs which ultimately affect performance. At present, there are many inputs which are not well understood or easily quantified. So, in the meantime, coaching will continue to be a blend of science and art.

UNANSWERED QUESTIONS FOR SPORTS SCIENTISTS

'The modern textbook on coaching methods tells next to nothing of a scientific nature of how to train the body for speed and endurance. We lack too many basic facts about the effects of muscular exercise on the human organism even for the most modern training regimes to be called scientific.'

Forbes Carlile, Australian swimming coach

Although sports scientists have recently begun to investigate some of the practical questions frequently asked by coaches regarding specific training interventions and their effect on athletic performance, there still remains much mysticism surrounding the way some athletes prepare for competition and why certain training techniques yield more successful results than others. For example, the question of whether base/foundation training in the high volumes currently undertaken by elite runners, cyclists, swimmers, rowers and triathletes is essential to their superior performances is difficult to say, and has not been systematically determined. From a scientific point of view it is difficult to explain how training several hours a day at speeds which are markedly slower than planned competition pace can possibly prepare the athlete for maximal competitive efforts. Research is also needed to establish whether base training *per se* results in better endurance performances compared to when the athlete trains at an intensity or effort that is more specific to the athlete's specialist event from the outset of a training cycle. Whether base/foundation training has any benefit to athletes whose speciality event has little or no aerobic component, such as sprint running or cycling, also remains speculative. Another question which needs to be addressed by sports scientists is just how many times a year an endurance athlete might realistically expect to peak for major competitive efforts. Finally, the effect of different pacing strategies on endurance performance has, until recently, received little scientific inquiry.

It is clear that more research of an applied nature is required in almost all endurance sports to determine the precise combinations of reductions in training volume and intensity that will subsequently result in the greatest improvements in performance. Answers to these and other practical questions should provide sports scientists with many fertile areas of research to investigate in the foreseeable future.

7

Training for team sports

'The players of today are much quicker. Technology has improved, training methods have improved, diet has improved. But make no mistake, the footballers of thirty years ago were just as skilful.'

Kevin Keegan, former England soccer captain

'The greatest concern among today's players in soccer, basketball, rugby, lacrosse, field hockey and most other team sports is how to improve playing speed—the speed of all movements, including starting, stopping, accelerating, changing the direction of the body, sprinting, and split-second decision making during competition.'

Coaches George Dintiman, Bob Ward and Tom Tellez, in their book *Sports speed*

'He only practises three times a week with his team. If I trained that little, I would be in serious trouble. An athlete has to train a lot harder than a rugby player.'

The wife of a former Springbok rugby player who was herself an international athlete

TRAINING FOR TEAM SPORTS: A MIXTURE OF TECHNIQUES

The training techniques required for successful sprint and endurance performance were discussed in the two preceding chapters. These contrasting and vastly distinct types of sporting event make unique physiological demands on the athlete and, as such, represent the extremes of the power production continuum (see Chapter 3). Team sports, on the other hand, require players to be able to sustain up to two hours of high-intensity intermittent activity. This is a phenomenal endurance feat in itself, made all the more impressive when one considers that much of this activity is conducted at close to maximal speed. In addition, there is normally little recovery between these intense work bouts, which can best be described as random and unplanned in nature. They may vary in length from a few seconds up to several minutes. So, unlike the sprinter or long-distance runner, both of whom have a precise knowledge of the requirements of their event, team sport players are not able to anticipate how any game will evolve. The tactics of the opposition, the prevailing weather conditions, injuries to key players, and a variety of other factors conspire to make it difficult to formulate a precise plan on how to play any given match. And, by definition, this means that there is no ideal blueprint for the training of all team sport players.

The scarcity of scientific studies dedicated to team sports and the reluctance of many top players to submit to physiological investigations make this a difficult subject to discuss. Additionally, many sports are conservative in their approach to physical training, relying solely on the input from managers, tacticians and coaches rather than trained fitness professionals. While many coaches possess superb tactical acumen, an ever-increasing number are former players who now train their teams just as they themselves were trained many years before. Because physical training was not considered a vital component of team sport success in past decades, coaches still tend to place greater emphasis on the skill aspect of a game, often at the expense of the players' fitness requirements.

Taken collectively, these observations mean that there are still many uncertainties concerning the physiological requirements of various team sports and the optimum method of training and conditioning for them. In the last few years, however, several sports scientists have made a concerted effort to provide hard data on the physiological demands of several popular sports. While acknowledging the importance of skill, tactics and the role of the coach in blending individual players into an effective playing unit, there can be no disputing that when teams of roughly equal ability meet, the one with the higher overall fitness level will have the advantage. This chapter provides a practical approach to the physiological preparation and fitness training for team sport players. Although there are a multitude of sports, all with slightly differentiated demands, the basic principles outlined here are likely to be applicable to most team sports.

DETERMINING THE PHYSIOLOGICAL DEMANDS OF TEAM SPORTS: MATCH ANALYSIS

'Victorious teams need to develop novel training methods and a more advanced style of play.'

> Bob Dwyer, coach of the Australian rugby team, 1990–94

'We would predict that the country that first introduces a more scientific approach to game analysis will be at a decisive advantage.'

> Professor Tim Noakes and Morné du Plessis, in *Rugby without risk*

There is general consensus amongst coaches that over the past decade most sports have become faster and are played at a higher intensity than ever before. In some sports such as Rugby Union, rule changes have had a direct impact on the physiological demands placed on players in specific positions. Before the laws governing the restriction of touch kicking outside the 22 metre line were enforced, the ball was in play for only 14 minutes, compared to nearly 30 of the 80 playing minutes after the rule change. Recent (1994) rule modifications in Rugby League now require players who are not in possession of the ball to immediately retire 10 m from their opponents after each tackle. Although no published data are available, it is likely that this may lead to an increase in both the total distance covered by all players, and the proportion and total amount of high-intensity running.

In other sports, such as field-hockey, the advent of synthetic playing surfaces has drastically altered both the physiological and technical demands of the game at all levels, but in particular at the elite level. Comparisons of women's international matches held on artificial and grass surfaces show that there were more touches per possession, players ran with the ball longer, the ball travelled quicker, and the speed of the game was, on average, faster on synthetic surfaces. Rule changes primarily designed to speed up the game by increasing playing time and decreasing the number of interruptions have also had a big influence on the physiological requirements placed on players.

One of the most frequently used methods of determining the physiological demands of any team sport has been to measure the distance covered by players during a match. Researchers usually estimate running 'performance' by filming an individual player during a match and dividing their activity patterns into discrete categories such as walking, easy jogging, running hard and sprinting. While such time–motion analysis provides a reasonable estimate of the total work undertaken

TABLE 7.1

Total running distances covered by players from different outfield positions from a variety of team sports

Sport and playing position	n*	Distance (metres)
Soccer		
Australian National league		
Full-back	5	11,980
Centre-back	5	10,169
Midfield	5	12,194
Striker	5	11,766
English First Division		
Full-back	8	8,245
Centre-back	7	7,759
Midfield	11	9,805
Striker	14	8,397
Rugby Union		
Club players		
Prop forward	1	3,635
Scrum-half	1	4,596
Inside centre	1	5,756
Fullback	1	3,657
Internationals		
Prop forward	1	6,100
Scrum-half	1	6,398
Rugby League		
Prop forward	1	6,530
Hooker	1	6,764
Half-back	1	7,921
Winger	1	6,750
Field-hockey		
Internationals		
Defender	2	5,140
Midfield	4	6,360

Note: n* refers to the number of players tested.

by players, a more detailed breakdown of the time spent performing different tasks would be more helpful to the fitness coach. For example, a comparison of the data collected from studies conducted over twenty years ago which determined the total running distances covered by professional soccer players and the data from more recent investigations shows little or no difference. In both cases, players covered around 10–11 km. In Rugby Union, top international players typically cover 6–7 km, a distance similar to that reported for top Rugby League players (see Table 7.1). However, taken alone, this information is of little value. It merely indicates that the *absolute minimum* fitness requirements for players from those sports is the ability to run continuously at a low-to-moderate pace for the specific distance. For example, during an 80-minute game of Rugby League, the ball is in play for 'only' 50 minutes, but physical confrontations (i.e. tackles) can be as high as 40 per player per match. The physical collision and subsequent confrontation between an attacking and defending player has been reported to last three to four seconds. And players reveal that either making or receiving a tackle is the most fatiguing part of a game. To neglect such activity in an analysis of the demands of the game would be a serious oversight.

In Rugby Union there are likely to be 40 scrums per match, of which 90% last up to twenty seconds, making a total scrummaging time of around ten minutes a game. Likewise, up to 70 loose rucks and mauls, each lasting approximately ten seconds, add up to close to twelve minutes spent rucking and mauling. Efforts such as these will inevitably place intense physical demands on players, and involve both upper and lower body. Indeed, these 'non-running' activities are a major characteristic of team sports where physical contact is considered a large part of any game and need to be considered when constructing physical training programs.

REST . . . IF YOU CAN!

Team sports are characterised by short bouts of high-intensity intermittent exercise interspersed with varying recovery periods of active rest, such as walking or jogging. And while energy to power intense exercise is derived predominantly from anaerobic processes (see Chapter 3), the energy for recovery processes is obtained almost exclusively from aerobic sources. For the team sport player, the ability to recover from the last work bout is crucial to subsequent performance.

Dr Paul Balsom and his colleagues from the Karolinska Institute in Stockholm have evaluated how different-length rest intervals during repeated high-intensity exercise affect subsequent sprint performance. On three occasions, they asked seven trained athletes to perform fifteen all-out 40 metre sprints from a standing start. The duration of the rest interval differed for each set of sprints and was either 30 seconds (short), one minute (medium) or two minutes (long). The direction of the sprints alternated so that the finishing position of the last sprint became the start of the next. Between the sprints the athletes rested at the start line.

With the long and medium recovery periods, acceleration over the first 15 m did not change between the first and the last sprint. But with the shortest recovery, acceleration over the first 15 m was slower after just seven sprints, and continued to get progressively worse for the last eight work bouts. The average running speed over the last 10 m of each sprint was maintained until the eleventh sprint with the long recovery and until the seventh sprint with the medium recovery. But when the recovery was short, running speed over the final 10 m was slower after just three sprints, and continued to get worse. Total 40 m sprint times did not differ between the first (5.58 seconds) or the last (5.66 seconds) sprint with the long recovery. With the medium recovery, sprint times were maintained until the eleventh repetition. But with the short recovery, there was a deterioration in 40 m time after just the fifth work bout.

This is an important study, as it shows that the capacity to accelerate from a stationary position is restored rapidly with adequate recovery. However, even with medium to long recoveries, there were still decreases in running speed towards the end of each sprint. It would appear that this component of performance is strongly affected by the preceding exercise bout. These findings have direct practical relevance for the coach, and indicate that similar testing protocols should be introduced when evaluating the fitness levels of players from team sports (see Chapter 4).

In addition to those studies which have investigated the energetics of team sports by time–motion analysis, several others have used heart-rate monitoring and blood lactate measurements to assess the physiological responses of players during a match. When examined in conjunction with the information gained from time–motion analysis, such data enable sport scientists to get a reasonably accurate estimate of the true energy demands of a game (see 'And don't forget the ball' on page 148). For example, in soccer, most of the flat-out sprinting is covered in short bursts lasting four to five seconds, with rest periods (jogging or walking) of approximately 30 seconds. The range of sprint distances is from 5 to 25 m, and players may start from a stationary position up to 70 times a game, and have to accelerate between 50 and 60 times. Perhaps the most interesting observation is that players change pace or direction every five seconds. It is perhaps not surprising, then, to find that top soccer players exercise at close to their maximal heart-rates for sustained periods throughout a game, spending over two-thirds of the entire match at about 85% of their maximal heart-rate (approximately 77% of their maximal oxygen uptake). Blood lactate measurements are also significantly elevated during a game, clearly indicating the role of anaerobic (oxygen-independent) metabolism (see Figure 7.1).

Data for Rugby Union and Rugby League also highlight the sustained high-intensity activity pattern of team sports and the stochastic (stop–start) nature of these games. For example, during international Rugby Union games there are up to 160 different 'activity cycles' of which a third last less than five

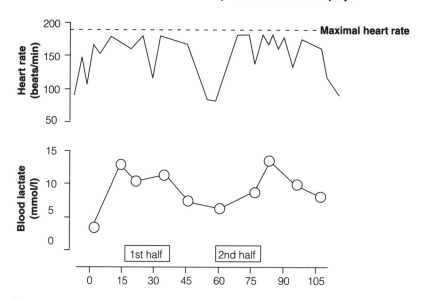

FIGURE 7.1

The heart-rate response and blood lactate profile measured in a professional soccer player

Source: Ekblom, B. 'Applied physiology of soccer', *Sports Medicine* 3, 50–60, 1986.

seconds, a quarter last less than ten seconds, nearly 30% last less than twenty seconds, and 10% last less than 30 seconds. In addition, about 85% of the 'recovery' periods have a duration of less than 45 seconds.

Of interest is the finding that the higher the quality of the team, the higher the absolute intensity and speed of a game. This is consistent with the observations that top players have superior aerobic and anaerobic powers compared to players from less experienced sides (see Chapter 4). But notwithstanding this fact, there is always a reduced running distance by players in the second half compared to the first half of a match. Studies on elite soccer players reveal that not only is the total running distance less during the second half of a game, but the distance at speed is reduced by as much as 50%.

AND DON'T FORGET THE BALL . . .

The running distance covered by players of team sports represents an underestimation of the true energy expenditure of most games. So says Professor Tom Reilly of the Centre for Sport and Exercise Sciences at John Moores University, Liverpool. Professor Reilly has investigated the energetics of many team sports, especially soccer, and is regarded as one of the leading authorities in the world on match analysis. He says that when routine time–motion studies are conducted on players from a variety of team sports, the extra demands of the game skills themselves are not accounted for in traditional methods of analysis. These movements include angular runs, changes of direction, jumping to contest possession, tackles and avoiding tackles. But there are also the many aspects of direct involvement in play, such as dribbling a ball using a body part (soccer and basketball) or an implement (hockey and lacrosse), or carrying a ball (Australian Football, Rugby League and Rugby Union). These techniques are all examples of the additional physiological demands of game skills over and above the physiological cost of locomotion.

In an effort to quantify these 'game-specific skills', Professor Reilly examined the additional cost of dribbling a ball on a motor-drive treadmill at a range of speeds typically encountered during normal match play. The protocol allowed players to control the ball, playing it against a rebound box at the front of the treadmill belt at a predetermined rate. Interestingly, the added cost of dribbling was the same, irrespective of the player's running speed. And the elevation in metabolism was paralleled by a higher blood lactate concentration and an increase in the player's rate of perception of effort for the task. The increased energy cost is, in part, attributable to the extra muscular activity required to control the ball and propel it forward. There is also an extra energy cost due to changes in the player's stride rate, which increases when dribbling in tight control. Professor Reilly also notes that the energy cost of dribbling may be even higher than he measured in the laboratory. In actual match play, players deliberately change stride pattern when they feign side-to-side movements in order to outwit an opponent. Clearly, improving the efficiency of game-specific skills should be a high priority for players and coaches.

Minimum physiological requirements for high-level team sports

From the results of scientific investigations it would appear that the minimum physiological requirements for any individual wishing to compete at a high level in team sports are:

- a moderate maximum oxygen uptake (50–55 ml/kg/min for females; 60–65 ml/kg/min for males), depending on the playing position;
- the ability to sustain a moderate-to-high percentage of aerobic power for the duration of a match;
- a high anaerobic power;
- the ability to recover quickly between high-intensity work bouts;
- the ability to accelerate from a stationary position at speed;
- the ability to change pace and/or direction at speed (speed-agility);
- the ability to resist fatigue during the latter stages of a match;
- sports-specific flexibility;
- a high degree of skill and technical proficiency; and
- tactical awareness.

In addition to the above prerequisites, in those sports which involve direct physical contact (such as Rugby League, Rugby Union or Australian Football) or dominance in the air (such as basketball, volleyball or soccer), the following requirements are necessary:

- a high degree of muscularity;
- exceptional upper and lower body strength;

- a high power to weight ratio; and
- superior vertical jump height.

PRINCIPLES OF TRAINING FOR TEAM SPORT PLAYERS

'More detailed scientific analysis will allow more specialised training programs specific to the different playing positions to be developed. This will be aided by the introduction of real professionalism which will allow players more time to train. These changes will increase the need for specific training programs that will optimise the unusual talents of this new breed of talented athletes.'

> Professor Tim Noakes and Morné du Plessis, in *Rugby without risk*

'The basis of any program is that it is highly structured and specific for each player, depending on his size, physique, strength and stamina.'

> Bob Dwyer, coach of the Australian Wallabies, who won the 1991 Rugby World Cup

The scientific principles of training for team sports are essentially no different to those outlined in Chapter 2. But because of the diverse physiological requirements placed on team sport players and the demands of playing more and more games each season with less and less recovery (both between games and seasons), there are several key concepts that need to be adhered to when constructing training programs. These principles, unique to team sports, are listed below:

- The fitness requirements for one team sport are not necessarily the same as for other team sports.
- There is a *minimum* fitness requirement which is common to all players in a team.
- Each playing position or playing style requires a slightly differentiated form of fitness. Training programs should be modified to match these requirements.
- Training programs may need to be adapted to suit the specific strengths or weaknesses of a player.
- Training sessions should be as sports-specific as possible (i.e. players should practise with the equipment to be used during games and competition).
- Training sessions should be structured so that aspects of

skill and technique are emphasised early in a session, and fitness later.

- Players cannot peak for every game during a season.
- Training programs should be planned in advance.

When planning a fitness training program for team sports, the first priority is to divide the year into the playing season and the off-season. Unfortunately, as the demands of professional sport increase, players are forced to participate in an ever-increasing number of games. The net result of this is to increase the playing season and drastically reduce the length of the off-season. Before winning their fifth National Basketball Association final play-offs in 1997, the Chicago Bulls had already played over 70 normal-season games. With the advent of Rugby Union's 'Super 12' series contested by state and provincial teams from Australia, New Zealand and South Africa, the off-season for some international players is now limited to less than a month. Clearly, such physiological demands are unrealistic and are likely to reduce the life-span of a top professional player, especially if they are involved in a contact sport. But they make it all the more crucial that training is soundly structured and periodised to the requirements of the playing season.

SOCCER TRAINING AT THE AIS

Doug Tumilty, exercise physiologist at the Australian Institute of Sport

Except at the professional level, it is unlikely that many coaches involved in team sports see their players for training more than a couple of times each week. On these occasions, time is most profitably spent imparting to players the coach's knowledge regarding the techniques and tactics of the game. An important question therefore is whether such training can be structured to also produce significant physical conditioning benefits?

Coaches in the soccer program at the Australian Institute of Sport (AIS) do not really have to consider this question: in their case, access to players is unlimited. Most of the squad are in residence at the institute and could train under the coach twice a day if necessary. But because the players constitute a development squad aged between fifteen and sixteen years, the aim of the program is to increase their game skills as much as possible during their 18–24 month AIS scholarship.

Different types of training sessions have been monitored by a variety of techniques—including heart-rate, blood lactate concentration and film analyses—in order to assess their intensity. These results have then been compared to measures determined during competitive games. Intermittently throughout a season, a standard battery of physiological and anthropometrical tests have also been administered in order to determine any changes in fitness.

The results from these observations indicate that:

- Lots of drills and small-sided game variations can produce exercise intensities that are comparable to, or even higher than, those observed in competitive match situations.

- These activities are usually much shorter than the real games, so they have to be suitably structured to prevent a drop in intensity. For example, if a ball goes out of play it must be retrieved quickly, or the activity must proceed immediately with another ball. Players will rest whenever they get the opportunity, as they would during the course of a match. If simulated activities are allowed to proceed with rest intervals, then there will be an associated reduction in the potential conditioning effect of such practices.

- Before any training session, coaches need to determine whether they want to emphasise coaching (skills and tactics) or conditioning (physical work). This could then apply to the whole session or within the individual activities scheduled. As discussed, stopping an activity frequently to make protracted coaching points will reduce the overall effectiveness of any training session considerably. In any case, coaches should consider that it may be more productive to highlight a few specific technical points at the beginning of a session, than to emphasise only these issues throughout the session, ideally without stopping play.

- Although the results of the AIS physiological testing reveals that a high *average* level of fitness can be maintained by a squad for the duration of a season by concentrating on game-specific training *during* the season, practical experience has also shown that the more traditional, basic, conditioning work is needed by players in certain circumstances, for example, when certain players need to develop speed, power or agility. At the AIS, 2–3 sessions weekly are devoted to weight training, sprints, and plyometrics, designed to improve acceleration, speed, agility and overall strength. These components are necessary in the modern game, since even the most highly skilled player can find themselves brushed off the ball all too easily by aggressive defenders, and there is also some evidence that the more robust player is more likely to survive the season without injury. There is also the need to address individual player's weaknesses; the physically inferior players may need resistance training to increase their muscle mass; a player with poor endurance (especially if they are a midfielder or outside back), should be encouraged to undertake additional aerobic conditioning, above their normal training. Sometimes game-specific training will be insufficient to bring a player up to the necessary level of fitness required because of the stop–start nature of training, and because all-round endurance development requires a spectrum of training ranging from protracted continuous work to regular, disciplined, interval sessions.

In summary, the coach should devote as much time as possible to improving their squad's playing skills. Conditioning work, as deemed necessary, should be left to the individual players to perform. If they are conscientious and knowledgeable, such an approach will meet with success. However, the assistance of specialists across a wide range of disciplines may be necessary with certain players: there are many team sport players who dislike all forms of activity unless it is playing the actual game!

KEEPING THE BIG MEN FLYING . . . AND FLYING, AND FLYING

Dr Mike McCoy, exercise physiologist and fitness adviser to the Richmond Football Club (Australian Football League)

There is no doubt that the periodisation of training and competition works most effectively with athletes from individual sports. These athletes have the opportunity to peak at specific meetings, to compete aggressively at minor competitions without necessarily having to produce a personal best performance or to miss competitions completely if they don't fall within the aims of their overall program. But periodisation is equally necessary for players from team sports. The factors which influence the fluctuations in training volume and intensity however, are often not of the players' choosing, making the task more difficult.

Aiming to have a team at peak fitness for a whole season in Australian Football is a plan destined to failure. It can take up to 35 games to get from the first pre-season practice match in early February to the ultimate aim, victory at the Melbourne Cricket Ground on the last Saturday in September. And to get there, you have to prove time and again throughout the season that your team is better than each of the other fifteen who are just as determined to reach the same goal. In other words, although your best results as a team will hopefully be at the business end of the season, if team performance was below par early in the season, it just won't matter how well your team might have played in September because they'll only be watching the action from the grandstands!

Regardless of the team's ultimate objective, it is important that the approach to attaining that goal is carefully planned out well in advance of the event. During the pre-season, when there are no games played, the volume and intensity of training can be cycled just as effectively as they might be for an athlete from an individual sport. During this period, some players will need to focus on the development of better endurance, others on speed and agility, strength and power, while a hopefully smaller group may be recovering from post-season surgery and may be in need of specific rehabilitation.

Once the season begins there are a number of external elements which might direct the coach in deciding when and how to attempt to have a team at their peak. The draw a team faces will often impose a rhythm on your in-season training. This rhythm is determined largely by two factors: who you are playing and how many days' break you get from the previous game before you're asked to play again. Others factors, such as where the game will be played (home or interstate), the expected success of your own team both for that game and for the year in general, and a knowledge of how your team actually responds to changes in the volume and intensity of training, both in the short and long term, will all influence your decision regarding the setting of training loads.

Consecutive games played against strong opposition will often require a reduction of training volume and intensity, while a couple of games in a row against less successful opponents might allow for more rigorous training sessions. Such phases, when plotted across the season as a whole, help to balance the need for an on-going training stimulus against that of sufficient freshness to allow the team to attack each game with aggression.

The second factor on deciding the weekly fluctuations in training load is the length of the competitive week. As the football codes become less tied to one state, the necessary consequence is that the team you support will often be playing interstate. There is now a fairly strong incentive for games to be scheduled to maximise their potential TV coverage, all of which means that for the footballer, the break between one game and the next can be as miserly as five days or as luxurious as nine. A five-day break means you are not going to work your players very hard regardless of who they are playing, especially if your opponent has an extra day or two to prepare for the game. A nine-day break gives you the chance to train hard for a few sessions and still have time to ease off before match day.

The underlying principle behind this division of the season into training phases is that the weekly game itself, no matter how intense, is insufficient to maintain adequate levels of fitness. This is not to say that playing the game isn't the best way of advancing your level of preparation—it is. The principle of specificity (Chapter 2) dictates this. But the intensity of such a stimulus, along with the consequences of the many high speed body-on-body and body-on-turf collisions which result from it, prohibits match-play more frequently than once a week. In fact, there is a growing argument that the game has become so intense that even an average seven-day break is no longer enough.

At the beginning of a season, not all teams will have the premiership as a legitimate target. Some might focus instead on a preliminary goal, like victory in the pre-season competition, or simply showing good early season form, both of which can help generate confidence and a winning attitude in young teams, and have the added advantage of boosting club memberships. Towards the end of a season, an appearance in the finals is an impossibility for some teams, so training might be adjusted to ensure the best chance of performing at optimal levels for the remainder of the home-and-away season, regardless of the effect that might have had by September.

All these factors must be integrated into the plan for the team's performance for the year and mixed together to produce a training program that anticipates peaks and troughs in performance and times them to occur to advantage. Ideally, those troughs are not so deep that you lose games you should properly have won, but the worst scenario is to go from one game to another, simply reacting to the success or failure of the team at the week-end game just past.

GET FIT TO PLAY. DON'T PLAY TO GET FIT

'There are many eminent physical educationists who have been urging for some time that [rugby] training should be continued on a year-round basis, with that part of the season traditionally looked upon as the "off-season" being taken up by endurance training.'

Tim Noakes, circa 1974

Until recently, off-season training was an activity team players tried to avoid. Endurance athletes might be disciplined enough to train all year round, but the physiological demands of team sports were different. After all, 'match fitness' could always be gained during the first few games of the new season. And as long as every team followed this dictum, then there should be no problems.

Then in the early 1980s a New Zealand physical education teacher, Jim Blair, popularised the idea that physical fitness (and fitness testing) be incorporated into the schedules of team sport players, particularly rugby players. Blair worked with the All Blacks and was so successful that at the inaugural rugby World Cup in 1987, which they won, the New Zealand team was considered to be the fittest and best prepared team in the tournament. Nowadays, players from all team sports are used to reporting for physiological testing throughout the year and know that they can ill afford to take too much rest, less they lose their hard-earned fitness. Now there is good scientific evidence to suggest that off-season training may be the most important time to undertake physical fitness training for team sport players.

Dr Dave Holymard and Rex Hazeldine from Loughborough University, England, have investigated the seasonal variation in the fitness characteristics of international rugby players. They studied eighteen players from the English National rugby squad over a 12-month period. Players undertook a series of physiological and anthropometrical tests during National squad training sessions at the end of a season (April), early off-season (June), pre-season (September) and mid-season (January).

During the off-season (April to June) there were significant decreases in the percentage of body fat, and substantial increases in the maximum aerobic power of the players. However, there were no further improvements in either of these two parameters during the playing season. In fact, aerobic power actually declined as the season progressed. Holymard and Hazeldine were unclear as to whether this reduction was due to a loss of fitness *per se*, or was a result of accumulated match fatigue. Although there were improvements in sprint ability (30 metre speed) during the first half of the season, anaerobic power (as determined by a high-intensity 20 metre shuttle run test) remained constant throughout the entire assessment period.

This is a particularly important study as it shows that the major improvements in aerobic power and body composition occur not during the playing season, but in the off-season. Furthermore, most aspects of fitness remained relatively constant throughout the entire season. The practical implications of these findings are that coaches should pay careful attention to the design of off-season fitness training programs. And, perhaps more to the point, they illustrate that if a player is not fit before the season begins, then they can't be expected to be fit at the end of the season.

THE EFFECTS OF RESISTANCE TRAINING ON KICKING PERFORMANCE IN SOCCER PLAYERS

The powerful quadriceps muscles at the front of the leg are largely responsible for the kicking action in a number of sports, including soccer, Rugby Union and Australian Football. So it would seem sensible to strengthen these muscles as much as possible in those players required to kick for both distance and speed. Not so, according to a study conducted by Dr Michael Trolle and his colleagues from the August Krogh Institute in Copenhagen, Denmark. During the players' off-season, they persuaded 24 male National league soccer players to undertake a 12-week strength training program. Players were split into one of four groups and undertook 36 training sessions in total. One group performed hydraulic strength training exercises at high resistance (low velocity). Another group undertook the same exercises at low resistance (high velocity). The third training group trained 'functionally' in a loaded kicking movement, but without the ball, while the last group acted as controls and did no training at all.

Maximal kicking performance was determined by terminal ball velocity during a standard indoor soccer kick. The velocity was measured by Doppler radar when the players kicked towards a goal from a distance of 11 metres. Each player performed twenty shots, with the fastest being compared to their performance before the study. Although high-resistance training improved knee extension strength, none of the strength training techniques had any effect on maximal ball velocity during the shoot-out. Peak ball velocity ranged from 85 to 115 km per hour among all players, but was not different before or after the training period. The investigators concluded that their elite players already had excellent kicking abilities prior to the study, but that such training could possibly benefit less skilled players.

THE INFLUENCE OF RESISTANCE TRAINING ON THROWING VELOCITY

A number of sports require players to perform overhead throws from various outfield positions. This technique is the most effective throwing action and is frequently used by cricketers and baseball players. The key components of a good overhead throw are speed and accuracy. But there is one sport which requires players to perform multiple overhead throws during a game, and it is not even conducted on land! In water polo, the overhead throw differs markedly from the on-land version, especially so when the player is shooting for goal. At release of the ball, the arm is almost fully extended and the hand flexed, thereby providing the ball with a slight backspin. Speed and angle of release are of paramount importance to the successful player. An increased throwing velocity and momentum reduces the time in which a goalkeeper may detect the path of a ball and deflect it. Also, at sufficiently high velocities, the ball can be made to bounce off the water. If this occurs, the ball may be projected to a point in front of the goal and still result in a goal. So, in an attempt to improve throwing velocity, many water polo players undertake strength training.

The results of an investigation conducted by Dr John Bloomfield and his colleagues at the University of Western Australia, however, suggest that such training does not result in an improved throwing velocity. They studied 21 elite male water polo players who were randomly assigned to either an eight-week strength training program, or to a control group, who maintained their usual swim training program. The strength training group undertook a progressive resistance program, three times a week using a Nautilus system for the duration of the study. The emphasis of the strength training was on the muscle groups of the upper body which were involved in the water polo throwing action. Specifically, the pectoralis major and minor, latissimus dorsi, teres major, trapezius, triceps, biceps and deltoid muscle were trained. Following the eight-week program, all players were assessed during a water polo throw in which the speed of release of the ball was measured during an accurate throw. Players were required to throw at a circular target 1 m in diameter which was positioned 50 cm above water level. The thrower was positioned 6 m away from the target, and five maximum-velocity throws were analysed by high-speed cinematography. The results revealed that there was no difference in throwing velocity between either the strength-trained or control group after the eight-week intervention period. The average throwing speeds were between 16 and 17 m per second irrespective of the previous eight weeks of training.

The investigators concluded that it was likely that their 'homogenous group of elite water polo players already possessed optimum levels of upper body strength, and that diminished strength returns were gained from the extra training'. It seems that only a certain level of strength is required for successful water polo throwing proficiency, and that further gains in strength do not improve throwing velocity. The concept of specificity strikes again!

BLACK MAGIC

Many articles in the lay press would have us believe that whites are supposed to be superior at some sports and blacks superior at other sports. And on the anecdotal evidence alone, they seem to have a point. Take professional basketball in the United States. African-Americans make up over 80% of the players on the floor for the National Basketball Association plays-offs. And the world's current best player, Michael Jordan of the Chicago Bulls, is black. Clearly there comes a point where it becomes foolish to deny the fact of black athletic prowess in some sports. But isn't some of this hype just stereotyping?

Yes, and no, says Malcolm Gladwell in a well-researched article entitled 'The sports taboo', which appeared in *New Yorker* magazine. Gladwell points out that there is definitely stereotyping in athletics—unwritten rules holding that blacks achieve success through natural ability, and whites through effort. He quotes a recent article in *Sports Illustrated* comparing the white basketball player, Steve Kerr, with his Bulls team-mate, Michael Jordan. According to the article, Kerr is a 'hard working over-achiever' distinguished by his 'work ethic and heady play' and by a shooting style 'born of a million practice shots'. But Kerr is one of the best three-point shooters in the game today, and a key player on one of the most successful teams in history. More to the point, there is absolutely no evidence to suggest that Kerr (or Luc Longley or Tony Kukoc, or any other white player on the Bull's roster) works harder than any of his black team-mates, least of all Jordan. In fact, Jordan's work habits and practice sessions are legendary. But, as Gladwell points out, you would never get that impression from the *Sports Illustrated* article.

Using track and field as another example African-Americans recently recorded the top 22 fastest 100 m times in the world, thirteen of the fastest 1500 m times, eighteen of the twenty fastest 5000 m times, and fifteen of the fastest twenty 10,000 m times. Clearly *something* is going on!

While the scientific evidence shows that African-Americans seem to have, on average, greater bone mass than whites, which suggests a greater muscle mass, comparing elite athletes of different races tells us very little about the races themselves. The best players in any team sport are the best not because they are like other members of their ethnic group, but because they are *not* like them (or like anyone else, for that matter). Elite sportsmen and women are elite because they are on the fringes of genetic variability. And the African continent just seems to create more of these genetic outliers than do most white populations.

SERVING NOTICE

Racquet design has changed substantially over the past twenty years. So, too, have the characteristics of tennis balls. And maybe today's players are fitter and stronger than their predecessors. Whatever the reason, the speed of the tennis serve has gone ballistic during the past few seasons. Whether or not this has made for a better, more entertaining game is not the question here. Technological developments have now made it possible to measure the speed of a player's serve within a tenth of a kilometre. In the late 1970s, Australian ace-expert Colin Dibley was credited with a serve measured at 232 kilometres per hour. But it is only since 1991, when photo-electric timing devices were introduced at most of the world's major tournaments, that 'official' results have been given any credibility. Table 7.2 lists the top ten fastest serves of all-time, measured during games on the official Association of Tennis Professionals' tour.

TABLE 7.2

The ten fastest recorded serves during official tournament play

Player	Speed of serve (km/hour)	Tournament (year)
Mark Philippoussis	227.2	Scottsdale, 1997
Greg Rusedski	225.0	Beijing, 1996
Richard Krajicek	220.0	Rome, 1996
Goran Ivanisevic	218.8	Wimbledon, 1994
Mark Rosset	215.6	Wimbledon, 1991
Thomas Enqvist	215.6	US Open, 1996
Alex Radulescu	215.6	Key Biscayne, 1996
David Witt	215.6	Newport, 1994
Markus Zoecke	215.6	Wimbledon, 1994
Shuzo Matsuoka	214.0	Wimbledon, 1996

Source: Sports Illustrated (South Africa), 28 April 1997, p. 15.

THE HOME COURT ADVANTAGE

Many teams have a great record when they play at their own stadium, but are not quite as impressive when they have to play away from home at another team's ground. Most coaches attribute this to the local crowd support, familiarity with the playing surface and surroundings, and, perhaps most important, the fact that players are able to maintain their normal eating, sleeping and training pattern more easily than when they are on the road. Whatever the reason, the home court advantage is a real phenomenon. History predicted that the United States would win more medals in the 1996 Atlanta Olympic Games than it did at the previous games in Barcelona. And it did (see Table 7.3). History would also predict that the host nation wins more medals 'at home' than when they have to travel to the next Olympiad. And a glance at Table 7.3 shows this to be true.

An analysis of the results from team sports confirms the home court advantage. Dr Richard Jehue and his colleagues from Beverly Hills, California, conducted a survey of the results of the American National Football League from 1978 to 1987. They analysed data from 27 teams who were grouped by time zone (Western, Central or Eastern). West Coast teams displayed uniformly high home winning percentages (75%) when playing either Central or Eastern teams. And overall, home teams won 57% of games, versus 43% for teams travelling to 'away' games. Although sports scientists have no way of predicting the magnitude of the home court advantage, it seems to be a real phenomenon that cannot be ignored.

TABLE 7.3

The number of gold medals won by host nations in the year of hosting the Olympic Games and in the preceding and following Games

Year	Host nation	Medals		
		Previous	Host	Next
1996	USA (Atlanta)	37	44	—
1992	Spain (Barcelona)	1	9	5
1988	Korea (Seoul)	6	12	12
1984	USA (Los Angeles)	—	83	34
1980	USSR (Moscow)	49	80	—
1976	Canada (Montreal)	0	0	—
1972	West Germany (Munich)	5	13	10
1968	Mexico (Mexico City)	0	3	0
1964	Japan (Tokyo)	4	16	11
1960	Italy (Rome)	8	13	10

8

Training aids and strategies: Do they help?

Previous chapters described the scientific principles of training. Such training prescription has been shown to vary markedly between different types of athletic events. But whatever the sport, there is always a need for ongoing assessment of the effectiveness of any intervention. Athletes wish to gain the maximum performance benefit from the minimum input. As such, they must continually monitor the effectiveness of their training methods. Any strategy that can increase the efficiency of training and lead to a performance improvement, however small, is of benefit to the athlete. In their quest for excellence, athletes often employ a number of training aids or tools. Some of these lack scientific credibility and are not likely to enhance performance. However, some strategies can aid the athlete during training and subsequently improve competition performances. A number of these aids or tools are evaluated in this chapter.

MONITORING PROGRESS

Methods for monitoring progress include training diaries and heart-rate monitoring.

Training diaries

'Training logs are important. They monitor how you feel and create a skeleton of how you train—what helps and what doesn't.'

Anne Marie Lauck, elite US distance runner

'It lets you see what works and what doesn't, to identify trends and pick up on over-training.'

PattiSue Plummer, US Olympian

'To improve incrementally, you must plan incrementally. And the best way to do that, to think it all through, to make sure you've missed nothing, is to write it down. Having a good record is vital. It's the first step in learning to put yourself on the hook, to being responsible to yourself.'

Michael Johnson, gold medallist 200 and 400 metres, 1996 Atlanta Olympic Games

Feedback from training sessions is of utmost importance to the coach, athlete and sports scientists alike. For the coach, the main application of such data is to prescribe and fine-tune systematic training to improve competitive performance. For the athlete, keeping a training diary acts as a motivational tool. For the sports scientist, a valid and reliable record of training allows the effectiveness of various interventions, and their impact on performance, to be assessed.

There are several ways in which training data can be recorded. The simplest is the training diary. Information about a particular workout, as well as other data about the environmental conditions, how the athlete felt during the session, and if they were successful in completing the prescribed training, is recorded for all sessions over a specified period. The coach can utilise the diary on a day-to-day basis to assess whether or not an athlete is recovering from successive workouts. Alternatively, a coach may wish to observe the effects of a more prolonged period of training to determine if an athlete is adapting to a particular phase or type of training intervention. Keeping a diary may result in better compliance with a training program. If so, this alone would be expected to improve subsequent performance.

MONITORING TRAINING INTENSITY: RATING OF PERCEPTION OF EFFORT

Quantifying training intensity is essential if a coach wishes to determine whether an athlete is complying with a prescribed training program, or if a self-coached athlete wants to ensure that their self-imposed training targets are being met. A training program that lacks specific high-intensity training will not improve the athlete's fitness (see Chapter 2). However, a program which is too difficult will lead to a decline in fitness and a subsequent drop-off in performance. There are several ways in which training intensity can be quantified, including:

- measurement of oxygen uptake;
- measurement of heart-rate;
- measurement of lactate concentration; and
- rating of perception of effort.

While the first three methods provide the sports scientist with direct physiological data about a training session, they are sometimes impractical. For this reason, both coach and athlete need a simple, quick method of assessing the severity of a workout. Table 8.1 provides such a measure. As soon as practical after a training session, the athlete is asked to rate how hard or easy the workout was. Alongside specific details of the workout (the number of repetitions, the rest interval, the times of the work bouts etc.), the athlete scores the whole session based upon how they *felt* while completing it.

If an athlete repeatedly rates their training sessions as ones and twos for a period of a week or so, it is likely the coach has set a program which is too easy for the current physiological status of the athlete. On the other hand, if an athlete is rating several successive sessions threes and fours, then the athlete is failing to adapt to the current training load. Athletes should paste this table in the front of their training diaries—and use it!

TABLE 8.1

Rating of perception of training effort

Score	Perception of effort during training session
1	Felt good during all parts of the workout. Maintained target pace and completed session. Could have done more.
2	Felt good during some parts of the workout. Completed session, but had difficulty in hitting target pace, especially near the end.
3	Somewhat difficult. Felt pretty bad during some parts of the workout. Only just able to complete the session.
4	Felt terrible throughout the entire workout. Very heavy and sluggish. Had to reduce pace considerably just to complete the session. Should have rested.

Heart-rate monitoring

The recent introduction of reliable, portable heart-rate monitors has enabled sports scientists to quantify the physiological
demands of a number of sports. Using a transmitter worn on
an electrode around the chest and a receiver which contains
a small microcomputer worn on the wrist, the athlete can get
instant feedback on their training intensity. A record of
heart-rates for an entire workout or match can be stored by
the memory of the microcomputer and downloaded on to a
personal computer for later playback and analysis (see Figure
8.1).

In order to prescribe training intensities based on heart-
rate, it is first necessary for an athlete to determine their
maximal heart-rate in their chosen discipline. This is best
carried out during an incremental, exhaustive test in the
laboratory (see Chapter 4). There are reports of some endurance athletes hitting higher 'maximal' heart-rates during a race
than those they attained during the lab. If this is the case,
then the highest heart-rate achieved should be taken as the
athlete's true maximal value. Under most conditions, providing
a work bout lasts longer than two to three minutes, heart-rate
accurately reflects the intensity of that exercise. Remember
that environmental factors such as heat and altitude will cause
heart-rates to be excessively elevated for a given exercise
intensity.

During very long training sessions lasting several hours,
heart-rate will tend to 'drift' upwards, sometimes by as much
as twenty beats per minute, despite a constant workload (see
Figure 8.1). Competition nerves and excitement may also
cause an alteration in the relationship between work intensity
and heart-rate. Caution should therefore be used when assessing the intensity of training sessions which are undertaken in
adverse conditions or for a long duration. Chapter 6 sets out
the appropriate training heart-rates for the different phases of
endurance training.

SPECIAL TRAINING TECHNIQUES

Special training techniques include altitude training, heat
acclimatisation, vision training, water running, indoor training,
hill training and stretching.

FIGURE 8.1

The average power output and heart-rate response of eight well-trained endurance cyclists performing a simulated 100 km road race in the laboratory. Note the progressive upward drift in heart-rate over the duration of the ride.

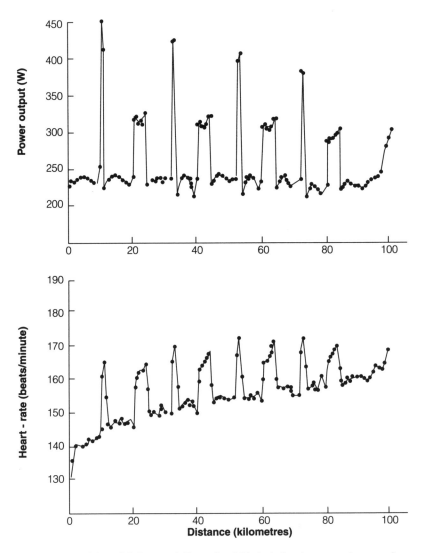

Source: Adapted from Schabort et al. 'A novel, reliable test of endurance performance for road cyclists', *Medicine and Science in Sports and Exercise* (in press 1998).

Altitude training

'Ninety per cent of our athletes should do this altitude training some-where prior to the anaerobic load . . . to enhance the process of anaerobic training, to facilitate recovery, to enhance the aerobic system.'

Dennis Pursley, American swimming coach

'The beneficial effects of altitude training for sea level performance remain to be convincingly demonstrated and should not be taken for granted.'

Dr François Péronnet, sports scientist

'I went from feeling great to feeling bad in about three strides. I felt as bad with 400 metres to go as I have at the finish of tough races in the past.'

Ron Clarke, Australian running great, describing the last lap of the 10,000 metres in the 1968 Mexico City Olympics

Any athlete born and raised at sea level and who has had to compete at an elevation of over 1500 metres will know that performance is affected by altitude. It seems that a greater effort is required to sustain the same pace in endurance events, while it can be especially difficult to perform repeated bouts of high-intensity activity so common to most team sports. Yet only 30 years ago athletes, coaches and sports scientists were unaware of the effects of altitude on athletic performance.

It was not until the 1968 Olympic Games that the world first became aware that the performances of those athletes who were born at sea level were consistently slower in almost all events when competing in the rarefied air of Mexico City (altitude 2300 metres). A few events benefited from the 'thin air', such as the jumping or throwing events and the short sprints. However, once the decrease in air drag was offset by a reduced exercise capacity, performance was hampered. Race times in events lasting longer than three or four minutes were impaired, progressively more so with increasing race distance. And almost every track medallist from the 1500 m to the marathon was either born at altitude or had trained at altitude for a prolonged period before the Games. An indication of the effect of altitude on performance is the fact that the American Athletics Union permits a 3% 'altitude allowance' for track performances at distances of 1500 m or longer when these are achieved above 1200 m.

Today, many coaches steadfastly believe that preparation for a major *sea-level* competition is incomplete until an athlete has undertaken a period of altitude training. The prevailing opinion among most coaches, athletes and, indeed, sports administrators is that altitude training can enhance performance at sea level for *any* athlete, irrespective of their event. There is so much anecdotal speculation suggesting that altitude training improves sea-level performance that the majority of elite athletes have incorporated such a strategy into their training regimens. There is also the underlying assumption that living and training at altitude is somehow responsible for the phenomenal success of the Kenyan runners. However, while some Kenyans live and train at altitude, many don't. And the competitive European track season requires many Kenyan athletes to live and race at sea level for extended periods. Their prowess does not seem to be diminished to any noticeable extent as a result of this!

So what is the purpose of altitude training? Does the scientific literature support the claims of athletes? Is sea-level performance really enhanced?

The physiological rationale of altitude training: Benefits and trade-offs

Altitude training evokes a multitude of physiological adaptations which are remarkably similar to those caused by regular endurance training at sea level, which include:

- an increase in the activity of several key enzymes in the muscles involved in aerobic metabolism;
- an improved capacity of those muscles involved in training to 'buffer' lactate;
- an increase in the volume of red blood cells;
- an increase in haemoglobin, the oxygen-carrying compound in the blood; and
- an increase in maximal aerobic power ($\dot{V}O_{2max}$).

Theoretically, an increase in one or more of these adaptations should result in enhanced performance, particularly in those events requiring a large contribution from aerobic metabolism. But our understanding of the physiological effects of altitude training has largely been gained from research undertaken on a few moderately-fit individuals living and training at altitudes over 3000 metres. In practice, athletes not born at altitude choose to train at more moderate elevations of 1500 up to 2500 metres. The reason for this is simple.

Going higher than about 3000 metres increases the frequency of discomfort from the effects of altitude, if not the symptoms of altitude sickness. These problems, which are particularly noticeable in the first few days of arriving at altitude, include:

- general fatigue;
- frequent headaches;
- dehydration resulting in a loss of weight of a couple of kilograms; and
- disturbances in normal sleep patterns.

But perhaps of even greater consequence for the athlete is that upon arrival at altitude, and for some time thereafter, the intensity at which they can train is significantly compromised. This is because acute exposure to altitude results in a decrease in an athlete's $\dot{V}O_{2max}$. The reduction in aerobic power seems to be related to the elevation: there is a loss of about 3% in $\dot{V}O_{2max}$ for every 300 metres' elevation above 1600 metres. Paradoxically, for a given altitude, $\dot{V}O_{2max}$ is reduced more in those athletes with the highest sea-level values.

Altitude training strategies

'Ultimately, the best situation would be to do your aerobic work in the mountains, then come back down to sea level for your speedwork. You'd have the best of both worlds.'

John Sinclair, US Olympic marathoner

'No clear case can be made for any athlete to train at altitude to enhance sea level performance.'

Dr Lynneth Wolski, Canadian sports scientist

A current focus of research for sports scientists is the determination of the optimal altitude at which athletes should train, and the time at which they should be exposed to such elevations in order to obtain any physiological adaptations which might benefit subsequent sea-level performance. As such, a variety of strategies have been tested in an attempt to optimise any advantages of hypoxic exposure, without the drawbacks of altitude sickness or a reduction in training intensity. These strategies include:

- constant, prolonged exposure;
- intermittent exposure; and
- live high and train low.

The traditional strategy for altitude training for those athletes who normally live at sea level has been a fixed, constant exposure to an elevation of around 2000 to 3000 metres for three to six weeks prior to a major sea-level competition. British athletics coach Frank Dick has stated that after such an exposure, maximum sea-level performance can be expected in the two to four weeks *after* altitude training. However, scientific research does not support such a contention. Several studies have shown that after three to seven weeks' constant exposure to altitudes varying from 2300 metres up to 4000 metres, there was no improvement in either $\dot{V}O_{2max}$ or running performance upon return to sea level. Even two to three weeks after re-exposure to sea level, maximum aerobic capacity and performance remain unaltered from pre-altitude values.

A strategy which might be more likely to improve sea-level performance is intermittent exposure to altitude, separated by periods of training at sea level. Such a practice might allow for any potential physiological benefits of altitude while still permitting athletes to maintain their normal training intensity at sea level. This strategy has recently been incorporated into the training programs of elite runners, cyclists and swimmers from a number of countries. Special altitude training centres have been built to cater for the needs of such athletes, and training communities have developed in 'altitude' cities such as Flagstaff, Arizona, Boulder, Colorado, and Albuquerque, New Mexico. The centres are practical in terms of cost, accommodation and disruption to the athletes' normal routines. And coaches are adamant that camps held at these centres or cities have beneficial results on sea-level performance.

Surprisingly, however, this practice has received only minimal scientific inquiry to date. One study conducted by Drs Jack Daniels and Neil Oldridge at the University of Wisconsin in the late 1960s strongly suggested that athletes might benefit from such a routine. They studied six champion runners (average $\dot{V}O_{2max}$ 73.9 ml/kg/min) over a ten-week period during which they trained alternately at sea level and 2300 metres altitude. The exposure to altitude was for periods of up to fourteen days, while sea-level training varied between five and eleven days. During the first month of this regimen, the results were disastrous! There was a 14% drop in $\dot{V}O_{2max}$ while running performances over one mile and three miles were 8% and 10% slower, respectively. But by the start of the second month of the study the runners started to undergo more positive adaptations to the training protocol. Indeed, during their regular trips to sea level, and immediately after the study was completed, they ran a total of fourteen personal best times over a wide range of distances, including two world records. These feats were no doubt helped by the fact that the VO_{2max} values for the six runners had improved an average of 5%. The conclusions from this investigation are that intermittent training at sea level and moderate altitude does not interfere with the process of altitude acclimatisation. And it was beneficial for improving sea-level endurance performance.

This strategy of altitude training, pioneered over a quarter of a century ago, was the front-runner to the 'live-high-and-train-low' practice now being advocated by a few sports scientists. This option is less practical, as it requires an athlete to be based in one place (altitude) and travel each day to another (no-altitude) training venue. Alternatively, the athlete might train and live at sea level and spend nights sleeping in a hypobaric chamber set to simulate altitude. Obviously this strategy has severe practical limitations, but, in theory, it should allow the athlete the best of both worlds: living high and training low. To date, however, the scientific studies to support such a practice are not convincing. There are major problems with many such studies. For example, there is often a lack of a good control group, where athletes of similar ability as those who train at altitude undergo the same training program at sea level. Without such a group, it is almost impossible to separate the improvement in fitness and performance caused by training, from the possible additional effects of altitude. Also, the response to altitude is very individual: some athletes are good responders, while others may actually show a decrement in fitness and performance. When scientists study such small groups of athletes and report the 'average' results, this individual variability is not readily apparent. Finally, some of the altitude training programs studied by sports scientists have not been scientifically sound and would not have been expected to result in any change in fitness, either at altitude or sea level. Perhaps these are just some of the reasons why there is disagreement between coaches and sports scientists on the value of altitude training to improve sea-level performance.

It is clear that further research with highly-trained athletes needs to be undertaken before firm recommendations can be made to coaches and athletes. While live-high-train-low might be the best way to acclimatise to altitude, at present there is insufficient scientific evidence to support the claims that altitude training can improve sea-level performance in endurance or power events. In a recent article reviewing the scientific literature on the effects of moderate altitude (2000–3000 metres) on sea-level performance, Dr Brent Rushall and colleagues from the San Diego State University concluded:

- The athlete or team that is successful in competition at sea level should be equally successful at altitude after a period of acclimatisation.
- There is no advantage for strength and power athletes to train at altitude.
- There may be an improved buffering capacity of the muscles with altitude acclimatisation.
- The $\dot{V}O_{2max}$ of highly-trained athletes does not always improve with altitude acclimatisation.
- Training at altitude might enhance sea-level performances of moderately-trained athletes.
- Upon return to sea level, performances of elite athletes are not always improved as a result of altitude training.

ALTITUDE TRAINING: THE BASICS

Dr Dave Martin, exercise physiologist and adviser to many of America's top distance runners, has formulated his top ten tips on altitude training. They are:

1 Experiment with altitude training.
2 Discover the best place to train which fits in with the athlete's lifestyle and convenience.
3 Do not wait until an important championship to try altitude training for the first time.
4 Use laboratory testing before and after altitude training to quantify the extent of any physiological changes.
5 Do not go so high or train so hard that the stress of altitude is excessive.
6 Ensure that the terrain used for training allows for flat as well as hilly running or cycling.
7 Stay long enough to allow sufficient adaptation.
8 Create a home-like lifestyle through advance planning.
9 If an important competition follows a period of altitude training, return home early enough to permit appropriate sea-level adaptations

(neuromuscular and ventilatory) before racing begins. This can take 7–10 days.

10 Be aware that altitude training does not benefit all athletes.

REDUCED PERFORMANCE OF HIGHLY-TRAINED ATHLETES AT ONLY 580 METRES ALTITUDE

Colorado Springs—home of the US Olympic training centre; altitude 1600 metres. The Australian Institute of Sport, Canberra—altitude 580 metres. Johannesburg, South Africa—proposed site for the new SA sports academy; altitude 1800 metres. Facilities such as these provide state-of-the-art testing and training opportunities for athletes. But do performance tests measured in such locations 'count'? Sports scientists know that the performances of athletes born at sea level are impaired at moderate altitude (above 2000 metres). But Dr Chris Gore and his colleagues at the Australian Institute of Sport have recently shown that an altitude of only 580 metres reduces $\dot{V}O_{2max}$ and maximal performance. They had twenty well-trained athletes (ten men and ten women) perform a five-minute maximal work bout and a $\dot{V}O_{2max}$ test on a cycle ergometer at sea level and in a hypobaric chamber in which the pressure was chosen to simulate an altitude of 580 metres. $\dot{V}O_{2max}$ decreased 5.9% for men and 3.7% for women at altitude. But more importantly, the work performed during the maximal five-minute ride was reduced by an average of 3.7% for both males and females. These data suggest that even low altitude impairs exercise capacity in events with high aerobic demands. An implication of this finding is that altitude must be taken into account when comparing results of tests undertaken in different labs and locations. For example, if the results of such tests and race performances are to be taken into consideration in the selection of National teams, this must not be in isolation.

THE TRAINING CAMP EFFECT: ALTITUDE OR ATTITUDE?

Many altitude training camps are held in remote locations, totally isolated from the pressures of everyday living. And most venues are located in mountainous regions, so there is usually a good view as well! As a result, the athletes who attend these camps don't usually have too many distractions or too much to focus their attention on, apart from the training itself. Life at altitude consists of training, eating, sleeping—and more of the same. Athletes are usually working towards a common competitive goal. The company of other highly motivated team members is very conducive to high-quality living and training. If the isolation of these altitude camps is the reason that performance is improved upon return to sea level, then maybe isolated sea-level camps would have just the same positive benefit? Obviously the same type of training camp will not be suitable for all athletes, and the length of stay might vary. But it may just be that *any* training camp, whether it is held at altitude or not, might be beneficial. It might just be a matter of attitude!

BAD BLOOD

It was called 'the drug of choice' at the Atlanta Olympic Games. An Italian professor claimed that EPO was being used by 60% of all professional European cyclists. News reports suggest that twenty athletes have died as a result of incorrect EPO administration. But what is EPO? Is it altitude training in a bottle? And does it improve performance?

Erythropoetin (known technically as rhEPO) is a naturally occurring hormone produced in the kidneys which stimulates the production of red cells in the body. By 1985, medical scientists had discovered a way to manufacture EPO synthetically. This breakthrough allowed doctors to treat patients in kidney failure, as well as a variety of other conditions where red blood cell production was compromised. But soon after it became commercially available, it was shown that EPO administration to *healthy* individuals for six to eight weeks resulted in significant improvements in $\dot{V}O_{2max}$ and endurance performance. Such enhancements were largely due to massive increases in the levels of haemoglobin and haematocrit (the proportion of the blood that is comprised of red blood cells, normally 45% in *untrained* individuals). Immediately, EPO was recognised as a threat to fair competition and it was banned by the International Olympic Committee in 1990.

In January 1997 the Union Cycliste Internationale (UCI) went one step further. In an effort to deter the international cycling community from condoning the practice of EPO, the UCI ruled that cyclists with a haematocrit of more than 50% would not be allowed to start a pro race. Such a stand is admirable but needs to be evaluated, since their 50% upper limit is a totally arbitrary figure.

According to Dr Dave Martin, physiologist to the Australian Institute of Sport's cycling team, there were no data available to the UCI to indicate that a 51% haematocrit is dangerous for a professional cyclist.

Nor do sports scientists really know the normal haematocrit levels of elite endurance-trained athletes. As Dr Martin points out, it is quite conceivable that many cyclists and other athletes have haematocrit values of 50% or higher *without* EPO. To back up his claim, Martin and his colleagues at the AIS conducted a retrospective analysis of some 360 blood samples collected from Australia's top road cyclists during the last ten seasons. They found that 2.8% of all samples exceeded the 50% haematocrit value set by the UCI as an acceptable limit. The highest value was 52% for one of the cyclists. Furthermore, Martin firmly believes that 'these cyclists were training and competing in a clean environment at the time of testing'.

In a much larger sample from the AIS, Martin and colleagues analysed blood from 12,359 athletes who participated in a wide range of sports, including athletics, water polo, rowing, tennis, soccer, basketball and weight lifting. In this case, 3.4% of blood samples had a haematocrit of greater than 50%. But interestingly, the incidence was very different between sports. For example, the percentage of tests where haematocrit was higher than 50% was only 0.3% among netball players, but a massive 25.7% for weight lifters.

So is the arbitrary 50% haematocrit value advocated by cycling's governing body unfair? Certainly. Any stand against cheating in sport is admirable and acts to deter the use of banned substances. However, there will always be a certain percentage of 'false positive' results and cases of 'clean' athletes being disqualified. And that number would seem to be around 3% in cycling and other endurance sports. So some of the cheats *might* be caught, but a few genetically gifted cyclists will be penalised unfairly.

Heat acclimatisation

The 1984 Soccer World Cup, USA. The 1992 Olympics, Barcelona. The 1996 Olympics, Atlanta. The 1988 Commonwealth Games, Kuala Lumpur. Many major international sporting events have been and will continue to be scheduled in hot locations. But exposure to thermal stress is a major threat to the health and performance of athletes who must compete in hot climates. This is especially so if the athlete is from a cool or temperate region. History is replete with stories of famous athletes who had the misfortune to compete in adverse environmental conditions and thus failed to perform up to expectations. Despite medical warnings that sporting events should be held in the early morning or late evening to reduce the risk of heat-related illnesses, many competitions are still scheduled in the heat of the day. Unfortunately, the athlete or coach usually has no say in the matter: the commercial push of major television networks is a far more powerful influence on the governing bodies of world sport. But what if a major competition is to be held in the heat? Are there training strategies the athlete can employ to try and reduce the adverse effects of such stress?

An athlete's ability to perform well in hot conditions depends on whether or not they have had exposure to similar conditions on a number of occasions before competition. The process of adapting to perform in temperatures hotter than those the athlete habitually trains in is called heat acclimatisation. There are a number of physiological changes which take place during this process which include:

- a reduction in heart-rate at any given speed or power output;
- a drop in body (core) temperature during exercise in the heat;
- an increase in the rate of sweating during exercise;
- an earlier onset of sweating during exercise;
- a decrease in blood flow to the skin;
- an increased blood flow to the working muscles; and
- lower skin and core temperatures.

These adaptations allow the acclimated athlete to perform better in the heat than if they had not been exposed to such conditions previously. But their performance will still not be as good as if they competed in a cooler environment. As such, the athlete should always adopt a pace or game tactics which are appropriate to their level of acclimatisation and the prevailing environmental conditions.

The optimal method of acclimatisation to a hot environment is to spend two to three weeks in that environment, gradually increasing the volume and intensity of the training stimulus. However, sometimes this is not possible, so the athlete must take advantage of any artificial acclimation they can, such as exercising in an environmental chamber in a sports science laboratory, or wearing clothing with a limited vapour permeability while training. The extent of the acclimatisation-induced physiological responses depends on a number of factors, including:

- the initial fitness level of the athlete and their current state of acclimatisation;
- the severity of the heat stress encountered by the athlete during their acclimatisation sessions;

- the total training load during the acclimatisation sessions (e.g. the volume, intensity and frequency of training sessions); and
- the time period available for acclimatisation.

It is important that any training session conducted in the heat during this acclimatisation process is of sufficient severity to raise the athlete's core temperature significantly and provoke substantial sweating. Merely travelling to a hot climate for a couple of weeks' holiday before a competition is not sufficient to induce complete heat acclimatisation! For most athletes, heat acclimatisation is a relatively rapid process. Athletes who train in the heat for several hours a day have accrued most of the physiological adaptations within two weeks.

The acclimatisation process seems to have two distinct phases. The first phase, which takes three to seven days, is characterised by early changes in the cardiovascular function of the athlete, such as an increase in plasma volume and a reduction in resting and exercising heart-rate. The second phase, from one to two weeks, includes other more subtle thermoregulatory changes that increase the athlete's sweat rate and decrease blood flow to the skin during exercise. But all of these adaptations are lost quite quickly. After acclimatising to the heat, athletes should aim to compete within the next five to seven days in order to gain the maximal competitive advantage over an equally fit but unacclimatised rival.

Unlike heat acclimatisation, there is no scientific evidence that an athlete can adapt to competing in the cold. Although performance will always be better in *cool* rather than *hot* conditions, extremely low environmental temperatures can cause extreme body heat losses, resulting in an impairment of exercise capacity and even collapse. But beware. Even in the coldest conditions, athletes who are exercising intensely can have sweat rates of over a litre an hour, and still need to consider their fluid losses.

Vision training

'There is no sport where vision does not play a vital role. Yet studies show that more than a third of all athletes, including professionals, suffer from a visual problem that adversely affects their performance.'

Sherryle Calder, international hockey player
and a sports vision specialist

Good vision is one of the most important physical assets an athlete can possess. It encompasses a chain of commands from the eyes feeding information to the brain, which in turn interprets a message and sends an appropriate signal to initiate a specific movement in space. This is a continuous, dynamic process that happens almost without thinking. But if the eyes consistently relay inaccurate or incomplete information to the brain, the consequences for the athlete can be disastrous. Like a computer, the brain receives input information from an external source and then decides on the best movement pattern. However, a computer is no better than the information it is programmed to receive. The most complex and powerful computer in the world will not solve problems correctly, or process data accurately, if the input fed to it is inaccurate, incomplete or untimely. In the same way, if the visual input sent to the brain is not accurate, complete and rapidly transmitted, then an athlete cannot be expected to perform up to their true potential.

So is 20/20 visual acuity all the athlete needs? Definitely not, according to Sherryle Calder, a sports vision expert and former international hockey player. Calder has identified several important visual skills that are vital to optimum sporting performance. These include:

- visual acuity;
- dynamic visual acuity;
- peripheral vision;
- visual reaction time;
- visual recognition; and
- eye–hand coordination.

Visual acuity refers to the athlete's ability to see clearly and sharply at a distance. Acuity merely refers to the sharpness of an image on the retina and is really the catalyst for vision. Good visual acuity is a prerequisite to superior dynamic visual acuity, which is the ability to see objects that are in motion (such as a ball). Dynamic acuity requires rapid, accurate eye movement. Good peripheral vision allows the athlete to maintain awareness of what is happening around them, while still being able to concentrate on the immediate task at hand. For example, a rugby player catching a high ball needs to concentrate not only on the path of the ball (dynamic acuity), but also on the opposition players who are bearing down on him in an attempt to gain possession or make a tackle (peripheral vision). If a player is forced to turn their head back and forth in order to gain visual information from the periphery, then the visual reaction time is being slowed down. If reaction time is longer, then performance is compromised. Although an attribute of all great team players seems to be their sixth sense in knowing where a team-mate is at any time during a game, or being able to 'read' a play, it should be noted that all players can improve their peripheral visual skills with appropriate training and practice.

Visual recognition time is the ability of a player to process visual information rapidly. The quicker the speed of recognition, the more time the player has to formulate and execute a skill. But even with good visual recognition time, a player must still possess the ability to respond to the information the eyes have sent to the brain and then to perform the best movement pattern. Eye–hand coordination is the ability of the body (mainly the hands and the feet) to react to input information rapidly and accurately.

These interrelated vision skills play a critical role in the well-coordinated and effective performance of many sports. And just as physical training can increase an athlete's speed, endurance or agility, then so too can vision-related skills be enhanced. Sometimes a vision problem will be noticed by the player or by the coach. Obvious examples are the player who wears glasses off the field, or who squints in order to see the ball coming from a distance or from a height. But other times visual problems go unnoticed. Poor vision can be the reason for bad technical skills. Players start to make mistakes that are uncharacteristic, such as dropping easy catches, swinging the bat too early or too late, or consistently overshooting during golf putting or free-throws in basketball. These visual problems lead to erratic performances and need to be identified, assessed and retrained.

In order to determine the effect of visual skills training on performance, Calder studied 29 international women hockey players who participated in a four-week training program. One group of players ($n = 11$) received visual skills training and a sports-specific vision coaching program in addition to their normal hockey practice session. Another group ($n = 10$) received only visual skills training plus their normal hockey practice sessions, while a third group ($n = 8$) acted as controls and participated in only the hockey training. The visual skills training program in which groups one and two participated consisted of five sessions a week of vision exercises in the laboratory. The sports-specific vision coaching program (group one only) comprised three one-hour sessions per week of specific practices with the hockey stick and ball that were designed to maximise the players' use of their visual system. For example, players were coached how to use their dominant eye to improve skill performance, to alter their body position to create better peripheral vision, and to position their head in relation to the dominant eye and the ball in order to improve hitting technique. Skill progressions were implemented to provide an ever-increasing level of difficulty. Players only moved on to the next or modified technique when the previous skill had been fully mastered. Before any intervention, all players were tested on 22 field-hockey skills. In order to perform these tasks successfully, players had to execute the skills accurately (the ball had to be placed or stopped within a certain area) and at speed.

The results were staggering. The control group, who only performed their normal hockey practice, showed a statistically significant improvement in only three of the 22 skills tested. This is no more than statistical chance, and clearly indicated that this training was not effective in improving visual awareness. In the players who undertook the visual skills training only, there was a significant improvement in nine of the 22 skills. However, in the players who undertook both visual skills training and the sports-specific vision coaching, there was an improvement in sixteen of the 22 skills. These data clearly show that elite hockey players who performed a four-week sports-specific vision coaching program improved their visual skills dramatically. Further, they suggest that for players of lesser ability, the increases in performance could be even better, as one might naturally assume that international players are already near the upper limits of their skills capacity. Calder recommends that the training of visual skills should be included in the normal training programs of sports where vision has a direct impact on performance.

Water running

Many athletes have taken to water running as a form of cross-training, to rehabilitate from soft tissue injuries or merely to supplement their normal workouts. Water running is performed in the deep end of a swimming pool with the athlete wearing a flotation device which keeps them upright and their head above the surface. Many anecdotal reports have described the benefits of such training. But, until recently, there had been no scientific studies to determine the effectiveness of these claims.

In 1996, Dr Randall Wilber and colleagues from Florida State University, however, examined the effect of a six-week deep-water running program on the maintenance of aerobic fitness in sixteen trained male runners. The runners were randomly divided into either a water run or treadmill run group. They then adapted their normal training programs, which consisted of five days of running per week, to either land or water running for the six-week study period. The training intensity was alternated in both programs: they ran for either one hour at 70–75% of $\dot{V}O_{2max}$, and the next day for 30 minutes at 90–100% of $\dot{V}O_{2max}$. After six weeks, there was no change in $\dot{V}O_{2max}$ for either group compared to before the two training programs. But more importantly, there were no changes in the running economy of the athletes when they were tested on the treadmill. This is a particularly important finding because it suggests that deep-water running can serve as an effective training alternative to on-land running for maintaining aerobic conditioning and running efficiency.

THERMAL PANTS: DO THEY PREVENT INJURY?

Several seasons ago only soccer players wore them. Now basketball and rugby players are seen with thermal pants under their regulation kit. This practice has evolved spontaneously without any scientific assessment as to the value of wearing such clothing. However, Paddy Upton, a biokinetician at the University of Cape Town Medical School, recently conducted a study to determine whether the use of thermal pants might reduce the risk of hamstring injuries in rugby players. The study followed 44 players who had previously suffered a hamstring injury during the 1992 season. Players were given the choice of whether or not to wear the pants. Players in the group who wore the pants had a significantly lower injury rate than those players who did not wear them (three injuries per 1000 playing hours for the pants, versus 57 injuries per 1000 playing hours without).

This finding is especially interesting, because players who believe the use of thermal pants might reduce the risk of injury would probably be more likely to wear them. So the pants may have produced an even greater reduction of injury than this direct comparison suggests. The authors of this study point out that although the wearing of thermal pans can reduce the risk of hamstring injury, other factors (such as pre-season fitness, warm-up and stretching, and rehabilitation before returning to activity) are probably more important.

UNDER PRESSURE

During a 10 kilometre training run, your feet hit the ground around 9000 times. If you are running on the flat, the ground reaction forces (how hard you hit the road) are about one and a half times your body weight. Run downhill, however, and these impact forces can be as high as four times body weight. Little wonder that most runners get injured eventually. But imagine if your feet were able to inform you that they were taking a pounding and needed an easy day.

A new American device called the Novel Pedar System (NPS) uses a special insole fitted with 100 sensors which measures the pressure distribution between the foot and shoe. A runner wears the special insoles and is wired up to a receiver strapped to their waist. Information from the sensors is stored in a microcomputer which can be analysed after a training run or race. The NPS yields information about the effectiveness of cushioning in a particular shoe and biomechanical data concerning the patterns of force distribution during the footstrike. You may need to alter your gait pattern. It may be time for a new pair of shoes. The NPS will provide you with the information to make such decisions. The device has already been used in several laboratory studies and soon the technology will be available for all runners, irrespective of how they run!

Training indoors

Many athletes, especially those who live in harsh climates, spend some of their time running indoors on a treadmill. This form of training has several advantages compared to running outdoors, in that it allows the athlete to:

- set a precise, steady-state pace;
- program hills into their workouts;
- simulate a specific race course; and
- practise nutritional strategies, including drinking on the run.

However, when running indoors on a treadmill, the lack of air resistance results in a lower energy cost compared to when the athlete runs outdoors at the same speed. All athletes will know that a slight gradient on the treadmill can be used to increase the effort of running. The question is, how much gradient? A recent study conducted by Drs Andrew Jones and Jonathan Doust at the University of Brighton in England found that a treadmill grade of just 1% reflected most accurately the oxygen cost of running outdoors over a wide range of running speeds (10.8–18.0 km/hour). So if you are training indoors, remember to hit that grade button, otherwise you are getting an easier session than you bargained for!

Hill training

'Hill training is beneficial for building strength and useful for racing which involves hilly courses.'

Cathy O'Brien, US Olympic marathoner

Sebastian Coe trained on hills, to devastating effect. Percy Cerutty had Herb Elliot run them until he dropped. The Kenyan distance runners' workouts always incorporate them. Some coaches say they help with form and technique. Do they really work? Does training on an incline make an athlete faster when they compete on undulating terrain? Does it make them faster on the flat? Surprisingly, these questions have not really been addressed by sports scientists.

The only study to investigate the effects of training on hills was undertaken by Dr Beau Freund and co-workers at the University of Arizona. They were interested in determining whether twelve weeks of running hills improved maximal oxygen uptake (VO_{2max}) in healthy but untrained subjects when they were subsequently tested in the lab using two different protocols: (1) where the treadmill *speed* was increased but the incline remained constant; and (2) where the *incline* was increased but the speed was the same. After hill training, subjects significantly increased their VO_{2max} on both protocols. But the improvement was greatest when the subjects were tested on the incline protocol (8.5%) compared to the flat protocol (5.3%).

On the one hand, these findings support the concept of training specificity (see Chapter 2). They also suggest that hill training *may* be beneficial for athletes whose event is on the flat. However, more studies employing highly-trained runners and cyclists are needed before sports scientists can recommend that all athletes head for the hills.

WHEN SCIENCE LEADS THE WAY

Normally any breakthroughs in training techniques come from the athletes themselves. Innovations in technology are left to the sports scientists. In the sport of speed skating, a Dutch scientist, Dr Gerrit van Ingen Schenau, has been analysing the biomechanics of the skating motion. He has concluded that the traditional skating technique may not be the most effective one for generating power during the 'push-off'. When the foot is fixed to the skate, normal range of motion is constrained. There is little plantar-flexion (driving off the forefoot) and the work done by the powerful quadriceps muscle is also reduced.

Ingen Schenau and his colleagues looked at the motion of the foot in other sports such as running, where motion is unrestrained. The result was a newly designed skate which allowed the shoe to rotate around a hinge connecting the shoe and the skate blade. As in running and jumping movements, the 'hinge' of the skate was positioned over the toe joint. The skater could now employ a more complete leg extension, deriving extra power from the push-off phase. The skate was christened the 'slapskate', since it allowed the skater to 'slap on' extra foot extension. And it works. In a preliminary study, eleven junior skaters agreed to switch over to the slapskates for a full racing season. Their performances were compared to 72 other skaters in the same region of the same ability and age. At the end of the season the slapskaters had improved their performances by an average of 6.2%, versus 2.5% for the skaters wearing normal footwear. The data left little doubt as to the positive effect of the new technology on performance.

By the 1996–97 season, slapskates were part of the international skating scene. But the transition from old to new is not always easy. Elite performers with years of training on old skates found it difficult to make the transition to the new technology overnight. Initially, the top male skaters were too strong for the new slapskate, breaking it at the hinge during sprint starts. And, like with many equipment changes, some skaters felt the skates were illegal and should be banned. But the skates are here to stay, having been fully endorsed by the International Speed Skating Federation. So those skaters who can make the transition to the new equipment quickly can probably profit for a season or two before the pack catches up. For the record, the idea of a hinged skate was patented over 70 years ago. Sports science just takes a while to catch on!

9

Competition: Getting it right on the day

'In the finals you do the exact same dives you did in the prelims. But as I climbed the platform the crowd were going nuts. This time I had to narrow my focus and shut everything out. I had to go into my own world: just the pool, the board and me. I had to be intensely aware of my body and my timing to make sure that everything was in synch. I couldn't afford to be distracted. And I couldn't let myself think that this was the last dive of my career.'

Greg Louganis, four-time Olympic gold medal winner

'It's not a very nice thing to say, but for a couple of days leading into a big race I'm totally selfish. I need to make my own decisions, to be independent of other people. I need to get stronger so I can cope and get through the race. In a race you're on your own and you've got to get used to it.'

Steve Moneghetti, champion Australian marathon runner

'To be prepared is half the victory.'

Pat Riley, professional basketball coach

'The race is the goal and the focus of preparation.'

Gennadi Touretski, coach of Alexandre Popov, the fastest swimmer in the world

Fit, rested, well-nourished and raring to go. The day of competition has finally arrived. There is nothing the athlete can do to improve their performance on the day. Or is there?

In most team sports, skill and tactics will have a major influence on the outcome of a match, and even the best plans can amount to nothing when the opposition plays a different type of game or when key individuals have an off-day. But in some athletic events, attention to small details might mean the difference between winning and losing.

WARMING UP AND WARMING DOWN

'Warming up before an event should include a series of exercises, including running on the spot.'

Philostratus, in *De Ante Gymnastica*, third century AD

'The competitors for the men's mile warm up outside the stadium. John Walker keeps away from the rest, away from the warm-up area. He chooses his own path along the road, up and down the hills. He runs hard, stretching out. He keeps at it for forty minutes. This is a race he has planned carefully. Soon he will attempt to execute those plans.'

Ivan Agnew, describing John Walker's warm-up before he became the first man to run under 3:50 for the mile

'I never warm up.'

Michael Jordan, Chicago Bulls basketball star

Warming up might be defined as a period of preparatory exercise in order to enhance subsequent competition performance. Empirical observations of many top sportsmen and women prior to competition reveal two major trends. First, the more intense the subsequent competition, the more extensive and prolonged the warm-up. Secondly, the greater the ability of the athlete, the longer they take to warm up. However, an examination of the current scientific literature on the effects of warm-up on performance show a remarkable lack of consistency. On the other hand, there is consensus on some of the physiological advantages of warming up. These include:

- an increased muscle temperature;
- an increased flow of blood to the working muscles, which improves oxygen and fuel transport;

- an increased speed of nerve impulse conduction, which would be expected to result in a faster reaction time;
- an increase in the speed of muscular contraction; and
- improved muscle elasticity, permitting a greater range of joint movement.

All of these physiological changes would be expected to improve, rather than impair, performance. But perhaps just as important as the physiological benefits of a warm-up are the psychological benefits. Warming up allows the athlete to prepare and rehearse the specific movement patterns for their event. Depending on the sport, many athletes also believe in stretching the major muscle groups to be used in competition during a warm-up. Again, while there may not be strong scientific support for such a practice, neither is there any evidence that performance is impaired.

WARM-UP AND PERFORMANCE

Athletes engage in warm-up routines of varying duration, intensity and specificity, depending on the physiological demands of their event, the prevailing environmental conditions, and the time-delay between warm-up and competition. Yet there are few scientific studies which have examined the effects of warm-up on performance. Just as scarce are investigations assessing the influence of different types of warm-up on exercise capacity. Those studies that have been undertaken have usually employed untrained or moderately-fit individuals. It is difficult to extrapolate the results of studies using these populations to highly-trained athletes. But Dr Joel Mitchell of Texas Christian University recently investigated the effects of high- and low-intensity warm-ups on performance in well-trained male collegiate swimmers. On separate occasions, the swimmers were tested after two different warm-up routines. These were compared to no warm-up. The warm-up protocols consisted of either a 400 yard swim at 80% of maximal heart-rate (low intensity) or four maximal 50 yard sprints (high intensity). Lactate levels were significantly higher five minutes after the high-intensity warm-up. But swim performance times were not significantly different between any of the experimental conditions. These results suggest that, for swimming at least, there appears to be no beneficial effect on performance of an intensity-specific warm-up.

With regard to warming down, again, there is very little scientific evidence to either support or refute such a practice. But from the observations of top athletes, it would appear that some form of active cool-down is beneficial. A physiological benefit of a cool-down is that a period of low-to-moderate-intensity exercise after a maximal effort promotes the removal of lactate from the working muscles into the blood, where it is taken up by the liver and later converted into glycogen. However, the best form of recovery after strenuous activity might be complete inactivity. If continued exercise produces additional muscle glycogen breakdown, this is disadvantageous to the overall recovery process. So cool down, but make sure the exercise intensity isn't long or too strenuous, as this will have a negative impact on the next training session or competitive effort.

CHILL OUT: HOW TO GO FASTER IN THE HEAT

Hot and humid conditions on race day have a detrimental effect on performance. The problem is, most athletes feel that so long as they train in the heat, their performance will not be affected. Before the Atlanta Olympic Games, sports scientist Dr Dave Martin of the Australian Institute of Sport tested the effects of heat (32°C) and humidity (60% relative humidity) versus cooler (23°C, 60% relative humidity) conditions on the time-trial performances of eleven members of the National road cycling squad. He found that the average power of the riders dropped a massive 6.5% in the heat, compared to that in the cooler environment. The trouble is, you can't do much about the weather. But you can do something for the athlete!

In order to prepare for racing in the heat, athletes should acclimatise appropriately, ensure adequate levels of hydration before and during an event, modify pacing strategies and tactics if necessary, and practise pre-event body cooling. Many studies have documented the effects of heat acclimatisation and fluid replacement in the heat. But the concept of pre-cooling an athlete before competition is a relatively new area of investigation in sports science. Basically it involves dropping the athlete's skin and/or core temperature fifteen minutes or so before competition. This lower temperature provides a greater temperature gradient for dissipating heat once the athlete commences exercise. This means they should be able to go faster.

Dr Allan Hahn and colleagues from the AIS were among the first to report the beneficial effects of pre-cooling on high-intensity exercise performance. They had twelve rowers pre-cool by exposing their skin to ice wrapped in wet towels for just five minutes prior to a maximal laboratory test. Then they asked the rowers to perform an all-out six-minute piece on the rowing ergometer in 30°C and 30% relative humidity. Nine of the twelve rowers went faster in the heat after pre-cooling compared to no cooling. On average, they were able to increase their power output by 1% after pre-cooling, which resulted in them rowing 17 metres further.

Hahn and his colleagues at the AIS began experimenting with a number of 'cooling devices' worn by athletes during warm-up and removed just before the start of a race. In an early design they had members of the National women's road cycling squad tape panels of ice over their jerseys while they warmed up. Pre-cooling significantly decreased the skin temperature of the chest and back and improved average power output during a laboratory time-trial by 1.1%. Encouraged by these results, the AIS physiologists designed a special neoprene jacket with pockets for carrrying ice pouches and tested its use before a 25 km time-trial held in hot and humid conditions. Cyclists wore the jacket during their warm-up (20 minutes) and removed it just before the start of the race. Again, skin temperatures were lower in those cyclists who wore the jacket before the race. Cyclists also rated their 'thermal discomfort' as less. Those competitors who pre-cooled felt it contributed towards their performance and were even interested in wearing the jacket during their cool-down after the race. The jacket has been subsequently tested in other sports, including rowing, hockey and running (track). It was used by many Australian athletes at the 1996 Atlanta Olympic Games and Paralympic Games, and is now available commercially (Cool-it Jacket™).

But specially designed jackets are not the only method of staying cool during the heat of competition. Dr John Booth and colleagues from Charles Sturt University, New South Wales, recently reported that athletes who were immersed in a cold-water bath for 20 minutes before exercise decreased their core temperature by 0.5°C. And when the pre-cooled athletes subsequently performed a maximal 30-minute run in the heat (32°C, 62% relative humidity), they ran 300 metres further than when they did not pre-cool. It appears that a performance improvement in the order of 1% seems to be the norm for athletes who pre-cool before competing in an event in hot and humid conditions. So, stay cool, and perform better.

CLOTHING: WHEN MORE IS LESS

In most sports, the trend is to wear less clothing in competition than in training, particularly in events held in hot and humid conditions. But for swimming, it may be a case of more is better. Several recent studies have shown that compared to a conventional swim-suit, body-suits and wet-suits reduce drag and result in faster performances. In one investigation, Dr Ray Starling and colleagues from Ball State University, Indiana, examined the effect on the physiological responses of wearing a form-fitting torso suit versus a standard swimming costume during a submaximal, fixed-pace 400 yard front crawl swim. They also determined whether the torso suit would allow the swimmers to glide further underwater. The energy cost of swimming was reduced by 4% when swimmers wore the specially designed suit. In addition, the distance covered with each stroke was significantly longer. In a prone, underwater push-off glide, swimmers covered a greater distance while wearing the suit, compared to a conventional costume. These findings clearly show that body drag in swimming can be reduced by wearing a torso suit, and that such a physiological effect would be expected to improve maximal swim performance. Indeed, in recent Olympics, several nations have unveiled special swim-suits of various materials and designs as their 'secret weapon'.

Wet-suits are another clothing choice of some athletes who swim in open water. Dr Jean-Claude Chatard and co-workers from St Etienne University in France examined the effects of wearing neoprene wet-suits on performance in swimmers and triathletes. Under newer race regulations, professional triathletes are now banned from racing in a wet-suit unless the water temperature is less than 21°C for a standard distance event (a 1500 m swim) and under 24°C for a long-distance triathlon (over 2000 m). However, thermoregulatory reasons aside, such suits have a flotation effect and have been shown to enhance swimming performance by up to 7% in a 1500 m open-water swim. But all competitors do not experience the same benefits. When well-trained swimmers wear a wet-suit, their performances over 400 m are not significantly different to when they swim without a suit. However, when triathletes wear a suit, they go, on average, about twenty seconds faster for the same distance. It appears that the effect of wearing a wet-suit depends on the ability of the swimmer. While it improves performance in less-efficient triathletes who swim at slower speeds and have lower buoyancy, specialist swimmers competing in the triathlon would be advised to leave the wet-suit on land!

And it is not just in the water that wearing specialised clothing can make a difference to performance. Modern cycling clothing and aerodynamic 'tear-drop' helmets have much lower 'drag coefficients' than do conventional clothing and headgear. At speeds of around 48 km/hour, the drag of a rider plus conventional cycling clothing is 2930 grams. Put the same rider in a rubberised skin-suit with long sleeves, however, and the drag drops to 2620 grams, a reduction of 12%. The effect of the aerodynamic helmet is just as impressive. At similar speeds, a good aero helmet can save the rider about 20 m for every hour of riding. So, if the hat fits, wear it!

DRAFTING

Drafting is the practice of following closely behind another competitor to reduce the energy cost of movement and thereby improve performance. In cycling, particularly mass-start, long-distance stage events like the Tour de France, drafting is an accepted and integral part of the race. The leading team controls the pace of the peleton, alternating the speed to a pre-race plan designed to protect a certain individual, often the race leader. In such situations, drafting makes sense. The lead rider can sit behind a team-mate and save considerable energy which can later be expended in a hill climb or a sprint to the finish line. But just how much of an advantage is this practice?

In cycling, when riding at speeds slower than 25 km/hour, rolling and mechanical resistance provide the main obstacles to movement. However, at speeds over 25 km/hour, air resistance is the major impediment to forward motion. For example, when riding speed increases from 12 to 32 km/hour, mechanical resistance increases by 225% and rolling resistance by 363%. In contrast, the addition in power required to overcome air resistance for this same increase in riding speed is a massive 1800%. The practical implication of this observation is that at the speeds encountered by most competitive cyclists, almost two-thirds of their power is necessary merely to overcome the resistance of moving through the air. Clearly, then, any practice to reduce such air resistance will dramatically change the cyclist's energy expenditure.

In order to determine the effects of drafting on the oxygen cost of riding at different speeds, Dr Steve McCole and colleagues from the University of Florida at Gainesville studied 28 competitive cyclists and triathletes. During their experiments, cyclists completed a total of 92 rides on a flat road at a range (32–40 km/hour) of speeds and under different drafting conditions. When riding, a vehicle followed alongside each cyclist and collected expired oxygen ($\dot{V}O_2$) via a breathing valve and mouthpiece.

The results, shown in Figure 9.1, were staggering. When drafting behind one cyclist at 32 km/hour, $\dot{V}O_2$ was reduced by 18%, compared to when riding alone. But the faster the riding speed, the greater the effect, so that riding behind a single cyclist at 30–40 km/hour reduced $\dot{V}O_2$ by 28%. Interestingly, it didn't make much difference to $\dot{V}O_2$ whether or not a rider drafted behind one or up to four riders; the reduction in energy cost was similar and consistent. However, riding at the back of a pack of eight riders at 40 km/hour reduced $\dot{V}O_2$ even further. Perhaps the single most impressive demonstration of the effects of reducing air resistance was when riding behind a vehicle at 40 km/hour. In this situation, when the rolling and mechanical resistance is not changed compared to when a cyclist rides alone, the reduction in VO_2 was a massive 62%. Although it is illegal to draft behind a vehicle in competition, the effect of drafting in a group of riders allows competitors to ride up to 5 km/hour faster than they would otherwise be able to manage alone. And that's a big advantage on any day.

In swimming, too, drafting can decrease energy expenditure. Dr David Bassett and co-workers from the University of Tennessee at Knoxville studied seven trained swimmers, once where they drafted behind another competitor, and again where they swam alone. They found that although the swimmers' stroke distance didn't differ between the two conditions, heart-rates were significantly lower in the drafting trial. In addition, post-swim lactate levels and VO_2 were decreased after drafting, and the swimmers' ratings of perceived exertion were lower. These data indicate that drafting is a considerable energy-saving strategy during front crawl swimming and should be used during open-water swims and triathlons.

Although there are no scientific studies of the effects of drafting on road running performance, it seems reasonable to suggest that competitors would benefit by such tactics. Many big-city marathons are held on out-and-back courses where

FIGURE 9.1

Reduction in the oxygen cost ($\dot{V}O_2$) of riding when a cyclist drafts at a speed of 40 km/hour

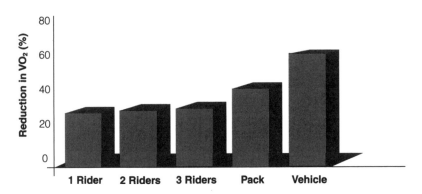

Source: McCole, S.D., Clancy, K. Conte, J.C., Anderson, R. and Hagberg, J.M. 'Energy expenditure during bicycling', *Journal of Applied Physiology*, 68: 748–53, 1990.

runners could gain a considerable advantage by sitting at the back of a large pack, particularly when running into a headwind. In major track events there is inevitably a rabbit (pacemaker) who leads the field through the first half of a race. Whether this is for pacing reasons or as a break from the wind is hard to determine. But at the speeds typical of middle-distance track events (7–8 metres per second, or 60–65 seconds per lap), about 8% of the runner's energy is used to overcome air resistance. By running directly behind another athlete, the second runner can save up to 80% of that energy. By employing such a drafting strategy, the athlete would benefit by about one second per lap.

THE COMPETITIVE EDGE: THE 1% SOLUTION

The greatest improvements in athletic performance over the long term are to be gained from a systematic training program (Chapter 2). However, there are several ways in which an athlete can gain that extra edge on the day of competition. Dr Tim Olds and colleagues at the School of Sport at the University of New South Wales have found that the following changes will reduce a cyclist's 40 kilometre time-trial performance by around 1%:

- use a 51 centimetre front wheel;
- inflate tyres an extra 35 psi;
- flatten back angle by four degrees;
- ride at an altitude of 375 metres above sea level;
- reduce the barometric pressure by 23 millimetres of mercury;
- reduce the weight of the rider by 5 kilograms; and
- reduce the weight of the bike by 18 kilograms!

On the other hand, raising $\dot{V}O_{2max}$ by 2.5% and increasing the sustainable percentage of $\dot{V}O_{2max}$ throughout the race by 3% are equally as effective; they just take more effort!

SHAVING DOWN

The removal of body hair, or 'shaving down', prior to a major competition is an accepted practice in several sports. Swimmers say it improves their feel for the water and allows them to go faster. Cyclists will tell you they shave only for safety reasons; if they crash, then it's easier to clean a wound. The post-race massage is also a lot more pleasant! But is it worth it?

From a scientific perspective, shaving, or any practice that reduces resistance to movement through water or air, will reduce the physiological demand of that activity. And in theory that should result in a faster performance. The trouble is, when athletes shave down, they usually do it during the taper phase prior to a major competition. So, when they compete, they are well rested and will go faster anyway. There is also the psychological aspect to consider. To provide answers to these questions, Dr Rick Sharp from Iowa State University studied thirteen male collegiate swimmers, nine of whom removed hair from their arms, legs and exposed trunk. Swimmers were tested during a 400 yard paced breast-stroke swim during which distance per stroke and heart-rate were determined. Post-swim oxygen uptake and lactate were also measured. In addition, all swimmers performed six 'velocity decay' trials before and after shaving. This part of the study was undertaken in order to examine how rapidly a swimmer slows down during a prone underwater glide after a maximal leg-push from the side of the pool. Underwater video analysis allows the sports scientist to produce a graphic image of the swimmer's velocity during the movement.

The results showed that shaving significantly increased the swimmers' stroke distance by an average of 0.24 metres. This increase in distance per stroke resulted in a reduction in heart-rate during the paced swim from 174 to 168 beats per minute. Post-swim oxygen uptakes and blood lactate levels were also much lower after shaving. Finally, the instantaneous accelerations of the swimmers who shaved were significantly greater during the maximal push-off, while the rate of velocity decay was less. These results clearly indicate that removing exposed body hair decreases the physiological effort required to maintain a given speed during swimming, and results in a reduction of active drag during the push-off. Shaving is therefore recommended for swimmers before a major competition and will provide a measurable performance benefit. Whether shaving the head provides benefits over wearing a swim cap is debatable. However, it certainly enables swimmers to present a ferocious image to other competitors in their event!

PACING: A MATTER OF STRATEGY

'I was running along . . . and I started reciting "Bob Hawke, Bob Hawke, Bob Hawke" in my head to keep me running to the finish. "Bob Hawke" over and over gave me good rhythm and cadence. It was lucky he was Prime Minister, because if it had been Paul Keating or John Howard, they're longer, slower names and I might have slowed down.'

Steve Moneghetti, during the 1990 Berlin marathon which he won in 2:08:16

Ask any coach about pacing, be it for a single event or match, or for the duration of a season, and they will tell you it is a vital component for success. Ask any athlete or player about the most appropriate pacing strategy to achieve peak performance, and they will probably say they have 'learned' the optimal pacing strategy for their event, more often than not by trial-and-error. Go out too hard and you will 'blow'. Go out too slow and you will get dropped by the pack and never be in contention. Often at the top level of competition there are very small differences between winning and losing. In the Olympic Games or World Championships, the margin between the glory of a medal and total anonymity is usually less than 1%. Given the importance of correct pacing in any sport which lasts more than a few seconds, the lack of scientific study of how different pacing strategies can influence competitive performance is surprising.

In those events where the sole aim of the athlete is to cover a set distance in the quickest possible time, the conventional advice to competitors has been that 'even-pace' is the best way to race. This sentiment was based on a single experiment conducted by Sid Robinson and his colleagues at Indiana University in 1958, in which three well-trained athletes were asked to run the same distance (1200 m) using three different pacing strategies. One strategy involved a fast start, one a slow start, and the other even-pacing. The fastest start produced the worst performance, while even-pacing produced the fastest time. Largely as a result of this single study, the advice to athletes for the next few decades was to delay the heaviest effort to as late in the run as possible.

More recently, Dr Carl Foster and colleagues at the Human Performance Laboratory, Wisconsin, have studied the effects of different pacing strategies on a 2000 m cycle time-trial. They had nine well-trained cyclists complete the first 1000 metres of the time-trial riding at a predetermined pace (very slow, slow, even-paced, fast or very fast) and then complete the second 1000 m as fast as possible. The difference between the slowest time-trial (the 'very slow' start) and the fastest trial (even-pace throughout) was 4.3%. As these workers point out, this difference is the gap between first and eleventh in an Olympic pursuit race (cycling) or between first and last in a middle-distance running event. They concluded that even-pacing, or even-effort, was the best strategy for middle-distance athletic events, and that there were 'negative consequences for even small variations in this strategy'. Further scientific evidence in support of this hypothesis comes from observations on Olympic gold medal cyclist Chris Boardman during an 80 km time-trial ridden on an undulating course (total elevation 400 metres). For the duration of the race, which he won in 1:44:49, Boardman sustained a heart-rate of 178 beats per minute with only a five-beat deviation from this average!

While a 'steady-state' even-pace strategy is likely to result in the best performance in events where the athlete has to 'time-trial' against the clock, racing directly against an opponent may call for changes in pace as a matter of race tactics and strategy. Often such races are won by those athletes with superior tactical skill. For example, in mass-start cycle races such as the Tour de France, it is very unusual to see the peleton all ride at the same pace throughout the day's stage. This is because cyclists in groups, whether riding for a team or as an individual, are nearly always drafting behind another competitor's wheel, or riding in a bunch. Further, there are random, variable changes in pace as groups of riders attack a hill, or try to break away from the main pack. Distance running races are also a matter of skill and tactics, with runners making use of their advantage (e.g. a fast finishing kick) or the course conditions (e.g. a hilly section) to break away from competitors at strategic times. These may be pre-planned, or in reaction to the prevailing race tactics.

To investigate the effects of pacing strategy on endurance cycling performance, Garry Palmer from Kingston University in England studied the effects of steady-state, even-paced cycling and stochastic, variable cycling on subsequent time-trial performance. He had six highly-trained riders perform two-and-a-half hours of cycling, followed by a 20 km time-trial. The rides undertaken before the time-trial were of the same *average* power or speed. During one ride, cyclists rode even-pace for 150 minutes. During the other they varied their pace within a 12% range above and below this average. Their 'paced' or 'random' efforts were immediately followed by the time-trial during which they covered the 20 km as fast as possible. Despite identical *average* power outputs during the first two-and-a-half hours of cycling, there was a significant improvement in the time to complete the 20 km time-trial following the even-paced ride. All riders went faster under these conditions by an average of 96 seconds. These laboratory results are in direct conflict with what actually happens in the field. But they are so convincing that further research is obviously needed to resolve the issue of the most effective pacing strategies for a variety of sports.

Perhaps a major point of difference between lab and field conditions is that in many races, the successful athlete dictates any change in pace to suit their own strengths and to exploit an opponent's weakness. The race winner is the first athlete to cross the finish line, rather than the fastest time-trialist. Future scientific investigations must examine the nature of stochastic or intermittent pacing strategies when they are manipulated and controlled by the athlete, rather than enforced by the researcher.

WHEN EVEN PACE JUST ISN'T ENOUGH

In most sports where an athlete has to complete a set distance as quickly as possible, an even-paced strategy from start to finish is probably the best way to optimise performance. Rowing, however, seems to be the exception. Rowers start a 2000 m race (which lasts between five and seven minutes) flat out, with ratings as high as 40–50 strokes per minute for the first 30–40 seconds. After this initial burst, the rating is dropped to around 35 strokes per minute, which is then maintained for the next four minutes or so. During the final minute of a race, there is an all-out sprint to the finish. The rating goes back up to 40 strokes per minute or even higher. If the 2000 m was divided into four 500 m segments, the first 500 would be the fastest, the middle two around three to four seconds slower than the first, and the final 500 the second fastest, about one to two seconds slower than the first. Such a pacing strategy seems a very uneconomical use of energy. When the rower goes out hard, heart-rate and oxygen uptake climb to near maximum values within 90 seconds of the start of a race, and blood lactate rises to peak concentrations very early in exercise. But this strategy seems to work, both on the water and in the lab. In one scientific study, rowers were asked to perform the same total work by adopting either even-paced tactics or a fast-start, fast-finish strategy. The uneven pacing resulted in the best performances on the row ergometer.

PACING STRATEGY FOR SPRINTING: JUST GO FOR IT!

Sprinting performances in events like running (100 and 200 m), cycling (1000 m time-trial), speed skating (500 m) and swimming (50 m) rely strongly on a fast acceleration from a stationary position at the start of a race, as well as on the capacity to reach a high maximal velocity and to maintain a high power output for as long as possible before inevitably slowing down (see Chapter 5). As such, sprinters need a large and rapid breakdown of the energy-rich phosphagens stored in the muscles during the first few seconds of a race (see Chapter 3). Although it has been widely recommended that after the start and acceleration phase, a more-or-less even-pace strategy leads to the fastest times in *all* events, such a scenario would be totally disastrous for the sprinter! For short-lasting sprint events, the best pacing strategy is a maximum all-out effort from the gun. Hit top speed as quickly as possible, and maintain this for as long as possible. Even if this strategy causes a rapid reduction in power output or speed during the latter stages of a race, it will still result in a faster performance than if an athlete attempts to produce an even effort throughout the duration of a race. Even-paced strategies should only be employed in events which last longer than 90 seconds.

PREDICTING RACE PACE BASED ON PREVIOUS PERFORMANCES

Most well-trained athletes enter a race with some idea of the performance they wish to achieve on the day of a competition. Often, this will be based on how well they have been training in the weeks leading up to a race. In addition, performances in races of shorter duration will be taken into consideration when deciding on a specific pace they hope to maintain. Assuming an athlete is well-prepared for an event, it may be helpful to have a knowledge of their best possible time based on both scientific data and their own previous performances.

One sport where race times from shorter distance events predict best possible times with a good degree of accuracy is running. Dr Dave Martin, a sports scientist from Georgia State University in Atlanta, has devised a set of simple formulae for estimating race times over a wide range of distances. His equations are based on the assumption that an athlete specialises in either short (1500 m), middle-distance (5000 m) or long-distance (10,000 m) events. From these three 'standard' distances it is possible to predict several other race distances which span the athlete's specialist event. Table 9.1 lists the formulas.

If your specialist event was the 10,000 m and you had a best performance over this distance of 35 minutes, then

TABLE 9.1

Predicting race times over varying distances based on previous best performances

Marathon = 4.76 Y		
10,000 metres = Y	10,000 metres = 2.1 Y	
5000 metres = 0.48 Y	**5000 metres = Y**	5000 metres = 3.63 Y
3000 metres = 0.28 Y	3000 metres = 0.58 Y	3000 metres = 2.15 Y
1500 metres = 0.13 Y	1500 metres = 0.27 Y	**1500 metres = Y**
	800 metres = 0.13 Y	800 metres = 0.48 Y
	400 metres = 0.06 Y	400 metres = 0.22 Y

Source: Martin, D.E. and Coe, P.N. *Training distance runners*, Human Kinetics, Champaign, Illinois, p. 149, 1991.

assuming you had trained sufficiently you might expect to run a marathon in around 166.6 minutes (4.76 multiplied by 35), or two hours 46 minutes. For the 15-minute 5000 m runner interested in racing over 10,000 m, a time of around 31 minutes 30 seconds would be a reasonable goal (2.1 multiplied by 15). There will undoubtedly be a few well-trained athletes who run faster than the formula would predict. However, for the most part, the estimations will be fairly accurate. Indeed, another way they might be used is to assist the coach in determining whether or not an athlete has attained an 'equivalent' running time for one distance in relation to their best time for another similar distance. But beware. Athletes who are unfamiliar with a new race distance often lack good pace judgment when it comes to competing in a longer event. They go out too hard, running the first half of a race faster than the second half. When this happens, performance will inevitably be worse than if they had gone out conservatively and run the second half of the race faster than the first. Indeed, athletes should, whenever possible, aim to cover the race at an even pace or to run negative splits. The advice to runners to 'go out fast and hang on' is not based on any scientific rationale. And besides, it hurts both the body and the athlete's pride to crawl home to the finish!

GETTING IT WRONG ON THE DAY

Never do anything on the day of the race that you haven't already tried in training. How often have athletes heard these words of wisdom from sports scientists and coaches alike, but ignored them nevertheless? Nutritional potions swallowed in the hours or minutes before competition are a common cause of race day disasters. But some athletes will even wear a new pair of racing shoes or make mechanical changes to their equipment on the morning of a race. There are many anecdotal reports of world-famous athletes making serious blunders in the critical moments before they compete. Some of them may have even got away with it. However, athletes are reminded not to throw away months of hard training and preparation for a quick fix. Most of the time it just won't be worth it. Here are a couple of examples where athletes got it totally wrong on the day.

Technically disadvantaged

The eight seconds by which American Greg LeMond defeated local hero Laurent Fignon in the 1989 Tour de France, after 22 days of riding, is the smallest winning margin in the history of the race. And although LeMond was a great and worthy champion, Fignon certainly contributed to his own downfall. Riding down the Champs-Elysées in Paris on the final day of the Tour, LeMond was the prototype professional cyclist. He utilised state-of-the-art, ultra-modern equipment. He dressed in aerodynamic clothing to reduce the wind resistance. And on the day, these innovations, along with a superb mind-set, were the difference between first and second. Dr Chester Kyle, one of the world's leading sports scientists in the field of sports equipment research, has calculated that LeMond was at least 60 seconds quicker on the final day's time-trial due to a combination of good equipment and a better riding position (see Table 9.2).

Get to the start line. And on time!

Going into the 1972 Munich Olympics, the United States had three of the top-ranked 100 m sprinters in the world. And traditionally, this event has been dominated by the Americans. Before the Munich Games they had won the 100 metres title twelve times in sixteen starts. And apart from a Russian, Valeri Borzov, the American trio of Eddie Hart, Rey Robinson and Bob Taylor were confident of one, if not two, medals in 1972. As expected, the Americans coasted through the first heat held on the morning of 31 August. But when the competitors settled on their blocks for the second round at 4.15 p.m. the same

TABLE 9.2				
Aerodynamic drag of different equipment chosen by Greg LeMond and Laurent Fignon during the final time-trial in the 1989 Tour de France				
Equipment	LeMond	Fignon	Difference in drag (grams)	Difference in time (seconds)
Aero helmet	Giro	No	+ 150	+ 29
Ponytail	No	Yes	+ 45	+ 8
Toe straps	Yes	No	− 10	− 2
Aero tubes	Yes	No	+ 140	+ 23
Disc wheel (front)	No	Yes	− 20	− 4
Low-profile bars	Yes	No	+ 250	+ 45

Source: Adapted from Kyle, C. 'Ergogenics for bicycling', in *Perspectives in Exercise and Sports Medicine*, vol. 4, *Ergogenics: Enhancement of Performance in Exercise and Sport*, Lamb, D.R. and Williams, M.H. (eds), Cooper Publishing Group, Carmel, Indiana, pp. 373–413, 1991.

day, there was no sign of the Americans. They were standing outside the Olympic television centre waiting for a bus to take them to the stadium. They saw the 100 m being run and presumed it was a replay of that morning's heats. Unfortunately, they were watching a live broadcast! They dashed to the stadium, but only Bob Taylor arrived in time to race. The assistant track coach, Stan Wright, had read the timetable wrong. The race was scheduled for, and took place at, 1615 hours, but Wright had read it as 6.15 p.m. It was a very costly mistake. Taylor went on to win the silver medal in 10.24 seconds, behind Borzov (10.14 seconds), who also won the 200 metres. Three Americans *did* make the final of the 200 m, but not the 100 m. To win, you must arrive at the start line. And on time!

FALSE START: WHEN TECHNOLOGY LAGS BEHIND

'There's no such thing as a perfect start. You just work hard on trying to react as quickly as possible to the gun, and to get your legs turning over as fast as possible. You know it's not perfect and it can never be perfect. You can't move faster than the gun, so the gun's always there to beat you.'
Linford Christie, 1992 Olympic 100 metre champion

Remember the disqualification of the reigning Olympic champion, Linford Christie, in the 100 m at the 1996 Atlanta Games? It is possible that he may not have been guilty after all. Although state-of-the-art judging technology ruled that the sprinter moved too early on two occasions, Christie may have just been guilty of an exceptional performance. The fact is, Christie did not move before the starting gun; rather, he reacted faster than the 'allowable threshold' of 0.100 of a second. The false-start criterion is an entirely arbitrary number, based on reaction times of untrained individuals. Consistent reaction times of below 0.100 of a second are easily attainable among well-trained sprinters who now use electronic biofeedback systems to train this aspect of their race. In addition, the starting blocks used in Atlanta did not record the first movement of the sprinter; rather, they activated the false-start detection system by compression on the blocks. Runners who employ the modern technique of applying a steady force against the blocks while in the 'set' position will therefore appear to react faster. Support for this assertion is that women sprinters record much slower reaction times when such blocks are used, even though there are no scientific data to indicate that females have slower reaction times than males. It may just have been that on this occasion, man beat the machine!

START SMALL . . .

There is no doubt that striking the ball with accuracy and consistency is the secret to successful batting performance in a number of sports, including cricket, baseball and softball. In this regard, there are reports that Australian cricketing legend, Sir Donald Bradman, improved his hand–eye coordination by continually hitting a golf ball against a wall with a cricket stump! This practice obviously paid dividends: Bradman retired with an average score of 99.94 runs for his test career. No modern cricketer comes anywhere near Bradman's record, so maybe it's time to go back to basics. Recent research conducted by Dr Richard Stretch of the University of Port Elizabeth, South Africa, and Professor Gerald Nurick and Dougan McKellar of the University of Cape Town, suggests this may not be such a bad idea.

In an effort to quantify whether the practice of striking the ball with a narrow bat would improve the accuracy and consistency with which a batsman hits the ball, these researchers instrumented a standard size cricket bat so that they could measure the exact point of impact of the ball on the bat. The accuracy with which a player strikes the ball is evaluated while a player bats against a bowling machine which delivers a ball at a constant speed of 100 km/hour. They studied a state squad of eighteen players who were randomly divided into two groups. All players, who were tested before any experimental intervention, underwent a four-week pre-season training program. In addition to their normal training, nine batsmen performed an intensive three-times-a-week, three-week skill training program, consisting of ten overs (60 deliveries) from the bowling machine using a narrow training bat (25 millimetres wide). The remainder of the squad (the control group) faced the same number of balls, but with the standard size bat. After the training intervention, all the players were re-evaluated using the standard sized bat.

The results revealed that the accuracy with which the test group hit the ball improved significantly when playing both defensive and attacking strokes off the front foot. These players consistently struck more deliveries closer to the centre-line of the bat, within a reduced band width, compared to the players who had not practised with the narrow bat. This is important, because coaches believe that the closer to the middle of the bat a player can make contact with the ball, the better the outcome of *any* stroke.

This study, conducted over just a short training period, shows that state-level cricketers can improve their batting technique with just three weeks of intensive training. The practical implications of these findings are that coaches should include drills aimed to improve hand–eye co-ordination in pre-season practices. This will ensure that skill development is optimised and therefore increase the· opportunity of success.

AND THE WINNER IS . . .

After each major international championship has faded from memory, sports scientists get out their computers and determine the medal count of each country. But this is no ordinary tally of bronze, silver and gold. Medals are expressed relative to a country's population, the amount of money spent on sport in that nation, and a multitude of other factors. Dr Stephen Seiler, a physiologist from Norway, has derived data combining the results from the 1994 winter and 1996 summer Olympic Games based on the population of various nations. The undisputed champions, based simply on medals won per number of inhabitants, are Tonga (silver medal for boxing) and the Bahamas (silver medal relay), who have populations of only 110,000 and 277,000 respectively. But the top ten nations from those countries with a population of over one million, based on gold medals won per million population, are:

1   New Zealand
2   Ireland

3   Cuba
4   Denmark
5   Australia
6   Norway
7   Jamaica
8   Czechoslovakian Republic
9   Bulgaria
10 The Netherlands.

And the biggest losers, apart from those 100-plus countries which have never won an Olympic medal? A tie between India and Indonesia. With a combined population of over 1.14 billion they emerged with just two medals. Seiler concludes that poverty and the absence of a sporting culture continue to make almost a quarter of the global population mute in the world of sport.

IF AT FIRST YOU DON'T SUCCEED . . .

by Dr Will Hopkins, statistics guru, University of Otago, New Zealand

As you must know from your own experience, performances of individual athletes vary from competition to competition. Thank goodness! If athletic performance was 100% predictable, sport would be boring. Why bother to compete if you know you're going to come last? Most events would end up with only three competitors, and there would be even fewer spectators! Sometimes there is a good reason for the variability: an athlete will perform worse if they are recovering from a serious illness, or do better when they get the right mix of peaking and tapering in the week or two before an event. Sometimes it is a matter of good luck or bad luck with terrain or tactics on the day. And sometimes an athlete will find themselves flying along or struggling for no good reason at all: they are just having a good day or a bad day.

Believe it or not, this variability in performance is an advantage to all but the best competitor in an event. Let's imagine that talent-wise, you are really a fourth place-getter in your event. *On average*, that means you will come fourth. But there is a chance that you will turn in one of your top performances, which will put you up to third or even second place. And there is also a chance that the best competitor will oblige you by turning in a bad performance. You go home with the first prize and the cheers of the crowd ringing in your ears, when by rights you should have come fourth!

Naturally, there are going to be days when instead of coming first or fourth, you will come tenth or worse. But this is all part of the grand scheme of competitive sport. You have to do poorly sometimes if you want to do well at other times. The person to feel sorry for is the best athlete in the field. He or she should come first every time, but it can't be.

How can you cash in on this variability in performance? Easy. Just enter as many events as possible. If there is only one chance in ten that you will win, you will average one win for every ten events you enter. It's just like buying lottery tickets: the more you buy, the more likely it is that you will win a prize. This strategy is particularly important for top professionals. For many sports, the margin separating the medal winners averages out to less than the variability between individual performances (typically 1–2%). So if you are up there close to the top of the field, it is inevitable that you are going to win sometimes. But you can't win if you don't compete.

There is one other way to make the most of the unpredictability of performance: switch to a sport that is even less predictable than your present one. This is not an option for most athletes, because you need innate ability and years of training to be good at a particular sport. Besides, research needs to be done to identify the less predictable sports. But at this stage of the game, is clear that if you can switch to golf successfully, you should. Golf is a very unpredictable sport, because the variation in a good competitor's score (about 4%) is similar to the variation in scores between competitors. So, everyone is in with a (sporting) chance!

Part III

EATING TO WIN

'The winners . . . will, without doubt, be highly talented, highly trained and highly motivated. At one time that would have been enough. But these days it is highly likely that everyone in the race will have these qualities . . . where everything else is equal, it's diet that can make the vital difference.'

Professor Ron Maughan, exercise physiologist from Aberdeen, Scotland, on the runners competing in the 23rd IAAF World Cross Country Championships, 1995

The first Olympians in Ancient Greece sought magical foods to make them strong and fast. The interest continues today, although hopefully most modern athletes pursue nutrition systematically and with purpose, instead of approaching it as a random and elusive search for a gold medal elixir. The goals of sports nutrition are to supply the athlete with the fuel and nutrients needed to optimise their performance during training sessions, and then to recover quickly afterwards. Of course, the athlete must also eat to stay in good health and good shape. Special strategies of food and fluid intake before, during and after an exercise session may help to reduce fatigue and enhance performance. These will be especially important in the competition setting.

Sports nutrition is a *practice* as much as it is a *science.* Athletes also deserve to enjoy food and the social aspects of eating. Often they will need to eat and drink at times that are awkward or inconvenient. Or to consume amounts that don't match their appetite, their access to supplies, or the typical eating practices of those around them. Creative thinking and forward planning are needed to find suitable foods and drinks, or to make them readily available.

These are the challenges of eating to win!

10

The training diet

THE TRAINING DIET—A BRIEF OVERVIEW

A good training diet must meet and balance the following goals:

- to promote an enjoyment of food and the opportunity to take part in social eating occasions;
- to keep the athlete healthy—now and long into their retirement;
- to get the athlete 'in shape'—with body mass (BM) and body fat levels that are good for performance;
- to provide adequate fuel for training sessions;
- to meet all requirements for protein, vitamins and minerals, including any increase in requirements that results from heavy training;
- to ensure the athlete is well-hydrated;
- to promote recovery after training sessions; and
- to ensure the athlete practises and fine-tunes competition eating strategies, particularly pre-event eating or intake during events.

These goals are also evident in many aspects of competition nutrition. The nutrition of athletes must be based on healthful eating guidelines that promote short-term health in terms of meeting all nutrient needs. In addition, it must consider issues of long-term health, for the time after sporting careers are generally over, by adopting eating patterns that reduce the risk of developing the chronic disease patterns of

211

affluent countries. To a large extent the healthy nutrition guidelines proposed for the community lend themselves well to the sports-related needs of athletes. These guidelines have been summarised in Table 10.1, and revised to emphasise these sports-related needs. The various chapters of Part III will reveal details of the specific background to these goals, their direct relationship to optimal sports performance, and strategies for achieving the goals in a typical athletic lifestyle. The rest of this chapter will focus on the practical challenges faced in the training situation, and on a key principle of athletic nutrition—adequate carbohydrate intake.

THE CHALLENGES OF THE TRAINING DIET

Since training is fundamentally a preparation, and sometimes a dress-rehearsal, for competition, it is not surprising that the

---

TABLE 10.1

Guidelines for the training diet

Guideline	Chapter
• Enjoy a variety of foods, with the emphasis on nutrient-rich choices.	15
• Eat sufficient energy intake to meet energy requirements and to promote levels of body fat and body mass that are ideal and individual to you.	11
• Match carbohydrate intake with the increased fuel needs of the training load. Pay special attention to intake before, during and after exercise sessions, since these strategies may improve performance and recovery from each session. Focus on nutritious carbohydrate-rich choices to ensure that all dietary goals are met overall, but identify times when practical issues dictate the choice of carbohydrate-rich foods and drinks. Practise all competition fuelling strategies so that you can be confident of success.	10, 12, 13, 14, 15
• Be moderate with fat intake, especially when total energy needs are low or when the focus is on carbohydrate eating.	11
• Pay special attention to total fluid needs in recognition of increased sweat losses in training. Focus on fluid intake strategies before, during and after training sessions. Fluid balance is important for optimising training performance, and all competition strategies should be well-rehearsed.	12, 13, 14, 15
• Pay special attention to calcium intake, since this is in short supply in the diets of some female athletes.	11
• Pay special attention also to iron intake, since some athletes may fail to meet their increased requirements.	15
• Keep things in perspective—eat to enjoy, as well as to meet nutrient goals.	10

same nutrition issues and goals should arise. Yet there is evidence that athletes may not be as successful in meeting some of their training nutrition goals as they are in the practice of competition eating strategies. It is understandable that an athlete will pay special attention to detail when everything is on the line. But many athletes fail to realise that it can be even more important to 'get it right' during training. After all, the balance of time leans heavily on the side of training. Most athletes spend hours training in preparation for a few moments of vital competition. It is the level achieved through adaptation to training that sets the platform from which competition performance is set. And in many cases, it requires practice and fine-tuning of specific eating strategies before they can be perfected for competition use.

There are a number of issues that stand in the way of optimal training nutrition practice:

- The athlete has not appreciated the importance of training nutrition, and is only interested in competition eating strategies.
- Many of the current sports nutrition education resources focus on competition situations. Even if there is discussion of training issues, often this is not supported by sufficient practical advice.
- The athlete often has to fit training into a busy schedule of work or school, travel, medical appointments and a personal life. Some things are not done optimally because there simply isn't enough time in the day. Only during competition can exercise and its demands take total priority.
- Competition often provides an infrastructure that supports nutrition goals. For example, during races there may be aid stations which supply the athlete's fluid and fuel needs. Or perhaps trainers and handlers are available to supply suitable provisions where they are needed during and after the event. Not only doesn't the athlete have to find these foods and drinks, in many cases they don't even have to remember that they need them. It is simply handed to them on schedule! During training the athlete is on their own and may be less able to access foods and fluids at important times.
- When financial resources are limited, the athlete may choose to save the best for the day of competition. For example, they may decide to buy a sports drink for a big race, but economise by drinking water during training.

- Training is tiring, draining and relentless. The athlete is often too tired and uninspired to be creative.
- In some sports, competition continually interweaves through and disrupts the training program. For example, professional team sport players may compete a number of times in the week and need to travel to their events. Although training is undertaken between these matches, the athlete is too concerned with the recovery or preparation for a match to think about the separate goals of training nutrition.

The nutrition chapters in this book will include attention to special training needs, and to strategies that are practical in both competition and training settings. A key issue that is essential to both situations is to meet the needs for the body's principal dietary energy source, carbohydrate. It is important to set this goal at the outset so that it enables other nutritional goals to fall into place.

THE CARBOHYDRATE NEEDS OF ATHLETES

Historically, population guidelines for healthy nutrition have considered carbohydrate as an 'energy filler', making up the remainder of energy requirements after the needs for other macronutrients have been met. Nutrition guidelines in Westernised countries generally recommend an increased carbohydrate intake, particularly from nutritious carbohydrate-rich foods, so that it provides at least 50–55% of total dietary energy. This tradition is based on the desire to encourage a relative decrease in fat intake to less than 30% of total energy, and to allow for protein requirements to be met. However, the recent research into the importance of carbohydrate in fuelling exercise performance makes it important to rethink these dietary recommendations. Athletes are one group who merit specific carbohydrate intake goals in order to meet the fuel needs of training, competition and recovery. These requirements are summarised in Table 10.2.

WHAT TYPE OF CARBOHYDRATES SHOULD ATHLETES EAT?

Although athletes are advised to eat 'carbohydrate' as if it is a single entity, in fact, carbohydrates are a family of compounds. More importantly, people eat carbohydrate in the form

───┤TABLE 10.2├─────────────────────────────────

Carbohydrate intake goals for the athlete

Goal	Carbohydrate intake target
• To support an extremely prolonged and intense exercise program—e.g. 5–6 hours of moderate–high-intensity exercise each day. To meet challenges of very high total energy requirements, daily muscle glycogen recovery, and continued refuelling during exercise (e.g. Tour de France cyclists) (see Chapters 13 and 15).	10–12 g/kg body mass (BM) per day
• To maximise daily muscle glycogen recovery in order to enhance prolonged daily training, or to 'load' the muscle with glycogen before a prolonged exercise competition (see Chapters 12, 14 and 15).	7–10g/kg BM/day
• To meet fuel needs and general nutrition goals in a less fuel-demanding program—e.g. a daily program of < 1 hour of moderate-intensity exercise, or many hours of predominantly low-intensity exercise.	5–7 g/kg BM/day
• To enhance early recovery after exercise, when the next session is less than 8–12 hours away and glycogen recovery may be limiting (see Chapter 14).	1–1.5 g/kg BM soon after exercise, and continued intake over next hours so that a total of ~ 1g/kg/2hrs is achieved in snacks or a large meal
• To enhance fuel availability for a prolonged exercise session (particularly competition) (see Chapter 12).	1–4 g/kg BM during the 1–4 hours pre-exercise
• To provide an additional source of carbohydrate during prolonged moderate- and high-intensity exercise, particularly in hot conditions or where pre-exercise fuel stores are sub-optimal (see Chapter 13).	30–60 g/hr in an appropriate fluid or food form

of foods which are varied in their carbohydrate composition, the content of other nutrients, their form, presentation and other features. Indeed, it is better to use the term 'carbohydrate-rich' foods rather than 'carbohydrate' foods. This recognises the presence of other nutrients and components of a food or mixed recipe, and the general complexity of food characteristics.

Traditionally, foods containing significant amounts of carbohydrate have been categorised according to the structure of the principally occurring carbohydrate. This has led to a simplistic division of carbohydrate-containing foods into 'simple' carbohydrate foods (containing glucose, sucrose, glucose polymers, etc.) or 'complex' carbohydrate foods (containing fibre or starch). A variety of beliefs about these carbohydrate-rich foods have become widespread, based on these categories:

- 'Simple' carbohydrate foods cause large and rapid changes in blood glucose levels on ingestion (a rapid rise, followed by a rapid and often greater fall). They are prized for their sweetness but are generally not nutritious. 'Simple' carbohydrate foods are the cause of dental caries.
- 'Complex' carbohydrate foods are nutritious foods which contain significant amounts of other nutrients, including dietary fibre. The digestion and absorption of 'complex' carbohydrate foods are slower, producing a flatter and more sustained blood glucose and insulin response.

While this classification system may have been developed as a simple nutrition education tool for the lay person, it is based on erroneous beliefs. In fact, each of the statements above is incorrect and has caused confusion in both nutrition science and practice. Such misconceptions have spilled over into the area of sports nutrition.

There is no single system that can do justice to the diversity of carbohydrate-rich foods. And even if it could judge individual foods, it would fail to appreciate that we eat meals, with a variety of food mixes and matches. Instead the athlete should recognise a number of different characteristics of foods, and match foods which promote these features to the situation in which this will be of major benefit. Priorities will vary with the athlete and with the specific situation. Generally there are three features that may be of importance.

Total nutritional value and similarity to nutrition goals

Whichever way it is expressed, it is recommended that carbohydrate-rich foods provide the major energy source in an athlete's diet (see the panel on the next page). However, for optimal health and performance, athletes must also achieve their requirements for protein and micronutrients, including any increase in requirement that may result from a heavy exercise program (see Chapters 11 and 15). Thus, carbohydrate-rich foods which provide significant sources of other nutrients are of value in allowing the athlete to meet a number of nutritional goals simultaneously. This is an important consideration in the everyday or training diet of the athlete, particularly for those individuals with very high carbohydrate needs and/or restricted energy intake. In other words, as carbohydrate increases its importance in the total food base, there should be an increase in the focus on nutritious carbohydrate-rich foods and combinations. This is particularly important when total food intake is limited, as in the case of athletes who are concerned with body fat levels.

CARBOHYDRATE TARGETS: GRAMS OR PERCENTAGES?

The terminology used to educate athletes about their carbohydrate intake goals has become a source of debate and confusion. It has on some occasions interfered with the interpretation of studies on carbohydrate and sports performance, and on others it has caused an athlete to have their diet unfairly criticised. Nutrition guidelines for the community express carbohydrate intake goals in terms of the percentage of energy that should be consumed from carbohydrate. This works because the message is general and the emphasis is on a relative change in fat and carbohydrate consumption. When the muscle fuel needs of an athlete are moderate, adequate carbohydrate intake should be provided by a diet that meets these guidelines for 'healthy eating'.

However, in situations where maximal glycogen storage is desirable and/or the athlete must meet the fuel bill of prolonged exercise sessions, carbohydrate needs become more specific. In other words, the muscle has an absolute requirement for carbohydrate (see Table 10.2). Therefore, we think that it is best to set definite carbohydrate intake goals for athletes in these situations, scaled to their body size and therefore, their muscle mass. The guideline to consume 7–10 grams of carbohydrate per kilogram BM is not only considerate of the muscle's needs, but is 'user-friendly' in setting a definite target for the amount of carbohydrate that the athlete should eat. With the advice of a sports dietitian, an athlete might be able to further narrow this target range according to their specific situation. This absolute amount of carbohydrate is greater than the typical intakes of most people, including other athletes, and it may require an athlete not just to eat more carbohydrate (in grams), but to devote more of their total energy intake to 'fuel foods' to do so. Typically, it might require the athlete to earmark 60–70% of their energy intake for carbohydrate needs. However, in practice, the total energy and muscle fuel needs of an athlete are not always synchronised, so this energy ratio is not fixed. For some large athletes with very high energy intakes, total intakes of 800–1000 grams of carbohydrate (representing 10 grams per kilogram of BM) may be consumed from only 45% of their energy budget. Other athletes may need to devote 70% of a restricted energy budget to achieve a carbohydrate intake of even 6–7 grams per kilogram. This makes it difficult and confusing to give carbohydrate intake guidelines on the basis of an energy ratio alone. It is not certain that this will guarantee the absolute amount of carbohydrate that the muscle needs.

There is an unfortunate tendency of those working with athletes to regard carbohydrate intake guidelines as rigid. Some judge that the fuel intake of an athlete or a group of athletes is 'deficient' or 'inadequate' based on the percentage of energy derived from carbohydrate. As in the situation described above, an athlete might be consuming a high *absolute* intake of carbohydrate, adequate in terms of their fuel requirements, but be judged to be following a 'low- or moderate-carbohydrate' diet from the perspective of energy ratio. Although total amounts of carbohydrate may be a better guide, they must still be regarded with some flexibility. In all areas of nutrition, judgments of adequacy or deficiency cannot be made from a single piece of evidence, particularly when it comes from a food record or another dietary survey tool. Such a judgment can only be made by working with an individual athlete and assessing their overall nutritional goals and nutrient needs from a number of sources of information. Specific information about an individual's training load and their ability to recover between sessions may help to fine-tune carbohydrate intake targets. It is important, particularly in terms of judging everyday carbohydrate intake, to regard guidelines as an approximation rather than a fixed rule. Generally, though, for athletes who have an important or increased need for carbohydrate, it is both more reliable and more practical to set guidelines in terms of a fixed amount of carbohydrate, rather than an energy percentage.

Many carbohydrate-rich foods provide valuable amounts of other nutrients, or at least can be constructed into a nutritious carbohydrate-rich meal using typical food combinations. Table 10.3 summarises nutrient-dense carbohydrate-rich foods and clever meal combinations which match a rich source of a key nutrient to a carbohydrate-food base. Note that there is no correlation between 'simple' and 'complex' carbohydrate classifications and the nutrient density of a food. Many carbohydrate-rich foods which contain mostly sugars can be nutrient-dense (e.g. fruits or flavoured yoghurt). By contrast, many foods that are full of complex carbohydrates contribute few nutrients and may be high in fat (e.g. potato crisps or pastry).

——|TABLE 10.3|————————————————————

Examples of nutritious carbohydrate-rich foods and meal combinations

Nutrient	Valuable source in a carbohydrate-rich food	Clever meal combinations
Protein	Flavoured low-fat yoghurt Flavoured milk drinks Fruit/milk smoothies Bread Legumes and lentils Baked beans Liquid meal supplements	Breakfast cereal + milk Baked potato + cheese Pasta + meat sauce Cheese sandwich Chicken kebabs + noodles Lentil curry + rice Baked beans + toast
Calcium	Flavoured low-fat yoghurt Milk/fruit smoothies Liquid meal supplements Tofu Flavoured milk and fortified soy milks	Breakfast cereal + milk Pizza with reduced-fat cheese Rice pudding made with milk Salmon casserole + rice Hot chocolate + toast Stewed apple + custard
Iron	Fortified breakfast cereal Legumes Baked beans Wholegrain bread and cereal Dried fruit	Beef kebabs + rice Pasta + seafood sauce Lamb stir-fry + rice Chilli con carne + rice Roast beef sandwich
Vitamins	Fruit Potatoes and corn Legumes Bread Breakfast cereal Wholegrain rice and pasta Liquid meal supplement	Salad sandwich Stir-fried vegetables and rice Fruit salad + icecream Toast and Vegemite Vegetarian pizza

Most naturally occurring carbohydrate-rich foods are low in fat, in keeping with general health guidelines. However, the athlete may also find low-fat and reduced-fat options among processed carbohydrate-rich foods or dishes, ranging from low-fat sweetened dairy products and bakery items to mixed dishes such as stir fries, pasta meals or pizzas made with minimal added fats/oils and low-fat ingredients. Moderation with fat intake will be an important strategy for athletes who have limited energy budgets. These include athletes trying to achieve or maintain a lower body fat level, or athletes in aesthetic/skill-based sports such as gymnastics and figure skating who must remain small and lean without the contribution of a high-energy expenditure training program (see Chapter 11).

In summary, athletes should focus on nutrient-rich carbo-hydrate foods and meals:

- in planning their everyday diets;
- when energy intake is restricted; and
- when requirements of key nutrients are increased (e.g. iron and vitamins—see Chapter 15, and calcium and protein—see Chapter 11).

The glycaemic index

The 'simple' versus 'complex' classification system provides a particularly inaccurate view of the effect of carbohydrate-rich foods and meals on blood glucose and insulin levels. Since the 1970s it has been recognised that carbohydrate-rich foods produce variable blood glucose responses that are impossible to predict from food composition data. For example, several carbohydrate-rich foods containing predominantly sugars (e.g. fruit and flavoured yoghurt) produce a flattened blood glucose curve when ingested, while other foods high in 'complex' carbohydrates (e.g. bread and potatoes) produce a high blood glucose response, similar to that following the intake of glucose itself. Curiously, the presence of dietary fibre in foods does not always seem to delay absorption and flatten the post-meal blood glucose curve. For example, blood glucose responses to wholemeal bread are similar to those following the consump-tion of white bread.

The glycaemic index (GI) was introduced in the early 1980s as a classification system that could systematically address the effects of carbohydrate-rich foods on blood glucose levels. Canadian researchers Professors David Jenkins and Tom Wolever are generally given credit for introducing this system. However, Australian researchers such as Dr Greg Collier from Deakin University and Associate Professor Jenny Brand-Miller from the University of Sydney have been prominent in undertaking research into GI.

The GI is a ranking of foods based on their actual post-meal blood glucose responses compared to the responses following a reference food of either glucose or white bread (see Figure 10.1). The GI is calculated by measuring the area under the blood glucose curve following the intake of a 50 gram carbohydrate serving of the test food, compared with the area under the blood glucose curve following an equal carbohydrate intake from the reference food. All tests are conducted after an overnight fast. Extensive research in this

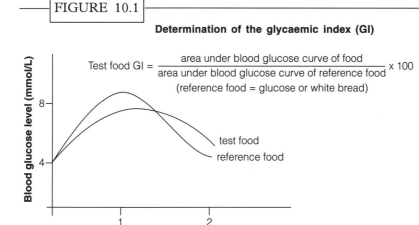

FIGURE 10.1

Determination of the glycaemic index (GI)

$$\text{Test food GI} = \frac{\text{area under blood glucose curve of food}}{\text{area under blood glucose curve of reference food}} \times 100$$

(reference food = glucose or white bread)

test food
reference food

area has shown that the GI can be reproduced within and between individuals and can be applied to a mixed meal containing carbohydrate-rich foods.

In essence, the GI reflects the rate of digestion and absorption of a carbohydrate-rich food. The factors which influence this are many and varied and include:

- the form of the food (e.g. the size of particles after milling or processing, the texture and viscosity, including the presence of soluble fibre and the presence of intact grains);
- the degree of food processing and cooking (e.g. how soluble the starch has become, how much the cell structure has been disrupted);
- the presence of fructose or lactose (both have a low GI);
- the ratio of amylopectin (branched) and amylose (straight) forms of starch. (The amylose form of starch has a slower rate of digestion.)
- interactions between starch and protein or starch and fat;
- other 'anti-nutrients' in food which block absorption (e.g. phytates in wholegrain foods); and
- the 'ripeness' of foods (involving the breakdown of starch into sugars).

Clearly, the permutations and combinations of these factors mean that it is impossible to guess the GI of a food. Table 10.4 summarises the GI of some common carbohydrate-rich foods, ranking them into general categories of 'high', 'medium'

TABLE 10.4

Examples of the glycaemic index of carbohydrate-rich foods

	Food	GI
High GI (>70)	Glucose	100
	Cornflakes	84
	Cocopops	77
	Instant mashed potato	83
	Baked potato	85
	Sports drink	95
	Jelly beans	80
	White or wholemeal bread	70
	Weetbix	70
	Watermelon	72
	Honey	73
	Typical Australian rice	88
Moderate GI (55–70)	One-minute oats	66
	Muesli flake cereal (e.g. Sustain)	68
	Muffins (cake style)	62
	Soft drink	68
	Basmati rice	59
	Arrowroot biscuit	66
	Icecream	61
	Mangoes	55
	Orange juice	57
	Sucrose	65
Low GI (< 55)	Porridge	49
	Mixed grain bread	45
	All Bran	42
	Milk	27
	Flavoured yoghurt	33
	Chocolate	49
	Ripe banana	52
	Unripe banana	30
	Apple	38
	Orange	44
	Pasta	41
	Baked beans	48
	Kidney beans	27
	Red lentils	26
	Fructose	23

Note: GI has been based on glucose as a reference food. Where white bread is used as the reference food, GI values are higher by approximately 1.4.

Source: Foster-Powell, K. and Brand-Miller, J. 'International tables of glycemic index', *American Journal of Clinical Nutrition*, 62 (suppl): 8715–935, 1995.

and 'low'. Knowledge of the GI of carbohydrate-rich foods has allowed researchers and clinicians to manipulate the glucose and insulin response to diets of equal carbohydrate content. Lowering the GI has been shown to improve the metabolic profiles of individuals with diabetes and high blood lipids and to increase post-meal satiety. Thus the GI has gained recognition as a useful nutrition education tool, particularly for people with metabolic disorders. A recently published book, *The GI factor* (by Dr Brand-Miller and colleagues), has made this information widely accessible. The importance of manipulating blood glucose and insulin responses to food in the context of sports nutrition will be discussed in other chapters (Chapters 12 and 14).

Practical issues

The athlete is often recommended to eat carbohydate at special times, or in quantities greater than that which would be provided in an everyday diet or dictated by their appetite and hunger. Therefore, carbohydrate-rich foods and drinks that are appealing, available or able to be easily consumed will have value in helping the athlete to meet their carbohydrate intake targets. Sweet-tasting foods and drinks are generally appealing to people. Studies show that the flavour of a carbohydrate-containing drink may encourage greater intake of fluid during and after exercise, thus promoting better hydration as well as achieving fuel intake goals at these times. Sports drinks are tailor-made for athletes to provide carbohydrate at a concentration suitable for optimal delivery of both fluid and fuel during and after exercise. The taste profile is manipulated towards preferences experienced while exercising or dehydrated. Excessive sweetness in these products is avoided by using a mixture of glucose polymers along with glucose and sucrose. A little sodium (salt) is added to enhance the flavour.

Sports bars are another convenience food in a compact form that can be easily carried and consumed 'on the run'; either literally during exercise, or as a general part of an athlete's busy day.

These sports products, together with high-carbohydrate powders and drinks, carbohydrate gels and nutrient-dense liquid meal supplements, offer the advantages of compactness, minimal preparation and known carbohydrate content (see Chapter 16). Since carbohydrate intake guidelines may specify a recommended amount to be consumed in a given situation, foods of known or standardised carbohydrate content are often a popular choices of athletes. However, food tables and ready

┌─────────────────┐
│ TABLE 10.5 │
└─────────────────┘

Ready reckoner of the carbohydrate content of carbohydrate-rich foods and drinks

Each of the selections provide approximately 50 grams of carbohydrate:

Cereals

Wheatbiscuit ceral (e.g. Vitabrits)	60 g (5 biscuits)
'Light' breakfast cereal (e.g. Cornflakes, Weeties)	60 g (2 cups)
'Muesli' flake breakfast cereal (e.g. Sustain)	65 g (1–1.5 cups)
Toasted muesli	90 g (1 cup)
Porridge—made with milk	350 g (1.3 cups)
Porridge—made with water	550 g (2.5 cups)
Rolled oats	90 g (1 cup)
Muesli bar	2.5
Rice cakes	6
Rice, boiled	180 g (1 cup)
Pasta or noodles, boiled	200 g (1.3 cups)
Canned spaghetti	440 g (large can)
Crispbreads and dry biscuits	6 large (e.g. Ryevita) or 15 small (e.g. Salada)
Fruit filled biscuits	5
Plain sweet biscuits	8–10
Cream filled/chocolate biscuits	6
Bread	110 g (4 slices white or 3 thick wholegrain)
Bread rolls	110 g (1 large or 2 medium)
Pita and Lebanese bread	100 g (2 pita)
Chapati	150 g (2.5)
English muffin	120 g (2 full muffins)
Crumpet	2.5
Cakestyle muffin	115 g (1 large or 2 medium)
Pancakes	150 g (2 medium)
Scones	125 g (3 medium)
Iced fruit bun	105 g (1.5)
Croissant	140 g (1.5 large or 2 medium)
Ricecream	330 g (1.5 cups)

Fruit

Fruit crumble	1 cup
Fruit packed in heavy syrup	280 g (1.3 cups)
Fresh stewed/canned in light syrup	520 g (2 cups)
Fresh fruit salad	500 g (2.5 cups)
Bananas	2 medium–large
Mangoes, pears, grapefruit and other large fruit	2–3
Oranges, apples and other medium-size fruit	3–4
Nectarines, apricots and other small fruit	12
Grapes	350 g (2 cups)
Melon	1000 g (6 cups)
Strawberries	1800 g (12 cups)
Sultanas and raisins	70 g (4 Tbs)
Dried apricots	115 g (22 halves)

Vegetables and legumes

Potatoes	350 g potato (one very large or 3 medium)
Sweet potato	350 g (2.5 cups)
Corn	300 g (1.2 cups creamed corn or 2 cobs)
Green beans	1800 g (14 cups)
Baked beans	440 g (1 large can)
Lentils	400 g (2 cups)
Soy beans and kidney beans	400 g (2 cups)
Tomato puree	1 litre (4 cups)
Pumpkin and peas	700 g (5 cups)

Dairy products

Milk	1 litre
Flavoured milk	560 ml
Custard	300 g (1.3 cup)
'Diet' yoghurt and natural yoghurt	800 g (4 tubs)
Flavoured non-fat yoghurt	350 g (2 tubs)
Icecream	250 g (10 Tbs)
Fromage frais	400 g (2 tubs)

Sugars and confectionery

Sugar	50
Jam	3 Tbs
Syrups	4 Tbs
Honey	3 Tbs
Chocolate	80 g
Mars Bar and other 50–60 g bars	1.5 bars
Jubes and jelly babies	60 g

Mixed dishes

Pizza	200 g (1/4 medium–thick crust or 1/3 thin crust)
Hamburgers	1.3 Big Macs
Lasagne	400 g serve
Fried rice	200 g (1.3 cups)

Sports products and drinks

Fruit juice–unsweetened	600 ml
Fruit juice–sweetened	500 ml
Cordial	800 ml
Soft drinks and flavoured mineral water	500 ml
Sports drink	700 ml
Carbohydrate loader supplement	250 ml
Liquid meal supplement	250–300 ml
Fruit smoothie	250–300 ml
Sports bar	1–1.5 bars
Sports gels	1.5 sachets
Glucose polymer powders	60 g

Source: NUTTAB 1995, Australian Department of Community Services and Health.

reckoners of the carbohydrate content of food can make everyday foods more 'user friendly'. Table 10.5 provides a ready reckoner of carbohydrate-rich foods.

Compactness and ease of consumption are food attributes that are important to an athlete with very high energy and carbohydrate requirements, or in the choice of a pre-exercise or post-exercise meal. The 'bulkiest' carbohydrate-rich foods are those which are high in fibre, particularly in combination with a high water content and an intact, rigid structure, (e.g. most vegetables). They involve greater volumes of food, longer eating time, and greater stomach fullness to provide a given amount of carbohydrate. This may prevent the athlete from reaching their carbohydrate intake targets, or may be a cause of gastrointestinal discomfort, particularly during exercise. Carbohydrate-rich foods that are less fibrous, require less chewing, or with a greater carbohydrate (lower water) density, may be more practical when carbohydrate has to be consumed in large amounts. For example, 'white' or refined bread and cereal products are less filling than most wholegrain products, and processed fruit and juices may be more easily eaten than fresh fruit. Sugars, jams and syrups may be added to foods or meals to provide an additional low-bulk carbohydrate source, while confectionery items and carbohydrate-rich drinks (e.g. soft drinks, nutrient-rich milk shakes and fruit smoothies) are also compact forms of dietary carbohydrate.

In the post-exercise situation, an athlete's refuelling plans may be challenged by fatigue and loss of appetite. Carbohydrate-containing drinks, or carbohydrate-rich foods with fluid-like appearance (e.g. flavoured yoghurt and other sweetened dairy foods), may have appeal to an athlete who is dehydrated. Food that can be presented in small portions (e.g. sandwich fingers and fruit pieces) may encourage continued nibbling and be more attractive to an athlete who has lost their appetite than large food pieces or whole foods with a rigid structure.

Conversely, for an athlete who needs to restrict energy intake, carbohydrate-rich foods which provide long eating times, large volume and stomach fullness, and high satiety value may assist with this goal.

Finally, the athlete may be required to eat carbohydrate in situations where access to food or the facilities for food preparation are poor. This may include the post-training or competition situation, or the 'grazing' pattern of frequent intake during a busy day that is characteristic of athletes with high-energy intakes. Thus, carbohydrate-rich foods which require minimal preparation, are portable or have good storage properties may be of practical value. These include both naturally occurring foods (e.g. fruit), as well as processed and convenience foods such as bars, confectionery and bakery items, and special sports foods.

Practical issues in choosing carbohydrate-rich foods and drinks are of most importance in the following situations:

- immediately before, during or after exercise when gastro-intestinal comfort is an issue (see Chapters 12, 13 and 14);
- when appetite will not cover carbohydrate needs;
- when total carbohydrate needs are high (see Chapters 11 and 15);
- when the athlete needs to calculate or ingest a specific amount of carbohydrate; and
- when access to food and food preparation is limited.

Summary

Dietary carbohydrate is provided by a wide variety of carbo-hydrate-rich foods and drinks. There is no universal system that can adequately describe the diverse metabolic, functional and nutritional features of these various foods. Nutrition guidelines for athletes make recommendations for everyday intake of carbohydrate as well as carbohydrate intake for specific situations before, during and after exercise sessions (see the panel below). Athletes are encouraged to meet these guidelines by choosing carbohydrate-rich foods that are suited to the requirements of the situation. Characteristics on offer may include nutritional value, a desirable glycaemic index, appetite appeal and practicality. In the following chapters (Chapters 12–15) there will be opportunities to examine these guidelines in more detail.

A SUMMARY OF CARBOHYDRATE INTAKE STRATEGIES FOR THE ATHLETE

- The athlete should be prepared to be different—a Western diet is not a high-carbohydrate diet. Carbohydrate-rich foods and drinks should make up at least half of all meals and snacks.

- Nutritious carbohydrate-rich choices should be the focus of most meals and snacks, so that requirements for all nutrients can be met. Meals or recipes should feature the following foods
  — breads and breakfast cereals
  — rice, pasta, noodles and other grain foods
  — fruits
  — starchy vegetables (e.g. potatoes, corn)
  — legumes (e.g. lentils, beans, soy-based products)
  — sweetened dairy products (e.g. fruit flavoured yoghurts, fruit smoothies).
- Many foods commonly believed by athletes to be carbohydrate-rich are actually high-fat foods (e.g. cakes, takeaway foods, chocolates and pastries). The athlete should be aware of low-fat eating strategies, particularly when they desire to maintain low BM and body fat levels.
- When carbohydrate and energy needs are high, the athlete should increase the number of meals and snacks that they eat, rather than the size of meals. This requires organisation to have snacks on hand in a busy day.
- Sugar and sugar-rich foods are useful for the athlete, especially when added to a nutritious carbohydrate-rich meal, or to refuel during and after exercise. Not only do they taste appealing, but they provide a more compact form of carbohydrate.
- Lower-fibre choices of carbohydrate-rich foods may be useful when energy needs are high, or when the athlete needs to eat just before exercise. These choices are more compact and less likely to cause gastrointestinal discomfort during exercise.
- Carbohydrate drinks (e.g. fruit juices, soft drinks, fruit smoothies) are also a compact source for special situations or high-carbohydrate diets. This category includes many of the supplements made specially for athletes (e.g. sports drinks, liquid meal supplements, sports bars).
- The athlete who needs to optimise muscle glycogen storage—either to recover between prolonged training sessions, or to fuel up for a competition—should aim to eat 7–10 grams of carbohydrate per kilogram BM per day. It may require expert advice to design an eating program to achieve these levels.
- The athlete should eat a high-carbohydrate meal 1–4 hours prior to competition. The type and amount of foods and timing of this meal will vary with the individual and their event. All strategies should be practised in training.
- Post-exercise recovery of muscle fuel stores is enhanced by eating a high-carbohydrate meal or snack within 15–30 minutes of exercise. An intake of at least 1 gram of carbohydrate per kilogram BM is recommended. Nutritious carbohydrate-rich foods and drinks can

provide protein and other nutrients that may also be useful in recovery. It may also be appropriate to focus on foods with a high glycaemic index in recovery meals and snacks.

- Carbohydrate should be consumed during lengthy training and competition sessions when additional fuel is needed. An hourly intake of up to 1 gram of carbohydrate per kilogram BM is suggested, and both foods and drinks can be used by athletes to achieve this. However, sports drinks offer the advantage of looking after fluid and carbohydrate needs simultaneously, and being specially designed for sports situations.

ARE HIGH-FAT DIETS BACK IN FASHION?

Ideas in nutrition often come in cycles. One idea that keeps resurfacing is to improve the athlete's use of fat as an exercise fuel. A short period on a high-fat (low-carbohydrate) diet has been shown to impair exercise endurance and performance because of reduced muscle glycogen levels. But what about the possibility of adapting an athlete over a longer period to make better use of fat as a fuel? The idea is intriguing. After all, even the leanest of athletes has an abundance of fat stored in adipose tissue and as triglyceride droplets in the muscle itself. Adapting the muscle to improve its capacity to oxidise fat is a well-known outcome of training. The prospect of enhancing this process further is tempting.

Support for adaptation to a high-fat diet by athletes includes a mixture of ideas and research, some credible and some flawed. Further confusion has arisen from many of the diets promoted in popular books and magazines. The authors of the Zone diet for example (see Chapter 16), seem to have jumped onto the high-fat bandwagon. Some commonly quoted arguments to support high-fat diets are as follows:

- Certain animals, such as rats and dogs, adapt well to high-fat diets. In fact, husky dogs, renowned for their efforts in the Iditarod sled races, train and race on high-fat diets (>50% fat).
- Dietary studies show that most athletes fail to meet the theoretical carbohydrate intake targets set by sports nutrition experts. It has been said, therefore, that they do not really need such high intakes of carbohydrate in order to perform well.
- Studies have failed to provide convincing proof that high-carbohydrate diets promote superior training adaptation and performance (see Chapter 15).

- Three well-quoted studies have shown that athletes who consume high-fat/low-carbohydrate diets for 2–4 weeks adapt to these diets. Performance is not impaired (the Phinney study) and may even be enhanced following this adaptation (the studies of Muoio and Lambert). There is evidence that the muscle 'retools' itself to become more efficient in burning fat. It becomes able to burn a higher fat mixture during moderate intensity exercise, sparing muscle glycogen stores.
- A study by Charl van Zyl and colleagues from the University of Cape Town showed that the consumption of Medium Chain Triglyceride (MCT) oils, in combination with carbohydrate, improved performance of a 40 km time-trial, undertaken after two hours of moderate-intensity cycling. These special fats are digested and handled by the muscle in a more efficient way than the long-chain fatty acids that make up most of our dietary fat intake. They may provide an additional fuel source for the athlete during prolonged exercise.

   However, these arguments have failed to convince most scientists that athletes should embark on high-fat eating plans. Here are some counter-arguments, followed by a weighing up of the overall picture.
- There are species differences in the ability to utilise various energy sources during exercise. Humans behave differently to rats and dogs.
- The benefits of a high-carbohydrate diet for athletes cannot be dismissed. There is clear proof of the benefits of maintaining adequate carbohydrate availability in acute situations of exercise. Dietary surveys which report that athletes do not eat high-carbohydrate intakes cannot tell us whether these athletes were eating or performing optimally; nor are they necessarily accurate. It is difficult to show clear performance benefits from high-carbohydrate intakes as compared with moderate-carbohydrate intakes, but this is as much an issue of research study design as it is of the fat versus carbohydrate debate (see Chapter 15).
- The current studies of performance in relation to high-fat adaptation suffer from flaws. In the (in)famous study by Dr Steve Phinney undertaken while at Massachusetts Institute of Technology in America, four weeks of adaptation to a high-fat diet produced clear evidence of a shift towards higher fat utilisation during moderate intensity cycling. However, the conclusion that fat adaptation did not cause a decrease in exercise endurance in the cyclists is questionable. The results of the study are skewed by the large improvement in performance of one subject in a small subject pool (five cyclists). The rest of the subjects showed small performance changes, both positive and negative. Of course, when you take an average of the results of such a group, the differences in each direction are counter-balanced and 'cancel out'. Thus the impression from the group data was that

'performance had not changed' after the diet. Importantly, this study showed no evidence of performance *benefit*.

- The study by Deborah Muoio and colleagues from the State University of New York at Buffalo claims to show performance enhancement following adaptation to a high-fat diet in runners. However, the results of the study are confused by the possibility of an 'order effect'. A cross-over design was used, and the runners were given the 'normal', 'high-fat' and 'high-carbohydrate' diets in a set order, rather than in a randomised fashion. This is not a good study design since performance may have been influenced by factors such as familiarisation, training, and the time of season rather than by the treatment (see Chapter 17). Most importantly, despite the titles given to the treatment diets, there were not great differences in their fat and carbohydrate content. Therefore this study did not really test adaptation to a high-fat, restricted carbohydrate intake.

- The study by Dr Vicki Lambert from the University of Cape Town, South Africa, exposed cyclists to two weeks of high-fat or high-carbohydrate eating and showed evidence of muscle retooling for increased fat oxidation. However, the performance results are confused as a result of the crowded design of the study. Subjects were asked to perform a number of exercise tasks of different intensities in succession. It is difficult to separate the effects of the previous bout of exercise from the performance of the next. Although there was evidence of glycogen sparing and increased fat utilisation at various exercise intensities, the validity of the performance results must be questioned. Clearly more studies need to be undertaken to resolve the question of possible benefit of fat adaptation.

- Fat adaptation is likely to be important only in sports in which carbohydrate availability is a limiting factor. The contribution of the various fuels to exercise is determined by the intensity and duration of the exercise, and fat oxidation cannot sustain the power output needed for high-intensity exercise (see Chapter 3). However, fat adaptation could, in theory at least, be beneficial in events in which it is useful to spare muscle glycogen, or to enhance the ability of muscle to generate power when glycogen is depleted, such as in ultra-endurance events. As such it is of interest to only a small and select group of athletes.

- The benefits are only useful to well-trained athletes, as an extension of the adaptations that occur as a result of training itself. Longitudinal training studies conducted by Dr Jorn Helge and colleagues from August Krogh Institute in Copenhagen, Denmark show that untrained subjects gain greater benefits from undertaking a training program while eating a high-carbohydrate diet than subjects who take up training while eating a high-fat diet.

- If 'fat adaptation' can be shown to enhance endurance and ultra-endurance performance, it is best achieved by a short period on a high-fat, low-carbohydrate diet (e.g. 7–14 days). It appears that most of the adaptation occurs within this period. The athlete can then avoid the long-term disadvantages of high-fat eating (e.g. cardiovascular risk, excessive energy intake, inadequate intake of some nutrients). Athletes feel better and train better on a high-carbohydrate diet, so the time spent on a high-fat diet is best kept to a minimum.

- A study by Asker Jeukendrup and his colleagues from the University of Maastricht in the Netherlands, did not find performance benefits when cyclists were fed MCT oils in combination with carbohydrate, during a long ride. Instead they reported that many athletes performed worse, due to gastrointestinal problems. They suggested that there is a risk of such problems when athletes ingest more than 30 grams of MCT oil during exercise. If use of MCT is to be a useful strategy for the provision of supplementary fat during exercise, it may require familiarisation-training by the athlete.

- The final outcome may see the endurance or ultra-endurance athlete use a combination of a high-carbohydrate training diet, a period of 'fat adaptation', and then carbohydrate loading to prepare for their events. Another possible strategy is the intake of both fat and carbohydrate during the event. Of course, these ideas are speculative and the area requires further study. However, it is clear that high-fat eating is not meant to be a long-term strategy for any athlete. Should future research support any benefit from high-fat intake, it will be as part of a plan to enhance all power systems, rather than as an attempt to 'overthrow' the importance of carbohydrate.

11

Changing body size and shape

'"There is a huge difference between fifth and first." With the advice of his trainer Dr Cecchini, Riis has completely changed his approach. Dr Cecchini sent the cyclist to ride up a mountain near his home in Tuscany carrying five kilograms of lead, to illustrate the improvement he could expect if he lost weight. The lesson hit home: in the past 6 years Riis has lost 8.5 kg and is now just "skin and bone".'

> Tour de France promotion describing the rise of
> Bjarne Riis, from domestique to fifth place in 1993,
> and then 1996 Tour winner

'I feel good, and at my current weight, I feel I have never trained better . . . But, my coach wants me (to lose weight) . . . because that's what I weighed last year when I set the world record . . . He reminds me of my weight a lot, and I have to train differently than I would like . . . After our afternoon workout, which lasts about 2 hours, most people on the team work out in the weight room. This is what I feel I need. Instead, I have to run to lose the weight.'

> Female Olympic swimmer, talking to psychologist,
> Professor Kelly Brownell about her weight problem

'I ran in one Great Britain team which consisted of six runners and a reserve. Of these seven, I know that as many as five were suffering from some kind of eating disorder, including me.'

> Alison Outram, member of Great Britain's Junior
> women's cross-country team in 1995 and 1996

Athletes come in a range of sizes and shapes that almost define the boundaries of the human body. They range from the tallest basketball player, to the most petite gymnast, and the sheer bulk of the sumo wrestler. On the other hand, muscularity can stretch from the bursting definition of the body builder to the almost wasted upper body of the distance runner. Physique and body composition play a vital role in the performance of many sports. Elite athletes typically show the characteristics that are suited to performance in their sport. This is a result of inherited features that first directed the athlete to an activity that they could do well in, as well as changes achieved through the conditioning effect of training. Some athletes naturally arrive at a physique that is ideal for top performance. Others may need to work on the features that can be moulded—body fatness and muscle mass.

HOW MUCH DOES BODY SIZE AND FATNESS AFFECT SPORTS PERFORMANCE?

In some sports, particularly those based on skill (e.g. golf, archery and shooting), performance is largely independent of body fatness. Both selection and conditioning factors tend to allow higher body fat levels in these athletes. In fact, top performers in these sports may actually be overweight (or over-fat) by community standards.

At the other end of the spectrum there are sports in which a low body mass, and in particular a low body fat level, are a distinct advantage to performance. The advantages of a low body fat level include physical and mechanical gains due to an increased power to mass ratio, or simply to a reduction in the 'dead weight' that must be moved by the athlete. This is a particular advantage where the athlete has to transport their own body mass over long distances (e.g. distance runners, triathletes, road cyclists) or to move vertically against greater gravity effects (gymnasts, jumpers, basketball players, or cyclists riding a hilly course). Higher body fat levels are seen in endurance athletes, most notably swimmers, who perform in a weight-supported sport. A high 'power to mass' ratio plays a role in 'stop–start' sports by increasing speed, agility and the ability to change direction quickly. In some team sports, players in mobile field positions or with a mobile playing style are often observed to have lower body fat levels than their team-mates. On the other hand, particularly in sports involving physical contact, a higher body fat level may be less problematic for 'set position' players. A certain level of body fat may help to protect body organs against injury from body contact, and to provide bulk against tackling. Nevertheless, a high body mass should be achieved principally through an increase in muscle mass.

A small body size *per se* is an advantage in distance events, especially in hot conditions where a greater surface area to volume ratio enhances heat dissipation. It also helps in acrobatic sports such as diving and gymnastics to assist the athlete to rotate or spin their entire body over a smaller area or in a faster time. Finally, in some sports there is an aesthetic component to performance. A slim, petite figure is currently deemed *de rigueur* in gymnastics, diving, figure skating and other subjectively judged sports. Extreme leanness is an obsession in body building, to allow muscularity to be maximally defined.

A number of studies of elite athletes have identified profiles of body fat and muscularity that confirm these principles. And in some sports, across a group of athletes of differing abilities or disciplines, there is a statistical relationship between performance and body fatness: a lower body fat level is related to better performance. These data help to promote the interest, and sometimes obsession, of various groups of athletes to achieve minimal body fat levels. But there are some limitations of these types of studies that are not taken into account by individual athletes. First, it is true that among heterogeneous groups of athletes, individual factors such as body fat levels or VO_{2max} are predictive of performance. However, among a group of top performers or athletes with similar ability, the importance of these factors alone disappears. Instead, a combination of factors begin to play interconnected roles. Even when there is an association between body fat and performance, this does not hold true for individual cases. Among a group it is likely that some of the best performers do not conform to the stereotyped lean model, whereas some athletes with very low body fat levels are not highly gifted.

Most importantly, these studies are cross-sectional rather than longitudinal. In other words, there are no good studies in which the performance of individual athletes have been monitored across a range of body fat levels. These studies would be necessary to confirm the absolute value of a certain, particularly low, level of body fatness. It is likely that if such studies were undertaken, they might confirm general tendencies towards benefits of size and body fat in some sports. But they might also confirm the observation of sports nutrition practitioners, that each athlete has a 'natural' body shape, and that they perform best within a range of this. Trying to achieve a stereotypical 'ideal' must always be balanced against the cost and disadvantages of fighting against their natural body fat levels.

A separate story of size, shape and performance involves sports with specific weight limits for competition. In sports such as boxing, wrestling, judo, light-weight rowing and weight lifting, weight divisions (commonly ranging from two to ten) have been set with the intention of matching competitors or opponents of similar size and strength. This is proposed to allow fair and equal competition. In horse racing, the horse is similarly handicapped in that they carry a certain weight, which then sets an upper weight limit for the jockey. Of course, athletes in these sports all want to compete in a lower weight class than they really deserve to be in, believing that this will mean competing against a smaller, lighter opponent. 'Making weight', the practice of reducing body mass to meet the competition weight limit, will be discussed later.

METHODS FOR ASSESSING BODY FAT AND MUSCLE LEVELS

Most people have some interest in assessing or monitoring their size and shape, and the bathroom or gym scales are usually where they first turn for information. This is at best a crude assessment technique, and in the case of athletes especially irrelevant, since such measures do not distinguish between body fat and lean body mass. This distinction is important in determining sports performance, and the levels of each tissue vary considerably among athletes. Apart from those athletes who need to weigh-in to meet a competition limit, the only other justified use of scales in sport is to monitor acute changes in body mass over the duration of an exercise session, or from day to day, to reflect body fluid losses (see Chapters 13, 14 and 15).

There are a number of techniques that attempt to assess body fat levels and muscle mass, or lean body mass. Some techniques use expensive equipment or require experts to make the measurements. These include underwater weighing (densitometry) and DEXA (dual X-ray absorptiometry). These are usually impractical for everyday use by athletes and are typically used for research purposes only. Techniques such as

TOBEC (total body electrical conductivity), bioelectrical impedance (e.g. 'Futrex') and air displacement (e.g. 'Bod Pod') are also available. However, more work is needed to ensure that the results obtained by these methods are valid for athletic populations. Often mathematical equations are involved in the final calculations, or assumptions are made in the method that are valid for sedentary populations but may not apply to well-trained athletes.

Kinanthropometry involves the measurement of body girths, circumferences and skinfold fat thicknesses to describe physique. It offers the advantage of being portable and cheap—a technique that can travel with the athlete into the field. However, accurate readings and interpretation of the results require considerable skill. Skinfold fat readings have been popular for many years as a method of estimating total body fat. There are many limitations to this technique, especially when percentage body fat is estimated using mathematical equations generated from general populations or even from general groups of athletes. Such equations are only accurate when they are derived from, and then used for, a specific group. This is important if accurate information is needed. An alternative to generating percentage body fat information is to work with the skinfold measurements themselves. In many countries, athletes have body fat measurements presented as a 'sum of skinfolds'. This represents the sum of the individual skinfold fat thicknesses from a number of specific sites (usually seven), taken according to a standardised procedure.

Whatever method is used to generate information about body fatness or physique for use by an athlete, the following guidelines should be met:

- The technique is valid and reliable. This means that the method needs to be validated on the specific type of athlete involved, and that errors are minimised by having an expert undertake the technique using a standardised protocol.
- The same method is repeated over time to allow the athlete to gain longitudinal information about their size and fatness, and how this relates to their training and performance. This allows the athlete to set targets that are individually suited. This strengthens the need for a reliable technique, and in the case of skinfold fat measurements,

it is preferable that the same expert take the readings on each occasion.

- The method can travel to times and places where useful information can be collected—for example, to allow the athlete to be assessed at their peak of competition. Quite often athletes are prepared to sacrifice the validity and impressiveness of high-technology methods, preferring the ease and practicality of a method such as skinfold measurements.
- The results are interpreted by an expert who understands the limitations of the technique and can assist the athlete to use the information appropriately.

SETTING IDEAL BODY FAT LEVELS

An athlete's ideal body fat level is an individual characteristic. Generally, the 'norms' for a specific group of elite athletes can provide a guideline to the range of levels that are compatible with good performances. But this information should not be used for making strict prescriptions or setting narrow standards that one or all athletes must adhere to. Another mistake made by some athletes and coaches is to set their sights on the body fat levels of a certain elite performer, or on minimum body fat levels *per se*. For a start, this makes the assumption that the observed body fat levels of elite athletes or a certain athlete are optimal. In fact, they may not be. Secondly, it fails to account for individuality.

An athlete's ideal level of body fat and body mass are specific to them, and can really only be judged by 'trial and error', over a period of time. They must encompass a range of health, nutrition and sporting issues. Or more specifically, they must achieve the following goals:

- be associated with consistently good performances over the long term;
- keep the athlete healthy—or without an added risk of injury and illness that can occur both from being overfat or underfat; and
- allow the athlete to eat a well-chosen diet with sufficient energy to meet all their other nutritional goals, and to be free of unreasonable food-related 'stress'.

In practice, the concept of ideal may change over an athlete's career, and may vary according to the time of the year and the athlete's immediate goals. The clever athlete works within a range of 'ideal' and may fine-tune for important competitions.

The dangers of very low body fat levels

If all athletes complied with the simple laws of physics, it might be easy to calculate an ideal power to weight ratio, or body fat level, for a given sporting situation. And in some cases, the lower the 'dead weight', the better the performance. However, humans carry body fat for a number of reasons, including to carry on the inherited characteristics of their parents, to provide insulation and protection for their body and its important organs, to preserve body hormone levels, and to provide an energy reserve for the 'lean times'. This last issue is especially relevant to females, whose gender is programmed to carry 'hard to shift' body fat on their buttocks and legs. This may not suit sports coaches, but it is part of Mother Nature's plan to ensure that females can support the energy cost of pregnancy and breastfeeding, come what may.

Some racial groups and individuals naturally carry low levels of body fat, or can achieve these without paying a substantial penalty. And some athletes vary their body fat over a season so that very low levels are achieved only for a specific and short time. However, in many cases where an athlete tries to adopt a very low body fat level, *or a level that seems unnatural for their inherited body characteristics*, problems occur. These problems remain mostly speculative, but include loss of body warmth and protection, as well as disturbances to hormonal balance and the immune system. Some of the disadvantages arise directly from the methods that the athlete used to try to lose body fat—severe energy or nutrient restriction, excessive training loads, or disordered eating behaviours. Typically, there is an immediate improvement in exercise performance accompanying the loss of body fat. However, after a honeymoon period, chronic problems gradually emerge. The athlete finds that they are often sick, or eventually suffers a consequence of disturbed menstrual status (see below). Unfortunately, it is hard to persuade many athletes to overturn what was initially a successful strategy.

MAKING WEIGHT

The typical practice in weight classification sports is to compete in a division that is substantially lower than normal training weight or the athlete's 'natural' level of body mass and body fat. Some of these athletes reduce their weight by minimising body fat levels through food restriction and extra training. Most athletes 'make weight' over the last days prior to their competition by dehydrating and restricting food. Some athletes need to use a combination of these methods in order to weigh in on target. In the case of body builders, similar techniques are used to 'cut up' so that the muscle and vascularity appear defined against minimum body fat levels and dehydrated skin tissue.

The rapid weight-making techniques reduce the athlete's body mass principally by reducing the mass of body fluid levels, food in the gastrointestinal tract, and muscle fuel stores. Some loss of muscle protein may also occur. Techniques include:

- dehydrating by exercising in the heat, or in 'sweat suits';
- sweating in a sauna;
- using diuretics or laxatives;
- restricting fluid intake;
- restricting food intake or fasting; and
- self-induced vomiting.

Making weight has been studied extensively in college wrestlers in the United States, where these athletes compete over a season of weekly competitions, in teams with up to thirteen different weight classes. Dr Suzanne Nelson Steen and Professor Kelly Brownell are two of the researchers who have documented the pattern of weekly cycling of weight loss and regain, as the wrestlers cut to a lower weight division to gain a perceived advantage in strength and leverage over a smaller opponent. They observed among college wrestlers who were trying to qualify for the National Collegiate Athletic Association (NCAA) competition that 80% of the subjects were always dieting during the season and that they were often or always preoccupied with food. The typical (median) weight loss each week was 6.8 kg, and on average the wrestler was required to make weight fifteen times a season. Some wrestlers reported losing up to 20 kg in one cycle, and to having to make weight 60 times in that season. They reported using several practices from the list above among their rapid weight-loss techniques. Clearly none were striving for a natural body fat level, since their post-season weight gain was 7 kg, similar to the level that they were continually trying to shed.

Similar practices have been observed in light-weight rowers, jockeys, weight lifters and other weight-making athletes, although the situations differ slightly. The frequency of making weight varies, from weekly in sports such as horse racing and wrestling, to once or twice a year as in the case of professional boxers who prepare only for specific fights. In most weight classification sports, athletes are required to weigh in at a specified time prior to their event, ranging from one hour to the day before. Jockeys are unusual in that they must certify their weight after their performance (i.e. after the ride) and may choose to ride at a number of weight handicaps on the same day's program. However, in all other sports there is a variable period between the weigh-in and competition during which the athlete can attempt to recover from the effects of their weight-making strategies. Unfortunately, most times, full or even significant recovery is not possible due to inadequate time, or due to the gastrointestinal limits on food and fluid intake immediately prior to exercise (see Chapter 14 for issues of recovery).

Clearly there are a number of disadvantages associated with severe and rapid weight-loss techniques. In the short term, the athlete is challenged by moderate to severe levels of dehydration—on some occasions in the order of 5–10% of body mass. Depleted glycogen stores in the muscle and liver arise from low carbohydrate intake, as well as utilisation during the exercise undertaken to produce sweat loss. These factors provide a challenge to the performance of exercise (see Chapters 12 and 13). In the long term, the athlete faces issues of protein loss, inadequate nutrient intake due to erratic food patterns, and changes to hormonal and metabolic function. In some cases this may be superimposed on the problems associated with restricted energy intake and unnaturally low body fat levels. The effect on psychology cannot be underestimated. Many studies comment on the increased feelings of fatigue, anger, anxiety and depression associated with continued food stress and repeated cycles of making weight. Although in some combative sports this is rationalised as a positive factor in competition aggression, it is more likely to detract and distract from good performances.

It is easy to condemn weight-making practices—even if only on the grounds that they try to 'cheat' the original goal of matching opponents of similar capability. But from the performance view, it is not as black and white as nutritionists and scientists outside these sports might first think. There are a number of arguments from the inside of these sports that must be noted:

- While the performance of some exercise tasks, notably prolonged aerobic activity, is severely impaired by dehydration and depletion of muscle carbohydrate stores, the effects on strength are equivocal. Therefore, in some weight-making sports (e.g. weight lifting) there may be a smaller penalty for employing dehydrating tactics.
- Performance is also affected by the environment. The performance of sports involving prolonged activity in the heat will be greatly affected (e.g. a light-weight rowing competition conducted in a hot climate). However, the penalty will be less for a sport of short duration that is conducted in cool surroundings (e.g. a weight-lifting event carried out in an air-conditioned theatre).
- In a few sports there is considerable opportunity for recovery. In many professional boxing matches, the contestants weigh in on the day before the match.
- In most of these sports, absolute performance is not the issue. Rather, success is judged in comparison to other contestants. Although weight-making strategies may reduce the performance of an individual, they may still be successful relative to their opponents. This is particularly relevant to combative sports. The culture of those involved in wrestling, judo and other 'one-on-one' competitions is that a larger person will maintain a strength and reach advantage over a smaller opponent despite performance losses due to 'making weight'. Also, the nature of the event allows a stronger competitor to play to this advantage rather than their weakness. For example, they may use their superiority to force an early end to the match with a fall or knock-out rather than allow the effects of dehydration to compromise their endurance. Research is needed to prove whether this theory is true.
- Finally, in some sports there are few weight divisions. Athletes in these sports will find it harder to find their true body weight division. And there will be a number of 'borderline' cases who are too small for an open category but significantly heavier than the lower division (e.g. open rowing versus light-weight rowing). For these athletes the choice is to 'size down' or not to compete at all.

Nevertheless, the extreme levels and techniques of current weight-making practices cannot be condoned. They persist despite the continued attention of medical, educational and research bodies, because they have been internalised and even romanticised within the cultures of the sports. The issues are too specific to the individual athlete and to their sport to provide general strategies that are of use. Instead, it is recommended that athletes in weight-making sports receive individual expert advice about determining their optimal competition weight division and achieving it with minimal compromise to their success or health. Meanwhile, the governing bodies and expert panels in these sports might consider that education strategies are ineffective without reinforcement from appropriate regulations and rule changes. For example, in wrestling, at least one state organisation in the United States has proposed or undertaken rule modifications to discourage severe weight-making practices. These include the certification of athletes at a weight division at the beginning of a season, measuring the level of hydration in competitors before the event, distributing weight divisions to better match the typical distribution of body mass in the sports population, and making the weigh-in closer to the event to prevent the notion of post-weigh-in recovery. Such strategies may be necessary to enforce safer athlete practice.

LOSING BODY FAT

Many people might think it strange that a book on sports nutrition needs to contain a section on fat loss. Shouldn't regular exercise keep an athlete in trim? However, being overfat, whether real or imaginary, is the major dietary concern of athletes. Female athletes suffer typical female fears and misconceptions about their body image, regardless of their sporting excellence. The issues of body fatness and performance that have been previously discussed are an additional angle, and occupational pressure, for both sexes.

Athletes may have a number of valid reasons for intentionally promoting a loss of body fat. Sometimes this is to augment their genetics and training to arrive at a lower body fat level that may promote better performance. Athletes in 'aesthetic sports' experience a particular mismatch between their body fat goals and their energy expenditure. In these sports, low body fat levels are regarded as necessary for optimal performance, yet these athletes are not assisted to achieve these levels through their typical training activities. Although they are committed to long hours of training, these primarily involve skill, flexibility, strength and short bursts of high-intensity work.

Another common case is the athlete who has gained body fat and may desire to regain their original ideal level. This can occur when there is a sudden change in the factors that determine an athlete's energy balance. For example, when an athlete suffers an injury or comes to the end of their season, they usually incur a dramatic reduction in activity levels. It is hard to respond immediately with an equal reduction in food energy intake. In fact, this is a time when many athletes are tempted to eat more. The result is a rapid gain of body fat. Athletes who are faced with a new or changing lifestyle often increase their food intake without realising the change in energy balance. This includes the travelling athlete who eats out of 'hotels and suitcases', the young athlete who leaves home to take up a sporting contract or scholarship, or the athlete who moves into an 'all you can eat' dining hall in an athletes village. Of course, some athletes in skill-based sports have reasons unrelated to sports for losing body fat—such as health, comfort or appearance.

The key to loss of body fat is to achieve a long-term scenario where energy intake is lower than energy output. Guidelines are provided in the panel on the following pages.

GUIDELINES FOR LOSING BODY FAT

- Identify 'ideal' body fat and body mass targets which are consistent with good health and performance, and are achievable. This will be individual to each athlete. It often requires professional advice from a sports scientist or nutritionist to set realistic targets since the athlete may be pressured by coaches, peers or the culture of body fat obsession.
- If loss of body fat is required, plan for a realistic rate loss of about 0.5 kg per week. It is a good idea to set both short-term and long-term goals.
- Organise your program so that fat loss can be achieved in a reasonable time-frame, and during a period where any side-effects or pressures are unimportant. For example, take care of this activity at the beginning of pre-season training (or even before) so that it is not an issue during important competitions.
- Examine current exercise and activity patterns. If training is primarily skill or technique-based, or a sedentary lifestyle between training sessions is observed, the athlete may benefit from scheduling in some

aerobic exercise activities. This should always be done in conjunction with the coach. Some athletes live a 'couch potato' lifestyle between training sessions and may be able to increase the energy cost of incidental activities.

- Keep a food diary for a week and take an objective look at your real eating patterns. Many athletes who feel that they 'hardly eat anything' will be amazed at their hidden or unintentional eating activities. Simple changes to prune unnecessary eating or unneeded portion sizes can make a long-term difference.

- Reduce typical energy intake by an amount that is appropriate to produce loss of body fat (e.g. 500–1000 kcal or 2–4 MJ/per day) but still ensures adequate food and nutrient intake. An athlete should not reduce their energy intake below 1200–1500 kcal/day (4–6 MJ per day) unless supervised by a sports dietitian. Meals should not be skipped. Instead, food should be spread over the day, particularly to allow for efficient refuelling after training sessions and to avoid the discomfort of hunger.

- Target occasions when you find yourself overeating. Useful techniques include making meals filling by choosing high-fibre forms of foods, and fighting the need to finish everything on the plate. People often overeat when they are hungry, or are eating 'on the run'. A well-chosen snack before training or in the afternoon can take the edge off evening hunger. Take the time to slow down and eat, even when you are busy. Your brain and your stomach both need to enjoy the experience of eating.

- Find ways to reduce intake of fats and oils.
  — Choose low-fat versions of meats, and trim all fat and skin.
  — Switch to low-fat and reduced-fat dairy products.
  — Minimise added fats and oils in food preparation (e.g. dressings, added butter and margarine, cream, fatty sauces).
  — Use cooking techniques that minimise the addition of fats and oils.
  — Enjoy high-fat snacks and sweet foods as occasional treats rather than everyday foods.
  — Select lower-fat versions of takeaway foods.

- Show moderation with alcohol and, in some cases, sugar since these may represent less nutritious sources of kilojoules. Since alcohol intake is associated with relaxation, it is often associated with unwise eating. Sugary foods and drinks may be useful to meet carbohydrate goals in some situations—for example, using a sports drink during exercise. Take advantage of these uses, but otherwise focus on bulkier and more nutrient-dense carbohydrate-rich foods.

- Focus on nutrient-rich foods so that nutrient needs can be met from fewer kilocalories. A broad-range low-dose vitamin/mineral supplement should be considered if energy intake is to be restricted below 1500 kcal/day (6 MJ/day) for prolonged periods.

- Be aware of inappropriate eating behaviour. This includes eating when bored or upset, or eating too quickly. Stress or boredom should be handled using alternative activities.
- Be wary of fad diets and supplements that promise weight loss. There are no special pills, potions or products that produce safe and effective weight loss. If something sounds too good to be true, it probably is.
- Consult a dietitian if you are having difficulties with your weight-loss goals, or would like a supervised program. Expert advice is needed for those who are struggling with an eating disorder or disordered eating behaviour.
- Making weight is another area that deserves individual and expert attention. In many cases, athletes walk a fine line between achieving their performance goals, and actually harming their health and performance. Finding a way to stay on the right side of the balance will be individual to the athlete and their situation.

GAINING MUSCLE MASS

In many sports, a high level of muscle mass and strength are important factors in performance. Methods to gain these have intrigued the sports nutrition world and muscle industry alike for most of this century. The key ingredients for success are:

- genetic potential;
- an appropriate resistance-training program; and
- a positive energy balance—intake of more kilojoules than are being expended.

Despite the interest in protein and muscle growth (see the panel on the following pages), the most important nutritional factor required for an increase in muscle mass is energy. Although protein is laid down to form muscle cells and other cells which support the new tissue, this accounts for only a small amount each day. It is the energy cost of building new tissue, and the cost of doing the exercise to stimulate its growth, that are most important. Inadequate amounts of carbohydrate to fuel the training, and inadequate energy intake, will both impair the rate of increase in lean body mass. Although it is understood that additional amounts of some minerals and other micronutrients are needed in the manufacture and support of new tissue, there are no systematic studies to quantify these additional requirements. It is generally deemed that a high-energy diet sufficient to promote the gain of lean body mass will contain additional levels of micronutrients. Further research is necessary to define the nutrient intakes that optimise gain of muscle mass. In the meantime, the most practical issue is to help athletes increase their total energy intake to a positive balance. This can be difficult for athletes who are already high energy consumers. The battle is against gastrointestinal comfort and finding time to consume kilojoules in an already overcommitted timetable. Guidelines are summarised in the panel on the following pages.

> GUIDELINES FOR INCREASING
> MUSCLE MASS AND ACHIEVING A
> HIGH-ENERGY DIET

- Follow a progressive resistance training program that will stimulate muscle development and growth.
- Set goals for weight and strength gain that are practical and achievable. Increases in body mass of 2–4 kg per month are generally considered a good return.
- Be organised. In order to increase your intake of food and to supply a daily energy surplus of approximately 500–1000 kcal (2–4 MJ), eating often requires the same dedication as training. This additional food should supply carbohydrate to fuel the training sessions, and adequate protein and micronutrients for the development and support of new tissue.
- Increase the number of times that you eat rather than the size of meals. This will enable greater intake of food with less risk of 'overfilling' and gastrointestinal discomfort, and will require a supply of nutritious high-carbohydrate snacks to be available between meals, particularly after training sessions.
- Increase the energy content of bulky carbohydrate-rich foods by adding sugar or low-fat protein. For example, jams and syrups may be added to toast or pancakes, and sandwiches may have two or three fillings. This adds extra kilocalories to a nutritious meal, without adding greatly to the volume of the food.
- Avoid excessive intake of fibre, and include the use of 'white' cereals with less bulk (e.g. white rice, white bread). It is impractical to consume a diet that is solely based on wholegrain and high-fibre foods.
- High-energy fluids such as milk shakes, fruit smoothies or commercial liquid meal supplements are useful. These drinks provide a compact

and low-bulk source of energy and nutrients, and can be consumed with meals or as snacks—including before or after a training session.

- Don't be surprised if you are not eating as much—or, more importantly, as often—as you think. Many athletes fail to gain weight yet report 'constant eating'. However, commitments such as training, sleep, medical/physiotherapy appointments, work or school often get in the way of eating opportunities. A food record will identify the hours and occasions of minimal food intake. This information should be used to reorganise the day, or to find creative ways to make nutritious foods and drinks part of the activity.

EATING DISORDERS AND DISORDERED EATING

There are many reports of athletes who set unrealistic fat loss goals; either seeking to achieve an unnecessarily low or harmful body weight or body fat level or trying to achieve it in an unacceptably rapid time. The pressure to set these goals comes from a number of sources. Athletes by nature are obsessive. The same personal characteristics that encourage good performance in athletes—perfectionism, dedication, 'tunnel vision', ability to deprive themselves—may lead them to overfocus on body fatness. Parents, peers, trainers and coaches are guilty of providing additional pressure and incorrect advice. In some cases of high-profile athletes, their physique (or perceived physique) may become public property via concentrated media attention. Simply being female carries a risk of being dissatisfied with one's body image.

Although there is some criticism of the methodology used in making diagnoses of 'eating disorders', many studies report a high prevalence of disordered eating behaviour and body image among athletes. More specifically, they observe a higher prevalence of these problems in female athletes and those involved in sports in which weight and body fat is an issue, than in sedentary controls or among sports in which weight/fatness is not a performance issue. The exact extent of this is unknown, as is the nature of the link with sport. It is likely that sport provides a permissive environment for the development of disorders in those who are prone. While some individuals obsessed with body fat seem capable of stopping disordered food and exercise behaviours once they are removed from the environment (e.g. at the end of a season or when they retire from sport), for others these behaviours become the *end*, rather than a *means to an end*. In other words, they lose control. Equally, there may be cases where individuals with existing eating disorders turn to sport because it camouflages and supports behaviour such as food restriction, low body fat levels and high energy expenditure. In fact, for a while it may promote good athletic performance! Many sports are currently examining ways to reduce the pressured environment that may contribute to the development of eating disorders, and to develop effective and early treatment for athletes who develop disordered eating and body image problems. Eating disorders in male athletes are also recognised.

The prevalence of cases that meet the full diagnostic criteria of anorexia nervosa or bulimia nervosa as set by psychiatric bodies remains low in sport. Instead there are a larger number of athletes who fit within the spectrum of eating behaviour between 'normal' and 'clinical eating disorder', but lie closer to the latter end. 'Anorexia athletica' or 'disordered eating' are terms sometimes given to describe these situations. The athlete is obsessed and dissatisfied with their body weight and fat levels, is driven to undertake unhealthy eating and exercise patterns while striving for an unhealthy or unnatural body fat level, and will persist with these behaviours despite the occurrence of obvious side-effects and problems. Indeed, this may be seen as an occupational hazard or a common personality trait of athletes competing at elite levels—in other words, it is 'normal' or necessary. However typical or common it appears, the side-effects must be recognised and minimised. More importantly, it is also a common occurrence at non-elite levels where it cannot be justified as one of the sacrifices that is undertaken for the reward and glory of excellence.

A striking feature of many dietary surveys is that female athletes often report energy intakes that seem too low to be true. Their kilojoule intake would seem able to sustain only their basal metabolic requirements without the added energy cost of a heavy training program. Some people have suggested that this 'energy discrepancy' is due to metabolic efficiency— that these athletes have lower basal metabolic requirements or have somehow lowered the energy expenditure of their training and lifestyle activities. Maybe this is true for certain individuals. There is some evidence and a believable hypothesis that the body will try to defend its 'natural' or critical lower level of body fat, particularly the sensitive body fat stores on the thighs and buttocks of females, in this way.

But the methodology of dietary survey work is famous for

being inexact. It is well-known that people under-report their food intake when keeping food records. Either they under-estimate the portions of food that they are eating and forget to record everything that was consumed, or they eat less than usual during the period of recording. Everyone does it, but it is possible that those who are more 'body conscious' do it to an even greater extent, thus exaggerating the extent of the energy discrepancy. A recent energy balance study on elite female runners by Dr Jeffrey Edwards and colleagues from Indiana University has provided data to support this. They measured the match between energy intake (estimated from seven-day food records) and energy expenditure over the same period (estimated using the double-labelled water technique). They found that mean daily intake only accounted for 70% of expenditure (8.5 MJ versus 12.5 MJ), yet none of the subjects lost body fat or weight over this time. This could indicate that the subjects were metabolically efficient and the double-labelled water technique overestimated their real expen-diture. But an anomaly in the group data stood out. There was an inverse relationship between body mass and the size of the energy discrepancy. That is, the heavier the athlete, the *less* they ate compared to their estimated energy expenditure. These athletes also had the poorest body images. It seems that the more stressed an athlete is about their body fat and body size, the more they are likely to underreport their intake—sometimes by as much as 50% of their intake.

Evidence of an 'energy drain' in an athlete may be important. The athlete who eats less than they 'deserve' or struggles to keep low body fat levels on a restricted intake may directly encounter some hormonal and metabolic side-effects from their efforts. But equally, this may be a warning sign that the athlete has a disturbed body image, poor recognition of their real dietary intake, and a tendency to cycle between dietary restriction and dietary excess. The combination of metabolic stress, nutritional stress and psychological stress can lead to real problems.

The female athlete triad

The existence of the 'female athlete triad' has recently been proposed to publicise the cluster of medical/nutritional problems that are frequently found together in female athletes. These are:

- eating disorders or disordered eating;
- amenorrhoea (disturbed menstrual function); and
- osteopaenia (reduced bone density).

These problems are of considerable consequence to the health and performance of the athlete. The development of strategic programs to minimise risk factors for their development, and to intervene with early and effective treatment, deserves support. However, there is some danger in turning the situation into a neat triangle, with the idea that simple solutions can be found. Each of these disorders is complex, with a multitude of causes that seem to vary in importance according to the individual athlete. And they can exist alone. One doesn't necessarily lead to another. Furthermore, male athletes may also suffer from two of the three elements of the triad.

The issue of menstrual disturbances in female athletes has received much attention in the last decade. It is now realised that numerous factors predispose to this, including:

- a history of menstrual irregularities prior to sport;
- the onset of heavy training before regular periods had been established;
- an excessive level or a sudden increase in training volume or intensity;
- excessive or sudden loss of body fat, especially from important body sites (thighs, buttocks);
- emotional stress;
- disordered eating; and
- general 'energy drain' syndrome, which encapsulates some or all of the previous four factors.

Each athlete seems to have a critical threshold for each of these factors. For example, some athletes continue to have regular periods while training hard and having very low body fat levels. It is important to recognise the individuality of the response to these factors. A common outcome of menstrual irregularity is the decrease in level of reproductive hormones, particularly estrogen. Since estrogen levels play an influential role in maintenance of bone health, it has been easy to demonstrate a general loss of bone density, or failure to gain optimal bone deposition, in female athletes with menstrual disturbances. This condition, called osteopaenia, is also multi-factorial with risk factors including race, small frame size, low calcium intake and inadequate bone loading. Interestingly, gymnasts are a group at high risk of impaired menstrual function—usually due to a failure to establish menses in the first place. However, their training appears to provide strong mechanical loading stress on the bone which compensates for a low estrogen environment. By contrast, amenorrhoeic female runners generally present with low bone density.

Low bone density is of concern to athletes in that it may predispose them to the development of stress fractures. And in the long term it may dramatically increase the risk and the earlier development of osteoporosis—the condition of fragile bone density that occurs with the ageing process. Athletes are generally more concerned with the here and now of their bone health. Again, the picture of stress fractures is complex. Low bone density is a plausible risk factor, but it interacts with other factors directly related to the impact on the bone. These include the amount and the change in training, cushioning provided by shoes, the surface on which training is undertaken, and the biomechanics of footstrike.

Clearly, the prevention and management of each of these issues is delicate and complicated. Individual attention from the appropriate experts is recommended.

Calcium intake and healthy bones

Bone is a living tissue that is continually breaking down and reforming. Sports science now recognises that hormonal status, particularly in females, plays a major role in the balance of bone remodelling. Nevertheless, a low calcium intake is one of the factors that may be involved in the development of osteopaenia. Adequate calcium intake helps to ensure gain in bone mass during adolescence and early adult life, and to minimise the bone loss that occurs with ageing. Recommended dietary intakes for calcium are set to provide additional calcium during times of increased need, such as growth, pregnancy and breastfeeding. It may be useful to provide higher calcium intakes to females with low estrogen levels to reduce the calcium drain. Therefore, an increased target is suggested for post-menopausal women and for athletes with absent or irregular periods. Recommended daily intakes for calcium are summarised in Table 11.1.

In a typical Western diet, dairy foods provide 60–75% of total calcium intake. Athletes who fail to consume enough or any dairy foods are at risk of inadequate calcium intake, unless alternative sources can be found. Low-energy consumers are one such group. Meanwhile, dairy products have received undeserved criticism and have been unnecessarily avoided by

TABLE 11.1

Calcium content of foods compared with daily calcium requirements of athletes

Recommended calcium intakes

Athlete	mg/day
• growing males (12–18 years)	1000–1200
• growing females (12–18 years)	1000
• adult males and females	800
• pregnancy (trimester 3)	1100
• breastfeeding	1200
• post-menopausal	1000
• amenorrhoeic athletes	1000

Calcium-rich foods for the athlete

Foods	Serve	mg calcium
Skim milk	200 ml glass	250
Buttermilk	200 ml glass	285
Calcium fortified low-fat Milk	200 ml glass	320
Whole milk	200 ml glass	230
Flavoured milk	250 ml carton	270
Reduced-fat cheese slice	20 g slice	220
Cheddar cheese slice	20 g slice	160
Cottage cheese	100 g (1/2 cup)	80
Ricotta cheese	100 g (1/2 cup)	225
Low-fat fruit yoghurt	200 g carton	360
Low-fat natural yoghurt	200 g carton	420
Light fromage frais	200 g carton	120
Custard	140 g (1/2 cup)	140
Low-fat icecream	60 g (2 tabsp)	80
Fortified soft-serve icecream or yoghurt	100 ml	300–400
Normal soft-serve yoghurt/icecream	100 ml	80
Pink salmon with bones	100 g (drained weight)	310
Anchovies	3 thin (15 g)	165
Sardines	100 g (drained weight)	380
Oysters	120 g (= 12)	135
Soy milk	200 ml glass	80
Fortified soy milk (e.g. So Good)	200 ml glass	220
Tofu	100 g	130
Tahini	20 g (tabsp)	70
Almonds	50 g	110
Parsley	1 tabsp (5 g)	190
Spinach	95 g cooked (1/2 cup)	85
Skim milk powder	1 tabsp (11 g)	140
Sustagen Sport Powder	1 scoop (25 g)	200

Source: NUTTAB 1995, Australian Department of Community Services and Health. National Health and Medical Research Council. *Recommended dietary intakes for use in Australia*, Canberra: AGPS, 1991.

groups worried about fat and cholesterol intake, 'allergies' or 'mucous formation'. While some vegans avoid dairy products for ethical or cultural reasons, there are few other causes to delete these calcium-rich choices from their eating plans. Strategies for achieving a calcium intake target within the athlete's total nutritional goals are summarised in the panel on the following pages.

GUIDELINES FOR PROMOTING CALCIUM-RICH EATING

- Eat at least three serves of high-calcium dairy foods each day. In the case of groups with higher calcium needs, aim for a regular dairy intake of four to five serves. High-calcium dairy foods include milk, yoghurt and cheese. Low-fat or reduced-fat versions are the best choice for those who are conscious of total energy intake or carbohydrate needs. Build these foods into everyday eating patterns.
- Be aware that some dairy foods are not particularly calcium-rich. These include cottage cheese, and many brands of soft-serve icecream and yoghurt. Fromage frais is significantly lower in calcium than yoghurt. These foods may be a good dietary choice for other reasons—for example, they may be a valuable source of protein or other nutrients, but ensure that you don't solely rely on these for a calcium boost. Cream is technically considered to be a dairy food but provides minimum calcium or other nutrient value.
- People who are lactose intolerant can still consume dairy foods. Yoghurt and cheese have low lactose levels. It is also possible to buy milk that has had the lactose 'pre-digested', or tablets that can perform this task in your own milk (e.g. Lactaid). Even so, lactose intolerance is rarely absolute. Many 'sufferers' can still tolerate small amounts of lactose-containing foods, especially when they are consumed with other foods as part of a meal.
- True allergies to cow's milk are rare and most babies who suffer from allergies or intolerances outgrow these in early childhood. There is no evidence to support 'old wives' tales' about milk causing mucous formation.
- There are many ways that dairy foods can be added to a high-carbohydrate diet or be incorporated into a carbohydrate-rich meal. Clever combinations include breakfast cereal with milk, fruit salad with flavoured yoghurt, a sandwich or pizza made with reduced-fat cheese, fruit–milk smoothies, or sweetened desserts made with milk (e.g. rice pudding).
- Vegans and those athletes with cow's milk allergies must find calcium-rich alternatives to replace dairy foods. Fortified soy products such

as enriched soy milks and other soy products are good choices, but they must be incorporated into daily eating plans to be of value.

- Other foods such as fish eaten with bones, nuts and seeds, and some vegetables and legumes provide an additional source of calcium to supplement the dairy or soy food base.

- Generally, athletes with higher calcium requirements who are unable or unwilling to consume adequate dairy products should seek the expert advice of a sports dietitian to find acceptable ways to meet their calcium needs. This is especially important in the case of athletes with menstrual irregularities, but any eating plan must be supported by a total management plan.

- Calcium supplements may be recommended in the case of high calcium requirements (particularly in low-estrogen states), or when athletes are unable to meet calcium intake targets from food sources. In most cases, this will be part of an overall dietary strategy. Seek expert advice rather than self-medicate.

CAN YOU SWIM TO LOSE BODY FAT—OR SINK IN THE ATTEMPT?

There seems to be something fishy in the connection between body fat and swimming. In a study where people undertook daily swimming as a fat-loss activity, not only was it unsuccessful, but many subjects actually increased their body fat levels! Competitive swimmers typically complete 4000–15,000 m per day in training, which theoretically burns several thousand kilojoules. However, the typical body fat levels of these athletes are significantly higher than those of runners or cyclists who expend similar or even smaller amounts of energy in their daily training. The battle that many female swimmers endure with their body fat levels (and their coaches) is well-known. They are generally prescribed 'land training' (running or cycling) in addition to their many laps of the pool in the belief that it is a necessary treatment to produce lower skinfold levels.

Two studies from Professor Dave Costill's lab at Ball State University, Indiana, have tried to pinpoint whether these energy discrepancies really exist in swimming, and to explain why swimmers seem to have drawn the short straw of body fat management. The first study attempted to gain a crude measure of daily energy balance, comparing collegiate swimmers and collegiate distance runners. Ten athletes of each sex from each sport participated in the study by keeping detailed food records (for three days) and activity records (for one day). The activity records, which were only kept by half of the groups, noted the time each individual spent sleeping, sitting, walking, standing or training. The energy cost of these was estimated for each athlete by duplicating the activity in the laboratory and collecting oxygen consumption data. This factor was multiplied by the time spent in each activity to produce an estimate of total daily energy expenditure. Body fat levels were lower in the runners by about 5% (7% versus 12% for male runners versus swimmers, and 15% versus 20% for females).

The results showed similar daily energy intakes reported by both groups: 3380 kilocalories and 3460 kilocalories for male swimmers and runners, and 2490 kilocalories and 2040 kilocalories for female swimmers and runners, respectively. Estimated energy output seemed to be in agreement for each group, with the values for the male athletes being equal and similar to their reported intake. The female swimmers were estimated to have a higher energy expenditure than female runners, and in fact appeared to be in slight negative energy balance. These results were not helpful in finding or explaining an energy dilemma, or major differences between types of athletes.

What we might have expected to see, based on various theories and observations, is:

- Swimmers have higher energy intakes than other athletes and take in more energy than they expend. It has been suggested that swimming doesn't cause the appetite drop that accompanies heavy running and cycling training. Many people observe that they feel like 'eating a horse' after they have finished a swim training session, and may overcompensate for the energy they have just burned. Some research suggests that this is due to the cool temperatures in which swimmers train. By contrast, runners and cyclists usually experience an increase in body temperature during training, which may serve to suppress appetite—at least in the short term. Although this effect does occur in some individuals, it wasn't reported in this group.
- Swimmers are less active outside their training sessions. They are so tired from the hours spent training that they sleep, sit or otherwise avoid any real energy expenditure outside their sessions. Again this is an anecdotal observation that may be true of individual swimmers, but wasn't observed in this particular study.

One of the limitations of this study is that each method of measuring the energy balance is subject to considerable flaws. It is almost impossible to measure usual energy intake from diaries. Apart from the errors in translating descriptions of food into calorie counts, it is unlikely that people eat 'normally' while they are recording. It is well-known that those who are conscious of their body fat underreport their food intake. It is also hard to complete and describe 'normal' by record. Maybe, on paper, athletes try to appear as 'good' as possible and thereby cover up the clues to any energy balance problems. The behaviour of individuals may also be masked by the 'averaging' of results.

Another investigation, under the leadership of Dr Mike Flynn, examined energy and fuel usage during training sessions and recovery in swimming and running. These scientists theorised that differences in hormonal patterns and the oxidation of fat might explain differences in body fat levels. Swimmers and runners did their specialised activity for 45 minutes at 75–80% $\dot{V}O_{2max}$, then recovered for two hours. Triathletes did one session of each, so that results could be compared within the same individual. During these periods, blood hormone levels, glucose and fatty acid levels, and gas exchange were measured. Thus the oxidation of various body fuels was monitored.

The results showed that there were no differences in total energy expenditure during training or recovery between groups. There were some differences in substrate utilisation and hormone levels. For example, swimming resulted in lower blood glucose levels than running, with some evidence of a greater reliance on carbohydrate as a fuel during swimming. This is likely to be further accentuated in the real-life training of swimmers who undertake a high proportion of high-intensity interval work. During recovery, fat oxidation tended to be greater after swimming than running. Overall, these differences were small, and could not explain why swimmers have higher body fat levels.

So, while theories abound, none can verify or explain a real difference. Perhaps a final idea that needs to be explored is whether a selection process is at hand. Elite swimmers may be predisposed to have higher body fat levels because it is a help, or at least less of a disadvantage, to their swimming. Rounded shoulders and smooth curves may be more biomechanically sound than bony angles. At least up to a point before the extra weight of body fat becomes a negative drag. And since higher body fat levels are a greater disadvantage to weight-bearing sports like running, perhaps those that are even slightly genetically inclined, but otherwise possessed of high-level endurance qualities, headed for the water at an early age!

PROTEIN: ENOUGH IS ENOUGH!

For a long time, sports nutrition has been fixated on protein—and the question of how much is enough. Early athletes ate whole beasts in order to gain their attributes of strength and speed. Later logic said that muscle, being largely protein, needed more of itself to grow bigger or replenish after exercise. After all, early studies of exercise metabolism mistakenly reported that protein was the major fuel during muscular activity. After the 1960s when muscle biopsy studies revealed the real story, endurance athletes turned their attention to carbohydrate. In fact, with carbohydrate-loading and Pritikin diets, protein was very much an afterthought for this group.

However, strength-training athletes stayed true to their protein supplements, raw eggs and big meals of meat. If anything, they increased their debate against the scientists who stated that the exercise had no effect on protein requirements. Scientists said that athletes could live by the protein RDIs (Recommended Dietary Intakes) of sedentary people— approximately 1 gram per kilogram of body mass (BM) per day. Meanwhile the view from Eastern Bloc muscle builders was that three to four times this intake was needed to enhance strength and size gains. For many years there seemed no way of bridging this gap.

Some meeting of the minds was reached in the late 1980s following more detailed research. The outcome was that both groups needed to shift towards middle ground.

- Endurance athletes undertaking heavy training have a significant increase in protein requirements. This is needed to cover a small proportion of the fuel costs of their training, and to assist in the repair and recovery processes afterwards. Protein requirements increase when carbohydrate is in short supply to the muscle, or when the athlete is in energy drain. So athletes with extreme exercise loads (e.g. Tour de France cyclists) can experience greatly increased protein needs. Revised protein recommendations for endurance-trained athletes are:

    general training = 1 g per kg per day
    heavy training = 1.2–1.6 g per kg per day
    extreme exercise loads = 2 g per kg per day.

- Strength-training athletes need additional protein for exercise fuel, for repair and recovery, and to increase their muscle mass. Their major interest is in the latter. However, the additional protein needed to build new muscle is quite small. There is insubstantial evidence to support that greatly increased protein intakes increase the rate of muscle growth. The revised protein recommendations for strength-training athletes are:
    — heavy training = 1.2–1.7 g per kg per day.

- Athletes who are growing must meet these needs in addition to sports-related requirements. Protein requirements for adolescent athletes undergoing a growth spurt are:
    — 2 grams per kilogram per day.

So, what does this mean to the meal practices of athletes? Is it time to throw out the pasta in favour of a side of beef? Is there a need for the latest body-building supplements with their 'ion-exchange whey protein hydrolysates' and 'free form amino acid enhancement'? Typically, no. Dietary surveys of athletes report that most groups already meet these targets simply by eating a high-energy diet and maintaining protein in the usual ratio that we eat it. Generally, protein accounts for about 12–15% of the energy in the Westernised diet. Athletes on low-energy diets, or those who eat fad diets that exclude animal foods and cereal foods, may find themselves with a low protein intake. However, average intakes of protein range from 70 to 200 g a day, or about 1–2 g per kg of BM in endurance-based athletes, and higher levels again in protein-conscious athletes such as body builders. In other words, most athletes are already eating more than enough protein, and those that are missing out are probably in need of a general dietary overhaul.

TABLE 11.2

Protein-rich foods for the athlete

Animal foods	2 small eggs
	300 ml reduced- or low-fat milk
	30 g (1.5 slices) of reduced-fat cheese
	70 g cottage cheese
	200 g carton non-fat fruit yoghurt
	150 g light fromage frais
	35 g lean beef, lamb or pork (cooked weight)
	40 g lean chicken (cooked weight)
	50 g grilled fish
	50 g canned tuna or salmon
Vegetable foods	4 sl (120 g) wholemeal bread
	3 cups (90 g) wholegrain cereal
	2 cups (300 g) cooked pasta
	3 cups (400 g) cooked rice
	3/4 cup (150g) lentils or kidney beans
	200 g (small tin) baked beans
	120 g tofu or soy meat
	400 ml soy milk
	60 g nuts or seeds
Supplements (expensive versions)	10,000 mg amino acids
	15–20 g high-protein powder or protein hydolysate
Alternatives to expensive supplements	150–200 ml homemade fruit smoothie
	150 ml liquid meal supplement
	40 g Sustagen Sport Powder
	20 g skim milk powder

Note: Each food serve provides approximately 10 grams of protein and fits other dietary goals such as keeping fat intake to moderate levels. Many of these food choices are rich in other nutrients.

Source: NUTTAB 1995, Australian Department of Community Services and Health.

Table 11.2 provides a ready reckoner of the protein content of foods, showing how easy it is to reach protein intake targets from a variety of food sources. When a protein-rich food is added to a carbohydrate-based meal, many other nutrient goals fall into place simultaneously. Now that athletes of all types can 'meet in the middle' on their protein issue, there is room for some to broaden their menu plans to work on these nutritious food combinations and varieties. Some can now feel safe to trim back the serve size of their obvious protein-rich choices and include more fuel-rich foods. Others need to reacquaint themselves with protein-rich foods and expand the nutrient value and variety within a carbohydrate-rich meal. Supplements have a role when an athlete cannot find a practical way to eat sufficient food or to eat it at an important time. However, the best supplement for this situation is one that provides a total energy and nutrient boost, rather than the protein alone. The new protein supplements are fancy but become more expensive as the amount of processing and 'technology' increases. There is no justification for the additional protein or for the cost.

12

Pre-event nutrition

During competition, an athlete strives to take their body to its limits. These limits are shaped by many factors, including some of a nutritional nature. Implementing strategies to reduce or delay the effects of such factors will enhance performance. Competition nutrition is largely based on this principle. Of course, the psychology of competition eating is also important. When the athlete approaches the start of an event, they must feel confident and ready to put everything on the line. This chapter will overview the steps involved in putting together a competition eating plan, with details of the strategies of pre-event nutrition.

NUTRITIONAL FACTORS CAUSING 'FATIGUE' DURING PERFORMANCE

A variety of nutritional factors can reduce an athlete's ability to perform optimally during exercise. In common sports science language, this is termed 'fatigue' (see the panel below). The risk and severity of an encounter during competition depends on various issues, including:

- the duration and intensity of the exercise involved;
- the environmental conditions—for example, temperature and humidity;
- the fitness and training preparation of the athlete; and
- the success of nutritional strategies before and during the event.

NUTRITIONAL FACTORS
ASSOCIATED WITH FATIGUE OR A
DECLINE IN PERFORMANCE

- Depletion of muscle glycogen stores.
- Low blood sugar, causing both central nervous system fatigue and a shortage of fuel to the exercising muscle.
- Dehydration.
- Gastrointestinal discomfort and upset.
- Low blood sodium (hyponatremia).

By examining the characteristics of their event and their past experiences in competition, an athlete should be able to pinpoint which 'fatigue factors' are likely to affect their performance. Competition nutrition should involve strategies which reduce or delay the onset of these factors. A combination of pre-event and during-event tactics will generally achieve the best results. However, in practice, the athlete sometimes has to bypass or take short-cuts with tactics in one of these areas. When this occurs, greater emphasis on tactics in the other area may provide a compromise. For example, an athlete who has not been able to adequately 'fuel up' *before* a prolonged event should place greater emphasis on consuming carbohydrate *during* the event. Conversely, in some events the opportunities to drink *during* exercise are limited and fluid intake falls well below the rate of fluid loss. In this situation, the athlete should pay extra attention to hydration *before* the event starts, and perhaps even experiment with 'fluid overloading' (discussed later in this chapter). In any case, the athlete should set a total competition eating plan for each event, with nutritional strategies that complement and enhance each other.

Pre-competition nutrition can include strategies that start a week before an event, as well as special tactics undertaken just before the event begins. An athlete's plan must balance the challenges that are likely to be experienced during the event, with how much they want to invest in strategies for 'damage control'. For example, it may take days or even a week to load up maximum fuel stores before an endurance event. Such an investment is reasonable and compatible with the training program of an athlete who has one or two important competitions each year. However, if the event is just one out of a busy race schedule, or is part of a weekly fixture for a team sport, such preparation is impractical and overstated. Many athletes undertake an abridged dietary preparation before unimportant events, or between events that are sandwiched together in a tournament or weekly competition schedule. Meanwhile, full preparation is saved for single events or the most important competitions. In other words, on many occasions, 'optimal' must make way for 'most practical'.

FUELLING UP FOR EVENTS

The depletion of muscle fuels is a major cause of fatigue during exercise (see Chapter 3). Body carbohydrate stores are critical for performance of many sports, and these vary considerably with the diet and training activities of the athlete. Stocking the liver and muscles with adequate carbohydrate fuel is a high-priority task in pre-event nutrition. The key ingredients for 'fuelling up' are an exercise taper and a high-carbohydrate diet. Just how long these strategies are carried out for will depend on how much fuel the athlete wants to store. However, it may also need to be balanced by how much preparation time the athlete can afford.

General refuelling

Studies show that in the absence of muscle damage, muscle glycogen stores can be normalised by 24 hours of rest and an adequate carbohydrate intake (approximately 7–10 grams of carbohydrate for each kilogram of the athlete's body mass—BM). Scientists typically measure glycogen stores in values of mmol per kilogram of the muscle's wet weight, and the normal levels in trained athletes are 100–120 mmol/kg ww. Such stores should meet the fuel needs of most sporting activities lasting less than one hour. So, when preparing for these events, athletes should set aside 24–36 hours for refuelling. This could be as simple as scheduling a day of rest or light training before the event, while continuing to eat a high-carbohydrate diet. But not all athletes typically eat enough carbohydrate to maximise glycogen storage—particularly females who restrict their total energy intake to control body fat levels. These athletes may need to take a day off from counting kilojoules and make refuelling the dietary priority on the day before competition.

Providing the muscle with the ideal rest to refuel may also be difficult. Many athletes have to balance the priorities of immediate competition against training for a longer-term goal. It may be hard to sacrifice an important training day—for example, a long session over the weekend—just to participate in a minor event the next day. And in a tournament or stage race, there may be less than 24 hours between competition sessions. However, some athletes who continue to train hard right up to a competition do this for the wrong reasons. Sometimes it is because of false logic—'I just need one last session under my belt', or 'It's good for team morale to have a final big workout together'. Sometimes it is because athletes fear they will gain body fat even with the briefest of tapers. In most cases, the muscle will benefit more from extra time and fuel, than from an extra training session. The panel on the following pages summarises guidelines for fuelling up before competition.

GUIDELINES FOR 'FUELLING' AND 'LOADING UP' FOR COMPETITION

- Decide how long you will spend loading up your muscle fuel levels, based on the challenge provided by the upcoming event and how your preparation must fit into your overall sporting goals. For most events, a short 'fuelling-up' period of 24–36 hours may be sufficient—or at least all that you can afford. For prolonged events in excess of 90 minutes of moderate-to-high intensity exercise, particularly for key competitions, aim for an extended fuelling-up or carbohydrate-loading preparation.
- A major ingredient in the fuelling-up plan is rest or an exercise taper. Plan this strategically rather than haphazardly. There are few good reasons to keep training hard right up to an event, especially a key competition. In most situations, it is best to save your muscle fuel for race day. In the case of weekly competition, plan your training schedule so that sessions that are fuel depleting or muscle damaging (e.g. exercise involving eccentric contractions or vigorous body contact) are done mid-week. Finish off the week with lighter exercise or a pre-event rest day.
- A carbohydrate intake of 7–10 g per kg of BM is the daily target for optimal muscle fuel storage. This is more than many people typically eat—350–500 g for a 50 kg runner, or 700–1000 g for a 100 kg football player. Ready reckoners of the carbohydrate content of foods provide a quick guide to ensure that you are meeting these targets (see Chapter 10). However, if you are extending your preparation to a carbohydrate-loading strategy, it is even better to consult a sports dietitian. Expert advice can help to individualise your preparation and 'trouble shoot' any potential or previous problems.
- Your everyday training diet should already include strategies to make carbohydrate-rich foods and drinks the focus of all meals and snacks.

For some athletes, fuelling up is simply 'more of the same, plus a rest'. However, some athletes may need to increase their total kilojoule intake and/or the concentration on carbohydrate in order to meet fuel requirements. With careful planning and a good balance between priorities, this should not upset the overall nutritional plan. Problems can arise when athletes compete so frequently that they are almost in a perpetual preparation, competition and recovery cycle—for example, the professional soccer player who plays two competition matches each week over the season. Again, professional help can assist the athlete to find a balance between competition needs and overall nutrition goals.

- Since the priority during competition preparation is for carbohydrate fuel, it can make sense to de-emphasise non-carbohydrate foods to save on stomach space or kilojoules. Certainly, fatty foods should not be eaten at the expense of carbohydrate-rich foods. Some traditional loading favourites are surprisingly high in fat, so be a discerning consumer. It may also help to reduce the protein serving on your plate, and other low-carbohydrate foods such as salads and leafy vegetables, in order to put 'fuel foods' first.

- Greater emphasis on low-bulk and compact forms of carbohydrate-rich foods is also useful for fuelling up, particularly in the carbohydrate-loading situation. This makes high carbohydrate intakes more practical, as well as reducing the risk of gastrointestinal problems and discomfort. A sudden increase in the total volume or fibre content of food intake may cause diarrhoea, bloatedness or other problems. Steer towards processed or lower-fibre forms of foods—for example, 'white' bread and cereal foods rather than wholegrain forms. In particular, take greater advantage of the compactness of sugar and high-sugar foods and drinks. This is a quick and less filling strategy to increase carbohydrate intake. A couple of litres of fruit juice, sports drink, fruit smoothie or soft drink can look after the day's fluid needs while adding approximately 200 g of carbohydrate to the total intake of fuel.

- Commercially produced carbohydrate-loading supplements take the guesswork (and the chewing) out of a high-carbohydrate diet. These come in the form of neutral-tasting powders or highly concentrated drinks. Although they typically contain little other nutrient value, they provide carbohydrate in an easily measured and easily prepared form—best appreciated in fuelling-up situations.

- Eat to a plan on your loading days. A pattern of small, frequent meals and carbohydrate-rich drinks is considered an efficient way to consume high intakes. However, this requires good preparation and memory on the part of the athlete. This can be a challenge when nerves, travel and loss of routine are all part of the pre-competition scenario. Don't leave it to luck.

Carbohydrate loading

People use the term 'carbohydrate loading' to describe any-thing from fuelling up for a marathon, to rationalising a food binge of great quantity and dubious quality. Strictly speaking, carbohydrate loading refers to practices that aim to maximise muscle glycogen stores prior to competition. Athletes who do this may elevate their muscle glycogen levels from normal levels of 100–120 mmol/kg w.w. to approximately 150–200 mmol/kg. This is an important strategy for events lasting more than 90 minutes, which would otherwise deplete the muscle glycogen stores. Athletes who have 'hit the wall' during a marathon will attest to its dramatic effect on performance—it can reduce them to a crawl! Carbohydrate loading doesn't allow the athlete to run faster, but to run at their optimal pace for a longer time. Removing or delaying the fuel crisis will help the athlete to sustain their power output or speed. This translates into a faster overall race time or, in the case of team sports, the ability to keep running in the last quarter of the game. Consuming carbohydrate during the event may also assist with this goal.

The carbohydrate loading technique currently in favour is known as a 'modified' loading strategy. The original carbohy-drate loading technique on which it is based was devised by Scandinavian physiologists in the 1960s, from research on healthy people rather than well-trained athletes. These pion-eering studies involved a seven-day protocol, starting with a three-to-four day 'depletion' phase of hard training and a low carbohydrate intake, and finishing with a three-to-four day 'loading' phase of high consumption of carbohydrates and an exercise taper. This technique empties the glycogen stores of the working muscles, stimulating the activity of the glycogen synthase enzyme involved in glycogen synthesis. With rest and a high carbohydrate intake, the once-depleted muscle glycogen stores bounce back to above normal levels and increase their potential exercise capacity.

It was largely the work of Dr Mike Sherman and Professor Dave Costill, undertaken at Ball State University in the United States in the early 1980s, that created the modification or simplification of this pioneering strategy. Dr Sherman showed that well-trained athletes are able to overload their muscle glycogen stores without a depletion or 'glycogen stripping' phase. The runners in their study elevated their muscle glycogen stores with three days of taper and a high carbohydrate intake, regardless of whether this was preceded by a 'depletion' phase or a more typical diet and training preparation. In other words, for well-trained athletes at least, carbohydrate loading is simply a matter of extending the practice of 'fuelling up' (rest and carbohydrate) over three-to-four days.

Although carbohydrate loading is so well-known that it has entered everyday language, it seems difficult for athletes to master even in its modified form. At least one study has shown that in real life, athletes may not have the knowledge to plan a taper, or the discipline *not* to train hard for three-to-four days. Furthermore, they may fail to reach the daily carbohydrate intake targets of 7–10 g per kg BM. Even when they can describe the research behind carbohydrate loading and name the enzyme involved in glycogen synthesis! And even when their success and enjoyment of a high-investment competition lies in the balance. Common reasons for inadequate carbohydrate intake in everyday eating are discussed in Chapter 15. These may also apply to competition preparation. However, some issues specifically related to carbohydrate loading deserve comment.

The tradition of regarding carbohydrate loading as 'pigging out' is widespread, but misguided. Some athletes use this period to eat large quantities of what they consider to be 'junk foods'—for example, takeaway foods and rich desserts. These foods often feature a greater fat than carbohydrate content. As a result, carbohydrate intake can be less than optimal—and sometimes even less than the athlete eats in their everyday diet. Some sports events provide carbohydrate loading banquets and parties for their competitors. Although the atmosphere is great, the menus are not always well-chosen.

Many athletes find it hard to depart from the nutritional beliefs that guide their everyday eating, even though they understand that their dietary goals while loading are different. Many feel that all foods must be wholesome and minimally processed to offer any nutritional value, and sugar has a bad reputation in some circles. However, a loading diet that relies heavily on bulky and high-fibre carbohydrate foods is difficult to eat in the volume required to meet fuel intake targets. And it may cause the athlete gastrointestinal upsets and feelings of bloatedness. Compact fuel sources are the priority during competition preparation. Some athletes need encouragement, and even 'permission', to modify their everyday food choices and load up on low-fibre, more highly processed carbohydrate sources. Sugar-added or sugar-rich foods and drinks are often overlooked or underutilised—even sports drinks and special carbohydrate loading products. It is hard to break away from lifetime prejudices, particularly when they are based on weight and body fat phobias.

While carbohydrate loading, many athletes travel interstate or overseas to their competitions, and undertake their dietary preparation away from the familiarity of their kitchens or local supermarket and restaurants. Travelling athletes can find it difficult to cope with new food choices or a new eating routine and may fail to eat sufficient carbohydrate.

Guidelines for fuelling up and a carbohydrate loading menu guide are presented in the panels on pages 264–65 and below.

CARBOHYDRATE LOADING: DO YOU NEED TO DEPLETE?

'The diet makes you feel like death warmed up. You have no energy at all, you're really in heaps of trouble . . . I could feel myself getting more tired and exhausted and run down. I was absolutely gone . . . It's the toughest thing about a marathon. I've enjoyed marathons a lot more since I've stopped doing it.'
Steve Moneghetti, winner of the Berlin, Tokyo and Commonwealth Games marathons, on his 'depleting' experiences before carbohydrate loading

'Personally I don't carbo-load (with a depletion). One of the principal reasons is that the hectic schedule of professional racing doesn't give me enough of a break to methodically carbo-load. While top marathoners rarely race more than two world-class marathons a year, I'm racing approximately once every three days. The depletion phase puts too much stress on the body to be practical. I think it's the kind of stress a top cyclist can do without.'
Greg LeMond, three-time winner of the Tour de France

The original carbohydrate loading protocol was probably one of the first modern sports nutrition strategies to receive widespread publicity. It had all the ingredients to make a good story—scientists using special techniques to directly study a muscle, evidence of performance improvements, and good timing. It hit sports science journals in the early 1970s, then found its way into popular magazines during the start of the popular running boom. For both elite and recreational runners, this new carbohydrate loading technique sounded like the best thing since, well, sliced bread!

The depletion phase in this protocol is defined and tough—a long exercise session one week out, followed by three to four days of minimal carbohydrate intake and continued exercise. If anything, the rigid instructions and the challenge add a sense of mystique. It has become part of the endurance athlete's folklore. So, it is both surprising and understandable that anyone would ignore the 1980s' development of a 'modified' carbohydrate loading technique which offers elevated muscle glycogen levels to well-trained athletes without the need for a glycogen stripping phase. But the word of mouth (or book) from many recent top athletes is that they still include a depletion.

The surprising part is that an athlete would submit to the unpleasant side-effects of depleting if given a choice. Runners like Australian marathoner Steve Moneghetti who have written about the experience of a severe depletion phase describe overwhelming fatigue, irritability, reduced tolerance to anything from people to bugs to injury, and a marked reduction of performance. The body, brain and muscles are being deprived of carbohydrate fuel, and nothing functions well in the short term. For some athletes, carbohydrate restriction means substitution with a high fat and protein intake. However, even if you start that way, after a day or so most athletes will experience loss of appetite as their metabolism shifts to ketone production. Since it is both practically and physiologically difficult just to eat fat and protein, most athletes probably end up eating a low-energy diet by the end of the depletion phase. And they hope that by pulling themselves down hard, the next phase of loading will spring them back to new heights.

So what is the understandable part about the persistence of depletion? Perhaps some athletes are old-fashioned and stick to what previous legendary athletes and coaches did. Perhaps they just read old magazines and studies. Certainly the ritual of a special practice is hard to break away from—especially if you are the kind of athlete who believes that gain must be preceded by pain, or that greater effort will bring greater rewards. Many athletes are guided by superstition as much as by experience. If an early competition was a success, or a rival used a depletion preparation and was successful, the athlete may want to stick to what seemed to work. In a sport like marathon running, athletes may only compete at their highest level a couple of times each year. Therefore, it is quite difficult to experiment with and assess the contribution of the many different variables that affect the final result. Athletes who dare to try the new modified approach may have a bad race for an unrelated reason but may blame their new loading approach. And, of course, maybe athletes just *say* that they deplete, without really doing it rigorously.

But perhaps there is a compelling reason to keep depleting that we don't understand. Maybe it works! Maybe it does increase the subsequent loading of muscle glycogen stores. Maybe it offers the athlete some metabolic improvements by serving as a shortened version of the fat adaptation technique that is currently under trial. Scientists may need to reopen the files on the metabolic, glycogen storage and performance outcomes following a depleted and non-depleted loading phase before we can put this issue to rest.

In the meantime, athletes will continue to do what they think works best for them. Some endurance athletes may never be able to consider a depletion/loading protocol, due to practical restraints. Athletes who compete frequently, such as those in weekly sports competitions, or those undertaking stage or tournament events, simply do not have the time to undertake such a long preparation between their events. Others will find that the downside of the depletion is not worth the risk, or that any small merits are greatly overshadowed. There are easier ways for the athlete and their muscle to enjoy carbohydrates than to starve themselves in anticipation!

A CARBOHYDRATE LOADING MENU

This menu provides a daily intake of approximately 600 grams, which is sufficient for a 60–65 kilogram athlete to achieve their carbohydrate loading goals. Athletes should scale this intake up or down according to their BM—the ready reckoner in Chapter 10 will help. Note that the priority of this menu is for fuelling up for competition—it doesn't meet all nutrient intake goals. An exercise taper should accompany this menu to optimise muscle glycogen storage.

Day 1

Breakfast:	2 cups cornflakes + 1 cup milk
	1 banana
	250 ml sweetened fruit juice
Snack:	250 ml carbohydate loading drink
Lunch:	2 large bread rolls each with 1 tbsp jam
	375 ml can soft drink
Snack:	Large coffee scroll or fruit bun
	250 ml sweetened fruit juice
Dinner:	3 cups cooked pasta + 1 cup pasta sauce
	250 ml sports drink

Supper:	50 g packet of jelly beans 250 ml fruit juice

Day 2

Breakfast:	Stack of 3 large pancakes + 90 ml maple syrup 250 ml fruit juice
Snack spread over the day:	150 g packet of jelly babies or jubes 1 litre sports drink
Lunch:	3 crumpets + ½ tablespoon of honey on each 375 ml can soft drink
Dinner:	2 cups boiled rice made into light stir-fry with vegetables 1 cup sweetened canned fruit + 1 scoop icecream
Day 3	Repeat day 1 or 2, switching to all white cereals. You may like to replace meals and snacks from lunch onwards with 2 litres of a carbohydrate loading supplement (e.g. 400 g of glucose polymer powder).

PRE-EVENT EATING

Foods and drinks consumed in the four hours prior to exercise have a fine-tuning role in competition preparation. These foods and drinks can be eaten largely for comfort or confidence. Or they may continue to contribute to refuelling and rehydrating goals. There has been much undeserved publicity about the negative effects of eating in the hour before exercise, an issue that will be discussed separately.

The pre-event meal

The goals of the pre-event meal are to:

- continue to fuel muscle glycogen stores if they have not fully recovered or loaded since the last exercise session;
- top up liver glycogen stores, especially in the morning when they are depleted from an overnight fast;
- ensure that the athlete is well-hydrated;
- prevent hunger, yet avoid the gastrointestinal discomfort and upset often experienced during exercise; and
- include foods and practices that are important to the athlete's psychology or superstitions.

The pre-event meal menu should include carbohydrate-rich foods, especially in the case where body carbohydrate stores are sub-optimal, or where the event is of sufficient duration and intensity to challenge these stores. In some cases there may even be adequate time for pre-event carbohydrate to be processed and stored within the muscle or liver. Alternatively, carbohydrate may be in the gut, ready for gradual absorption and release during the event. Indeed, several studies have shown that a large carbohydrate meal (200–400 g of carbohydrate), eaten two to four hours pre-event, improves endurance during prolonged exercise by increasing carbohydrate availability during the event.

In real life there isn't the opportunity or need for a large meal before all sporting events. For example, it is unlikely that an athlete will want to get up at 3 a.m. to eat heartily before a 7 a.m. race start. Most will settle for a light snack before early morning events, and use carbohydrate intake during the event to balance up missed fuelling opportunities. A smaller pre-event meal also makes sense for athletes predisposed to gastrointestinal discomfort. There are many ways to juggle the timing and size of meals.

Foods with a low-fat, low-fibre and low–moderate protein content are the preferred choice for the pre-event menu since they are less likely to cause gastrointestinal upsets. Liquid meals and action-packed drinks are useful for nervous tummies or for brief pre-event timetables. The bottom line is that athletes should choose a strategy that suits their situation and their past experiences. The most important guideline for pre-event meals is that they should have been tested and fine-tuned! The panel below provides some pre-event meal ideas that fit the general recommendations above. But there is no single meal or food type that suits all athletes. Many successful performances have followed a variety of other menus—some, quite bizarre!

PRE-EVENT MEAL IDEAS—HIGH-CARBOHYDRATE, LOW-FAT EATING

- Pasta* with tomato-based or other low-fat sauces.
- Steamed rice* or noodles* with low-fat sauce.
- Creamed rice* made with sugar and milk.

- Breakfast cereal* with milk or yoghurt.
- Pancakes with syrup.
- Toast* or English muffins* with jam.
- Crumpets* with honey.
- Rice cakes or bread rolls* with sliced banana.
- Fresh fruit or fruit salad.
- Baked potato with low-fat sauce or filling.
- Toast* with canned spaghetti or baked beans.
- Fruit smoothie made with milk, yoghurt and fruit.
- Commercial liquid meal supplement.
- Sports bars.

* for low-fibre meals, choose 'white' types of cereal food.

Sugars consumed in the hour before exercise

In 1979, a study published from Professor Dave Costill's lab created much panic and confusion among athletes. It showed that when a large amount of glucose was consumed 30 minutes prior to exercise, it actually *reduced* the time that subjects could exercise at an intensity of 80% of VO_{2max}. In other words, carbohydrate ingestion in the hour prior to the event impaired their performance.

The key to interpreting this finding is to know that the timing of the carbohydrate snack causes blood glucose and insulin levels to be elevated at the start of the exercise. Raised insulin levels blunt the rate of fat oxidation during exercise and increase the reliance on carbohydrate fuels. Although muscle glycogen wasn't measured in this particular study, the researchers speculated that its rate of use may have been faster, leading to premature depletion of muscle stores. This could explain the earlier onset of fatigue in their subjects. The increased rate of carbohydrate oxidation also caused a drop in blood glucose levels soon after the start of exercise. Since blood glucose didn't reach extremely low levels, it is unlikely that it caused central nervous system fatigue. Nevertheless, the phenomenon of 'rebound hypoglycaemia' after eating sugar is a popular fear.

The results of this study were so well-publicised that many sports nutrition guidelines began to recommend that athletes *avoid* carbohydrate-rich foods and drinks during the hour before exercise. Unfortunately, this advice and fear persist even today, in spite of overwhelming evidence that pre-exercise carbohydrate feedings do *not* cause a performance disadvantage. At least a dozen more recent studies have experimented with various forms and types of carbohydrate, feeding these to their subjects during the hour before running and cycling. All have found that pre-exercise carbohydrate improved performance or, at worst, had no effect on performance. These studies confirm the insulin rise before exercise, the drop in blood glucose levels at the start of exercise and an increased rate of carbohydrate oxidation. However, they generally show that these changes are small and short-lived, being corrected within 30 minutes of exercise. In most cases, any early increases in carbohydrate oxidation are more than offset by the intake of the extra fuel. As previously discussed, athletes who reach the 'final hour' of their preparation without being fully refuelled may find an advantage in the extra carbohydrate.

Nevertheless, there seems to be a small percentage of athletes who respond negatively to carbohydrate feedings in the hour before exercise. These athletes experience an exaggerated rate of carbohydrate use and a drop in blood glucose concentration at the start of exercise. As a consequence they suffer a rapid onset of fatigue, sometimes to the point of 'getting the shakes'. Why some athletes experience such an extreme reaction is not known. However, these effects are so clear-cut that athletes will be easily able to identify themselves. Preventative action for this small group includes a number of options:

- Experiment to find the critical time before exercise that carbohydrate intake should be avoided.
- Choose low glycaemic index carbohydrate-rich choices which promote a more gentle blood glucose and insulin response.
- Include some high-intensity sprints during the event warm-up. High-intensity exercise prods the liver to release glucose into the blood.
- Consume carbohydrate during the event.

Pre-exercise meals and the glycaemic index

Eating low glycaemic index carbohydrate-rich foods and drinks causes a slower and more sustained change in blood glucose and insulin levels than eating the same amount of carbohydrate from high glycaemic index sources (see Chapter 10). This might provide a way for an athlete to consume their carbohydrate needs without causing such a sharp metabolic response.

A study by Australian researchers first publicised the use of the glycaemic index (GI) in sport. Dr Diana Thomas and co-workers from the University of Sydney found that a low GI carbohydrate-rich meal (lentils), consumed one hour before exercise, enabled cyclists to ride significantly longer before they fatigued at a work intensity of 65% of VO_{2max} than when they ingested an equal amount of carbohydrate from a high GI food (potatoes). The low GI meal resulted in more stable blood glucose and free fatty acid levels during exercise. Although muscle glycogen levels were not actually measured, these researchers suggested that a slower rate of muscle glycogen utilisation may have occurred, and that such 'glycogen sparing' might explain the increased endurance.

However, other studies have not been able to repeat these findings. Another Australian research team led by Dr Mark Febbraio from the University of Melbourne had cyclists eat 45 minutes before an exercise trial, which consisted of riding at a steady pace for two hours and then completing a time-trial. This is considered to be a more reliable and appropriate measurement of athletic performance than an 'exercise until exhaustion' task (see Chapter 17). They found no differences between performance following a high GI carbohydrate meal (pasta), a low GI carbohydrate meal (lentils), or a placebo meal of low-joule jelly. Muscle biopsy samples revealed no overall difference in glycogen use between any of the trials. The low GI meal caused small metabolic changes early in the exercise trial, and a brief period of glycogen sparing cannot be ruled out. But it seems that the pre-event meal does not dictate the whole outcome of an exercise session.

Of course, if performance in an event hinges on carbohydrate availability, the athlete's key strategy is to consume carbohydrate during exercise (see Chapter 13). The interaction between pre-event meals and carbohydrate intake during the event has not been well-studied—particularly with the recent twist of the glycaemic index added. However, significant intake during the event may override or at least 'smooth out' any bumps from pre-exercise carbohydrate.

In summary, it seems premature to claim universal benefits from switching to a low GI pre-event meal, although some sports nutrition guidelines have already taken it on board. It may benefit athletes who are sensitive, or have an exaggerated metabolic response, to pre-exercise carbohydrate intake. And it may be useful for prolonged events in which the athlete is prevented from taking in significant amounts of carbohydrate. In the big picture, pre-event eating needs to balance up a number of factors—including the athlete's food likes, availability of choices, and gastrointestinal comfort. The glycaemic index is only one on the list of issues.

PRE-EXERCISE HYDRATION

Dehydration poses one of the most common nutritional problems occurring in sport. Chapter 13 details strategies to enhance fluid balance during training and competition sessions. Since on most occasions, fluid intake during exercise will be unable to match the rate of sweat loss, it is critical for the athlete to start the session well-hydrated. Special attention is needed to ensure full restoration of fluid balance after previous exercise bouts (see Chapter 14), particularly if unusually large fluid losses have become a sudden way of life, leading to chronic dehydration (see Chapter 15).

Pre-exercise hyperhydration

Many athletes undertake events in which significant dehydration is inevitable, and this poses a challenge to both their health and performance. Such dehydration can occur when an athlete's sweat rate is extremely high, when there is little opportunity to drink during the event, or when these factors are combined. Some athletes have experimented with 'loading up' with fluid in the hours prior to the event to try to get a head-start on hydration. While this has been shown to improve fluid balance during subsequent exercise, a lot of the fluid ends down the toilet rather than in the body. After all, the body has a well-developed system to regulate the volume and concentration of its fluid content both at rest and during exercise. Fluid overloading may have a detrimental effect on performance if it causes the significant interruption of a trip to the bushes during the event, or just the discomfort of excess fluid in the gut! On rare occasions, if taken to extreme levels and in susceptible individuals, it may lead to 'water intoxication'. Symptoms include headaches and nausea due to the expansion of the brain blood volume (see Chapter 13). Clearly, fluid overloading just before an event is a strategy that needs to be researched before any more firm recommendations can be made to athletes.

One recent study by Estela Kristal-Boneh and colleagues from Israel examined the effect of chronic periods of fluid overloading. They asked heat-acclimatised subjects to double their usual fluid intake for a week, which led to a mean daily fluid intake of about four litres. They found that this tactic caused the body to reset its normal fluid balance and retain an extra 600 ml of fluid. They also described increased heat tolerance and improved cycling performance undertaken in the heat. More work is needed to confirm these results. Certainly it supports advice often given to athletes competing in a hot climate, to increase their fluid intake over the days leading up to the event. Whether this advice merely ensures fluid balance, rather than promoting fluid overload, has not been adequately tested prior to this study. Of course, the potentially negative impact of any gain in body mass might need to be taken into account in some sports.

GLYCEROL HYPERHYDRATION

A method of hyperhydration under current study involves the consumption of a small amount of glycerol along with the fluid overload. Glycerol is a fat that is rapidly absorbed and distributed throughout the body compartments. It exerts a concentration or osmotic effect that allows the body to retain extra fluid, at least until the glycerol is excreted over the next 24 hours or so. Several studies have reported that when subjects consume 1 g of glycerol per kg BM along with plenty of water about two to three hours before exercise, they are able to better retain this extra fluid compared to drinking plain water. Hypothetically this might allow them to undertake exercise with better maintenance of blood volume, assisted thermoregulation and sweating, and improved performances. Several studies have found one or more of these effects, but so far there is no consistency in the observations. Further, most of these trials have been performed using moderately-trained subjects.

A study conducted at the Australian Institute of Sport, led by Sam Hitchins, had elite cyclists try this strategy before undertaking an hour of high-intensity exercise in the heat. On one occasion the cyclists hyperhydrated with a glycerol and fluid mix, and on another with fluid alone. The glycerol treatment resulted in greater retention of the fluid load—in fact, it allowed cyclists to start the cycle trial with an extra 600 ml of fluid on board. More importantly, glycerol hyperhydration improved performance of a time-trial by 2.4% compared with the other trial. More work is needed to confirm these findings of performance improvement and then to explain the mechanisms behind them. In this study there were no obvious changes in the cyclists' sweat rates, temperature regulation, heart rate, metabolic measurements or their perceived effort. Perhaps the changes were too subtle to be detected by the laboratory measures, yet enough to improve performance. Alternatively, entirely different factors might be involved.

Not all athletes see a benefit with glycerol hyperhydration, however. Side-effects may include gastrointestinal upsets and headaches. Nevertheless, many athletes are convinced of its value, particularly when they are preparing for competitions undertaken in hot and humid conditions. Those who want to try it out can buy glycerol from a pharmacy, or use one of the commercial glycerol hyperhydrating products that have recently been introduced on to the market. These can take the guesswork out of knowing how much to use. Nevertheless, since this technique is still in an experimental phase, it is preferable that athletes do their own 'studies' under the supervision of a sports scientist. Being part of a properly designed research project is even better, since the results can be more widely and objectively shared.

Priming the stomach with a fluid bolus

Even if the athlete is not aiming to 'fluid overload', there can be good reasons to have a drink just before exercise. Effective rehydration during exercise depends on maximising the rate of fluid delivery from the stomach to the intestine for absorption. It is well-known that gastric emptying (the rate at which fluid leaves the stomach) is increased when the stomach is slightly stretched. It is clever to take advantage of this volume effect when trying to maximise fluid intake during an event. In other words, the athlete should keep filling their stomach to the point of a comfortable but slight stretch, letting it empty, then topping up again (see Chapter 13). This requires the athlete to start the event with the stomach 'primed' for quick action. Obviously the athlete will need to experiment to determine what is a comfortable amount and, in particular, how comfortable this feels once exercise has commenced. However, as a general rule of thumb, most athletes can tolerate a bolus of about 5 ml per BM (i.e. 300–400 ml) of fluid immediately before their event starts. This may provide a useful start to fluid intake tactics during exercise. Guidelines for pre-exercise hydration are summarised in the panel on the following pages.

GUIDELINES FOR FLUID INTAKE PRIOR TO COMPETITION

- Ensure that fluid losses are recovered each day by monitoring changes in BM. A loss of one kilogram or more from one day to the next reflects dehydration, and highlights the need to rethink current fluid intake practices.
- Make sure that you are well-hydrated in the lead-up to an event that is held in hot and/or humid weather, or likely to cause significant sweat losses. Look after fluid needs well in the days leading up to the event.
- Be aggressive in reversing pre-existing dehydration—for example, from a previous exercise session, or from strategies used to 'make weight'. Fluid recovery techniques include replacement of lost sodium—for example, by eating salty food or meals, or drinking oral rehydration solutions (see Chapter 14).
- Consider pre-event hyperhydration if it is likely that significant dehydration will occur during the event. Further research is required before general guidelines can be made for techniques such as glycerol hyperhydration. If you intend to experiment, do so with the advice and supervision of a sports scientist.
- Drink with the pre-event meal, allowing sufficient time for toilet stops to get rid of excess fluid before the start of the event.
- In situations where an aggressive plan of fluid intake is to be undertaken during the event, 'prime' the stomach with a fluid bolus immediately before the start of exercise. Experiment to find the amount that puts the stomach at a comfortable stretch to enhance gastric emptying, without causing discomfort or upset.

THE TRAVELLING ATHLETE

'. . . after flying here and getting settled into a hotel . . . I spent more than an hour looking for a health food store and still came up empty . . . I guess I'll be running the 200 fuelled by whatever we can get out of room service. It's a perfect example of why we're usually better off at home.'

Carl Lewis, track superstar, on travelling interstate to a running meet.

Travel is an exciting feature, but an occupational hazard, in the lifestyle of an elite athlete. Most athletes undertake the final preparation for their most important competitions from five-star hotels, budget digs, athletes villages or family billets—anywhere other than their own homes. Each provides a special nutritional challenge, especially when it is located in a foreign country. The athlete may have to battle against language problems, different food cultures, inadequate finances, poor hygiene standards, and a daily timetable that clashes with that of the local food outlets. They may be away from the person who normally organises or supervises their food intake. Or they may have to pit their wits and discipline against an 'all you can eat' smorgasbord in the food hall of an athletes village or group accommodation. And then there is the disruption to the athlete's usual routine caused by travel, jet lag, sightseeing and preparation activities. The environment itself may impose new nutritional challenges—a sudden change in temperature or altitude may result in increased needs for fluid, energy, carbohydrate and other nutrients.

The result of this uprooting can be unwanted weight loss, weight gain, chronic dehydration, inadequate carbohydrate for fuelling up, nutritional deficiencies, and gastrointestinal upsets, including traveller's diarrhoea. This is definitely not the glamourous side of a jet-setting life. There are a number of strategies to reduce the risk of problems:

- Be aware of your nutritional needs—including special needs arising from your new location. Younger athletes will need assistance and supervision.
- Investigate the food resources at your destination *before* you leave, especially if international travel is involved. People who have travelled previously to that country, competition or accommodation facility may be able to warn you of likely problems. Being forewarned can allow you to make a plan.
- Special menus and meals in restaurants, hotels or aeroplanes can often be organised in advance.
- Find out about the food hygiene and water safety in countries that you are visiting. You may need to restrict yourself to bottled or boiled drinks, and to avoid foods that are high-risk for contamination (e.g. unpeeled fruits and vegetables).
- If important foods are likely to be expensive or unavailable, take some food supplies with you. Foods that are portable and long-lasting include breakfast cereals, milk powder, tinned and dehydrated foods, dried fruit, sports bars and other cereal bars, liquid meal supplements and other sports products.
- Be aware of your eating behaviour in cafeterias and 'all you can eat' restaurants. These are often found in athletes villages, and are a common trap for new and old players. Eat what you need, instead of what is there, or what everyone around you is eating. It is easy to lose the nutritional plot when faced with a dazzling and unending choice of food.

13

Fluid and fuel intake for competition and training

'Don't take any nourishment before going 17 or 18 miles. If you do you will not go the distance. Don't get into the habit of eating or drinking in a marathon race: some prominent runners do, but it is not beneficial.'

Advice from J.E. Sullivan in his 1909 book on marathon running

'If the eating of sugar candy during a race was encouraged by Athletic Organisations, it seems possible that new records might be achieved in very long-distance running.'

Grace Eggleton, quoted in a 1936 textbook on muscular exercise

'In those days it was quite fashionable not to drink [during a distance running event] until one absolutely had to. After a race runners would recount with pride "I only had a drink after 30 or 40 km". To run a complete marathon without any fluid replacement was regarded as the ultimate aim of most runners, and a test of their fitness.'

Jackie Mekler, South African ultra-distance runner and five-time winner of the Comrades Marathon (90 km event) during the 1950s and 1960s

'One drink break may be taken during each session of play. However, this may be discarded at the discretion of both captains.'

Official MCC rules of cricket, 1992

'A thick carbohydrate solution may even have been the key to my victory . . . without it I might have bonked and fallen behind or dropped out. I also ate some rice snacks to complement my intake. As the race neared its conclusion I avoided taking anything but a glucose solution; my body was in the midst of a tremendous effort and needed the nutrition as quickly as it could be delivered. At the finish I had won the world championship.'

Greg LeMond, three-time winner of Tour de France and 1983 world champion cyclist, on his nutrient intake during a road race

'I was looking pretty good at half-way . . . It was at the 35 km drink station, a shocking place for a drink station and they have moved it since, when I missed my drink. We came around this corner . . . both Douglas Wakiihuri and I missed our drinks . . . Salah noticed—he didn't take one himself, but surged and sprinted off.'

Marathon runner Steve Moneghetti describing how tactics in getting drinks at an aid station in the 1989 London marathon played a role in race placings

'The runner is encouraged to drink 100–200 ml of fluid at each aid station, every 2–3 km.'

Advice from the American College of Sports Medicine 1987 position stand on prevention of thermal injuries during distance running

'. . . slow runners (running at 10 km per hour and drinking 100 ml at aid stations 3 km apart) will receive 330 ml each hour, whereas fast runners (running at 20 km per hour and drinking 200 ml each 2 km) will receive 2000 ml per hour . . .'

Scientists Professor Ed Coyle and Dr Scott Montain commenting that a literal interpretation of the 1987 ACSM guidelines is neither practical nor useful

As an exercise session increases in duration, so does the risk of being challenged by nutritional factors that reduce performance (see the panel on page 260 in Chapter 12). On the other hand, it provides sufficient time to take fluid and nutrients on board to reduce the severity of these problems. Like many things in sport, the line between help and harm can be fine and variable. By consuming fluid and carbohydrate during a training or competition session, an athlete can tackle three of the factors that may challenge their performance—dehydration, depletion of muscle glycogen and the effects of low carbohydrate status on the central nervous system (the brain). But unless these strategies are executed properly, they may fail to be effective. Worse still, failed strategies may actually cause some of the other problems listed in the panel referred to—such as gastrointestinal problems and low blood sodium levels. Clearly, each athlete needs to get the balance right.

For many athletes, food and fluid intake during exercise is considered a competition issue. However, as discussed in Chapter 10, the benefits to training performance may be of equal or greater importance. Certainly, since many things can go wrong on the day, it makes sense to practise and fine-tune all competition strategies well in advance. The athlete needs to decide which drinks and foods best suit their taste buds and stomachs, learn how to consume these items 'on the run' or under the stress of exercise, and learn how much is enough. In some sports there are regulations about when and what items can be consumed during the event. In others these issues are determined by the logistics of getting access to supplies. Each athlete needs to tailor a plan for their event.

FLUID LOSS AND REPLACEMENT

The effects of dehydration

Water is the body's most important nutrient. Deprive an athlete of it in sufficient quantities, and they will not only slow down, but will eventually die. Results of the latest research on dehydration and exercise reveals that:

- The effects of dehydration vary according to the type of exercise being undertaken. Whether dehydration reduces muscular strength and power is unclear. The type of exercise that seems most susceptible to the effects of dehydration is prolonged moderate and high-intensity activity.
- Dehydration causes an increase in the athlete's heart-rate and a small rise in body temperature for a given workload. The volume of plasma is reduced and its concentration is increased. Most importantly, the athlete's perception of effort is increased for the same workload. In other words,

the athlete will either feel more fatigued despite the same workrate or will reduce their self-selected pace when dehydrated.

- The performance effects of dehydration are greatly magnified when the exercise is carried out in a hot environment. Perceived effort is greatly increased, and the athlete may not be able to handle the extra challenge to control body temperature.
- These effects occur at all levels of dehydration and increase in magnitude as the degree of dehydration increases. This is contrary to the popular belief among athletes that dehydration can be 'tolerated' until a certain critical level (i.e. fluid losses of 3–5% of body mass—BM). In fact, any level of dehydration will reduce performance and the athlete must decide what is a 'significant' loss in their own situation. In laboratory studies, fluid losses of less than 2% of BM reduce performance according to the statistical view of significance. In real life, the difference between a winning performance and a losing performance is much less (see Chapter 17).
- The different methods of producing dehydration cause variation in the source of body fluid losses. For example, diuretic-induced dehydration is more likely to increase the fluid losses from the extra-cellular water and blood volume rather than the fluid inside the cell, compared with sweat-induced dehydration in which the majority of fluid is lost from the intra-cellular space. This will be of greater disadvantage to performance.
- Dehydration reduces mental functioning and the skills of motor performance, particularly when tasks are undertaken in the heat. Therefore, dehydration may severely disadvantage performance in team and racquet sports, or other activities requiring precise motor control, decision making and concentration. Laboratory studies which test the performance of physiological tasks are likely to underestimate the effect of dehydration on performance in real-life sports.
- There is no situation in which dehydration is of advantage to sports performance; an athlete cannot train themselves to adapt to, or tolerate, dehydration.
- Moderate to severe dehydration (fluid loss of greater than 3–4% BM) is linked with a significant increase in the risk of gastrointestinal upsets and impaired gastric emptying. An athlete who becomes significantly dehydrated during exercise will find it difficult to rehydrate, since fluid

delivery from the stomach is compromised. In fact, fluid intake is likely to cause discomfort and stomach upsets.

Although there is substantial research on the effects of dehydration on exercise performance, in the future high priority should be given to studies that use or mimic situations of real-life sport.

Fluid balance during exercise

There is no question that full hydration is a prerequisite for optimal sports performance. Whether this is a practical goal for all athletes to achieve is entirely another issue. The body produces heat as a major by-product of exercise. In fact, about 75% of the energy expended during exercise can be transformed into heat rather than mechanical work, and can be equivalent in heat production to a small bar radiator. Without mechanisms to dissipate this excess heat, the body temperature would quickly rise and eventually an athlete would die. When the environmental temperature is cold to mild (i.e. less than about 20°C), heat transfer can occur through convection and conduction into the air. However, these mechanisms are of minor value when the temperature is hotter or where there is little airflow for convection (e.g. inside a poorly ventilated stadium). In these cases the evaporation of sweat becomes the dominant way to lose heat and control body temperature. The rate of sweat loss is primarily determined by the athlete's metabolic rate or power output. However, other factors such as individual variability, degree of acclimatisation of the athlete, and the environmental conditions also play a role. Some athletes who undertake very high intensity exercise in very hot conditions can lose in excess of 2 litres of sweat each hour. American Alberto Salazar's sweat loss during the 1984 Los Angeles Olympic marathon was reported to be 3.7 litres an hour, for a total race loss of over 7.5 litres. Typically, most athletes exercise in less extreme conditions, and average sweat rates during sport are in the range of 1–1.5 litre/hour. An athlete must replace these sweat losses during exercise to maintain fluid balance.

However, studies that have measured the voluntary fluid intakes by athletes in a variety of sports show that the majority become mildly to moderately dehydrated over a training or competition session. Professor Tim Noakes has reviewed fluid balance studies on endurance athletes involved in 'continuous' activities (e.g. distance runners, cyclists and canoeists). He found that athletes typically replaced less than 50% of their sweat losses, drinking only 300–600 ml/hour. Studies conducted at the Australian Institute of Sport by Elizabeth Broad and colleagues, found that some team sport athletes were slightly better at replacing sweat losses—in some cases the team averaged a fluid intake that replaced 70–75% of sweat losses, by drinking at slightly higher rates of intake of 500–700 ml/hour. However, all studies show considerable variation between individuals in their chosen fluid intake patterns and their ability to cover sweat losses.

Of course, just because athletes do things in a certain way now does not make this an optimal practice. However, these studies are useful in uncovering issues that influence behaviour which may need to be tackled if new strategies are to be implemented. There appears to be a genetic component to self-selected fluid intake. Some people are good drinkers and are able to maintain fluid balance in most situations, while others are 'reluctant drinkers' even when significantly dehydrated. The factors which determine fluid intake during exercise include:

- the athlete's awareness of their sweat losses;
- the athlete's awareness of the disadvantages of dehydration;
- the availability of fluid;
- the opportunity to drink;
- the palatability of the drink;
- gastrointestinal comfort;
- fear of weight gain (e.g. avoidance of energy-containing fluids, use of dehydration to 'lose' body mass); and
- fear of needing to urinate during the exercise session.

Education is needed to raise awareness of the advantages of being as well hydrated as possible. In the past, athletes have worked on the principle of avoiding severe dehydration and conspicuous impairment of performance, rather than aggressively hydrating to promote optimal performance. Becoming familiar with typical sweat losses is a useful tactic for setting a fluid intake plan (see Figure 13.1).

The logistics of drinking during sport must also be considered. The athlete must have both an opportunity to drink and access to suitable fluids. These factors vary according to the sport and the event, and may sometimes be dictated by the official rules of a sport. For example, the International

---

FIGURE 13.1

Quick calculations of sweat losses and fluid balance during exercise

① ② ③

1   Change in body mass (kg) = body mass measured accurately in minimal clothing before exercise (kg) – body mass measured after exercise in same clothing, towel dried (kg).
2   Fluid intake (ml) = difference in mass of water bottle before and after exercise (g), or volume of fluid consumed (ml).
3   Urine or toilet losses (ml) = change in body mass before and after going to the toilet (kg × 1000 = ml).

Calculations:
Total sweat loss during exercise (ml) = change in body mass (kg × 1000) + fluid intake (ml) – urine losses (kg × 1000)
Sweat rate (ml/hr) = total sweat loss (ml) ÷ duration of exercise (hr)
Fluid deficit (ml) = change in body mass (kg × 1000)
% dehydration = change in body mass (kg) ÷ pre-exercise body mass (kg) × 100
Note that 1 kg = 1000g = 1000 ml of water.

Amateur Athletic Federation (IAAF) regulates the placement of official aid stations during distance running events. The 1953 rules dictated that aid stations could be placed each 5 kilometres, starting only after 15 kilometres of the race, and allowed water as the only provision. By 1990 the rules had gradually evolved to allow carbohydrate drinks and water to be provided at aid stations each 3 kilometres from the race start. Thus there has been an increase in the timing, frequency and choice of fluids available. FIFA, the national governing body of soccer, has recently relaxed its rules to allow fluid to be consumed during stoppages in play during game halves. Prior to this, fluid was only available pre-game and at half-time.

Sometimes it is custom and the natural flow of a sport that dictates opportunities to drink. In many sports, activity is continuous and the athlete must literally drink 'on the run'. This presents a dilemma to the athlete who must balance the benefits and disadvantages of drinking (see section below). In team sports, there are various opportunities to drink when the athlete is stationary. These include premeditated and formal breaks in play (quarter and half-time breaks), as well as spontaneous and informal breaks (game stoppages, substitutions). Table 13.1 summarises various opportunities for fluid intake in a number of team and intermittent sports.

Fluid may be made available to athletes in various ways. In some sports, athletes must carry their own supplies or prepare their own provisions. In other sports a network of aid stations may provide refreshments to athletes, or team management may look after the fluid needs of its players. Clearly it is easier to drink when fluid can be taken to the athlete on the field (e.g. drink bottles taken out by trainers) than when the athlete must find their way to the supply of drinks. Of course, fluids that are palatable are more likely to be consumed in adequate quantities. Temperature and flavour are important issues in the acceptability of drinks. The commercial potential of sports drinks has led to great interest in making drinks taste good to athletes who are hot and sweaty. A sweet flavour, and the addition of small amounts of sodium (salt), has been shown to increase the voluntary intake of fluids during and after exercise (see Chapter 14).

Finally, the athlete may have real or irrational reasons for limiting fluid intake that must also be considered. Gastrointestinal discomfort provides a significant limitation to fluid intake which varies according to the type of sport, the intensity of exercise and to the individual. It is often suggested that an athlete can 'train' themselves to drink greater amounts of fluid in preparation for situations where sweat losses are extreme. Research is needed to determine whether physiological adaptations occur to allow an athlete to tolerate great fluid volumes.

┌─────────────┐
│ TABLE 13.1 │
└─────────────┘

Opportunities to drink fluids during various team games and intermittent sports

Sport	Game characteristics	Opportunities to drink	Special comments
American football	4 × 12 or 4 × 15 mins + substantial 'time on',[a] unlimited substitutions,[b] timeouts	Quarter-time breaks; timeouts, substitutions, pauses in play	Trainers may run on to the field with drink bottles during breaks or pauses in play.
Australian Rules football	4 × 20 mins + substantial 'time on', unlimited substitutions	Quarter-time breaks; substitutions, pauses in play.	Trainers may run on to the field with drink bottles during pauses in play.
Basketball	4 × 12 or 2 × 20 mins + substantial 'time on', unlimited substitutions, timeouts	Quarter- or half-time breaks; substitutions, timeouts	Fluids must be consumed on the court sidelines.
Cricket	Test: 3 × 2-hr sessions, limited over: 2 × 50 over innings	Rest breaks between sessions One official drink break per session In some competitions, pauses in play—drink bottles kept on ground	MCC rules provide one official drink break per session. In practice, individual competitions, umpires or team captains may agree on more frequent breaks, or allow drink bottles on to the ground.
Field-hockey	2 × 35 mins, unlimited substitutions	Half-time, substitutions, pauses in play	Drinks must be consumed at the sidelines. Drinks cannot be carried or thrown on to the field. Players must not leave the field unless substituted.
Ice hockey	3 × 20 mins + substantial 'time on', unlimited substitutions, timeouts	Breaks between periods; substitutions, timeouts, pauses in play	Players must drink at the bench.
Netball	4 × 15 mins or 2 × 20 mins, timeouts, limited substitutions	Quarter- or half-time breaks; timeouts, substitutions	Fluids must be consumed on the court sidelines.

Rugby League	2 × 40 mins, unlimited substitutions	Half-time break; substitutions, pauses in play	Trainers may run on to the field with drink bottles during pauses in play.
Rugby Union	2 × 40 mins, unlimited substitutions	Half-time break; substitutions, pauses in play	Trainers may run on to field with drink bottles during pauses in play.
Soccer	2 × 45 mins. Players can be replaced, but cannot return to play.	Half-time break; pauses in play (drink must be taken at sideline)	Official rules amended in 1994 to allow drinks during play stoppages. Fluid cannot be carried or thrown on to the pitch. Players cannot leave the field.
Tennis	Each match contains 3–5 sets made up of individual games. Duration can vary from 1 to 5 hrs.	Players may drink at change of ends between games	
Volleyball	First to 3 sets; limited substitutions, timeouts	Breaks between sets; timeouts, substitutions	Official rules prohibit fluid on the court—drinks must be taken on the sideline.
Water polo	4 × 7 mins + substantial 'time on', unlimited substitutions, timeouts	Quarter-time breaks; substitutions, timeouts,	

Notes: a 'Time on' refers to additional time played to compensate for 'stopping of clock' when the ball is considered out of play. Adds considerably to the duration of the total session time.

b 'Substitutions' refers to players who are able to return to the game after substitution. 'Unlimited' means that any number of players may be rotated during the game; 'limited' means that the rules restrict substitutions to a finite number per game.

Source: Burke, L.M. and Hawley, J.A. 'Fluid balance in team sports. Guidelines for optimal practices', *Sports Medicine*, 24:38–54, 1997.

Such advice might be useful if only to allow an athlete to discover their maximum 'comfortable' fluid intake schedule.

CARBOHYDRATE REPLACEMENT

The observation that carbohydrate intake enhances performance during prolonged exercise events dates back to the

1920s. Scientists observed that some runners studied during the 1923 Boston marathon finished the race with low blood glucose levels. The next year they fed candy to runners during the second half of the marathon and found that this prevented the hypoglycaemia and improved their race performance.

During the next years, laboratory experiments confirmed the importance of carbohydrate fuel during prolonged moderate-intensity exercise, and showed that improved carbohydrate status led to improved endurance. Muscle biopsy studies in the 1960s provided more direct evidence of this, but focused interest on strategies raising pre-exercise muscle glycogen stores. Curiously, carbohydrate intake during exercise was then ignored until the 1980s. It is intriguing to speculate about why this happened, and why the observation of improvement in real sports events held little sway. Perhaps one reason is that the regulations under which some sports were conducted actually hampered or prevented opportunities to consume carbohydrate during an event. For example, the IAAF rules, discussed previously, made carbohydrate intake an illegal as well as impractical strategy. Another reason for the reluctance to consider carbohydrate feedings during exercise was concern over problems with stomach emptying and fluid delivery—a product of 1960s' and 1970s' research (see below).

It wasn't until the 1980s that carbohydrate intake during exercise finally received widespread recognition. This change was in part due to the emergence of new study techniques such as tracer labelling of carbohydrates to follow their metabolism during exercise. This allowed scientists to 'rediscover' the same facts from 60 years previously, except in greater detail! However, much of the impetus for this change came from the commercial interests of sports drink companies. They realised that there were both financial and performance benefits of producing products that could supply carbohydrate to athletes during exercise. Much of our present knowledge about carbohydrate intake during exercise has been stimulated, if not directly funded, by this commercial interest.

There are now many dozens of studies which show that carbohydrate intake can enhance the performance of prolonged moderate-intensity exercise (greater than 90 minutes). Many of these have used an 'exercise to exhaustion' protocol and show evidence of increased endurance. However, other studies have shown improved performance of a set task or an actual sports activity.

Carbohydrate replacement and the muscle

Early theories and studies suggested that carbohydrate intake during exercise enhanced endurance performance by 'sparing' glycogen levels due to increased blood glucose utilisation by the exercising muscles. Thus carbohydrate feedings might delay the time before the athlete 'hit the wall' of glycogen depletion. However, in 1986 a landmark study by Professor Ed Coyle now at the University of Austin in Texas, provided evidence of a different mechanism of performance enhancement. He studied cyclists riding to exhaustion at a moderate intensity while drinking a placebo sweetened drink. Muscle glycogen levels were measured at the beginning of the exercise task and 'at the point of fatigue'. The following week, cyclists repeated the task while drinking a carbohydrate drink. Muscle biopsies were taken at the time-point corresponding to 'fatigue' in the previous trial, but the cyclists were asked to keep riding if possible. An average of an extra hour's exercise was possible during the second week (4.02 hours versus 3.02 hours). Analyses showed that carbohydrate intake did not change the pattern of muscle glycogen utilisation during exercise. Rather, it maintained blood glucose levels throughout exercise, which provided a source of fuel once the muscle's own stores became depleted (see Figure 13.2). Curiously, subjects still fatigued after about four hours of cycling even though blood glucose levels were still well maintained at this point. Obviously fatigue has no simple or single cause. However, carbohydrate intake during exercise seems able to delay the onset of fatigue, or to maintain optimum performance for a significantly longer period.

Other studies have confirmed that muscle glycogen sparing does not typically occur during continuous cycling when carbohydrate is fed. But in some activities where there is intermittent activity, or periods of low-intensity exercise, there may be an opportunity to store glycogen in the non-active muscle fibres from the carbohydrate that is consumed during the exercise. This may be why Tour de France cyclists can find fuel in their fast twitch fibres to sprint to the line at the end of a long day's cruising in the peleton. The major effect of carbohydrate consumed during exercise is to spare liver glycogen stores, thus allowing the liver to maintain high rates of glucose output late in exercise to sustain the muscle's fuel needs.

FIGURE 13.2

Carbohydrate intake during prolonged cycling provides an additional fuel source when muscle stores are depleted

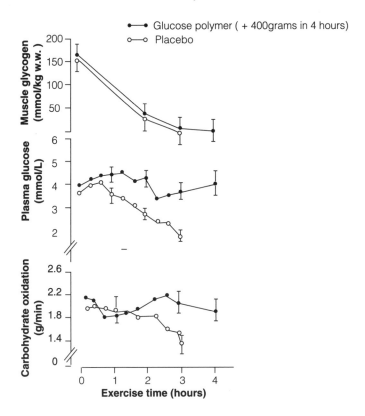

Source: Coyle, E.F., Coggan, A.R., Hemmert, M.K. and Ivy, J.L., 'Muscle glycogen utilisation during prolonged exercise when fed carbohydrate', *Journal of Applied Physiology* 61: 165–72, 1986.

Carbohydrate replacement—the 'central effect'

The benefits of carbohydrate intake during exercise extend beyond the muscle. The early studies showed that some athletes in some endurance sports experience low blood glucose levels. This deprives the muscle of an ongoing source of fuel, as well as causing some negative central nervous system effects in certain individuals. The brain is reliant on glucose for its own fuel, and carbohydrate intake will prevent or reverse symptoms of glucose deprivation to the brain. Even when frank hypoglycaemia doesn't occur, the central nervous system may respond positively to refuelling during exercise. Optimal brain function may be important to reduce feelings of effort or fatigue. It is likely to be even more important in sports involving skill, concentration and tactical decision making. For example, in a field study of soccer, researchers found that carbohydrate intake before the game and at the half-time break allowed players to run further and at higher speeds during the second half of the match. But it also seemed to preserve game skill levels, with fewer mistakes being made by the players who refuelled.

Central mechanisms of fatigue (involving the brain and central nervous system) are often blamed when peripheral mechanisms (involving the muscle) can't completely explain an observation. Unfortunately it is difficult to measure what is occurring in the brain, so scientists are often left to speculate on what is happening. Changes in the activity of various neurotransmitter chemicals in the brain are undoubtedly important. One such chemical is serotonin, which is linked to feelings of drowsiness and fatigue. Serotonin levels in the brain are thought to increase as a result of prolonged exercise, due to changes in blood levels of amino acids. The intake of branch-chain amino acids has been suggested as a way to correct this imbalance and prevent the resulting 'central fatigue' (see Chapter 16). However, carbohydrate intake also achieves this same effect. Clearly, central mechanisms of fatigue, or of performance enhancement, are an area needing further research.

Benefits of carbohydrate intake during exercise of one hour or less

Until recently sports scientists have believed that carbohydrate intake would be of greatest benefit during exercise that would otherwise deplete muscle and liver glycogen stores. Understandably, guidelines to refuel during exercise have been directed to activities of moderate-intensity exercise (65–75% of $\dot{V}O_{2max}$) lasting longer than 90 minutes. Another worthy situation is exercise of a shorter duration which is undertaken with sub-optimal body carbohydrate stores. For example, in team sports played in a tournament, or back-to-back training sessions, there may be inadequate time to recover or prepare body carbohydrate stores. Since fuel stores may be limiting on these occasions, carbohydrate supplementation during the exercise is also recommended. However, until recently it has been considered unnecessary to take on fuel for events of one hour or less. In fact, many sports nutrition publications have recommended that 'water is the best fluid' during these activities.

Some new studies have provided evidence to question this belief. All have examined performance of high-intensity exercise (80–90% of $\dot{V}O_{2max}$) using reliable performance tasks lasting approximately one hour. A study by doctoral student Paul Below, conducted at Professor Ed Coyle's laboratory in Texas, had trained cyclists undertake a time-trial lasting approximately 10 minutes after completing 50 minutes of cycling at a high intensity (85% of $\dot{V}O_{2max}$). Carbohydrate intake during the trial reduced the time taken to complete the final workload by 6% compared to when no carbohydrate was consumed. A similar protocol which employed high-intensity steady-state exercise followed by a time-trial was used by Dr Mindy Millard-Stafford in a study conducted at the Georgia Institute of Technology. Highly-trained runners ran 15 km on a treadmill, with the first 13.4 km being monitored at a high-intensity steady-state pace, and the last 1.6 km being raced as a time-trial. Carbohydrate intake before and during the trial reduced running time (i.e. improved performance) by a similar margin as in the Below study. Both of these studies were conducted in a hot environment. The period of steady-state exercise was used to compare metabolic responses to each treatment but could not uncover a cause for the performance improvement. Certainly there was no evidence of benefits to carbohydrate oxidation.

Finally, at the University of Maastricht in the Netherlands, Dr Asker Jeukendrup used a simple design to focus on performance of well-trained cyclists during a time-trial to complete a fixed amount of work. This trial was conducted in a mild environment, and without any measurements or interventions that might otherwise interfere with the reliability of the performance task. Drinking a carbohydrate drink before and during the time-trial significantly improved performance by 2.3% (60.1 versus 57.7 minutes). The average workload was increased with the carbohydrate feedings; however, there were no differences in heart-rates between trials.

So if carbohydrate ingestion can improve performance during high-intensity exercise lasting 60 minutes, might it not also enhance performance in events lasting less than an hour? Where is the 'cut-off' point where the benefits of supplying extra carbohydrate cease to exist? In an effort to answer this question, Garry Palmer and colleagues from the University of Kingston in England and the University of Cape Town, South Africa, studied fourteen well-trained cyclists who performed two 20 km time-trials. Before the rides, cyclists consumed 8 millilitres per kilogram BM of either a coloured, flavoured placebo, or a 7% carbohydrate–electrolyte solution. Irrespective of the type of drink ingested, the time taken for the 20 kilometres was identical (27 minutes 41 seconds). Therefore, although carbohydrate ingestion before and during intense exercise lasting one hour has a beneficial effect, it does not improve high-intensity steady-state cycling performance lasting approximately 30 minutes. These and other studies show that we must explore further possibilities for the benefits of carbohydrate intake during exercise. And then find ways to explain it!

REPLACING NUTRIENTS DURING EXERCISE

Before water and nutrients can enter the blood and be transported to the muscles and other parts of the body, they must:

- be consumed;
- empty from the stomach into the small intestine;
- be absorbed from the intestine into the blood; and
- in the case of some nutrients, pass through the liver, which regulates their release into the general circulation.

There has been considerable interest in studying each of these stages to see which might be the rate-limiting step. During the 1970s and 1980s, gastric emptying was the topic of focus. Study techniques used nasogastric tubes to introduce various solutions into the stomach and measure the residue after a certain period or an exercise task. A number of factors were identified which influence stomach emptying from its typical rate of approximately 600 ml per hour. These include the temperature and acidity of the food or fluid intake, high-intensity exercise, dehydration, and the size of food particles (whether it is solid, semi-solid or liquid). However, the two major factors are:

1   stomach volume; and
2   energy (kilojoule) content and concentration of food/fluid intake.

These factors can be included in strategies for exercise refuelling and rehydration. First, as the concentration of a fluid increases, it slows down the rate of stomach emptying. With the study techniques used in the 1970s it was found that solutions of a concentration greater than 2–3% carbohydrate (2–3 g per 100 ml) caused a significant drop in stomach emptying rates. Concern over the effect on fluid delivery led to advice that water or very dilute carbohydrate solutions were the only beverages that should be consumed during exercise. Subsequent research has found that these studies overstated the problem. In fact, although there is a small drop in gastric emptying, carbohydrate solutions of 4–8% (e.g. sports drinks) are emptied quite efficiently, and provide a good balance between carbohydrate and fluid delivery. Nevertheless, solutions of 10–12% (e.g. soft drinks) and above are more slowly emptied.

The volume or distention of the stomach contents can also be manipulated during exercise to promote greater fluid and carbohydrate delivery. Studies show that an increased stretch on the stomach wall increases emptying rate, so that approximately 50% of the stomach contents are emptied every 10 minutes overall. By starting exercise with a comfortably filled stomach and topping it up each 10–15 minutes, maximum fluid emptying rates can be achieved (see Chapter 12). There is considerable individual variability in what is comfortable and what can be emptied. Athletes who wish to maximise fluid delivery during exercise of high sweat rates need to experiment with their own plan. However, it appears that fluid can be emptied at rates of 800–1200 ml/hour.

During the 1990s, techniques were developed to measure intestinal absorption over sections of the small bowel. These studies are somewhat artificial and invasive, since they involve subjects swallowing triple barrel tubes right down to the site of study. However, they have shown that solutions containing a variety of carbohydrate types are best absorbed since they take advantage of various transport processes. They also show that highly concentrated beverages (for example, 10–12% carbohydrate drinks) must first be diluted by drawing water into the bowel before they can be absorbed. This is not optimum for maximising rehydration during exercise.

These studies of gastric and intestinal function during exercise have been given much attention over the past 30 years. However, there is a need to put this area of research into perspective. Undoubtedly, various factors are important in modifying these stages of nutrient delivery into the body. But the most simple issue should not be overlooked—that is, the intake by the athlete. After all, this represents the maximum nutrient supply that the muscle or body might receive. It is reassuring to note that new guidelines to athletes recognise strategies to promote better intake of fluid and carbohydrate in the first place. It is clever to know whether a characteristic of a fluid (e.g. its temperature or carbohydrate type) might alter gastric emptying. But the most important issue is whether it encourages voluntary intake by the athlete.

Guidelines for fluid replacement

Ideally an athlete should try to fully replace sweat losses during exercise, especially when exercise is carried out in the heat. In practice, this might translate into drinking fluid at a rate of at least 80% of sweat rates. However, when sweat rates exceed the gastrointestinal limit of approximately 1–1.2 litres/hour, this is not possible. Nor might it be practical to gain access to or an opportunity to drink even these volumes in many sports situations. The bottom line is that each athlete should replace as much fluid as is practical and comfortably tolerated in their sport and in their own situation. And the benefits of this must be weighed against the disadvantages.

Although the timing of fluid intake may largely be dictated by the opportunities provided by the sport, it is worth considering whether there are any physiological advantages to adopting a certain drinking pattern. Studies show that the total volume of intake is the most important factor in rehydration. However, from the comfort angle it is sensible to drink well-tolerated amounts frequently rather than trying to replace very large volumes on a couple of occasions. The value of frequently 'topping up' stomach fluid volume to maximise the gastric fluid emptying rate has already been discussed. Finally, the athlete should begin to drink early during an exercise bout, so that the strategy is to minimise the build-up of dehydration rather than reverse a severe fluid deficit.

Guidelines for carbohydrate replacement

In the early stages of exercise, muscle glycogen stores provide the major source of carbohydrate for oxidation. In fact, studies show that carbohydrate consumed during the first hour of exercise provides less than 20 g towards the muscle fuel bill during this time. After about 90 minutes of exercise, ingested carbohydrate can be used by the working muscles at a rate of about one gram per minute and contribute nearly a third of the body's total carbohydrate needs. Carbohydrate intake strategies should be individualised to the athlete and their event. A variety of strategies appear to work for various athletes and may benefit performance through effects other than muscle fuelling. General answers to the typical questions asked by athletes include:

- *Amount of carbohydrate.* Studies generally show performance benefits when carbohydrate intake is greater than 30 g/hour and more typically approximately 50–60 g/hour. From the muscle's point of view, a carbohydrate supply of about 60 g/hr must be available to sustain fuel needs after muscle glycogen levels are depleted. Therefore, the athlete must eat in advance of, and perhaps in greater quantities than, the muscle need, to ensure that this supply is available later in exercise. This is a matter for individual experimentation.
- *Timing of intake—how often? how early?* To date, studies have not found important differences arising from the issue of frequency of intake. Carbohydrate oxidation and performance effects appear to be similar following a variety of feeding schedules, ranging from a large amount as a single feeding to a series of smaller snacks. This might be best determined by the opportunities provided by the sport. The athlete who waits until they are fatigued before consuming carbohydrate will receive some benefit. However, it is more effective to consume carbohydrate well in anticipation of fatigue. Interestingly, a recent study suggests that it is most effective to begin carbohydrate intake at the start of exercise, even when it is known not to contribute significantly to muscle fuel needs over this period. Dr Glenn McConell from Monash University in Melbourne tested eight well-trained cyclists who cycled for two hours at moderate intensity then raced over a 15-minute time-trial. On one occasion, cyclists consumed 160 g of carbohydrate during the 30 minutes before the time-trial. On another they consumed this carbohydrate spread evenly throughout the first two hours, and in the third option they completed the trial while drinking an artificially sweetened placebo. Consuming carbohydrate throughout the ride enhanced time-trial performance compared to the control trial, with all but one subject doing their best 'race' under this protocol. Time-trial performance during the later feeding trial was not significantly different from the control (placebo) trial.

- *Form of carbohydrate.* Both liquid and solid forms of carbohydrate can be consumed by athletes during exercise. Carbohydrate drinks offer the advantages of being a simultaneous and rapidly absorbed source of fluid, and have become perhaps the preferred way to refuel during exercise. Meanwhile, carbohydrate-rich foods are useful in other ways. They are compact and portable—it is easier to pop a banana or sports bar in your cycle jersey than to carry the equivalent volume of carbohydrate in sports drink. During very prolonged exercise or sports events, many athletes may enjoy some solid food to stave off feelings of hunger. Generally, however, solid foods are more likely to cause gastrointestinal problems during exercise, especially if these foods also contain large amounts of fat or fibre. The athlete should experiment with their own choices
- *Type of carbohydrate.* All carbohydrate types that have a moderate–high glycaemic index (see Chapter 10) provide a rapid increase in blood glucose levels and an effective muscle fuel source. During the 1980s glucose polymers, made of short chains of glucose molecules, were promoted as a more rapidly delivered carbohydrate source. It was believed that superior gastric emptying would result because these solutions could maintain a moderate concentration of carbohydrate for a lower osmolality (a smaller number of individual particles). Studies have subsequently shown that any gastric emptying advantages are short-lived and small. Nevertheless, glucose polymers continue to be a popular component of sports drinks because they provide a mildly sweet taste instead of the sticky sweetness of other sugars. In general, sports drinks contain a mixture of carbohydrate types. This allows manufacturers to fine-tune the taste and mouth-feel so that drinks are as palatable as possible. It may also be of benefit to intestinal absorption to have various carbohydrate types being transported simultaneously. Fructose is the only carbohydrate that is not used in high amounts in sports beverages. Since it is not well absorbed in large doses, too much fructose can lead to gastrointestinal upsets and diarrhoea.

GETTING THE BALANCE RIGHT

Refuelling and rehydrating during exercise is a matter of experience, individuality, creativity and balance. Each athlete needs to assess their needs and their opportunities to match these. Often there are competing issues that require balance or compromise to be found.

Fluid versus carbohydrate

Carbohydrate replacement and fluid replacement offer different advantages to sports performance. The Below study, previously mentioned, used a clever design to test the effects of each. Subjects cycled at high intensity in the heat for nearly an hour on four occasions, receiving various permutations and combinations of fluid and carbohydrate, carbohydrate, fluid, or no treatment. At the end of the study, statistical analysis was able to separate and combine the effects of each treatment. It was found that aggressive fluid replacement improved time-trial performance by approximately 6%, and that carbohydrate intake caused a separate improvement of similar impact. The combination of both carbohydrate and fluid improved performance by approximately 12%, meaning that these effects were independent and additive.

The results of this study make a strong case for trying to meet both fluid and carbohydrate requirements during exercise. But these do not always follow the same formula. In some sports events, the athlete has large sweat (fluid) losses with a smaller need to replace fuel (e.g. an athlete who has dehydrated to make weight). In other sports events, the athlete may deplete fuel stores without losing great amounts of sweat (e.g. a long-distance swimmer or skier who is exercising in cold conditions). Important factors to consider are the athlete's preparation, the environmental conditions and the intensity of exercise.

Sports drinks provide carbohydrate and fluid in a ratio that suits the 'average' sports event. The typical concentration of 7% provides 50 g of carbohydrate when consumed at an hourly rate of 700 ml of fluid. When you are dealing with a mass market or the average sports event, this is a sensible approach. And it is associated with an effective rate of fluid and carbohydrate delivery. However, individuals may want to change this ratio in favour of the balance that suits the specific needs of their event. When fluid needs are of greater significance, and when even a small effect on gastric emptying is significant, the athlete might consider a 4% carbohydrate solution. When carbohydrate needs take priority, then the solution might be made more concentrated (e.g. 10–15%). Of course, this will reduce fluid delivery by reducing the amount of fluid that is consumed as well as by reducing the rate of

───┤ TABLE 13.2 ├─────────────────────────────────────

Quick guide to balancing fluid and carbohydrate needs by changing concentration of sports drinks

Drink concentration (% carbohydrate = g/100 ml)	Carbohydrate intake target (g/hr)	30g	40g	50g	60g	70g	80g
2%	Drink volume	1500	2000	2500	3000	3500	4000
4%	(ml/hr)	750	1000	1250	1500	1750	2000
5%		600	800	1000	1200	1400	1600
6%		500	670	830	1000	1170	1340
7%		430	570	715	860	1000	1140
8%		375	500	625	750	875	1000
10%		300	400	500	600	700	800
12%		250	330	420	500	580	670
15%		200	270	330	400	470	530
20%		150	200	250	300	350	400
25%		120	160	200	240	280	320

Shaded area = preferred range of fluid intake (600–1200 ml/hr)
<< 600 ml = low fluid replacement
>> 1250 ml = high risk of gastrointestinal upsets, volume >> gastric emptying
Source: Adapted from Coyle, E.F. and Montain, S.J. 'Benefits of fluid replacement with carbohydrate during exercise' *Medicine and Science in Sports and Exercise* (supplement) 24: 324–30, 1992.

gastric emptying. Table 13.2 summarises the range of fluid and carbohydrate ratios that might be useful in sport. Some athletes vary the priority of nutrient replacement given to different events in which they compete. Others may even vary the balance over the duration of a long event—for example, they start the event with the priority on fluid replacement by drinking dilute drinks, then switch to greater emphasis on carbohydrate intake with more concentrated drinks as the muscle fuel supplies dwindle. The success of these experiments depends on the response of the individual, whether their sport provides an atypical challenge, and whether there is opportunity for the athlete to provide their own supplies. In some cases, it is an advantage to be an individual. In other sports it is more convenient to 'go with the flow'.

Gastrointestinal problems during exercise

When lists of factors impairing performance are prepared, 'gastrointestinal problems' seems paltry compared to the spectacular collapses witnessed when athletes hit the wall or fall victim to heat stroke. To be truthful, symptoms like flatulence, burping and cramp may seem a minor price to pay during exercise. However, they may still detract from the concentration, enjoyment and performance of sport. On the other hand, problems of vomiting and diarrhoea are more than a major distraction. They directly add to fluid and carbohydrate balance problems, and hamper any attempts to replace body losses. Studies have identified a number of factors that increase the risk of gastrointestinal discomfort and upset, including:

- being female;
- being undertrained;
- undertaking exercise of unaccustomed high-intensity;
- undertaking exercise involving running or whole body movement or 'joggling';
- having pre-existing gastrointestinal problems;
- being dehydrated;
- suffering from stress or nervousness; and
- improper fluid and food intake before and during exercise.

The pre-event meal can be a cause of gastrointestinal problems. Problem foods or practices are usually specific to the individual. However, the size and timing of pre-event meals may need to be reassessed, and food choices should be kept low in fat, protein and fibre (see Chapter 12). During exercise, the intake of fat, fibre or solid foods, or just too much food or fluid can cause problems. Sometimes an athlete can find an alternative way to provide the same nutrient intake. Other times, the only solution is to cut back on total intake. This might mean that less fluid or carbohydrate can be consumed. However, in some situations the gastrointestinal discomfort overrides the physiological advantages of rehydration and refuelling. For example, a study by Dr Tracey Robinson and colleagues, undertaken at the University of Cape Town in South Africa, showed that cyclists who were forced to replace their total sweat losses while undertaking high-intensity exercise actually performed worse than when fluid wasn't replaced. Although most cyclists did not suffer from overt gastric upsets, the discomfort of having a full stomach was enough to interfere with their time-trial performance.

Time lost 'on the run'

Athletes who undertake continuous activities such as triathlons, road cycling, cross-country skiing and distance running have a special challenge. Any intake must be achieved, literally, 'on the road'. Eating and drinking while exercising increases the risk of gastrointestinal upset. Furthermore, getting access to supplies will mean that the athlete has to slow down from their optimal pace. For example, a runner or cyclist will have to slow down to accept a drink at an aid station or from a handler, and then to consume it. The cyclist or skier will have to move out of their aerodynamic position to reach for or consume their fluid/food supplies. Chaos can ensue in mass-participation races as athletes converge on aid stations, particularly when searching for their own special supplies. Any physiological advantages from rehydrating and refuelling must be balanced against the time lost in consuming it and the extra risk of gastrointestinal problems.

Each athlete must make their own decision about this balance. Of course, it is difficult to measure the subtle performance losses due to less successful replacement of fluid or carbohydrate needs. Many athletes appear to side on the balance of conservatism when it comes to sacrificing time for fluid and carbohydrate intake. They regard their outcome as successful if they avoid obvious performance disasters. It will take time and many studies to convince athletes that small performance losses do occur, and may be the real difference between winning and losing.

In the meantime there may be creative ways to improve the athlete's ability to refuel and rehydrate on the run. Devices such as pressurised fluid pouches are available, and can be carried on a rower's back or under the cyclist's saddle. They feed fluid straight to a straw near the athlete's mouth, freeing them from the need to change position or use their hands to obtain exercise refreshments. Light plastic bottles or squeezy packs are preferable to cups for athletes who need to drink during a running or skiing event. These allow fluid to be squeezed into the mouth without losing a stride, a breath, or most of the drink to the road.

PUTTING IT INTO PRACTICE

Scientists have always struggled to provide the 'bottom line' to athletes. After all, athletes usually demand precise instructions, and scientists are trained to be precise. Early attempts to prepare guidelines for fluid and food intake during exercise failed because they failed to grasp the individuality of sports and people. At the beginning of this chapter, the seemingly sensible advice on fluid intake provided by the 1987 statement of the American College of Sports Medicine (ACSM) was shown to be nonsensical. The 1996 guidelines by the ACSM on rehydrating and refuelling during exercise reflect a new understanding of the science and practice of sports nutrition. They incorporate new scientific knowledge into state-of-the-art advice. But they also respond to the bigger challenge—to strike a balance between giving athletes sufficient guidance to be useful, but sufficient flexibility so that each individual is encouraged to find their own balance. The panel on the following pages expands on these guidelines in a similar manner, providing a framework of advice and allowing athletes to 'colour in' their own picture.

GUIDELINES FOR FLUID AND CARBOHYDRATE INTAKE DURING EXERCISE

- Refuel and rehydrate to a plan rather than good luck or thirst. Most athletes underutilise opportunities to drink during exercise and thus become unnecessarily dehydrated.
- Counter false beliefs about exercise fluid and fuel intake. Any 'weight loss' that occurs during exercise is a temporary fluid loss and should not be seen as a way to control body weight. An athlete cannot train or 'toughen' themselves to cope with dehydration. And although carbohydrate intake involves the intake of kilojoules, this may improve performance and recovery for the weight-conscious athlete. In other words, aim to train and compete with the benefits of clever exercise nutrition strategies at all times.
- Use training sessions to practise and fine-tune exercise refuelling and rehydration strategies. Rehearse all competition strategies as closely as possible to develop an individualised and optimal plan.
- Become aware of your typical sweat losses in a variety of environments. Monitor changes in body mass and fluid balance on a number of typical occasions (see Figure 13.1). Use this information to plan rehydration strategies during and after exercise. Complete fluid replacement during exercise (i.e. fluid intake at 80–100% of sweat rates) is an ideal, but is not always practical. Usually the athlete must be satisfied to drink as much as is comfortable and practical, and then replace fluid losses fully after the session (see Chapter 14).
- Fluid intakes of 500–1000 ml per hour are generally possible across a variety of sports. This will vary with the individual sport and the

athlete. The athlete should take advantage of all opportunities that arise in their sport to match fluid intake to fluid needs.

- Fluid intakes of 1000–1200 ml per hour are possible and useful for some athletes who experience extremely large sweat losses. Gastric emptying can be maximised by drinking a volume of fluid just prior to the event, thus priming the stomach to a comfortable stretch. Top up with a drink each 10–15 minutes to maintain rapid fluid emptying. Since this strategy carries a risk of gastrointestinal problems it should be well-practised.

- In team sports and other intermittent activities, the athlete has chances to drink while stationary. These include formal breaks (time-outs, quarter-time breaks, change of ends), as well as spontaneous opportunities during play time (e.g. during stoppages due to injuries or rule infringements). These opportunities will vary from sport to sport (see Table 13.1). Each athlete should identify and use their opportunities to drink.

- Providing access to fluids is an important issue in promoting fluid intake. The methods will vary across sports. Event organisers and team managers play a role in optimising this by providing aid stations and communal drink tanks. In some sports, handlers may be able to take drink bottles to athletes during play. Individual drink bottles help the athlete to increase their own access to fluid, as well as providing them with continual feedback about the volume they have consumed. In other sports the athlete is responsible for their own fluid supplies. All should be aware of the benefits of aggressive hydration strategies during exercise, and create special strategies to make fluids readily available.

- During continuous activities such as distance running, cycling, triathlons and cross-country skiing, the athlete must consume fluids and fuels 'on the run'. Each athlete must balance the benefits of increased intake against the sacrifice of losing time to access and consume supplies, and the increased risk of gastrointestinal problems. With practice, and with the use of devices that make fluid/carbohydrate intake easy, an athlete can minimise the downside of rehydration and refuelling strategies. Experiment with squeeze-packed drinks, pressurised pouches with straws, and convenient carbohydrate gel pouches to find a strategy that works for you.

- Update your views on carbohydrate intake during exercise. In events lasting over 90 minutes, or events undertaken with less than optimal body carbohydrate reserves, the benefits of refuelling are easily shown. However, carbohydrate intake may benefit performance in some shorter sports—even events lasting 30–60 minutes. Experiment to find if there are advantages to your sport. While most sports nutrition resources still list water as the 'best' fluid source during exercise, it is fairer to say that it is 'adequate' for many situations. In fact, carbohydrate-containing drinks are suitable for all situations, and preferable in many sports.

- Begin fluid and refuelling strategies early and to a plan, rather than waiting until you begin to feel fatigued during your event. In the case of fluid intake, work from a position of minimising a fluid deficit, rather than reversing dehydration after it has become significant. Carbohydrate intake throughout the event may provide benefits in addition to supplying fuel to a depleted muscle. Arrange the timing of intake according to the opportunities provided in your sport.

- If refuelling is a tactic, experiment with carbohydrate intakes of 30–60 g per hour to find a plan that works for you. Some athletes may need to consume even larger amounts of carbohydrate (e.g. 1 g per kg BM per hour), particularly towards the end of prolonged events, to provide for the fuel needs of a depleted muscle.

- A variety of fluid and food options are available for refuelling. Sports drinks are a tailor-made option, generally providing a 4–8% carbohydrate concentration. This provides a suitable carbohydrate to fluid delivery ratio across a range of sports. Some athletes may experiment with different concentrations to alter the priority of fluid and carbohydrate replacement.

- Solid foods or gels provide a more concentrated carbohydrate source which may be handy for a large fuel boost, or for the situation where supplies must be portable. They may also take care of hunger pangs during prolonged events. Practise with such foods so that gastrointestinal risks are identified. Don't neglect fluid needs.

- Choose foods and fluids that are palatable, since they will encourage greater intake. Keep fluids cool but not cold, and experiment to find a flavour that you like. During very prolonged events, a change of flavours or the occasional intake of food may reduce the 'taste fatigue' that is often found after consuming litres of the same drink. The low levels of sodium found in sports drinks help to increase their taste appeal to athletes who are hot and sweaty.

- If gastrointestinal problems occur, look carefully at your strategies. Dehydration is a hidden cause of many problems. Athletes often blame the sports drink that was consumed mid-race for their upset, rather than their failure to drink it earlier, thereby reducing their level of dehydration. Solid foods with a high fat or fibre content may also cause problems for some athletes. Sometimes it is just a matter of too much while moving too fast. Modify your intake until the problems disappear.

- Ultra-endurance events call for special strategies. Make sure that fluid needs are balanced—noting that it is occasionally possible and undesirable for an athlete to overhydrate if sweat rates are sufficiently low. Refuelling is important—and some athletes are experimenting with intakes of Medium Chain Trigylceride (MCT) oils as well as carbohydrate (see Chapter 10). The replacement of sodium in rehydration fluids may help to reduce the risk of developing hyponatremia (low blood sodium levels).

HYPONATREMIA: TAKING EXERCISE FLUIDS WITH A GRAIN OF SALT

Professor Tim Noakes of the University of Cape Town is no stranger to speaking his mind and challenging truths. During the late 1980s he made a 'splash' in sports science by proclaiming that the advice to athletes to drink during exercise was overstated. He noted that runners and other athletes in 'continuous' endurance sports seemed unable or unwilling to drink the volumes of fluid recommended in sports science guidelines. Furthermore, he showed cases of hyponatremia (low blood sodium levels) occurring during ultra-endurance sports as a result of 'water intoxication'. Some athletes managed to be overzealous in replacing fluids lost during long-distance events. Often these athletes were exercising at slow paces so that sweat losses were low. And they were making ample use of the aid station network, taking plenty of time to stop and drink. Several individuals who were found collapsed in the medical tents of these races were found to be in significant fluid gain. In some cases, low sodium levels were associated with potentially fatal symptoms, starting with disorientation and leading to convulsion and coma. A routine screening of race finishers found a small percentage with lowish blood sodium levels—but fortunately, most athletes showed no symptoms of distress. Coming from South Africa, Professor Noakes has had plenty of experience with ultra-distance sports such as the Comrades 90 km marathon run. His initial advice was to warn athletes about the dangers of overdrinking during exercise.

However, his findings and interpretation met with plenty of opposition, particularly from Dr Doug Hiller and his colleagues from the Hawaiian Ironman Triathlon race. Their medical team had also seen cases of reduced sodium levels in race finishers. However, their competitors tended to be dehydrated rather than overhydrated. Their interpretation was that these triathletes were losing large amounts of sodium and water through sweat losses, and were diluting blood sodium levels by partially replacing water losses without sodium replacement. Their advice was to continue to rehydrate but to include sodium in race fluids. Sports drinks were promoted as a better choice than low-sodium water and cola drinks.

The debate has continued to rage, although some common ground has been reached. The present position is as follows:

- Hyponatremia is a rare but potentially serious problem that usually occurs in some athletes in ultra-endurance events.
- There may be several ways in which low blood sodium levels occur. One mechanism concerns the athlete who has lost significant amounts of fluid and sodium through sweat losses, who then overconsumes and absorbs a large amount of fluid. Plasma volume is increased and sodium levels are diluted. For unexplained reasons this athlete experiences difficulty in using the usual mechanisms to regulate fluid balance and sodium levels. They seem unable to produce adequate volumes of urine to rid the body of excess fluid.
- Another mechanism, suggested by Professor Noakes, sees the athlete consume, but not absorb, large amounts of fluid. This fluid may be residing in the gut and is technically outside the body. However, the body reacts to equilibrate sodium levels throughout all body fluid compartments, and moves sodium into the gut to achieve this balance. The result is a dilution of blood sodium levels. Again, normal mechanisms that would guard against this problem, or solve the crisis (i.e. to experience diarrhoea), appear to fail. Note that this is just a theory and the evidence to support this needs to be well investigated.
- Nevertheless, these mechanisms both require the convergence of the right people (predisposed to failure of body fluid regulation during exercise) and the right situation (consumption of large amounts of low-sodium fluid). This explains why the occurrence is rare.
- Ultra-endurance sports require specialised sports nutrition practices. Athletes should take note of the small risk of hyponatremia and should take the advice to 'drink plenty of fluid' during their race with a grain of salt, literally and figuratively. In other words, they should also drink to a schedule that is balanced against their sweat losses and their ability to empty and absorb fluids. And they should choose fluids that contain small amounts of sodium. Most sports drinks contain 20 mmol/L sodium—a small contribution towards replacing the massive sodium losses experienced over many hours of hot, sweaty work.
- The controversial advice to athletes to limit fluid intake during exercise has proved to be contrary to the balance of scientific knowledge. The publicity about hyponatremia has helped us to realise that balance is important with all aspects of sports nutrition. We have learned that occasionally it is possible to have too much of a good thing. However, the typical situation is that most athletes need help to increase their fluid intake during exercise so as to enjoy the benefits of better hydration.

DO YOU SWEAT IN WATER? (AND OTHER MYSTERIES OF LIFE)

Do athletes who train and compete in water, such as swimmers, water polo players, devotees of water aerobics and surf lifesavers, need to worry about dehydration during their exercise sessions? Is it possible to sweat when you are fully immersed in water? Is sweating needed to lose body heat produced by exercise in water, or is your body sufficiently cooled by the water it is immersed in? In attempting to find an answer to some of these questions, researchers from the Nutrition Department at the Australian Institute of Sport actually found some other unsolved mysteries of life: Why do you want to go to the toilet as soon as you get into a pool? And how do you know if a swimmer has peed in the pool?

The AIS study monitored fluid balance in members of the Australian National Swimming Team during a three-week training camp held in Atlanta, in the United States, before a major swim meet. Training was carried out in an indoor pool without air-conditioning. Therefore, although the swimmers were protected from direct sunlight, they did their training in hot (30°C) and humid (60% relative humidity) conditions, with the pool temperature ranging from 28° to 29°C. Sweat losses, dehydration and fluid intake were calculated by carefully weighing the body mass of each swimmer before and after the session, and changes in the weight of their drink bottles (see Figure 13.1). The swimmers were asked to be particularly honest in directing all urine losses to the toilet and to the attention of the weigh-in procedures. These calculations were made for thirteen training sessions and a total of 295 observations. Since the swimmers had done different types of training and different mileage in the pool, the results were compared by expressing them per kilometre of swimming. The study also looked at the different types of training sessions (called 'aerobic', 'anaerobic threshold', 'maximal oxygen consumption' and 'race pace/speed work' by the coaches) to see if this influenced sweat losses and fluid intake measurements. The results are summarised in Table 13.3.

TABLE 13.3

Fluid intake and loss during swimming training

	Sweat rate (ml per km of training)	Fluid intake rate (ml per km of training)
All swimmers ($n = 295$)	123	127
Females ($n = 140$)	107	95
Males ($n = 155$)	138	155
Aerobic sessions ($n = 81$)	92	109
Anaerobic threshold ($n = 23$)	167	117

The results showed that swimmers lost about 600 ml of sweat during their typical training session (mean distance = 4 km, mean time = approximately one hour of training). Therefore, although swimmers do incur sweat losses during training, it is less than is found in athletes who train on land. Since these swimmers were undertaking training at high exercise intensities, the most likely explanation is that body heat is partially dissipated by conduction into the surrounding water.

Of course, the mean values of fluid balance tend to disguise the behaviour of individuals. Within each session there were swimmers who lost larger amounts of sweat or failed to drink enough to replace their losses, and who became mildly dehydrated. On the other hand, some swimmers drank more fluid than they had lost as sweat, and actually 'gained weight' by the end of the session. Male swimmers sweated more and drank more than female swimmers. And the 'sweatiest' sessions were ones based on anaerobic-threshold training. Not only did these sessions increase the rate of sweat loss, but the swimmers seemed less successful in drinking enough fluid to replace their losses.

Of course, the sources of error in this study must be acknowledged. Urine losses in the pool would not only breach pool etiquette, but would inflate the calculated sweat losses. The researchers made a special comment that the swimmers needed to 'jump out' for a visit during a training session more often than any other athletes they had studied. Maybe this is due to the fact that swimmers remain in general fluid balance, and sometimes even drink more fluid than they are sweating. One swimmer in the study managed a total urine volume of 1 litre during several visits during one training session! However, there also seems to be an increased urge to urinate that comes from being immersed in water, and perhaps from the body fluid redistribution that comes from exercising in a prone rather than upright position.

In addition, the researchers could not be sure that they measured all fluid intake during the session. Although they monitored what was being consumed on purpose from drink bottles, they were not able to measure if water was being swallowed by accident from the pool. Swimmers tell you this happens, particularly during backstroke, or when the water is turbulent from high-intensity training and lots of swimmers are in your lane. Is this volume of fluid significant in the study calculations or in the swimmers' fluid balance? We don't know.

In summary, these results showed that swimmers do sweat, although at rates that are lower than land-training athletes. Most of them are able to replace their fluid losses during the session by drinking from water bottles kept at the end of the pool. But this occurred under what might be deemed an 'optimal situation'. The swimmers were part of the National swim team, and were motivated and well-educated. Sports drinks and water were provided at every session for them, and coaches reminded them to bring their drink bottles to the session and to drink between sets. It doesn't come much easier than that!

But these also may be the conditions that are most desirable for swimmers who want to train at their best. Of course, fluid balance isn't the only reason to drink during a training session. If the drink bottle contains a sports drink or cordial, it will provide the muscles with an additional source of fuel. This is important for optimising training during prolonged hard workouts or in a heavy training week. In fact, for swimmers this is the best reason for having a drink bottle and drink plan in place during a swim training session. If your muscles are doing the work, they deserve the best treatment!

14

Eating for recovery

'I like to get replenishment in the first half hour after my race with high carbohydrate drinks and foods. Especially when I have a busy program with more than one race each night. I have to fit in swim downs, massage, drug tests, the next race, coaches, the media. It can be frantic. I have my own supplies organised—a sports drink, bananas, or something sweet.'

> Michael Klim, sprint swimmer, 1998 World Champion for 100 metre butterfly and 200 metre freestyle, and world-record holder in 100 metre butterfly

'My team has discovered that it's important to ingest a small amount of carbohydrates, usually by eating a bowl of cereal, immediately following the race. This is quite a change from the traditional approach in cycling, in which riders were told not to eat anything until many hours after . . . supposedly to allow their bodies to recuperate before ingesting. In fact, they were losing four hours of precious glycogen storage time.'

> Greg LeMond, three-time winner of the Tour de France, on eating after a day's stage

The finish line has been crossed, the final whistle blown, the winning shot played, or the last set in the training session completed. Should these have involved a medal-winning performance, a premiership cup or the athlete's retirement, then this chapter may not be necessary. But for the vast majority of athletes, even if the immediate schedule reads 'rest', it is likely that another workout or competition event is looming on the horizon. Therefore, recovery is an important item on the athlete's agenda. As outlined in Chapter 2, recovery is the desirable process of adaptation to physiological stress. In the training situation, with correct planning of the workload and the recovery time, adaptation allows the body to become fitter, stronger or faster. In the competition scenario, however, there may be less control over the work to recovery ratio. A simpler but more realistic goal may be to face the next opponent, or the next round or stage in a competition, in the best shape possible.

Recovery encompasses a complex range of processes which include:

- refuelling the muscles and liver of their expended energy;
- replacing the fluid and electrolytes lost in sweat;
- allowing the immune system to handle the damage and destruction caused by the exercise bout; and
- manufacturing new proteins, red blood cells and other cellular components.

In other words, although an athlete may appear to be 'resting', a lot of activity is occurring within the body. The traditional approach to recovery is a passive one—'let it happen'. Other athletes take an even less effective route—the 'make it even harder approach'. This might involve activities such as drinking excessive alcohol, further heat exposure via sun or saunas despite already being overheated, or failing to get sufficient rest or sleep. Such activities hamper recovery processes and/or add to the damage that must be repaired.

The best approach is a proactive recovery. In dietary terms, this means providing the body with all the nutrients it needs, in a speedy and practical manner, so that refuelling, rehydration, repair and regeneration processes are all optimised. Where specific recovery processes have been identified and studied, clear nutritional guidelines can be stated. This is the case for rehydration and refuelling. Unfortunately, the post-exercise workings of the immune system, protein metabolism, anti-oxidant defence and many other issues relating to recovery remain unclear. This chapter will outline the guidelines that can be made with a good degree of certainty, and include a safety margin for ideas that are intuitively sensible. Future research will help to fill in the gaps.

REFUELLING

The muscle biopsy technique, introduced into sports science research in the 1960s, has made possible a large number of studies of muscle glycogen storage. Thanks to this technique, a number of factors that promote speedy resynthesis of the carbohydrate stores in a depleted muscle have been identified (see Table 14.1). Not surprisingly, athletes have been less willing to submit to having needles poked into their livers, so there have been few direct studies of the 'ins and outs' of liver glycogen storage in humans. However, it is known that the liver can deplete and restore its fuel levels quickly—it can empty after a few hours of heavy exercise, or after 10–12 hours without food (e.g. overnight). But it can also rapidly refuel within two to four hours after a high-carbohydrate meal. After exercise, the body gives priority to the recovery of muscle glycogen stores over liver stores. In fact, if the athlete does not eat carbohydrate immediately after exercise, the liver will work hard to convert compounds such as lactate and amino

---

TABLE 14.1

Factors affecting muscle glycogen recovery

Factors which enhance the rate of recovery

- Depleted stores—the lower the stores the faster the rate of recovery.
- Immediate intake of carbohydrate after exercise. Adequate amounts of carbohydrate:
  —1–1.5g CHO/kg BM within 30 minutes after exercise
  —7–10g CHO/kg BM per 24 hours.
- Focus on carbohydrate-rich foods with a high glycaemic index.

Factors which have minimal or no effect on the rate of recovery

- Gentle exercise during recovery.
- Spacing of meals and snacks (provided the total amount of carbohydrate is adequate).
- Other food at meals (e.g. fat- or protein-rich foods) provided that the total amount of carbohydrate is adequate.

Factors which slow the rate of recovery

- Damage to the muscle (contact injury or delayed-onset muscle soreness caused by eccentric exercise).
- Delay in intake of carbohydrate after exercise.
- Inadequate amounts of carbohydrate.
- Reliance on carbohydrate-rich foods with a low glycaemic index.
- High-intensity exercise during recovery.

acids into glucose, and promote a low rate of muscle glycogen recovery. However, muscle refuelling is best achieved by supplying the body with carbohydrate-rich foods and drinks.

THE MUSCLE BIOPSY

For subjects who have taken part in sports science studies, a muscle biopsy scar is something like a badge of honour or courage. Certainly, it is an invasive process and not many athletes like the sight of needles. However, in skilled hands, a muscle biopsy is a safe and relatively painless procedure, and has assisted scientists towards greater under-standing of exercise metabolism. Today it is just one of a number of techniques used to study fuel usage and exercise performance. But in the 1960s when exercise scientists began to experiment with muscle biopsies, it allowed great leaps in 'proof' or support for certain exercise science theories. Muscle glycogen levels were one of the first factors to be measured and manipulated by different diets and training programs. Once it became possible to monitor changes in muscle fuel levels before and after exercise, scientists were able to correlate endurance capacity with the size of glycogen stores, and fatigue with fuel depletion. Today, many features of the muscle can be measured from tiny muscle samples.

Before a muscle biopsy is performed, a small amount of local anaesthetic is injected just under the skin. Once the area is numb, a scalpel is used to make a small incision in the skin and underlying muscle fascia (muscle sheath). The size of the biopsy needle is determined by the amount of muscle that is needed—tiny samples from 10 to 100 mg are typical—but is generally thinner than a ball-point pen. The biopsy needle is hollow, with a small 'window' at its end, and another smaller cylinder that slots inside it. This second cylinder has a sharp end or blade. Once positioned through the muscle fascia and into the muscle belly, a syringe can be attached to the outer end of the needle and some suction applied. This causes a small amount of muscle to be drawn into the window of the needle, which can be sliced off by dropping the inner cylinder with blade. With a relaxed subject and an experienced doctor, the sensation can vary from no feeling at all, to a deep pressure inside the muscle. Some exercise scientists have even been known to perform biopsies on themselves!

Scientists take samples from the major muscle groups involved in various exercise types—for example, from the vastus lateralis (quadriceps) of cyclists, from the gastrocnemius (calf) of runners, and from the deltoid muscles of swimmers. Some studies have required a muscle sample to be taken within seconds of finishing exercise or in the middle of a race. This requires expertise and good cooperation from the subject. Studies often program a series of biopsies to be taken to monitor changes in the muscle content of some compound over a short time period—for example, before and after exercise, or before and after recovery. Where possible, each sample should be taken from different sites—for instance, in opposite legs or through a new incision at least 3 cm from the first one. This is because the biopsy itself causes temporary damage to the muscle and can interfere with the storage of the compound that is being monitored at that site. A muscle biopsy generally leaves the subject feeling a deep bruise for 24–48 hours, and leaves a small scar which fades with time. However, as part of a well-conducted study it may also leave behind a new piece of information about the science of exercise.

Refuelling and the amount of dietary carbohydrate

The most important dietary factor affecting muscle glycogen refuelling is the amount of carbohydrate consumed. There is a direct relationship between the quantity of dietary carbohydrate consumed and post-exercise glycogen storage, at least until the muscle storage capacity has been reached. The daily upper limit for conversion of dietary carbohydrate into muscle glycogen appears to be 7–10 g of carbohydrate for each kg of body mass (BM)—or around 500–700 g of carbohydrate per day. This amount will vary between athletes according to the size of their muscle mass and other factors. However, when the aim is to maximise muscle glycogen storage, these are the carbohydrate intake targets to reach.

Refuelling and timing of dietary carbohydrate

Eating immediately after exercise also promotes speedy refuelling. The results of several studies have led to guidelines that the athlete should consume carbohydrate-rich foods and drinks, providing at least 1 g of carbohydrate for each kg BM (50–150 g of carbohydrate for most athletes) within 30 minutes of the completion of their exercise session. Since it is often difficult or unappealing to eat large meals after exercise, many athletes prefer to have a post-exercise snack and then ease back into a meal routine a couple of hours later.

One study by Dr John Ivy from the University of Texas has suggested that muscle glycogen storage is slightly enhanced during the first couple of hours of recovery, because exercise has left the muscle more sensitive and with a greater capacity to take up blood glucose. After a couple of hours these benefits dissipate, and glycogen storage slows to more typical rates. While this finding has received much publicity, the more important message is that unless or until carbohydrate is consumed, muscle refuelling is very slow. Optimal refuelling is important when the first exercise session has substantially depleted glycogen stores and the recovery period until the next session is short (e.g. less than 4–12 hours). Therefore, when minutes count, it makes sense to provide the muscle with an early supply of carbohydrate and promote glycogen storage at full capacity.

Over the day, it is not important whether carbohydrate is eaten as a series of small snacks, or as 'three square meals', provided that carbohydrate intake targets are met. Studies have shown that glycogen storage over 24 hours of recovery was similar when a high-carbohydrate diet was consumed as two huge meals or as seven smaller meals, or when four high-car- bohydrate meals were redistributed into sixteen hourly snacks. The frequency of eating affects blood glucose and insulin profiles over the day, and each of these affect glycogen storage. So there may be some influence on muscle glycogen storage when it is working below its full capacity. However, if sufficient carbohydrate is consumed, this doesn't appear to be an issue. Whether the athlete prefers to 'nibble' their way through the day, or 'gorge' on a few larger meals, is a matter of individual preference and timetabling within a busy day.

Refuelling and type of carbohydrate foods and drinks

The choice of carbohydrate foods and drinks in the recovery diet is probably also more of a practical concern than direct physiological importance. Studies have found no difference in the rates of refuelling between liquid and solid forms of carbohydrate. However, there are confusing results from stud- ies of carbohydrate food types, largely because researchers have looked at carbohydrate foods according to the 'simple' and 'complex' classification—a system that is unhelpful and somewhat misleading (Chapter 10).

Research involving the Australian Institute of Sport and Professor Mark Hargreaves has investigated the glycaemic index (GI) of carbohydrate-rich foods and recovery. One study compared post-exercise recovery on a high-carbohydrate diet composed of foods with high GI, with a diet of an equal amount of carbohydrate provided by foods of low GI. The high GI diet produced significantly greater glycogen storage during 24 hours of recovery from prolonged cycling (106 mmol/kg) compared with the low GI diet (71 mmol/kg). However, this does not provide a major change to sports nutrition education, because in real life athletes don't eat diets composed only of low GI carbohydrate-rich foods such as lentils, legumes, oatmeal and sweetened dairy foods. Although recovery nutrition guidelines can include an encouragement to focus on foods of higher GI, this is largely a reinforcement of typical eating patterns.

Since the major hurdle for most athletes is to consume sufficient carbohydrate—particularly immediately after exercise—the 'best' foods and drinks are those that lend themselves to these goals. Practical issues such as taste and appeal to the athlete are important factors to consider, especially when the athlete is hot and exhausted after exercise. Portability and ease of 'eating on the run' also need to be considered in a busy lifestyle. Athletes may favour 'compact' carbohydrate-rich foods and carbohydrate drinks, rather than bulky high-fibre food choices, in order to meet high carbohydrate intakes without feeling uncomfortably full.

Other nutrients and overall nutritional needs

It has been suggested that other nutrients eaten with carbohydrate-rich foods or meals could alter the rate of glycogen refuelling, primarily by changing blood glucose and insulin responses to meals. One study has reported that protein added to a post-exercise carbohydrate drink stimulates glycogen storage. However, subsequent research from the Australian Institute of Sport, using real foods, has shown that the protein and fat content of meals does not affect glycogen storage during 24 hours of recovery from prolonged exercise when adequate carbohydrate is consumed. The problem with eating large amounts of protein and fat in post-exercise meals, or recovery diets in general, is that most athletes will not have the stomach capacity or energy budget to consume their carbohydrate goals as well. Therefore, the advice to athletes is to focus on carbohydrate needs first, and look after other nutritional needs or concerns accordingly.

There may be other reasons for including protein and other nutrients such as vitamins and minerals in snacks and meals eaten immediately after exercise. These nutrients are important in other recovery processes—for example, repair and rebuilding activities and immune responses—and an immediate intake may be useful in promoting these activities. This issue is still awaiting research. In the long term, eating patterns must balance carbohydrate recovery goals with many other nutritional concerns. Choosing carbohydrate-rich foods that are also good sources of other nutrients can help to achieve a number of everyday nutrition goals simultaneously. In tricky situations, particularly during or immediately post-exercise, the practical aspect of meeting a carbohydrate need may be the first priority, and the nutrient content of carbohydrate foods or drinks may be of less importance. However, in the bigger picture of the everyday training diet, or competition seasons lasting over weeks and months, the focus on nutritious carbohydrate-rich foods and drinks makes good sense. With a little creativity, the athlete can find foods that are both practical and nutritious.

The panel on the following pages provides guidelines to eating for post-exercise refuelling which take all these factors into account.

GUIDELINES FOR PROMOTING POST-EXERCISE REFUELLING

- Consume a high-carbohydrate meal or snack within 30 minutes of completing a strenuous exercise session. Be organised to have suitable food and drinks available—at the exercise venue if necessary.
- Aim for an intake of typically 1.0–1.5 g of carbohydrate per kg BM (typically, 50–150 g of carbohydrate) immediately after exercise, and repeat after two hours or until normal meal patterns are resumed (see the panel on the following pages).
- A daily carbohydrate intake of 7–10 g per kg BM (typically 400–700 g) is required to optimise muscle glycogen storage.
- When carbohydrate needs are high, and appetite is suppressed or gastric comfort is a problem, focus on compact forms of carbohydrate—low-fibre forms of carbohydrate foods, sugar-rich foods and special sports supplements such as sports bars.
- Carbohydrate-containing fluids are also low in bulk and may be appealing to athletes who are fatigued and dehydrated. These include sports drinks, soft drinks and fruit juices, commercial liquid meal supplements, milk shakes and fruit smoothies.
- Low glycaemic index (GI) carbohydrate foods such as lentils and legumes may be less suitable for speedy glycogen recovery and should not be the principal carbohydrate source in recovery meals.

This is generally not a problem, as typical Western diets are generally based on carbohydrate-rich foods of moderate and high GI.

- Small, frequent meals may assist the athlete to achieve high carbohydrate intakes without the discomfort of overeating. However, organise your routine of meals and snacks to suit your individual preferences, timetable and appetite/comfort. As long as enough carbohydrate is consumed, it doesn't appear to matter how you space it over the day.

- When gastric comfort or total energy requirements limit total food intake, high-fat foods and excessive amounts of protein foods should not be consumed at the expense of carbohydrate foods. Focus on high-carbohydrate foods and meal choices first.

- Nutritious carbohydrate-rich foods and drinks may provide protein and other nutrients (vitamins and minerals) that are important in other post-exercise recovery processes. These will be important in the overall diet. Future research may show that intake early after exercise could enhance other activities of repair and rebuilding.

- Muscle damage interferes with glycogen storage—this may be partially offset by increasing carbohydrate intake during the first 24 hours of recovery. Carbohydrate needs may also be increased if exercise is undertaken during the recovery period.

CARBOHYDRATE RECOVERY SNACKS AND MEALS

Each of the following selections provides approximately 50 g of carbohydrate. Eat one to three of these portions to ensure speedy recovery after a heavy exercise session, and repeat this pattern after two hours or until normal eating patterns have been resumed.

- 650–800 ml of sports drink
- 800 ml of cordial
- 500 ml of fruit juice, soft drink or flavoured mineral water
- 250 ml of carbohydrate loader drink
- 60 g packet of jelly beans or jube sweets
- 3 medium pieces of fruit
- 1 round of jam or honey sandwiches (thick-sliced bread and plenty of jam/honey)
- 3 muesli bars
- 1 large Mars bar or chocolate bar (70 g)
- 2 breakfast bars

- 3 rice cakes with jam or honey
- 2 crumpets or English muffins with Vegemite
- Cup of thick vegetable soup with large bread roll
- Jaffle/toasted sandwich with banana filling (using whole banana)
- One sports bar (check the label to see total carbohydrate content)
- 115 g (1 large or 2 small) cake-style muffin, fruit bun or scones
- 330 g (1 cup) of creamed rice
- 300 g (large) baked potato with salsa filling
- 120 g (1–2 large) pancakes with 30 g syrup

50 g carbohydrate snacks which also contain at least 10 g of protein:

- 250–350 ml of liquid meal supplement
- 250–350 ml of milk shake or fruit smoothie
- Some sports bars (check labels to see carbohydrate and protein content)
- 2 × 200 g cartons of fruit-flavoured yoghurt
- Bowl of breakfast cereal with milk
- 200 g carton of fruit-flavoured yoghurt or fromage frais topped with 1 cup of breakfast cereal
- 250 g tin of baked beans or spaghetti on 2 slices of toast or in jaffle/toasted sandwich
- 1 round of sandwiches, including cheese/meat/chicken in filling, plus 1 piece of fruit
- 1.5 cups of fruit salad with ½ carton of fruit-flavoured yoghurt or frozen yoghurt
- Carton of fruit-flavoured yoghurt and a muesli bar
- 2 crumpets or English muffins with thick spread of peanut butter
- 250 g (large) baked potato with cottage cheese or grated cheese filling
- 200 g thick-crust pizza
- 1 cup fruit crumble with ⅓ cup custard

Source: NUTTAB 1995, Australian Department of Community Services and Health.

REHYDRATION

Despite consuming fluid during exercise, most athletes will become mildly to moderately dehydrated. Studies show that most athletes typically replace between 30% and 70% of their sweat losses when they train or compete. More importantly, studies also report that even when the session is over and drinks are freely available, athletes do not fully replace their fluid losses. There can be a time lag of up to 24 hours before body fluid levels are competely restored. And in cases of severe fluid losses, or a sudden change to a hot or high-altitude environment, athletes may carry a fluid deficit from one day and one training session to the next. This is clearly not conducive to optimal recovery or peak performance in future exercise sessions. Ideally, an athlete should aim to fully restore fluid losses between exercise sessions. Difficulties arise when the fluid deficit is moderate to high (2–5% of BM or greater) and when the recovery interval is less than six to eight hours.

One aspect of post-exercise rehydration is to ensure that the athlete consumes an adequate intake of fluid. However, there is an additional challenge. During recovery, the athlete will continue to lose fluid—partly due to continued sweating, but mostly through urination. The athlete will need to plan their fluid intake to account for physiological issues, such as overcoming inadequate thirst responses and minimising urine production, as well as practical difficulties such as poor opportunities to drink.

Making athletes drink—is thirst sufficient?

Thirst is not a sensitive and reliable indicator of dehydration. Most people are already mildly dehydrated (2% of BM) before they even feel thirsty. And then when they drink, thirst shuts off before fluid needs are fully replaced. In addition, there appears to be considerable individual variability in the reaction to thirst—some people are 'big drinkers' when they are dehydrated, while others are reluctant to drink much at all.

What is on offer to drink makes a difference to how much fluid a dehydrated athlete will consume. Factors such as the taste, general palatability and temperature of a fluid can all influence the volume that is drunk. It is hard to know each person's individual preference, but a sweet taste appears to be attractive to most. A small amount of salt (sodium) also enhances the palatability of drinks offered to people who are dehydrated after exercise. Sports drink companies spend millions of dollars to find a taste profile that is appealing, and it appears to be money well spent. A study from the Exercise Research Laboratory of Professor Carl Gisolfi at the University of Iowa measured voluntary fluid consumption in dehydrated athletes after they had sweated 2% of BM by cycling in the heat. On two occasions, these cyclists were observed during three hours of recovery, while they rested, and were given free access to fluids. When the choice was water, subjects drank enough to replace 63% of their sweat losses. However, on the other occasion when sports drink was offered, total fluid consumption was significantly greater—replacing 79% of sweat losses. Interestingly, on neither occasion did the athletes fully meet their fluid needs. It is a paradox that advertisements for many sports drinks promote them as 'thirst quenchers'. In fact, the ideal sports drink should probably be the opposite! It should keep the athlete thirsty so that they want to keep drinking. Better rehydration for the athlete; better sales and profits for the company.

The temperature of a drink also seems to be an important factor in encouraging intake. When an athlete is hot and sweaty, a cool drink is more welcoming than luke-warm or hot fluids. However, sometimes the perception of palatability and actual intake may not always go hand in hand. Studies suggest that while very cold water (0°C) might be rated as the most pleasurable drink, it is hard to quaff in large quantities. Therefore, cool drinks (10–15°C) are likely to promote greater intake.

Rehydration and urine losses

Urine is produced to help eliminate the body's waste products, and to keep body water and electrolyte concentrations in balance. An obligatory urine loss occurs over the day for this first purpose. When athletes sweat, they lose water and a small amount of electrolytes—principally sodium. Exercise dehydration produces a reduction in total body water and blood volume, and a mild increase in blood concentration and sodium content.

Consuming large amounts of plain water after exercise causes dilution of blood contents, before the entire blood volume has been restored. In order to preserve blood concentrations within healthy limits, the body shuts off thirst to stop the athlete drinking, and produces urine to reduce the dilution. In effect, the athlete can produce large amounts of dilute urine, even though they are still dehydrated. However, by consuming some sodium in the rehydration fluids, volume and concentration can be restored in better harmony, without the need for excessive urine production.

Professor Ron Maughan, an exercise physiologist from Aberdeen in Scotland, recently conducted a series of elegant rehydration studies. In his trials, athletes exercised to dehydrate by approximately 2% of BM and were then required to consume a specified quantity of fluids of varying compositions. Urine production and the restoration of blood volume and contents were monitored over six hours of recovery. Figure 14.1 shows the effect of the sodium concentration of various drinks on urine production and fluid balance. Low-sodium drinks (those containing either no or small amounts of sodium—25 mmol/L) produced significantly greater urine losses than drinks with higher sodium concentrations (those containing 50 and 100 mmol/L sodium). By the end of the recovery period, the difference in total urine production

---

FIGURE 14.1

Effects of adding sodium (salt) to rehydration drinks. These measurements were taken six hours into recovery after subjects had dehydrated (about 1.3 litres) and then consumed large volumes (about two litres) of various drinks

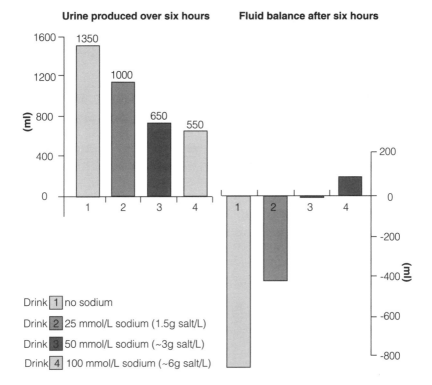

Urine produced over six hours   Fluid balance after six hours

Drink 1 no sodium
Drink 2 25 mmol/L sodium (1.5g salt/L)
Drink 3 50 mmol/L sodium (~3g salt/L)
Drink 4 100 mmol/L sodium (~6g salt/L)

Source: Maughan, R.J. and Leiper, J.B. 'Sodium intake and post-exercise rehydration in man', *European Journal of Applied Physiology*, 71: 311–19, 1995.

amounted to approximately 800 millilitres. With the low-sodium drinks, subjects were still dehydrated despite having consumed volumes equal to 150% of their fluid deficits. Studies from other laboratories have confirmed that until sodium losses are replaced, even forced intake of large volumes of water will not restore fluid balance after dehydration. Instead it will merely result in more urine production. This can be confusing for the athlete who thinks it is a sign of overhydration. And it can interfere with sleep patterns if the athlete has to continually get up in the night!

Some fluids exacerbate urine losses in other ways. Caffeine and alcohol exert a diuretic effect on the body—that is, they increase urine production. A study from Professor Ed Coyle's laboratory at the University of Texas compared the efficiency of rehydrating after exercise with a sports drink (containing a small amount of sodium), water (no sodium) or a diet cola (no sodium, plus caffeine). Subjects were made to consume a volume of these drinks equal to their fluid deficit (2.5% of BM), and were monitored over two hours of recovery. The diet cola resulted in increased urine losses and a retention level of only 54% of fluid lost, while the sports drink (73% retention) was slightly superior to water (65% retention), probably due to its higher sodium content.

Professor Maughan has also studied post-exercise rehydration with alcoholic beverages of 1–4% alcohol content and showed increased urine losses with the higher alcohol drink. This confirms the experience of many athletes who have found themselves making frequent visits to the bathroom while 'recovering' their fluid losses at a local hotel. While it is sometimes said that alcohol and caffeine drinks 'dehydrate' the athlete, this is not strictly true. When consumed, they add fluid to the system and improve hydration levels. However, the increase in urine losses compared to other drinks means that they are less efficient and effective as recovery fluids. When the situation calls for speedy rehydration, better fluids can be found.

A recipe for fluid replacement

When fluid deficits are greater than 1.5–2 litres, the athlete should consider both a plan of drinking and a considered choice of fluids. The 'ideal' will depend on the athlete and the situation. It appears sensible to actively replace sodium losses when the fluid deficit is significant and the time for rehydration is short. Common examples are when the athlete has dehydrated to 'make weight' before competition and there is only an hour or two between the weigh-in and the event, or where an athlete has just finished one event (e.g. a singles match in a tennis tournament) and the next session is scheduled within hours (e.g. a doubles match).

If a meal or snack is eaten during this time, it is useful to include high-sodium foods or to add a little salt to what is consumed. Bread, breakfast cereals and pretzels are examples of carbohydrate-rich foods with a signficant salt content. Alternatively, salt may be provided in the sauces, fillings or dressings added to carbohydrate-rich foods. Commercial oral rehydration solutions provide a ready-made fluid and salt replacement alternative when solid food cannot be eaten. Typically they have a sodium concentration of 50–90 mmol/L (2–5 g or a teaspoon of salt per litre) which is specifically designed to maximise rehydration in clinical settings such as following gastrointestinal upsets. However, they taste quite salty—beyond the usual taste preferences of most people—and the athlete needs to be encouraged to drink a set amount of such drinks rather than leave it to voluntary intake. Sports drinks contain smaller amounts of sodium (10–25 mmol/L) and may promote more efficient rehydration than plain water. However, additional sodium intake from food sources may be necessary over the next hours to correct the final body fluid/sodium balance. In most situations in Westernised countries, people consume sodium far in excess of their requirements. Therefore, with time and food intake, balance will be restored.

The most important issue for most athletes is to drink fluid in sufficient quantities—in excess of their fluid deficit and their thirst. Setting targets of intake and keeping a supply of fluids on hand are practical strategies that will assist in this goal. The panel on the following pages summarises guidelines for post-exercise rehydration.

GUIDELINES FOR PROMOTING POST-EXERCISE REHYDRATION

- Drink to a plan rather than relying on thirst or opportunity. The 'hit or miss' approach may be acceptable when fluid deficits are one litre or less, but when fluid losses are greater, there will be more 'miss' than 'hit'.

- Monitor changes in body mass from pre- to post-exercise to evaluate the success of drinking strategies during exercise, and the residual fluid deficit that must now be replaced. A loss of one kilogram equals a fluid deficit of one litre.
- Remember that you will continue to lose fluid during recovery via urine losses and ongoing sweating, and that these losses must also be replaced. Typically you will need to consume about 1.5 times the volume of your post-exercise fluid deficit over the subsequent two to four hours to fully restore fluid balance.
- Ensure that an adequate supply of palatable drinks is available. This may be difficult when you are at a remote competition venue, or travelling in a country where bottled water must be consumed instead of the local water supply.
- In situations where you need to encourage fluid intake, try a flavoured drink rather than plain water. Most people prefer sweet-tasting drinks.
- Keep drinks at a refreshing temperature to encourage greater intake. Cool drinks (e.g. 10–15°C) are preferred in most situations. Very cold fluids (0–5°C) may seem ideal when the environment or the athlete is hot; however, it is often challenging to drink them quickly.
- Carbohydrate-containing drinks are also useful in assisting with refuelling goals—you can tackle a number of recovery goals simultaneously.
- Replace sodium losses to help maximise the retention of ingested fluids by minimising urine losses. Options include sports drinks, commercial oral rehydration solutions, salty foods, or salt added to post-exercise meals. This is particularly important when fluid deficits are greater than 2–3% of BM or 2 litres. A high-sodium beverage such as an oral rehydration solution (50–90 mmol/L or 2–5 g of salt per litre), or salt added to post-exercise meals, may be the best way to guarantee efficient and rapid rehydration after significant fluid loss.
- Caffeine-containing fluids (e.g. cola drinks) and alcohol are not ideal rehydration beverages since they may increase urine losses.
- Where possible, avoid post-exercise activities that exacerbate sweat losses—for example, long exposure to hot spas, saunas or the sun.

A FEW WORDS ABOUT ALCOHOL AND RECOVERY

It is hard to imagine the end of a Grand Prix race or a premiership final without champagne spraying from the victory dais. Alcohol and sport are closely linked—sponsorship money plays a big part in making many sports possible. And while there is no necessity to include alcohol in an athlete's diet, neither is there any reason to exclude it totally. One of the unfortunate ways that alcohol has been linked to sport is in the post-event (or post-training) drinking binge. Whereas once every now and again there may be a special celebration that warrants the inconvenience of a sore head the next morning, some athletes repeat this pattern at frightening frequency and with frightening ferocity, and to a level that affects their heath, other people and their performance—in both the short term and the long term.

In some sports, but notably team sports, the tradition is to 'relax' and 'celebrate' or 'commiserate' the outcome by drinking alcohol together. This is often undertaken when the athlete is dehydrated and hasn't eaten for a number of hours, thus potentiating the absorption and effects of the alcohol. Often good sense goes out the window after a couple of drinks, and in a spirit of camaraderie or even competition, the athlete may overindulge considerably. There are many rationalisations about its benefits ('team bonding') and acceptability ('everybody else is doing it'), and minimisation of the disadvantages ('I can run it off the next day').

However, alcohol is a drug and, in large amounts, a poison. Excessive intake causes harm to the body—depending on the frequency and the level of the dose. It impairs the physiology of body recovery processes in a number of ways, including:

- vasodilation—swelling of blood vessels—and a likely increase in the fluid accumulation in damaged tissues;
- increased urine losses, thus reducing the rate of rehydration (see above); and
- interference with metabolic processes, such as glycogen recovery in the liver and perhaps muscle.

Most importantly, however, it interferes with good judgment and common sense. Athletes who are drunk rarely undertake the guidelines for recovery eating and drinking well—it simply isn't a priority. Alcohol may also have a small impact on the muscle's ability to store glycogen. But it has a major effect on whether the athlete cares about, and is capable of, meeting their carbohydrate intake goals. Most athletes fail to eat sufficient fuel-replacement foods when they are drinking— they drink rather than eat, or choose unsuitable high-fat takeaway foods. Carbohydrate intake is also sacrificed the next day as they sleep off their nausea and hangovers. In other words, recovery is considerably impaired and will affect the ability of the athlete to train (or compete) again the following day. Repeated occurrences of this pattern will greatly diminish the fitness and performance of the athlete. Ironically, the worst offenders are often professional team sports players who face the challenge of weekly (and sometimes, daily) competition, but appear to ignore the incentive of huge rewards and salaries for good performance.

Alcoholic binges cause the same poor compliance to matters of treating injury or muscle damage. In fact, they increase the chance of accidents and high-risk behaviour off the field. In many sports there have been an unfortunate number of fatalities and major injuries occurring from accidents and motor vehicle crashes after the game or competition, involving alcohol-impaired athletes. It would be a shame if the excitement and celebration of fantastic sporting performances couldn't be toasted! However, alcohol intake is definitely an area in which the athlete should know and respect their limits (see the following panel).

GUIDELINES FOR SENSIBLE INTAKE OF ALCOHOL AFTER SPORT

- Avoid alcohol for 24–36 hours after sport or exercise that results in muscle damage or injury. Alcohol promotes vasodilation and may impair the recovery and repair processes.
- Rehydrate and refuel as a first priority after intense exercise. Ban alcoholic drinks from the locker room and have appropriate drinks and snacks available instead.
- Remember that alcoholic drinks (more than 4% alcohol) are not ideal rehydration beverages. Nor do they provide a significant source of carbohydrate. These 'myths' are often used as a rationalisation to approve/excuse the heavy alcohol intake of some athletes.
- Once fluid and carbohydrate needs have been met, alcohol may be consumed in moderation. 'Drink-driving' education messages may provide a guide for sensible intake of alcohol.
- The vasodilation caused by alcohol may increase heat loss in cold environments (e.g. in winter sports). Take care to stay warm in such environments.

POST-EXERCISE EATING—THE PRACTICAL CHALLENGES

In an ideal world the athlete would tackle recovery with hunger, enthusiasm, organisation and knowledge. And the ideal world would supply all the athlete's food and fluid needs within easy reach. Unfortunately, these conditions rarely coexist. Instead the athlete is faced with a number of practical challenges. Advice from a sports dietitian can provide specific ways to tackle the various obstacles. The following guidelines may provide some general ideas

PROBLEM

Fatigue—the athlete is too tired and lacking motivation to obtain or prepare suitable meals and snacks.

Eating out requires time to find a restaurant and then wait for the meal to be ordered and prepared.

Poor access to suitable foods immediately after exercise:
a The athlete must travel a significant distance to their home base.
b The competition or training venue does not provide (suitable) food and drinks.

The athlete is too tired to eat or has a reduced appetite after intense exercise.

SOLUTION

1 Be organised and manage time well in order to have food ready to eat or requiring minimal preparation when you are most tired. Batch cook and store/freeze meals in convenient size portions. Prepare your meal before training.
2 Eat out.

1 Pre-arrange the restaurant or catering so that a suitable menu is established and available immediately you arrive.
2 In large groups, arrange buffet-style catering for quick service and to allow athletes to choose the individual type and quantity of food they need.

1 Bring suitable foods/drinks to the venue. Portable carbohydrate-rich snacks include sandwiches, sports bars and sports drinks, liquid meal supplements, breakfast cereal, fruit, flavoured yoghurt, dried fruit and rice cakes. Have a snack, and top up later with a more substantial meal when access to a better range of foods is possible.
2 Organise 'team' snacks or meals where teams or clubs of athletes face similar problems.
3 Take over or assist the venue catering/kiosk to improve their menu.

1 Choose a snack rather than a meal, and choose foods according to the environment and your appetite. When you are hot and sweaty, foods that are cool and high in liquid content may be most appealing. These may include juices, sports drinks, fruit smoothies and milk shakes, liquid meal supplements,

or flavoured/frozen yoghurt. In cold weather, a hot soup, toasted sandwiches or pizza squares may be appetising.
2 Offer food in 'bite-size' pieces rather than overbearing amounts. Fruit portions, sandwich fingers or small pizza squares may tempt a tired and timid appetite.

The athlete's attention is demanded by other post-event activities—coaches' post-mortems, media interviews, drug tests, equipment handling, watching other events, etc.

1 Look after first things first!
2 Choose foods and drinks that are portable and can travel along to other post-event activities.

The post-competition tradition is to celebrate or commiserate the results.

Look after first and important things first, and don't worry about what everyone else is doing. Stick to your recovery goals and then join in (sensibly) later.

TO IV OR NOT TO IV? THERE SHOULD BE NO QUESTION

You may have noticed dehydrated and heat-stressed athletes in the medical tents of marathons and triathlons receiving intravenous (IV) fluids to manage their medical problems. However, in recent years there has been a growing interest by athletes in using IV feedings as a recovery tool rather than a medical treatment. It has become trendy in tennis tournaments, stage cycle races and other multi-day sports events for athletes to request an IV to speed their recovery for the next day's performance. Some professional athletes and teams make their own arrangements for this. But medical directors of some races—for example, Ironman triathlon events—see healthy athletes walking into their medical tents and asking for an IV to boost their recovery.

Standard intravenous fluids provide saline (water and sodium) in various concentrations and, sometimes, a low level of glucose. In medical practice they are used to correct fluid, electrolyte and carbohydrate deficits in people who are unable to do this by eating and drinking. If someone is unconscious, asleep or has a non-functioning gut (e.g. has severe vomiting, diarrhoea or gastric shut-down), an IV drip provides an alternative and effective means of getting fluid and carbohydrate into the body. In rare medical cases, people may receive substantial nutrition via IV means. And the solution may also contain lipids, amino acids, vitamins, minerals and trace elements. However, this is expensive, and carries a high risk of infection and nutritional imbalances. Such nutrient-rich solutions generally have to be given via a large 'central' vein rather than a peripheral arm vein, since the concentration may cause a small vein to collapse. This is more trouble.

It might sound dramatic and state-of-the-art for an athlete to receive intravenous fluids or intravenous nutrition after prolonged intensive exercise. Many athletes claim that it makes them feel better and helps them to recover more quickly. However, most race medical directors dispute that this is anything more than a placebo. They counter that the main benefits are the novelty and attention, and being forced to lie still for one to two hours after the event. Many are reluctant to provide these services to healthy athletes, particularly if this ties up resources and attention that are required for athletes with real medical problems arising from the race.

It is possible that IV fluids may even be worse than 'low-technology' drinking. A recent study from Dr Larry Armstrong's group at the University of Connecticut in the United States showed an interesting difference in the outcome of oral and IV rehydration. Males were dehydrated by 4% of BM by two to four hours of mild exercise, then rested for a couple of hours. During this recovery period they either received no fluid, drank 1900 mls of (saline) fluid, or were infused with 1900 ml of IV saline. Then it was back to mild exercise (walking at 50% $\dot{V}O_{2max}$) in the heat. Although all exercise was conducted at the same intensity, the subjects rated the experience without fluid replacement as the hardest, and reported being 'very, very thirsty'. This is hardly surprising. However, subjects reported feeling *thirstier* and having to work *harder* at the exercise following IV rehydration compared with the trial after oral rehydration. One explanation is that the sensation of drinking—having cool liquid pass from your mouth into your stomach—sends important signals to the brain about thirst. And this may impact on how you feel during subsequent exercise. So, it may not be enough to top up plasma and other body fluids. To fully benefit, all of your body needs to join in the experience. Whether this holds true for athletes working at higher intensities, and whether it affects performance, needs further investigation.

There is also the issue of fluid overload. Some athletes finish ultra-endurance events with low blood sodium levels. This is generally associated with *over*hydration, rather than *de*hydration. And in some cases the athlete appears to have a kidney malfunction which stops excess fluid from simply being urinated out. It can be dangerous—even fatal—to pour litres of fluid into such athletes.

The bottom line for someone who has just finished a marathon or ultra-distance triathlon is that there is little real need to be concerned about aggressive, abnormally-delivered recovery nutrition. Particularly when there is adequate time for rest and recovery before the next exercise session, and they are perfectly capable of eating and drinking, and absorbing the nutrients and fluid provided.

But what about the athlete who is in the middle of Wimbledon or the Tour de France? It is likely that this athlete has a lot on the line, is severely fluid- and fuel-depleted from one day's effort, and has a date to do it all again the next day. Some of the components of the secret IV formulae reportedly used by pro-cyclists are unstudied and of dubious benefit. But there is still no proof that even the basic ingredients of IV preparations are of special help in recovery. Studies need to be undertaken before we will know if IV carbohydrate promotes faster glycogen storage than dietary carbohydrate, or whether IV fluids promote superior rehydration to post-event drinking.

No doubt there is a psychological edge from using an IV during these recovery challenges. And there may also be a practical edge. It is often hard to juggle the priority of eating and sleeping during busy competition schedules. With an IV the athlete can be given a known amount of fluid and carbohydrate, and be 'consuming' these while sleeping. The last word is that if IV recovery is used, medical supervision and strict control over the conditions in which it is given are essential.

15

The tired athlete

'All top international athletes wake up in the morning feeling tired and go to bed feeling very tired.'

> Brendan Foster, 1976 Olympic Games 10,000 metre bronze medallist

Tiredness is an occupational hazard for an athlete. An intense training routine increases the need for sleep, and most athletes know how it feels to hit the pillow exhausted at night. An increased level of tiredness is an expected, but hopefully transient, reaction to an increase in training volume or intensity.

However, tiredness is a fine line to straddle and on occasions the athlete may find themselves on the wrong side. Instead of being a by-product of a successful exercise program, tiredness can start to intrude into the athlete's enjoyment of training and to impact on other aspects of their life. Sports performance often decreases rather than improves. Everything can move in a downward spiral. This might be termed 'overtiredness' (see Table 15.1).

There are a multitude of causes of overtiredness, just as there are multiple definitions and terms to describe it. There are two broad categories—the acute overtiredness that disappears with short-term management and rest, and the long-term problems which take much longer to respond to management strategies. Medical reasons for overtiredness are numerous and require expert diagnosis and management. These problems have been deliberately omitted from this book since they require specialised attention. Athletes should consult a sports physician for help, and treat all medical matters or illnesses, even something as simple as a cold, with common sense and respect. In most cases a reduction in the training load, and a re-evaluation of the training program, is at least part of the treatment for overtiredness.

TABLE 15.1
Signs and symptoms of 'overtiredness'

- Elevated basal heart-rate.
- Elevated training heart-rate.
- Elevated recovery heart-rate.
- Increased feeling of effort during training. Inability to handle or complete workouts.
- Sudden drop in performance.
- Muscular soreness and pain.
- Heavy muscle feeling.
- Sudden weight loss.
- Loss of appetite.
- Thirst during the night.
- Gastrointestinal disturbances.
- Poor healing of wounds.
- Lower resistance to infection.
- Generalised apathy and lethargy.
- Irritability.
- Poor coordination.
- Short attention span.
- Loss of enjoyment and interest in training.
- Sleep disturbances.
- Depression.
- Low sex drive.

WHAT'S IN A NAME?

Leading haematologist Dr Randy Eichner has noted that just as Inuits (Eskimos) have 23 words for snow and Arabs have 23 words for desert, sports scientists have 23 terms for overtiredness. Various experts talk about over-reaching, staleness, overtraining, chronic fatigue, burnout, stagnation, overstress and rundown, to name just a few. Some people use the terms to denote slightly different issues—sometimes to distinguish between acute and chronic problems. Other people use the terms interchangeably. However, all describe the problem of unusual and limiting tiredness, and the 'more is less' outcome. Until there is uniform agreement on terminology, it will be hard to get to the bottom line of advice for the athlete. In the meantime, this book will simply refer to the problem as 'overtiredness'.

Poor nutrition and lifestyle can also cause or contribute to symptoms of overtiredness. This can also require expert diagnosis and dietary counselling. However, since these problems are largely preventable and easily reversed, they merit further discussion. This chapter will now focus on describing risk factors and strategies for avoiding the nutritional causes of tiredness.

OVERCOMMITTED LIFESTYLE

Most athletes overcommit their resources—be it time, finances or emotions. Most athletes know that the 'stresses of the rat race' and a constant, unfulfilled pressure to produce are unhealthy. It may be caused by the complex effects on the hormonal or immune systems, or simply as a by-product of an inadequate quantity and quality of sleep, or inadequate nutrition. In any case, tiredness is an expected hallmark of a chaotic and stress-filled lifestyle. However, many athletes are still surprised when they burn out from an overload of training, family, work, study or other commitments. This book is not designed to provide advice in time management or lifestyle balancing. But it does provide a reminder that all athletes must allow sufficient time for sleep and relaxation, plan to eat well, and achieve a balance between their various goals and commitments. This should be the first undertaking to prevent overtiredness and the first issue for reassessment if overtiredness occurs.

GENERALLY INADEQUATE ENERGY AND NUTRIENT INTAKE

Some athletes eat sub-optimal diets. Sometimes this develops into a diagnosable nutrient deficiency with biochemical and clinical symptoms (e.g. iron deficiency anaemia). Most times the athlete simply stumbles on, feeling slightly below par, with inadequate nutrient intakes and sub-clinical problems. It is hard to prove that this directly affects performance—be it work, sporting or mental performance. However, many 'sub-par' eaters will at least feel better, if not significantly enhance their performance, by improving their nutrition. These people often report such improvements when they take a course of vitamins or follow the advice of the latest best-selling diet book. There is obviously a psychological boost attached to this, since these changes usually still fall short of optimum nutrition. However, sometimes even these programs represent an improvement on the old eating patterns.

As explained in Chapter 10, the keys to peak nutrition are an adequate energy intake and a variety of nutrient-rich foods. A quick way to sabotage your nutritional status is to sacrifice one of these. Sacrificing both is asking for major trouble! (See the panel on the following pages.)

TOP TEN WAYS TO SABOTAGE PEAK NUTRITION—SACRIFICING THE QUALITY AND QUANTITY OF YOUR EATING

---

1   Battle chronically to reduce body fat or weight, particularly to a level below what seems 'natural' or 'healthy'. Count every kilocalorie twice, and eat meagrely and miserably most days. Break out with a splurge on high-fat, low-nutrient value foods and then start counting all over again. Think about food constantly. Drink diet soft drinks by the bucket-load instead of eating.

2   Be busy with an overcommitted lifestyle. Forget to eat at all or live from tins, on takeaways or from the junk food dispenser. Keep the fridge and cupboards bare. Eat on the run and never evaluate your total food intake.

3   Focus entirely on getting your carbohydrate needs from sports bars, carbo loader supplements and sports drinks. Forget about eating real food.

4   Become obsessive about only eating 'good' foods, and start to read every label, recipe or the fine print on the menu. Eliminate anything with fat, sugar, alcohol, chemicals and toxins, to the point where there are more things that you *can't* eat than you *can* eat. Out-Pritikin Pritikin.

5   Become a vegetarian who thinks that this means replacing the chop on their plate with more salad or vegetables. Go vegan or macro-biotic rather than vegetarian. Fail to explore the world of grains, legumes and pulses, soy products, nuts and seeds to find alternative sources of protein and minerals.

6   Go on fad diets—swallow a best-seller or make up your own. Pick ones that tell you to eliminate whole food groups, or work on 'food combining'. Fail to realise that food combining tells you not to eat foods together, rather than encouraging a range of food at meals.

7   Never learn to cook or prepare foods, beyond peeling a wrapper. Ignore your mother and never eat any fruit or vegetables. Make M&Ms the only brightly-coloured food in your diet.

8   Be a boring and fussy eater. Have a few favourite foods and eat them every day. Never try anything new or vary your routine. Know that you won't like something even before you have tasted it.
9   Travel all the time, particularly to countries with a limited food supply or with a cuisine that you don't like or won't try. Live on snack foods.
10 Develop an eating disorder.

Failure to eat enough food, or enough foods that are nutrient-rich, can see the athlete running low on energy or falling short of the body's nutritional requirements. Feeling jaded may be only one of the penalties. However, it may take the advice of a sports dietitian to help overcome the specific problems that prevent an athlete from putting these into practice, or from achieving their balance of dietary quantity and quality. The long-term and 'Big Picture' answers to peak nutrition are best found in well-planned and creative eating, rather than a visit to the vitamin counter of the health food shop or pharmacy.

VITAMIN SUPPLEMENTS—CAN THEY 'PICK YOU UP'?

The typical advertisement for a multivitamin preparation shows a business executive or hard-working woman of the nineties battling their overcommitted lifestyle. There is stress, long hours, late nights—and perhaps even fat-rich business meals, smoking, and too much alcohol. The person struggles with their workload and snaps at their family. It is all too much. However, brand X vitamins turn the situation around, and create spring in the step, harmony in the home, and productivity in the workplace. Or do they?

Advertisers know that Joe Average worries about getting enough vitamins. This probably dates back to the Bad Old Days, and war rationing, when food supplies were limited in quantity and variety. However, the major problems of our modern executive are smoking, excess alcohol, excess stress, inadequate sleep, overweight, too much fat or too little carbohydrate. Unless a person addresses these problems simultaneously with taking a course of multivitamins, the only benefit they can hope to receive is psychological. In other words, a poorly balanced diet or a poorly managed lifestyle need major surgery rather than a cosmetic facelift. Only if a person has a pre-existing vitamin deficiency can a vitamin supplement improve health and performance. In Western countries, true vitamin deficiencies are rarer than the problems of energy, fat and carbohydrate imbalance.

Even when athletes follow all the guidelines for healthy eating and living, some still like to have 'an insurance policy'. If everything else is in place, then the addition of a broad-range, low-dose multivitamin/mineral preparation may offer the final peace of mind they seek. However, since intake of vitamins is limited in situations where dietary variety and quantity is restricted, there are some athletes who might be advised to follow a similar program. For best results these athletes should consult a sports dietitian to optimise food intake possibilities as well as to make the best choice of supplement. These athletes include:

- Athletes on low-energy diets—for example, daily intakes of less than 1200–1500 kilocalories (5–6 MJ) for females and 1500–1800 kilocalories (6–7 MJ) for males.
- Athletes who are 'picky eaters' and who have a limited food range.
- Athletes who are travelling constantly and whose dietary routines are reliant on planes, trains and hotels.
- Athletes travelling to countries with an irregular and limited food supply—for example, Eastern bloc countries, and parts of Africa, Asia and South America.
- Athletes with eating disorders and disordered eating patterns.
- Athletes undertaking a prolonged competition schedule where normal meal routines are interrupted and overshadowed by the goals of competition eating—for example, cyclists in a tour, or players in a hectic tournament.

INADEQUATE CARBOHYDRATE TO FUEL TRAINING OR COMPETITION

Anyone who has attended a sports nutrition lecture or read a sports nutrition book will be familiar with Figure 15.1. It is perhaps the most well-known weapon in a sports nutritionist's education armoury. The figure was originally drawn in 1980 by Professor Dave Costill to illustrate the importance of carbohydrate intake to muscle glycogen recovery during heavy training. In this diagram, muscle glycogen gradually declines when an athlete undertakes daily training while eating a diet of moderate carbohydrate level (40% of energy), similar to Westernised eating patterns. However, with a higher carbohydrate diet (70% of energy), muscle glycogen levels are almost totally recovered between daily training sessions. The irony of

FIGURE 15.1

The famous Costill figure

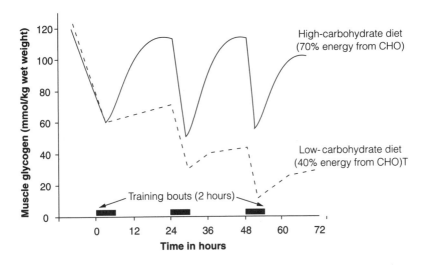

Source: Adapted from Costill, D.L. and Miller, J. 'Nutrition for endurance sport: carbohydrate and fluid balance', *International Journal of Sports Medicine*, 1: 2–14, 1980.

the fame of this figure is that it was not based on a real study. Rather it is a hypothetical situation proposed by Professor Costill, summarised from his considerable research undertakings. Many nutritionists and sports scientists, however, describe it as real data!

Since then, Professor Costill's theory has been proved correct by several studies. Table 15.2 summarises a number of studies of endurance-trained athletes who have undertaken intensive daily training programs over a period of time, eating either a 'moderate' or 'high' carbohydrate diet. The universal finding is that a high-carbohydrate diet, providing amounts of carbohydrate similar to that recommended in Chapters 10 and 14, is superior in promoting daily recovery of muscle glycogen stores. Generally, a diet that is moderate in carbohydrates leads to incomplete recovery of muscle fuel stores from one day to the next. The result is a gradual decline in these stores.

In many of these studies, and in the real-life experience of sports dietitians, such muscle glycogen depletion is associated with training fatigue and lethargy. Athletes often complain about 'heaviness' and increased effort during training. Sometimes they even fail to complete the desired workload for the

| TABLE 15.2 | | | | |

Studies comparing high carbohydrate intakes (HCHO) and moderate carbohydrate intakes (MCHO) on the training adaptation and performance of athletes in intensive training

Athletes	Length of study	Daily CHO intake (g/kg BM)	Muscle glycogen	Effects on performance
Swimmers	10 days	8.2 versus 5.3	↓ in MCHO. Maintained in HCHO.	↓ in training performance in MCHO, but swim trials unchanged.
Runners	5 days	8.0 versus 3.9	↓ in both groups, but greater ↓ in MCHO.	↓ in running economy and ↑ feeling of effort during training sessions in MCHO.
Swimmers	5 days	12.1 versus 6.5	Not measured.	No performance difference.
Rowers	28 days	10 versus 5	Maintained in MCHO. ↑ in HCHO.	Power output maintained during ergometer trials in MCHO. Small ↑ at end of study in HCHO.
Runners	7 days	10 versus 5	↓ in MCHO. Maintained in HCHO.	No ↓ of high-intensity run to exhaustion in either group.
Cyclists	7 days	10 versus 5	↓ in MCHO. Maintained in HCHO.	No ↓ of high-intensity cycle to exhaustion in either group.

session (see Table 15.1). In some cases, irritability and general tiredness can overwhelm the day's activities. An athlete may recognise the crippling feeling of 'hitting the wall' due to muscle glycogen depletion when it occurs during a single long event, such as a marathon. But when the symptoms creep up over a week or more, they may be more subtle.

Two tactics seem important to optimise the recovery of muscle glycogen stores during periods of heavy training. The first is adequate carbohydrate intake. The other is the scheduling of 'easy' days or rest days into the training program (see Chapter 2). In some types of exercise, particularly running, even a very high carbohydrate intake does not guarantee full recovery of muscle glycogen stores on a daily basis. Muscle damage or other factors may slow the rate of glycogen storage. Therefore, some lighter training days are necessary to allow the muscle fuel stores to play 'catch up'.

Causes of inadequate carbohydrate intake

With all the hype about high-carbohydrate eating in the sports world, it seems strange that a modern athlete could fail to refuel. Some athletes, notably in team sports, seem to be a bit slower to catch up with the message. However, most sports dietitians observe that it is not a lack of recognition that limits the carbohydrate intake of most athletes. The most common factors or situations leading to inadequate carbohydrate intake are:

- The background dietary patterns of the country. People tend to eat according to local traditions and the food that is available. Westernised eating patterns are not high in carbohydrate.
- Very importantly, a low energy intake. Low total food intake means low intake of all nutrients. Athletes who restrict energy intake to keep body fat levels low may pay a greater penalty of inadequate muscle fuel levels.
- Overemphasis on 'healthy' eating—exclusive choice of high-fibre foods and avoidance of sugar. Bulky carbohydrate foods cannot be eaten in sufficient quantities by most people to meet high carbohydrate targets.
- Fad diets, particularly the Zone diet and other energy-restricted unbalanced eating plans.
- Chaotic eating patterns as a result of minimal food preparation skills, hectic travel and lifestyle commitments, skipped meals and poor access to food.
- Poor food knowledge and lack of distinction between 'quasi' carbohydrate foods and real carbohydrate-rich foods. Many of the foods commonly believed by athletes to be high in carbohydrate are actually high in fat.

Chapters 10 and 14 provide information to assist an athlete increase their carbohydrate intake to meet the fuel needs of training and competition. Together with a short period of rest or reduced training load, inadequate fuel stores can be recovered and energy levels regained.

IS A HIGH-CARBOHYDRATE DIET CLEARLY SUPERIOR FOR TRAINING ADAPTATION AND PERFORMANCE?

The studies summarised in Table 15.2 show clearly that a high-carbohydrate intake promotes better recovery of muscle glycogen than a moderate-carbohydrate diet. However, these studies have also raised a controversy. Surprisingly, they failed to show convincing and unanimous evidence of a reduction in performance in the moderate-carbohydrate group when an exercise trial was undertaken at the end of the study period. Equally there was no clear evidence of superior performance or better training adaptation in the group ingesting high-carbohydrate intakes. Some argue that this fails to support the case for advising athletes to eat a high-carbohydrate diet. And that athletes can adapt to reduced glycogen levels.

However, there are other interpretations. One possibility is that the performance protocols used in these studies were not sensitive enough to determine small changes or differences in performance. This difficulty is explained further in Chapter 17. Another issue is that the studies were not conducted over sufficiently long periods to allow clear differences between groups to occur. Most were conducted over a week or less, and studies where athletes cease or dramatically reduce their training show that a week isn't long enough to lose performance adaptations (see Chapter 2). In other words, over a short period, despite fatigue and loss of training performance, the athletes in the moderate-carbohydrate groups were able to lift themselves for a single trial or 'competition'. Had reduced muscle glycogen and reduced training been allowed to continue for a longer period, then a clear reduction in performance may have been seen. Another complication is that in some trials, what was considered a 'moderate'-carbohydrate intake may have been enough to provide adequate fuel for the training undertaken by the athletes. If enough is enough, more is not superior!

Further studies are needed to provide definite proof that high-carbohydrate diets promote superior training adaptations and long-term performance. In the meantime, there is overwhelming evidence that in an acute situation, better body carbohydrate stores and availability are linked with better endurance and performance of prolonged exercise. Intuitively, training sessions should be tackled with greater success if the athlete has preserved their fuel stores. And this should eventually pay dividends. Therefore, the guidelines remain prudent and scientists are challenged to devise better studies.

IRON DEFICIENCY

Iron plays an important role in exercise metabolism. First, oxygen transport into the muscle is reliant on haemoglobin as a blood carrier and on myoglobin as the muscle carrier. In addition, some of the muscle enzymes involved in metabolism require iron as a co-factor. It is understandable that inadequate iron status might limit these functions and reduce performance. This is clearly demonstrated when a person has anaemia, in which iron deficiency has progressed to the stage where blood haemoglobin levels fall below a critical level. Anaemia causes tiredness and exercise intolerance to an extent that, in severe cases, even walking one flight of stairs can induce puffing and fatigue.

Iron deficiency is the most commonly occurring nutrient deficiency in the world. However, in Westernised countries only a small number of people become sufficiently iron-deficient to develop anaemia. The more typical situation is to develop low iron status. Athletes are identified as one of the groups at high risk for this condition. Unfortunately, the situation with athletes is complicated by the effect of exercise on the blood measurements used to determine iron status. A session of heavy exercise causes an acute increase in serum ferritin levels, the iron storage compound used as a predictor of early iron deficiency. And training produces an increase in blood volume (fluid content) which dilutes the concentration of several blood components, including haemoglobin. Thus, haemoglobin can appear artificially low in some athletes, particularly at the start of a training program, without having any detrimental effects on exercise performance. As a result, iron deficiency has most certainly been overdiagnosed in the sports world. However, the issue of low iron status is made murky by two as yet unanswered questions:

- If iron is involved in exercise metabolism, what is the optimal iron status for an athlete, particularly an endurance athlete? Should athletes aim for a higher iron status than sedentary people?
- At what stage of low iron status is exercise performance impaired? At what stage should it be treated?

The current evidence from studies is that exercise performance is not affected until the athlete's haemoglobin levels fall. This suggests that athletes who develop a low ferritin level, indicating a fall in iron stores, are not at risk while haemoglobin levels are unchanged. However, in practice, many athletes complain of fatigue and inability to train effectively, which corresponds to a fall in their ferritin status. They describe general tiredness, present on waking in the morning, an increased risk of catching infections, and a failure to recover between sessions. It may be that studies only monitor a single exercise effort, and fail to take into account the athlete's ability to repeat this the next day. Some athletes find relief from their symptoms when iron status is improved.

Currently, universal standards for optimal iron status measurements for athletes are not possible. Nor can a single blood test always tell what is normal or abnormal for an individual athlete. Therefore, the diagnosis and management of iron deficiency should always be undertaken by an expert such as a sports doctor or dietitian. They will use a number of measurements, including blood results, clinical examination and the presence of risk factors to make the diagnosis. Monitoring *changes* in blood results, such as a drop in ferritin or haemoglobin, is more helpful than a single reading. Therefore, periodic screening of the iron status of athletes at 'high risk' is helpful since it may help to identify what levels are associated with good training and performance, and where the 'danger territory' lies for each individual. In addition, it may detect a potentially harmful drop in iron levels at an early stage, before it has progressed into full-blown symptoms.

Cause of iron deficiency in athletes

Low iron status can occur in athletes for a number of reasons. Iron imbalance can occur through increased iron requirements and losses, or inadequate iron intake. Often a combination of these factors may occur, at a subtle level, over a long period. Situations of increased iron need in athletes are partially reflected in the recommended iron intakes in Table 15.3 and include:

- growth spurts during adolescence;
- menstrual losses in women, especially where heavy periods are experienced;
- pregnancy;
- blood loss caused by medical problems such as an ulcer;
- increased destruction of red blood cells due to the high training loads of high-impact exercise such as road running and perhaps court sports;

TABLE 15.3

Iron content of foods compared to daily iron requirements of athletes

---

Estimated iron requirements of athletes

Athlete	mg/day
General training:	
• males and non-menstruating females	7
• menstruating females	12–16
• growing adolescents	10–13
Pregnancy (trimesters 2 and 3)	22–36
Endurance training—especially running and high-impact sports:	
• males and non-menstruating females	7–17
• menstruating females	16–23

Iron-rich foods for the athlete

Foods	Serve	mg iron
Haem iron foods		
Liver	100 g (cooked weight)	11.0
Liver paté or liverwurst	40 g (2 tbsp)	2–3
Lean beef or lamb	100 g (cooked weight)	3–4
Hamburger patties	100 g (2 medium)	3.5
Bolognaise sauce	100 g (½ cup)	1.8
Veal	100 g (cooked weight)	2.0
Chicken (dark meat)	100 g (cooked weight)	1.3
Lean pork or ham	100 g (cooked weight)	1.3
Fish	100 g (cooked weight)	0.6–1.4
Chicken (white meat)	100 g (cooked weight)	0.7
Oysters	100 g (10)	3.9
Salmon	100 g (small tin)	1.5
Sardines	100 g	2.2
Non-haem iron foods		
Eggs	100 g (2)	2.0
Breakfast cereal (fortified)	30 g (1 cup)	2.5–5.0
Breakfast bar or muesli bar	30 g	0.6
White bread	50 g (2 slices)	1.2
Wholemeal bread	60 g (2 slices)	1.4–2.2
Wholemeal pasta	80 g (½ cup cooked)	1.4
Spinach (cooked)	145 g (1 cup)	4.4
Kidney beans/lentils/soy beans (cooked)	100 g (½ cup)	2.25
Baked beans	100 g (½ cup)	1.6
Tofu	100 g	1.9
Raisins	50 g	2.1
Sultanas	50 g	1.0
Dried apricots	50 g	1.6
Cashews	50 g	3.1
Almonds	50 g	1.9

Source: NUTTAB 1995, Australian Department of Community Services and Health.

- frequent blood donations;
- altitude training, and perhaps heat training;
- gastrointestinal bleeding during high-intensity running, or from use of some anti-inflammatory medications; and
- repeated or severe episodes of bleeding from injuries in combative or contact sports.

Iron is found in foods in two forms (see Table 15.3). Foods containing iron in the form of haemoglobin or myo-globin are said to contain 'haem' iron and include offal, red meat, shellfish, and the darker cuts of poultry and fish. This haem iron is found in small amounts but is relatively well absorbed. The non-haem form of iron, found also in animal foods but as the sole iron source in eggs and foods of plant food origin, is poorly absorbed. The absorption of the non-haem iron can be both increased or reduced by other dietary factors. Diets which are likely to be inadequate in iron include:

- Popeye's diet. Despite the publicity, spinach and green leafy vegetables are not an excellent source of iron. Although iron is present in quite high amounts according to food tables, its absorption is poor.
- a low energy diet;
- a vegetarian diet, reliant on non-haem iron-rich foods;
- a very high carbohydrate diet which has pushed aside the meat to make way for more pasta and carbohydrate powders; and
- fad diets, 'food combining' diets and other unvaried, unbalanced eating programs.

The following panel summarises guidelines to assist the athlete to meet their iron needs, and thus prevent or reverse the fatigue associated with low iron status.

GUIDELINES FOR PROMOTING IRON-RICH EATING AND PRESERVING IRON STATUS

- Recognise if you are in a high-risk category for increased iron needs due to physiological requirements or high iron losses. Minimise losses where possible. Have routine screenings of blood iron measures such as ferritin and haemoglobin, so that you can identify your optimal range for these parameters and know when to treat a falling level.

- Eat meat regularly. Don't eat half a cow at a barbecue and consider that your iron needs are met for the next six months. Instead, include smaller amounts of meat frequently in your meal plans—for example, three to five times a week.
- Think beyond a slab of steak—particularly if you are a fussy eater who finds this 'too heavy'. 'Lighter' red meat options include strips in a stir-fry, lean mince in burgers or pasta sauces, or grilled kebabs.
- Liver (and liver paté) and shellfish are other excellent iron sources. These can be considered a meat alternative for your iron intake goals.
- Darker cuts of poultry and fish contain more iron than white cuts—for example, a chicken thigh is higher in iron than the breast.
- Mix and match 'meats' into a high-carbohydrate meal. Small serves added to a carbohydrate-rich base allow iron goals and fuel goals to be met simultaneously. More importantly, the haem iron-rich foods contain a factor that enhances the total iron absorption from the meal in which they are eaten. Add 'meats' as a filling in a sandwich, in a stir-fry with noodles, in a pasta sauce, as kebabs served with rice, or as a pizza topping—the ideas are endless.
- Identify the foods that are rich in non-haem iron, such as eggs, wholegrain cereals, dried fruit, legumes, soya products and green leafy vegetables. If you are a vegetarian or are eating a vegetarian meal, make these a focus of the meal. Additionally, enhance the absorption of the iron in these foods by including a food rich in vitamin C in your meal. For example, drink juice with your breakfast cereal, or have tomatoes and capsicums in a kidney bean stew.
- Make use of commercial breakfast cereals that are iron-fortified. Check the label to see which ones have added iron. Don't forget to have a vitamin C fruit at the same time.
- Factors that inhibit the iron absorption from non-haem iron-rich foods include phytates in cereal fibre and tannins in tea. This can be significant if your iron intake is mostly from non-haem iron sources and if you have increased iron needs. If so, you may be wise to drink your tea between meals rather than with them, and to avoid extra bran added to meals. It is likely that you already eat enough fibre.
- Take iron supplements only on the advice of a sports nutrition expert. Don't self-diagnose your own 'iron deficiencies', and remember that iron supplements will not correct other dietary inadequacies. A sports dietitian can help you to improve your iron eating along with other dietary goals. If you have become iron-deficient, it is likely that other dietary problems exist or that medical issues need to be checked.

CHRONIC DEHYDRATION

Monitoring body mass (BM) each morning, first thing after waking and visiting the bathroom, provides a guide to daily fluid balance. A sudden drop of a kilogram or more from one day to the next largely reflects a body fluid deficit. Real loss of body fat is measured in weeks, not days. A crash diet produces a sudden 'weight' loss by tricking the body to shed some water as it excretes ketone compounds produced by a body starved of carbohydrate fuel. Of course, it regains that water quickly, appearing to reverse all the good results of the diet, as soon as normal food intake is resumed. For athletes, a more common reason to see the scales suddenly lighter, is through the failure to replace large fluid losses from one day to the next.

The signals provided by thirst are not sufficiently immediate or strong to ensure full recovery of fluid losses in the short term. The fine-tuning of fluid balance is largely achieved by planning and behavioural strategies rather than by 'listening to the body' (see Chapters 13 and 14). Often when an athlete switches to a situation involving a sudden increase in fluid loss, there is a lag period until the new fluid plan catches up with the demand. Dehydration may carry over from one day to the next until the imbalance is remedied, and may contribute to a feeling of lethargy and tiredness. Common situations include:

- a sudden change to a hot climate or a sudden burst of hot weather;
- a trip to altitude (which increases respiratory fluid losses);
- a long plane flight; or
- a sudden increase in the training/competition load and its sweat losses.

It can take up to a couple of days for the body to adjust its fluid balance hormones.

The athlete can reduce the likelihood or the length of chronic dehydration by immediately adopting new fluid intake strategies, and by monitoring BM to assess the results. This is one of the few times when scales are a useful tool for the athlete, or when frequent weigh-ins are a good thing. The athlete is encouraged to keep a record of BM before and after exercise, and first thing each morning, at least during the adjustment period. This can be used to set fluid intake targets and to check that these targets are being met. The advice in Chapters 13 and 14 should allow the athlete to set a good plan for fluid intake.

Part IV

DOES MAGIC EXIST?

16

Pills, potions and supplements

'Of course you'll try a product that could increase your performance by 22%. You may be masochistic, obsessive/compulsive, and have serious denial issues. But you're not crazy.'

> Advertisement for a glycerol-containing pre-exercise hydrating supplement

'Even after 30 years, research still shows that nothing replaces fluids, minerals and energy faster than sports drink X. It enhances performance and speeds recovery. Talk about the "Power of Positive Drinking™" . . . Life is a sport. Drink it up™.'

> Advertisement for a sports drink

'Choose your weapons wisely. These are the finest products in the world for your body building needs. Tested and proven by the greatest body building athletes all over the world . . . It is not like the stuff the pros use. It is the stuff the pros use.'

> Advertisement for a range of body building supplements

'Technological breakthrough. 25 years of research unleashes incredible results: 48% greater rate of fat loss.'

> Advertisement for a body building supplement containing pyruvate

'Tap the ultimate energy source: your own body fat . . . "I gave the X Bar and program a try. After 6 weeks I lost 7 pounds of

353

body fat and my training and recovery has improved dramatically. I'm glad I got off the high-carb roller coaster that has hindered my performance all these years"—testimonial from a high profile athlete.'

Advertisement for a 40:30:30 sports bar

'Find out about a potent combination of three supplements that are so powerful that they should be listed in the Physicians Desk Reference, instead of the Sports Supplement Review . . . Discover a new "anabolic cocktail" (it's completely legal) that may help to put more black-market steroid dealers out of business than 100 DEA agents!'

Advertisement for a 'supplement encyclopaedia' on body building products

Sports supplements are one of the most visible, and lucrative, examples of sports nutrition. There are an almost endless array of pills, potions, drinks, bars and powders which compete for the attention and the wallets of athletes. In fact, to some athletes these supplements *are* sports nutrition. But it is confusing to be bombarded with so many products that all claim to provide the winning edge. Clearly not all of them can live up to this promise. Yet many supplements play an invaluable role in allowing the athlete to achieve their nutritional goals and their optimal performance. Which are which?

Part of the reason that this question needs to be asked is that the supplement industry is largely unregulated. In most countries there is little legislative control and supervision of supplements, compared with the way that foods or pharmaceutical products are regulated. In Australia and New Zealand, food legislators are currently forming guidelines to create a new area of 'sports foods', since items like drinks and bars fall within their boundaries. Typically, though, supplements of the pills and potion kind fall into a grey area of the law. Some manufacturers may take advantage of this by being less than stringent in ensuring that their product ingredients match the description on its packet, or by making exaggerated and unsubstantiated claims about the benefits the product (allegedly) provides. This hasn't appeared to hurt the commercial viability of the industry—it is a thriving, competitive, billion-dollar concern. The players range from international food and pharmaceutical companies, to small operators who pack and label the goods in their own homes. And the products range from supplements that are supported by extensive research and nutrition education programs, to items that reflect a short-lived fad. But it is often difficult to tell just by appearances into which end of the spectrum a product fits.

Most sports supplements are packaged, presented and promoted with enthusiasm, flair and vigour. They all look state-of-the-art, must-have and used-by-the-champions. It would take a couple of volumes, rather than a chapter, to cover all the supplements available. And even at the point of publication, these would no longer be up to date, since new products appear by the month. A simpler way is to divide supplements into categories, and to judge a product according to the major characteristics of the category in which it belongs.

CATEGORY 1: DIETARY SUPPLEMENTS FOR ATHLETES

Products which assist athletes to meet their nutritional requirements and goals are the supplements most accepted and recommended by sports nutrition experts. These might be termed 'dietary supplements for sport' or 'sports supplements' and fit the following description:

- They provide the nutrients found in everyday foods in a form that is convenient or practical for an athlete or a sports situation.
- Alternatively, they provide doses of nutrients such as vitamins or minerals that will prevent or treat a nutritional deficiency. However, these should be used only after the diagnosis of a sports nutrition/medicine expert.
- They allow the athlete to meet a specific nutritional need in training or competition, and thus improve their performance.

The key feature of these supplements is that they offer 'tailor-made' or practical nutrition. From the previous chapter it is clear that science can offer the athlete many general and specific nutritional strategies to help optimise their health and performance. Unfortunately, while knowledge and enthusiasm are prerequisites for achieving these goals, this is not always enough. There are numerous practical challenges that prevent athletes from using everyday foods to meet their nutritional goals. Sports supplements address these practical difficulties in these ways and more by:

- providing a low-bulk and compact form of energy and

nutrients so that total intake can be increased, or consumed at a time when the athlete wants to avoid feeling full;

- providing a concentrated source of a nutrient for an athlete who is unable or unwilling to meet their requirements from a food source;
- packaging a 'convenient' amount of nutrient(s) so that an athlete can easily calculate how to meet a nutrient target;
- providing nutrients in a concentration that balances the body's needs against its ability to absorb various nutrients;
- removing components such as fat and fibre from pre- and during-exercise snacks that might otherwise increase the risk of gastrointestinal problems;
- being manufactured or packaged in portable, non-perishable or 'easy to get at' forms so that the athlete can consume them 'on the run'—often, literally;
- appealing to the taste and appetite of someone who is hot and sweaty, either during or after exercise, so that they are more likely to consume what they need.

So while these supplements can be part of the nutrition program that allows an athlete to perform at their best, a number of conditions apply. First, the athlete must realise that it is the *use* of a supplement, rather than the supplement itself, that is important. In the world of advertising hype, it is expected that manufacturers will 'talk up' the benefits of their product and perhaps suggest that it is better than the direct competition. However, the best products and companies are those that focus attention on teaching athletes how to use their product correctly, rather than just selling the product to them. Correct use involves matching the product to the right situation, with the right timing and in the right quantity.

The second condition is the financial consideration. Supplements are usually more expensive than everyday foods, especially those that come straight from Mother Nature. (She doesn't have to worry about overheads and reporting company profits.) Therefore, it makes sense to rely on food for everyday needs, and to save supplements for situations when the convenience or practical advantages justify the cost. Undoubtedly, some athletes (and non-athletes) buy products that are of little value to them other than as a status symbol or placebo (see Chapter 17). On the other hand, there has been some overstated criticism about the expense of certain supplements— for example, that sports drinks are a 'waste of money' for non-elite athletes. Indeed, many athletes can't afford to use such specialised products on all occasions. However, a key point to remember is that it is the effort undertaken in sport or exercise that creates a nutritional need, rather than the expertise of the person involved. Joe Public sweats when he is playing basketball, just like Michael Jordan. Although his success in replacing fluid and fuel losses with a sports drink is unlikely to win him an NBA championship, it is still likely to improve his game by his own standards. And that is probably important to him.

Table 16.1 summarises the types of products that fall into the category of sports supplements, along with the situations in which they are best used. Of course, the conditions of correct use and cost effectiveness will vary between athletes and various sports situations. Specific advice from a sports nutrition expert is the best way to ensure that the athlete is getting good value from sports supplements in all senses of the word, and is essential in the area of diagnosing and treating nutrient inadequacies. We have not considered it necessary to summarise individually the research that supports appropriate use of specific or general groups of these supplements. It interweaves the well-documented sports nutrition information that has been presented in previous chapters. In fact, some of our present knowledge has either direct or indirect association with sports supplements. For example, many of the companies who make these products fund independent as well as in-house research. Or conversely, supplements have been developed in response to research findings, as a practical means of achieving a successful nutritional intervention. Such a working relationship looks after sports scientists, athletes and companies alike.

CATEGORY 2: NUTRITIONAL ERGOGENIC AIDS

The second category of supplements are best described as nutritional ergogenic aids. 'Ergogenic' is a term meaning 'work enhancing' and could be applied to a number of products such as biomechanical aids, drugs or psychological interventions. In this case, it is used to describe supplements which fulfil the following characteristics:

- they generally contain nutrients or food chemicals in amounts greater than would be found in dietary sources and everyday eating; and

TABLE 16.1

Types of sports supplements

Supplement	Forms	Composition	Major uses
Sports drinks			
Gatorade, Powerade, Isosport, SportPlus, Energade, Replace, Isostar	Drink, or powdered form for making into drink	5–8% carbohydrate 10–25 mmol/litre sodium	• Fluid and/or carbohydrate replacement during exercise (see Chapter 13) • Post-exercise rehydration and refuelling (see Chapter 14)
High-carbohydrate source (= carbohydrate loaders)			
Gatorload, Exceed High Carbohydrate Source, Refuel powder, Maxim, Ultrafuel	Powder (for making into drink or adding to foods) or ready-made drink	100% carbohydrate powder, usually glucose polymers. Drinks usually made up at 20–25% carbohydrate concentration, sometimes with B vitamins added.	• Supplement to a high-carbohydrate diet (Chapters 10 and 15) • Carbohydrate loading or 'fuelling up' (see Chapter 12) • Concentrated carbohydrate drink during exercise (Chapter 13) • Post-exercise refuelling (see Chapter 14)
Gels			
Gu, Power Gel, Ultragel, Clif Shot, Hammer Gel, Leppin Squeezy, Relode	30–40 g sachets or larger tubes of thick syrup for a 'quick squeeze' of carbohydrate	60–70% carbohydrate gel—provides ~ 25 g carbohydrate per sachet	• Concentrated form of carbohydrate during exercise (see Chapter 13)
Liquid meal supplements			
Sustagen Sport, Gator Pro, Exceed Sports Meal	Ready-made drink, or powder for mixing in water or milk to make drink	When made as drink: 1–1.5 kcal per ml. 50–70% carbohydrate 15–20% protein low-moderate fat 500–1000 ml of drink provides 100% of RDIs of vitamins and minerals	• Compact energy and nutrient supplement for a high-energy diet (see Chapters 10 and 11) • Pre-event meal (see Chapter 12) • Post-event recovery (see Chapter 14) • Nutrition for the travelling athlete and the athlete 'on the move' (Chapters 12 and 14)

Supplement	Forms	Composition	Major uses

Sports bars
1   Power Bar,
Refuel bar, VO2
max bar, Clif Bar
2   PR bar,
Balance bar
	50–70 g
	bar—chewy or
	'muesli' bar
	consistency
		1 40–50 g
		carbohydrate +
		5–10 g protein.
		Usually low in fat.
		Often fortified
		with 50–100%
		RDI of vitamins
		and minerals.
		2 40:30:30 ratio
		of carbohydrate,
		fat and protein
		for use in Zone
		diet (Chapter 17)
			• Supplement to a
			  high-carbohydrate diet
			  (see Chapters 10 and
			  15)
			• Pre-exercise meal or
			  snack (see Chapter
			  12)
			• Carbohydrate source
			  during exercise (see
			  Chapter 13)
			• Post-exercise
			  refuelling (see
			  Chapter 14)

Vitamin/mineral supplements 1 Multi-vitamins/ minerals 2 Iron 3 Calcium	Capsule or tablet	1 Broad range, 100–300% RDI 2 30–125 mg ferrous iron 3 500–1000 mg calcium	1 Supplement to a low-energy or restricted variety diet (see Chapter 15) 2 Supervised treatment or prevention of iron deficiency (see Chapter 15) 3 Supplement to a low-energy or diet inadequate in calcium. Perhaps useful in treatment or prevention of osteoporosis (see Chapter 11).

• they propose a direct effect on performance, often suggested to occur as a supra-physiological effect.

This is the arena in which product companies and advertising executives have been able to exercise their greatest flair and use of hyperbole. The sheer number of nutritional substances which have been proposed to enhance performance, along with the various permutations and combinations in which they might be packaged together, is the reason for the stacked shelves in many health food shops and supplement outlets. For example, a 1993 survey examined the advertisements in five popular body building magazines and counted 624 different nutritional products promoted for strength and body building activities, with over 800 performance claims. It is likely that a similar number would appear in the latest editions of such magazines. However, perhaps half would be new products with new ingredients.

Although this is not necessarily a defining characteristic of nutritional ergogenic aids, it is fair to note that a common feature of these products is their reliance on testimonials and theories rather than rigorous research testing. Most products make strong claims to enhance performance. Unfortunately, this is most often backed up by elegant 'scientific' explanations, marketing exaggeration, anecdotes from famous athletes or happy consumers, or reference to research in a related field. This is emotive and generates sales, but, as discussed in Chapter 17, it does not provide proof. The overwhelming majority of supplements, or the individual compounds in them, have either not been adequately tested in well-controlled trials, or when tested have failed to live up to their performance claims.

Not surprisingly, sports scientists and nutritionists are not supportive of most nutritional ergogenic aids. In some cases, their disdain may encompass the whole family of these products. It is easy to understand this view. But, on closer inspection, it is possible to sub-categorise nutritional ergogenic aids into those that may be of use to athletes, those which have received some attention but await a final verdict, and those which have no substance to their claims. This chapter will overview some of the commonly discussed compounds.

Level 1: Products which have scientific proof of performance enhancement

Although there are details still to be fine-tuned with regard to each of these compounds, there is significant evidence that each can be used to enhance sports performance. The following conditions apply:

- There is no universal improvement in sports performance resulting from the use of these products. Rather, each aid is directed to a specific setting or type of physiological challenge. Athletes who wish to use such products should ensure that they are applying them correctly and in the correct setting.
- Individual athletes may respond differently—with effects ranging from clear benefit, to no response, and in some

cases, a negative response. Therefore, the athlete should experiment with the use of these aids, and should trial any intended competition use well before it is considered for an important event.

* At present there are ways to use these products within the law, if not the spirit of anti-'doping' control. Nevertheless, the athlete should keep abreast of the doping policies of the International Olympic Committee (IOC) or their national sporting bodies in case future rulings place such products on banned lists. Already in the case of caffeine, the intake of large doses is likely to contravene doping laws.

Caffeine

Caffeine is the most widely used drug in the world, with people including it in social rituals as well as taking it deliberately for its well-known buzz. It affects numerous body tissues in a variety of ways, making it difficult to isolate the specific mechanism for any observed changes. There is a long history of caffeine use in sport to mask fatigue and improve performance. However, it wasn't until the late 1970s and the publication of several studies from Professor Dave Costill's group at Ball State University in the United States that caffeine use by athletes gained real momentum and legitimacy. These studies reported that caffeine, taken approximately one hour prior to moderate-intensity exercise, increased exercise capacity and work output. Evidence suggested that caffeine increased free fatty acid levels and fat oxidation during exercise, sparing muscle glycogen use. Although black coffee and cola drinks became a favourite pre- or during-race beverage of many endurance athletes, the studies undertaken over the next decade showed inconsistent results.

More recent research has enabled scientists to form confident views on caffeine and sports performance. Our present understanding is summarised briefly:

* Caffeine supplementation of 3–6 mg/kg body mass (BM) in the hour prior to exercise may benefit the performance of endurance events (moderate-intensity exercise lasting more than 90 minutes), high-intensity exercise of approximately 20 minutes duration, and short very high intensity exercise lasting approximately 5 minutes. Most studies rely on laboratory measurements of performance, and further research needs to be undertaken in real-life athletic settings.

- Although increasing the dose may also increase the exercise benefits, caffeine intakes of above 9 mg/kg BM increase the risk of achieving 'illegal' urine concentrations of caffeine. At intakes above 13 mg/kg BM, the risk of side-effects is significant (e.g. headaches, insomnia, gastro-intestinal side-effects).
- Caffeine is considered a restricted substance by the IOC, and urinary levels above 12 ug/ml are considered to be 'doping'. These levels are not easy to reach via conventional dietary means, and are usually only achieved by using caffeine tablets or suppositories. A few athletes have fallen foul of these restrictions during international competition and have received severe penalties. Athletes who intend to use caffeine as a performance agent should check whether this use leads to illegally high urinary caffeine levels. There is some individual variability in caffeine excretion.
- Sources of caffeine for the athlete include coffee (typically 50–100 mg per cup), brewed tea (typically 30–60 mg per cup), cola drinks (typically 50 mg per 375 ml can) and over-the-counter medications (typically 100–200 mg per tablet). Some of these sources may be part of the normal competition practices of an athlete. However, other athletes may take caffeine before or during an event specifically to improve their performance.
- Caffeine exerts its effect on performance in a number of ways. At doses of above 5 mg/kg BM it appears to stimulate fat metabolism early during exercise, with increases in the oxidation of both free fatty acids and intramuscular triglyceride. However, these glycogen sparing effects are limited to the first 15 minutes of exercise. Other effects include an increase in adrenalin (probably not important), a direct effect on muscle contraction, and stimulation of the central nervous system to change the perception of effort.
- The metabolic effects of caffeine are more variable in untrained people. The greater reliability of performance in well-trained athletes also increases the likelihood of seeing a significant performance benefit (see Chapter 17).
- There is considerable individual variability in the metabolic and performance response to caffeine. Factors additional to training status include habitual caffeine use. While some athletes are definitely responsive to caffeine, others at the other extreme suffer side-effects that may reduce performance.

- Although caffeine is known to have diuretic properties and may increase urine losses during post-exercise rehydration, consumption before and during exercise has not been shown to impair fluid status or temperature regulation.

Bicarbonate

The primary power source for short-term (less than five minutes) exercise of near maximal intensity is the anaerobic glycolytic system (see Chapter 3). The progressive build-up of hydrogen ions in association with the production of lactate causes a limit to the power output of this system. The rise in acidity within the cell interferes with the muscle's ability to contract, and this power system becomes self-limiting. When the buffering capacity inside the cell is exceeded, lactate and hydrogen ions diffuse outside the cell and into the bloodstream. The most important buffer (outside the cell) is bicarbonate.

It has been hypothesised that an increase in the blood bicarbonate pool might delay the onset of muscular fatigue during prolonged anaerobic exercise, by increasing the extra-cellular buffering capacity and the muscle's ability to dispose of excess hydrogen ions. 'Bicarbonate loading' or 'soda loading' has been trialled by athletes and scientists for over 50 years. The types of events that are most suited to this intervention are those involving three to seven minutes of high-intensity work—such as 800 and 1500 m running, 400 and 800 m swimming, and various rowing, kayaking and canoeing events. The general protocol is to ingest 0.3 g sodium bicarbonate per kg BM (about 20 g for a typical 70 kg male athlete), one to two hours prior to the exercise task. This can be taken in the form of household 'bicarb soda', although some athletes prefer the taste of over-the-counter pharmaceutical urinary alkaliser products such as 'Ural'. It is generally recommended that the bicarbonate dose be consumed with plenty of water (e.g. 1–2 litres) to help prevent hyperosmotic diarrhoea. Gastrointestinal symptoms are a frequently mentioned side-effect of bicarbonate loading.

There have been over 50 studies of bicarbonate loading on exercise performance. One way to collapse the sometimes inconsistent results of this research is to do a statistical overview, called a meta-analysis. Such a summary was recently undertaken, collecting all studies which fulfilled the criteria of being conducted in a randomised double blind method (see Chapter 17). This overview, which included twenty-nine studies, showed that most experiments were performed on male college students—ranging from 'healthy' to moderately trained. Cycling was the most frequently used form of exercise, with duration ranging from 30 seconds to seven minutes, or repeated intervals of one minute with short rest times. Performance was measured in a number of different ways. This included the measurement of changes in power output over a given time period, total work output in a specified time, or the time for which a specific intensity could be maintained (i.e. time to exhaustion). Many of these have a low test–retest reliability (see Chapter 17) which makes it difficult to detect real changes in performance. Only five studies have measured performance time for a specific event to mimic the effect in a real sporting situation.

Despite the shortcomings of the design of many studies, the meta-analysis concluded that the ingestion of bicarbonate has a medium-sized and positive effect on exercise performance. From a statistical point of view, this effect would be made larger by using adequate doses of bicarbonate, by ensuring that the exercise task is sufficiently anaerobic, and by using trained groups of athletes to reduce the variability of the measurement of performance. This would also make the studies more applicable to the world of sport!

It was noted that there was significant variability within the group responses in most studies. This indicates that bicarbonate ingestion has an individual effect on different subjects. It is possible that non-responders have already max-imised their body buffering capacity. This might be more likely in elite or well-trained athletes whose training or genetic excellence have conferred these advantages. Alternatively, an event, or the athlete's pacing of the event, may not challenge their ability to dispose of hydrogen ion build-up. Further research is needed on bicarbonate as a whole. However, individual athletes must experiment carefully to judge their own case. Practice in a competition-simulated environment is crucial to discover the potential of performance enhancement, as well as the likelihood for side-effects.

Creatine

An estimated 300,000 kg of creatine was sold in North America in 1996, making it one of the most rapid supplement success stories of all time. The creatine tale began in 1992, inspired by the Barcelona Olympics and the almost simulta-neous release of a study by English and Scandinavian scientists. The study reported that a high-dose creatine supplement taken over a number of days increased muscle levels of creatine and creatine phosphate levels, particularly in trained subjects. Linford Christie, and other successful British track and field athletes, provided testimonials that creatine loading had been used in the preparation for their gold medal winning performances. The worlds of sport and sports science were captured!

Creatine is a dietary component found in meats and eggs, with a typical daily intake being about 1 gram. Ninety-five per cent of the body's creatine pool is found in the muscles. Since daily turnover of creatine is about 2 g, the rest must be manufactured by the body and transported to the muscle cell.

Whole body synthesis is depressed when intake is high. However, vegetarians who eat little or no dietary creatine may not be able to fully make up for the remainder of their creatine needs, and may have lower muscle levels. The average muscle creatine level is about 125 mmol/kg dry muscle, with most of this being bound to phosphate.

Creatine phosphate performs a number of important functions in exercise metabolism. First, it provides a limited but rapidly operating power system to regenerate ATP and is the most important fuel source in the performance of all-out sprints of five to ten seconds (see Chapter 3). But it also provides a buffer for the hydrogen ions produced within the muscle cell during anaerobic glycolysis. And lastly it transports the ATP generated by aerobic metabolism inside the muscle cell mitochondria to the part of the cell where the muscle's contractile machinery can use it. It is not surprising that an increase in the muscle creatine phosphate level sounds attractive.

There has been a big effort to study creatine—to determine how to optimally load the muscle, and how performance may benefit as a result. Our current understanding is as follows:

- The quickest way to 'creatine load' is to take large and frequent doses of a creatine supplement for a number of days (e.g. 5 g doses, four to five times each day for five days). Eating a moderate amount of carbohydrate (100 g) with each dose increases creatine uptake via the stimulatory effects of insulin. Some supplement manufacturers recommend a total daily dose of 3–5 g/day. This will eventually load the muscle, but it may take up to 28 days before the muscle becomes saturated.

- The muscle cell has a creatine threshold or saturation point. Typically, creatine loading increases total creatine and creatine phosphate by 25% above normal levels. The response is individual and some athletes may improve their stores by 50%. Some research has suggested that those whose levels were initially lowest might respond best to supplementation. Vegetarian athletes are considered a target group since their dietary intake of creatine is low. Other researchers suggest that a high proportion of type IIb (fast twitch) fibres might also predict a good response to creatine. Why some athletes respond minimally is presently unknown. Across research studies in which muscle biopsies have been undertaken, the 'success' rate in increasing muscle creatine levels ranges between 60 and 100% of subjects. Obviously only those who increase muscle creatine levels will show a performance improvement.

- Following loading, muscle creatine stores gradually drop. Some studies have shown that it takes four to six weeks to return to resting levels. A 'maintenance' supplemental dose of 2–3 g creatine per day keeps the loaded muscle at elevated levels.

- Creatine loading is associated with an immediate weight gain of 1–2 kilograms. This is most likely to be due to the retention of fluid stored with the creatine inside the cell. Indeed, one study has shown a simultaneous decrease in urine output during the loading phase. However, there are many testimonials from athletes who continue to gain weight over the next months—often in excess of 5 kg—claiming this to be predominantly muscle gain. This effect is yet to be well-studied. If creatine supplementation does result in long-term gains in lean body mass, it may be due to creatine stimulation of protein synthesis, or simply because the athlete is able to train harder when loaded.

- Performance studies have shown consistent evidence that creatine supplementation improves recovery between repeated bouts of high-intensity exercise. An increased level of total creatine in the muscle appears to increase the rate of resynthesis of phosphocreatine during the rest periods between sprints, providing the muscle with greater stores for the next bout. This is most important when the recovery period is brief—for example, from 30 seconds to less than three minutes. Most studies show that the extra creatine is insufficient to improve the performance of the initial bout or a single high-intensity exercise sprint.

- Creatine studies have generally been undertaken in laboratory settings with recreational or moderately-trained subjects. More studies are needed to confirm performance benefits in elite athletes and in real-life settings. The description of 'repeated bouts of high-intensity exercise with short rest periods' fits both the interval training undertaken by some athletes, and the competition setting for team and racquet sports. Future work should target these specific situations.
- Creatine does not appear to enhance the performance of aerobic or endurance sports. In fact, one study of cross-country runners showed a performance impairment following creatine supplementation which was attributed to the corresponding weight gain.

Level 2: Products which are still under active scrutiny

A number of compounds are currently under the sports scientist's scrutiny. This can be a long and painstaking process (see Chapter 17). Scientists want to replicate their results, and to ensure that observations of performance enhancement are valid and relevant to the world of sport. They also like to investigate a mechanism to explain and further support their findings. And to explore that there are no side-effects or problems associated with large or long-term doses of the compound(s) involved. Then once the science is confirmed, it must be translated into practical guidelines for use by athletes. Details of recommended occasions of use, optimal timing and correct dosages all need to be sorted out.

The following compounds might be considered to be in this process. Some show early promise but need more work before they have achieved sufficient proof to be considered for level 1 status (see above). Others have not lived up to the first positive signs. More in-depth study may actually push them down to the next level.

Glycerol
Glycerol is under consideration as a hyper-hydrating agent that may assist athletes to load up with extra fluid before undertaking a dehydrating event. Further work is needed to support early results and to determine practical guidelines for use (see Chapter 12).

Medium-chain triglycerides

The idea of providing an additional source of fat to fuel ultra-endurance events is attractive. Medium-chain triglycerides bypass a number of the slow points in the transport and metabolism of the long-chain fatty acids that make up most of our dietary fat intake. This makes them an ideal fat source to experiment with during prolonged, low-to-moderate intensity exercise. The research is still in a preliminary stage and may grind to a disappointing halt if the reports of gastrointestinal upsets become a universal finding (see Chapter 10).

L-carnitine

Carnitine plays a number of important roles in exercise metabolism. It is well-known as a transport molecule for taking fatty acids inside the mitochondria of muscle cells where they are oxidised. It also plays a role in regulating the balance between key chemicals in other metabolic processes. A couple of studies have reported that after a period of carnitine supplementation, well-trained subjects increased their $\dot{V}O_{2max}$. The key claim of this supplement is that it can enhance fat metabolism by increasing the transport of fat to its site of oxidation. Thus it is a popular ingredient in 'fat loss' supplements, as well as making claim to increase exercise capacity. This background has provided sufficient foundation to encourage further study.

However, the updated and better-controlled studies have found flaws in this claim, and have failed to replicate the findings of improved performance in athletes. Muscle biopsy studies have failed to find evidence that heavy training reduces muscle carnitine levels, or that these levels are increased by carnitine supplementation of up to one month. A change in muscle content after supplementation is a prerequisite if any benefits are to take place. Therefore, it is no surprise that performance changes have not been detected in the newer studies. Currently there is insufficient evidence to recommend that athletes take L-carnitine to improve their performance. The effect on loss of body fat has not been systematically studied. However, there is no indication from any study that subjects underwent any change in body composition.

Branch-chain amino acids

Amino acids have also been a marketer's dream during the last decade. The amino acid theory that seemed most credible concerned the role of branch-chain amino acids (BCAAs) in the prevention of central fatigue during prolonged moderate-intensity exercise. During endurance events, the blood levels of BCAAs drop in response to the growing carbohydrate fuel crisis. This is a sign that amino acids are being recycled by the liver to make new glucose for muscle fuel. However, a side-effect of the change in amino acid ratios in the blood is an alteration in the ratio of amino acids that compete to cross the barrier into the brain. A drop in BCAAs allows more of the amino acid tryptophan to enter the brain, which then leads to an increased production of a chemical called serotonin. This chemical is known to cause drowsiness and 'central' or brain fatigue, as opposed to the muscular fatigue of fuel depletion (see Chapter 13). It has been suggested that the intake of BCAA supplements during exercise might prevent this from occurring. Indeed, two studies have reported that athletes who supplemented with BCAAs during their event improved their sports performance and cognitive function.

Most scientists are critical of these studies. 'Performance' was assessed in an unusual manner in one case, and there seemed to be some juggling of numbers in the other to achieve a statistically significant outcome. More importantly, other research has shown that there is a better way to reduce the risk of central fatigue scenario. This is, simply, to feed carbohydrate during exercise. This reduces the amino acid drain by providing the muscle with a direct source of glucose. And it keeps tryptophan levels pegged. When blood glucose is high, fatty acid levels are suppressed. These travel around the bloodstream bound to the protein albumin, which also acts as a carrier for trytophan. When fatty acid levels are high, as in the case of prolonged exercise, tryptophan loses its spot and is 'free' in the blood. It is only the free tryptophan that has right of entry into the brain. Carbohydrate intake during exercise works to keep both sides of the amino acid competition under control. Studies show that it is effective in reducing the risk of central fatigue as well as in supplying fuel to the muscle.

There is still interest in studying the role of BCAAs in post-exercise recovery. However, the balance of evidence does not support BCAA supplementation during exercise. In fact, since amino acid supplements may be a source of ammonia production during exercise, and ammonia is another chemical associated with fatigue, there may be reasons to *discourage* athletes from using amino acid supplements or sports drinks containing BCAAs during events.

Vitamins E and C (anti-oxidants)

The destructive effects of free-oxygen radicals on various body tissues are now well-known. Exercise is known to increase the oxidative stress on the body, and anti-oxidant supplementation might reduce the oxidative damage to muscle cells and other body sites. Some studies support this view. There is evidence that supplementation with vitamin E (with and without other anti-oxidants) increases anti-oxidant potential, leading to a reduction in the signs of oxidative damage following an acute exercise bout. Other studies have reported that vitamin C supplementation bolsters the immune system against the onslaught of an exceptional exercise task, such as running a marathon or an ultra-marathon.

However, there are some methodological problems that make it difficult to track the cellular evidence of oxidative damage. Furthermore, some studies show that repeated exposures to exercise allow the body to develop adequate anti-oxidant protection on its own. Finally, even if anti-oxidant supplementation can be of benefit at a muscle cellular level, it may be too subtle to cause significant benefits at the level of exercise performance. It may take a long time before these effects, if any, are noticed. Several studies undertaken during the 1970s failed to detect any improvements in the performance of athletes who took vitamin E supplements for periods of up to a month.

For the moment there is insufficient evidence to justify recommendations that athletes take anti-oxidant supplements to improve their performance. However, supplementation might be of some use to athletes who suddenly increase their exposure to oxidative stress—for example, an athlete who undertakes a sharp increase in their training, or moves to a high-altitude location. This may offer a short-term boost until the body can adapt to the new stress.

Level 3: Products which have no scientific support

The majority of nutritional ergogenic aids fall into this class. Sometimes this is because they simply haven't been tested. But others which have had preliminary or even extensive scrutiny by researchers have failed to show any substantial evidence of performance benefits. Often the research stops because the scientist can't see any likelihood of a positive outcome. The list below is unfinished but includes products of recent promotions, as well as compounds that were fashionable some years back. The fact that these have disappeared, at least from the front pages or 'what's hot' topics of conversation, provides extra proof of a lack of efficacy. After all, if they did what they were claimed to do, athletes would still be using them. The world of ergogenic aids is like the world of fashion—it goes in cycles!

- bee pollen
- choline
- ferulic acid (Frac) and gamma oryzanol
- other free-form amino acids—for example, arginine and ornithine
- ginseng
- inosine
- B15—often but inaccurately called a vitamin
- chromium picolinate
- vanadium and vanadyl sulphate
- spirulina
- pyruvate
- poly-lactate
- magnesium

TO SUPPLEMENT OR NOT TO SUPPLEMENT?

Athletes have many reasons for taking supplements. These vary from the justifiable (correct use of dietary supplements) to the innocuous ('just in case', 'everybody else is doing it') to the dubious (it will make up for a poor diet or messy lifestyle). Ultimately, such decisions are a personal choice. However, there are a list of important considerations that should be checked off when making an informed decision. The advice of a sports nutrition expert may help to provide information if the athlete is unable to answer any of the following questions.

- Is it safe? Are there any side-effects?
- Is it legal? Does it (or any other of its ingredients) contravene doping laws?
- Does it work? What is the scientific consensus? What are my own experiences?
- Do I know how to use it correctly?
- Can I afford it?
- Am I doing everything else that is possible to optimise my performance? Am I looking at this product as an adjunct to good practices or am I looking for 'short cuts'?

YOU ARE ABOUT TO ENTER THE ZONE

Here are some tips for writing a best-selling diet book:

- Have impressive sounding qualifications in a medically-related field.
- Be controversial. Slam the current world experts on health and nutrition, and the guidelines for healthy eating.
- Claim an amazing new scientific understanding. Fill pages with complicated biochemistry explained in simple language.
- Claim that your diet will cure all manner of diseases and health problems, including heart disease, cancer, diabetes and AIDS. Prove this with case histories.
- Provide a complicated set of rules about foods which can't be eaten, or even better, foods which can't be eaten *at the same time.*
- Have sports stars, film stars and political heavyweights follow and flourish on your diet—or at least be rumoured to.
- Best of all, promise that weight loss will occur while the dieter can eat *as much as they like.*

Dr Barry Sears has used these techniques to captivate the market of weight watchers, athletes, health food eaters and celebrities with his 'Zone diet', and to cause controversy and debate among sports scientists and nutritionists. His books *Enter the Zone* (1995) and *Mastering the Zone* (1997) are complicated reading—full of scientific discussions, emotive claims and repetitive nutrition messages. 'Every time you open your mouth to eat, you are applying for a passport to the Zone.' The Zone promises optimal health, physical performance and mental alertness for the rest of your life.

According to Dr Sears, the Zone is reached by finding a correct balance between the 'good' and 'bad' hormones in our body—between the 'good' and 'bad' eicosanoids, and between insulin and glucagon. He soundly attacks current healthy eating guidelines and research. He claims that high-carbohydrate, moderate-fat diets actually *cause* weight gain and the current disease patterns of the Western world, principally by causing an overproduction of insulin. Although the Zone books and publicity provide a confused picture of the diet, it answers to the following description:

- A 'Zone favourable' meal or snack must be eaten at least every five hours during the day, to set insulin ratios for the next period.
- Forty per cent of the energy from each meal or snack should come from carbohydrate—with the emphasis on low glycaemic index choices.

- Protein requirements are set according to activity level and lean body mass. Daily eating patterns should neither under- nor over-achieve these levels, and this should form 30% of the energy in each meal and in the total diet.
- Fat, particularly from monounsaturated sources, should provide 30% of meals and snacks.

This explains why the diet and its related food plans and products are also titled '40:30:30'. In real life, it is difficult to organise food into such an energy ratio. Opposition comes from the complex nutrient composition of foods, and from the typical mixes and matches that we are used to eating. Sears suggests that food can be divided into 'blocks' of good carbohydrates, fat and proteins, and provides a formula for assembling meals and snacks from these blocks. The latest book provides some recipes based on these. Or you can purchase meal plans, or a computer program which generates these, from companies such as Eicotech and Envion (which have a past or present association with Sears) or PR (started by Sears' sister). Interestingly, a recent study which crunched the nutrient numbers on some Zone meals provided in the book found that they don't actually reach the magic ratio. In fact, it is likely that they provide less carbohydrate (around 30–35%) and more protein than advertised.

Of course, the most convenient (if not more expensive) option is to purchase food products already made to macronutrient measure. '40:30:30' sports bars come with the purchase of the specially devised meal plans from the companies above (well, vice versa, actually). A liquid meal powder is also on the market, and there are a range of everyday 'Zone favourable' food products available through network marketing schemes, 1-800 numbers and internet websites. Some trendy restaurants advertise Zone cuisine or meals. So supposing you do enter the Zone— what are the benefits?

If you are interested in losing body fat, and can follow instructions to the letter, then the Zone is likely to produce results. But for less than magical reasons. Although Dr Sears is coy about this, the Zone is actually a low-energy eating plan. We calculated the formula for a mythical female doing an hour of training each day (a bit like one of the authors of this book) and found a daily allowance of 960 Kcals (4 MJ). The claims that the Zone 'provides access to stored body fat' are not surprising in the light of this. Whether the Zone does this more effectively than any other low-energy food combination has not been tested. What is does, like a number of other recent diet best-sellers, is surreptitiously help people to reduce their food and energy intake. With the focus on special and difficult-to-find food combinations and scientific breakthroughs, people fail to realise that they are actually eating less. At least in the short term.

But what's in it for athletes? This is where the book becomes confusing, despite dazzling accounts of the success of top athletes on the Zone. It is claimed that athletes do better on a high-fat intake. But the Zone is a *low*-fat diet, however you look at it. Thirty per cent of energy is in line with the healthy guidelines for moderate-fat eating. And 30% of 960 Kcals only allows 32g of fat a day—a very modest amount. Some athletes may be pleased to lose body fat. However, extreme energy restriction such as this is likely to reduce training and competition performance. Although the athlete may be able to slog through low-intensity sessions, inadequate carbohydrate intake will interfere with their ability to perform high-intensity or quality sessions.

It is unclear how athletes who don't want to lose body fat can make up their energy requirements while on the Zone. The book hints that the athlete should increase their intake of monounsaturated fat, but is light on the practical details of how to do it. Of course, this manoeuvre will break away from the famous 40:30:30 ratio. Conflicting advice from one Zone-based company is that athletes should stick to the ratio and just eat more of everything. In turn this may lead to very high protein intakes—something that Dr Sears claims to be against. In practice, athletes appear to adopt a variety of ways of doing their own Zone thing. Many just seem to like the bars and eat them as snacks, while manipulating meals to steer away from 'bad carbohydrate foods' and increase their protein serves. Zone bars are more exotic than the strict high-carbohydrate bars—a significant fat and protein content lends itself to the territory of chocolate, peanut butter, fudge and other flavoursome options. However, there is no published evidence that the Zone diet in any of its forms improves sports performance.

Best-selling diets come and go. Whether the Zone diet will stand the test of time and the test of scientific scrutiny remains to be seen. For the moment, it is simply untested.

17

Where's the proof? Evaluating claims for new products or training interventions

'Experiments in the laboratory are not of much practical value to athletes. There is, in fact, little scientific evidence in favour of many things done in training.'

Sir Roger Bannister, first man to break
four minutes for the mile

'A scientific approach refers simply to one in which techniques that have been evaluated scientifically and shown to "work" are preferred to those which have yet to be evaluated scientifically. The scientific approach does not hold that traditional methods are necessarily wrong. It simply argues that until they have been evaluated scientifically, they should not be accepted as "dogma". Indeed, scientists are very suspicious of any dogmas and believe that all truths, even those which they have discovered themselves, are suspect and must be continually re-evaluated.'

Tim Noakes and Morné du Plessis, in
Rugby without risk

'No theory can be proved correct. The best we can hope for is that no test can be devised that proves our theory incorrect! The repeated testing for failure affords a measure of confidence in the knowledge that coaches bring to the training process.'

Dr Victor Katch, exercise physiologist

In the preceding chapters, it has become obvious that successful sports performance is dependent upon many factors, including genetic endowment, state-of-the-art training techniques, appropriate competition strategies, and proper nutrition before, during and after an event. Athletes continually seek to maximise these (and other) performance-related components. But most serious performers are also constantly searching for the 'magic bullet' that will give them a competitive edge over their opponents. This might take the form of a pill, potion or supplement, a new training technique, or a novel piece of sports equipment. Many companies, coaches and writers make a healthy living from athletes who are willing to include their product or idea in this search.

Nevertheless, sports careers are too short and most budgets are too limited to try every new thing on the market. This book can't pinpoint every magic bullet or winning edge. But the next best thing is to provide guidelines for narrowing the search, and then evaluating the targeted item swiftly and correctly. In other words, the clever athlete is the one who targets their resources to those products or strategies which have the most likelihood of working, then gives them a fair and efficient trial. Successful items can be integrated into the program or fine-tuned for maximum effect. Meanwhile, things that don't appear to provide any benefit, or have a low return for the investment, can be discarded. This chapter will discuss the methods by which evidence can be amassed to 'prove' the benefits of an intervention.

LEVELS OF PROOF

In the world of science, as in real life, there are very few things that are certain. Rather, people act on beliefs that are based on the best information available to them. Often such a decision is arrived at by taking an idea and scrutinising it as far as is possible. There is a search for evidence to support it. Attempts are made to challenge the evidence, and while it survives intact, it is accepted. In other words, there are different levels of 'proof', which will now be discussed.

The scientific theory

Everything starts with a good idea. Creative people can often look at a situation and speculate that a certain modification might improve the outcome. The ideas for the modification come from observing a similar situation, or from understanding the way things work. In the case of athletic performance, a knowledge of biochemistry or physiology or biomechanics may provide the idea for a new dietary supplement, training strategy or training aid. And it may colour in quite a complex mechanism to explain likely changes.

Supplements provide a good example of the way that theories can be developed. Many of the current 'in vogue' nutritional ergogenic aids are chemicals found in the body that take part in key reactions or processes in exercise metabolism. The rationale for taking these in supplement form is a 'golden oldie'—simply, that if a little bit of something is good, then more must be better. It is suggested that high levels of intake of these products might 'supercharge' the metabolic processes and allow them to proceed faster or longer. This may form an interesting hypothesis for testing.

The limitation of a scientific theory, no matter how complicated and well thought out is that it exists on paper. There may be other factors that have not been considered in the theory, which in fact interact to prevent the desired outcome. For example, a compound which has all the right qualifications to appear like a nutritional ergogenic aid may, in fact, not be absorbed or retained in the body in larger amounts. Quite often the body has regulatory processes to prevent excesses of various substances. Or the substance may not be taken up at the important site of its desired action. It is not useful if it is sitting in the blood, when its main activity should be occurring inside the mitochondria of a muscle cell. On the other hand, some interventions interfere with other processes to cause unexpected damage in another area. For example, a training intervention may cause improvements in one area, but cause concurrent injuries by overloading another. Finally, sometimes an intervention may 'work' in that it improves its own area of influence. However, in the final analysis this wasn't found to be the rate-limiting or most important contributing factor to performance. For example, certain training may be designed to make an athlete more aerobically fit, or stronger. And it may achieve these goals. But it may not translate into improved performance in the athlete's specific sport.

In summary, the scientific theory is a good place to start thinking about an intervention. But while it remains a theory, there is *no proof* of performance improvements. Unfortunately, the manufacturers of some products seem to take good ideas from the drawing board to the market, before they have been tested. The advertisements for some supplements and training aids appear to support the performance claims for their products with references to scientific papers. On closer examination these references turn out to be biochemistry textbooks or medical trials (i.e. theories) rather than meticulous testing of the actual product. Theory is not proof.

Testimonials and anecdotal support

'I tried it and it worked for me.' Humans are swayed by the experiences of others. Particularly if the 'others' are famous and successful. Testimonials provide a key advertising tool used by companies in all areas of marketing. However, it is noticeable that they can form the highest level of support for the claims made for many athletic products. This is most evident in the world of nutritional ergogenic aids, but it also occurs with some training and exercise aids.

The testimonial is an emotive and powerful form of advertising. Many companies claim that their product is responsible for the success or performance improvements of well-noted athletes. Often the athlete will provide a moving testimonial or quote. Or perhaps they quote a 'before and after' situation where the performance of an everyday athlete is lifted well beyond their previous level. Generally these endorsements are bought, which can sometimes, but not necessarily, colour the authenticity of the athlete's support. Endorsements can be a major source of income for top athletes, enabling them to earn far in excess of the prize money available in their sport. Sometimes the athlete has a heavy financial interest in the company itself. Other athletes have a smaller role—for example, as distributors for products sold through network marketing schemes.

But not all testimonials are paid for. The world of sport provides an arena for the continual swapping of ideas. Most athletes are in constant receipt of advice about the use of supplements or training programs or aids from their peers, coaches and trainers. This is often based on direct recommendation of someone who has had success, or on hearsay. There is always speculation about how the best athletes and teams achieve their success.

The limitations of anecdotes and testimonials are many. Most are based on crude observations of performance and are unable to link any performance successes or improvements to a single variable. Real life is a messy experiment, with many variables and constant change. In single cases it is hard to tell if an intervention had any effect or made any contribution to a certain performance. Many athletes are so good that they succeed without, or in spite of, intervention. The placebo effect is a major issue in the experiences of athletes who undertake their own 'experiments' (see the panel below). In other words, observations and anecdotal reports are powerful in advertising but of little value as scientific proof.

One good feature of testimonials and case histories is that they may help to move a theory to the point of testing. Scientists who tinker with interesting products and interventions may be interested in the experiences of those who have tried them. Often 'pilot testing' is undertaken before resources are committed to a sophisticated scientific trial. Here a small number of subjects may be given a treatment to note side-effects or to fine-tune the most suitable dosages or timing of use. Athletes who experiment with various products may consider themselves as pilot-testers. However, this is at best a prelude to proof.

THE PLACEBO EFFECT—IS IT WORTH BOTTLING?

We often talk about the power of positive thinking. The benefits of a positive psychological outlook are quite large, and can be expected when athletes or subjects in a study try a new intervention that they think will help them. 'Placebo' is a Latin term meaning 'I please', which is used to describe the effects that are simply due to a shift in psychological outlook. Psychologists have further defined various types of placebo effect. One effect is called the 'Hawthorne effect' after the company town whose participation in a study first drew attention to it. In this study, a series of changes were made to the lighting in a factory environment in which people worked. No matter in which direction it changed, the measured work output of their subjects improved. In other words, simply because they were being observed and participating in a study, subjects worked harder. Maybe this provides the athlete with an incentive to participate in a study! But it is also a reason to explain why an athlete who is having special attention paid to them—for example, having a coach monitor their performance more closely while they are trying something new—is likely to do better. And this has nothing to do with the product or intervention being trialled. It is just their reaction to being watched or being treated specially.

The placebo effect is mostly used in sport to describe the benefits that an athlete might feel if they expect a change to occur after trying a new product or intervention. If they believe strongly that something will happen, and are looking closely for evidence, it is likely that they will report a change. This may not be a real or long-lasting change. In some cases the effect is subjective anyway. An athlete might *feel* that they have more energy or are better recovered. However, this in itself may inspire them to improve performance in a study or, even better, to train harder and make a *real* performance gain. Again, this is without the intervention actually contributing an effect of its own. Many scientists suspect that the placebo effect explains the major benefits of most of the nutritional ergogenic aids, or new training devices that flood the market. Armed with a new magic potion or toy, and the expectations inspired by emotive advertising, an athlete may psych themselves into feeling and performing better. At least in the short term, or at least while they believe in it.

Some doctors or health professionals use the placebo effect in a clinical setting. Their patients expect to receive a treatment—usually some pills—regardless of their diagnosis, and feel disappointed to leave the counselling office empty-handed. This is not likely to help their recovery. But sometimes no real therapy is necessary or available. So the health professional provides a treatment to the patient that they believe to be essentially inactive and harmless, such as a vitamin B12 injection, or a course of multi-vitamins. If the patient feels satisfied that they have been listened to and treated, they often go away and get better. The therapy often has treated their concern rather than their problem. It inspired them to feel better, or to stop worrying and allow the body to heal itself.

Clearly, it is important to counteract the placebo effect when trying to undertake research on a new product, training strategy or piece of equipment. After all, the point of the study is to measure the real changes due to the new intervention, and not mix it up with the 'buzz' that the new experience may provide. That is why experimental design is made better by including a placebo treatment in a study. Basically, an inactive treatment is given to another group of subjects, or to the same subjects in another trial. This placebo should preferably be indistinguishable from the real treatment, or at least plausible enough so that the subjects believe that they are being given something. Then it should be OK for both groups to get psyched. And any differences in the outcome of the placebo and real treatment should be due to the true effects of the treatment.

The degree to which a placebo effect can improve sports performance has not been adequately measured. Funnily enough, although scientists are aware of it, and frequently observe improvements in the placebo group in an experimental trial, there have been few sophisticated attempts to isolate and measure the benefits. This is an area that deserves some scientific attention. Many scientists have been known to joke that it would be a lucrative activity to bottle an inert substance and call it placebo. The key is to make it look impressive—space-age, exotic, exclusive and expensive—and accompany it with a powerful story of performance improvements. Even have a famous athlete attribute their success to it. Under these conditions it is likely that some athletes would be prepared to give it a trial and their trust. And undoubtedly, it would pay dividends both to the athlete and to the scientist!

The scientific trial

The scientific trial remains the only way to evaluate the effects of a new training aid on the market, or the latest 'break-through' nutritional product. It sets out to isolate an intervention, apply it to a number of athletes under controlled conditions, and accurately measure the outcome. Of course, the hope is that the subjects and the trial adequately represent the real world of sport, so that the results are meaningful to athletes and their performances.

In lay publications it is often suggested that one study 'discovers' something. This is rarely the situation. Often the results of a well-designed study can make a great advance in our understanding of a certain area. But, usually, further studies must be conducted to support or replicate the results. It takes a body of evidence, examined from a number of angles which have explored some of the underlying mechanisms, to build up a good case to support an intervention.

There are a number of features that should be built into the design of a scientific trial. These help the study to find a clear outcome, and then to have confidence that the outcome is valid and reliable (see Chapter 4). Badly designed studies are likely to report results that are invalid and confusing. It is difficult to draw rational and objective conclusions from messy data. These detract from sports science knowledge rather than add to it. The features of a good study design are:

- The addition of a placebo treatment to allow comparison with the intervention. This means that on a separate occasion or in a separate group, subjects will receive a sham or inactive treatment which they believe to be the real thing. This allows the psychological effects of being in a study or believing in the power of a treatment to be separated from the *actual* effects of the treatment. Some-times this is difficult to organise because it is hard to find a suitable but inactive match for the product or intervention being tested.

- A double blind presentation of the intervention and the placebo. This means that neither the scientist nor the athlete knows which treatment they are receiving at any time during the experiment. Obviously this helps the athlete to get the full psychological boost from being involved in the experiment. But it also ensures that scientists are unbiased in their collection and interpretation of the data.

- Sufficient numbers of subjects to ensure that the statistical power of the study is adequate. With small numbers, the intervention or treatment will need to have a large effect to be noticed. To detect a small change, a large sample size is needed.

- A good match between the groups of subjects receiving treatment and the placebo. The subjects and the treatments should be randomly allocated to the groups. It is useful to check that key characteristics of the group, such as age, fitness and training status, are matched as closely as possible. Otherwise the group response to an intervention may be different, and the comparison between groups is clouded by this.

- If possible, a cross-over design, which maximises the match between subject groups by making them one and the same. This means that each subject is tested twice—once with the treatment and once with the placebo. This is a strong study design. However, to protect the design, the order in which subjects receive each treatment should be balanced. Half should receive the active treatment first and the other half, the placebo. This prevents what scientists call an 'order' or 'learning effect'. It refers to the situation where a subject gets 'better' or 'improves' their performance simply due to the course of time. They may learn to perform an experimental task better, they may get fitter or stronger during the course of an experiment, or sometimes, subjects may react (positively or negatively) to receiving the interventions in a certain order. If there are lasting effects from the treatment, then a suitable 'washout' period should take place before the subject receives the reverse intervention.

- A selection of subjects who represent the population to whom the conclusions of the experiment will be generalised. This is vital if a product or intervention has been designed for, and will be targeted to, a specific group of athletes who possess certain unique characteristics. Most specifically, if a product or intervention is intended for elite athletes, it should be tested on elite athletes.

- Familiarisation of the subject to any novel practice or piece of equipment to be employed in the testing procedure. This prevents an apparent 'improvement' in performance occurring merely because the subjects have learned how to undertake the task better. Since scientists are only interested in detecting changes due to experimental intervention, they must be confident that testing protocols are reliable (see the panel on the following pages).

- Strict control of pre-trial diet, hydration status, sleep and activity level. Remarkably, this important criterion is often overlooked, or not rigorously controlled by the sports scientist. Pre-experimental control is important during *all* experiments, but particularly during those where performance is likely to be affected as a result of small changes in diet or training status. In some of the experiments conducted in the authors' own laboratories, we often ask athletes to wear heart-rate monitors in the couple of days before an experimental trial. This is because although instructed to 'train easily or not at all' before a performance trial, we are aware that subjects often underreport their true activity levels! Similar care must be taken to ensure that diets are standardised during important periods.

- Standardised laboratory or other testing environment (see Chapter 4).

- Appropriate and conservative statistical analyses of the results. Eventually, the results of the study will be summarised into a series of numbers, which need to be analysed and interpreted. This is a science in itself. If the researchers do not have sufficient statistical knowledge to set an appropriate experimental design or to 'crunch numbers' at the end, then the services of a statistician should be sought.

From this discussion it should be clear that scientific trials are complex, and all-consuming of time, money, ingenuity, precision and enthusiasm. They are also dependent on the scarce resource of willing and suitable athletes who are able to incorporate the demands of the study into their training or competition program, and their already overcommitted lives. In a perfect world, full testing of all proposed performance-enhancing products and strategies would occur quickly and efficiently. And conclusive results would be available as soon as the athlete or coach asks, 'Will X help my performance?' In real life it is easy to see why research can't keep up with the questions. And why a company would not necessarily want to invest in the expense and risk of research, when it can sell products on the strength of testimonials and advertising hype. The risky part is that a study might find that the product is *not* an effective performance-enhancing agent.

Despite these limitations of research, it remains our best critical tool. It is crucial that researchers battle against the odds and continue to undertake well-conducted studies. But it is also important that athletes and coaches have a reasonable understanding of the efforts involved in research. It may help with their willingness to participate in a study, and with their cooperation in complying with the requirements. Certainly it is the athlete, in the long run, who stands to gain most from any scientific breakthroughs. It may also help the coach and athlete to critically analyse the work that does exist. Unfortunately, some studies in scientific literature—and, in particular, the 'pseudo' studies quoted in product advertisements—are poorly designed or incorrectly interpreted. An appreciation of research design can allow the scientist, athlete and coach to draw their own valid conclusions from the research that is available. This provides the bottom line for whether a product, training idea or piece of equipment might be used by the athlete.

MEASURING PERFORMANCE IN THE LAB

Sports scientists often need laboratory measures of 'performance' in order to determine whether or not an experimental intervention has been effective. Obviously the best (and only) measure of performance is the actual performance of that athlete in their chosen event in the field under normal competitive conditions. But for the scientist, this scenario is far from ideal. There are just too many external variables (ambient temperature, wind speed, track or road surface, etc.) over which they have little or no control. This, in turn, makes it difficult, or sometimes impossible, to make meaningful and accurate conclusions about the effects of their intervention. And the bottom line is that the wrong practical message may be preached to the sports world. So, in order to standardise as many factors as possible, the scientist will often resort to testing an athlete in the laboratory, hoping that the information gained from this process can readily be applied to the athlete in the field (see Chapter 4).

Most readers will be aware of studies which have claimed 'performance' improvements using one or other nutritional strategy. Sometimes 'performance' has been further qualified as an improvement in 'endurance' or 'endurance capacity'. In fact, these investigations have gauged 'performance' as the time an athlete can exercise for at a predetermined, submaximal work rate or speed until they become 'exhausted'. In this type of test, the time to exhaustion is typically defined as the inability to maintain a desired pace. If 'time to exhaustion' is increased, then supposedly, performance has improved. In real sporting situations, however, there are no events in which competitors are required to cycle, run, swim or row for as long as they can before they collapse! Races are not won by the athlete left standing at the end of the day, but by the competitor who can cover a set distance as quickly as possible.

The reliability of this 'performance' measure must also be questioned. Open-ended lab tests are largely dependent on scientists being able to persuade highly-motivated athletes to push themselves longer or further than before, not just once, but on several occasions. Often boredom and the monotony of the task are the *real* variables being measured, since neither athlete nor scientist has any clue of when such a test is likely to end! Furthermore, in cycling trials, a sore bottom is as likely a culprit for 'exhaustion' as any physiological variable. It is hardly surprising to find that the variability or error for such a test (termed the coefficient of variation, by statisticians) is very high—sometimes as great as 42%.

At last, sports scientists are realising that these types of tests should not be used to measure 'performance'. Several modern studies have employed protocols that more closely mimic what the athlete actually does in the competitive situation. And when this is done, the coefficient of variation drops from a massive 42% to, in some instances, less than 1%.

Garry Palmer and his colleagues at the University of Cape Town were probably the first sports scientists to study true performance measures in the laboratory. They recruited endurance-trained cyclists and asked them to complete a number of 20 and 40 km time-trials in the lab. The cyclists rode their own bikes, which were mounted on a specially designed air-braked ergometer. They found that when the cyclists were asked to ride a set distance as quickly as possible, the coefficient of variation for three different rides was 1% for 20 km time-trials and 0.9% for 40 km time-trials. Another study from the same laboratory undertaken by Elske Schabort revealed that trained rowers were even better able to reproduce their performances in the lab than the cyclists. When these athletes undertook three 2000 metre races on a Concept II rowing ergometer, they were able to reproduce their performance to within 0.6%. Such small variability highlights the importance of having athletes undertake laboratory tasks which closely mirror their normal race distance and also, wherever possible, use their normal racing equipment.

Sometimes it is not practical for scientists to measure an athlete's performance in the lab. For example, having a marathon runner perform 42 km on a motor-driven treadmill is neither ethical, nor likely to meet with the approval of coach or athlete! Furthermore, sometimes the scientist wishes to take some metabolic measurements which may, later, explain the observed differences, or lack of, in performance. In these situations, a compromise is reached. The scientist will usually have an athlete ride or run for a predetermined time or distance at a submaximal intensity so that they can collect blood and gas measurements. Then, after a specified time, the athlete will be asked to finish off their exercise bout by performing a given amount of work as fast as possible. The variability in these types of tests is better than the open-ended exhaustion-type protocols (at around 5%), but not as good as the true all-out performance test. The type of test used by a scientist largely determines whether or not they are likely to find an effect of their treatment. If small differences are expected as a result of a specific intervention, then this is unlikely to be detected with a gross and unreliable measure of 'performance'. For example, if the variability of a performance task is, say 5%, an intervention must improve performance by at least 5% in order to be detected. Only very dramatic effects will be noticed when studies employ performance measurements that are highly variable. In such a case a 'no significant change' verdict may be returned, with the conclusion that the intervention or product is ineffective. In fact, a small improvement may have occurred. This is one of the major sources of debate between athletes and scientists (see the following panel).

'SIGNIFICANT' FOR ATHLETES BUT NOT SPORT SCIENTISTS

Dr Will Hopkins, sports scientist and statistician

What would you regard as a significant improvement in sport performance? Let's think about it as a per cent improvement. What about 10%? With that sort of enhancement, a good 100 metre runner with a personal best of 10.5 seconds would run a whole second faster. A good 10 kilometre runner with a best of 33 minutes would cross the line at just under 30 minutes. An elite high jumper would clear an extra 20 cm, while a weightlifter could add 15 kg or more to the bar, depending on their weight class. In fact, whatever the sport, a 10% improvement is massive. It would take you from the back of the bunch right up into the medal winners.

But what about a 1% improvement? That would amount to 0.1 sec in the 100 metres race, 20 seconds in a 10 kilometres, two centimetres in the high jump, and just two kilograms in weightlifting. Yet, in most events an extra 1% would still get you a medal if you were up there close to the front runners. In some events even half a per cent could be useful, but let's assume that 1% is the smallest enhancement that athletes would regard as significant.

Sport scientists are the people who try to sort out for sure whether performance is enhanced by a new item of equipment, a new dietary supplement or a new way of training. Can they detect a 1% enhancement? Well, um . . . no, actually! Let's see why, and then we'll see how to interpret what scientists tell athletes about performance enhancement.

Sport scientists study performance enhancement by measuring the change in performance of a group of athletes treated with something. As you know, an athlete's performance varies a bit from day to day, so a group of athletes will sometimes show an overall improvement in performance purely by chance and not as a result of any treatment. The sport scientist gets around this problem by having a reasonably large number of athletes in the study. That way, the variations in performance of individual athletes tend to cancel each other out, and any effect of the treatment stands out clearly.

So let's get back to our 1% enhancement. How many athletes should the sport scientist study to be sure of detecting it? That depends on a few more factors—things like the variability of the performance of individual athletes from day to day, and the way the scientist uses a 'control' group. Put all these factors together, and the total number of athletes usually needs to be more than a hundred! Very rarely, the scientist might get away with studying twenty. Unfortunately, most sport scientists do not realise that they should be chasing a 1% enhancement, and even when they do, most do not work out the number of athletes needed to detect it. Instead, they opt for the number of athletes that other scientists have used in similar studies. Usually that's about eight or ten, way short of the number they should be studying.

What are the consequences when there aren't enough athletes in a study of performance enhancement? If the treatment enhances performance by three or more per cent, there's no great problem. Analysis of the data will show that the result is 'statistically significant', a bit of statistical jargon that means 'this stuff works'. Of course, when something works *that* well, it's usually obvious to athletes and coaches anyway. But what happens if the treatment enhances performance by only 1%? When there aren't enough athletes in the study, the result will be 'not statistically significant'. At this point many scientists conclude, quite incorrectly, that 'this stuff doesn't work'. The correct interpretation is that the treatment *may* work, but that more athletes need to be studied to be sure. So whenever you see a scientist claiming that something doesn't work, chances are she's jumping to conclusions too soon.

Use of the word 'significant' is so misleading to so many people that some scientists now report their results using something called confidence limits or intervals. For example, an enhancement of 2.1% with a 95% confidence interval of 0.3% to 3.9% means that 'in our study, this stuff enhanced performance by 2.1%, but the true enhancement is likely to be anywhere between 0.3% and 3.9%'. The 0.3% and 3.9% are the confidence limits, and 'likely' means 'we are 95% sure'. With this way of reporting results, you can see at once how good or how bad the treatment *might* be, and you can decide for yourself whether to invest in the treatment or wait for more athletes to be studied.

THE BOTTOM LINE

Ultimately, the athlete and coach must make their own decision about the products, supplements, training styles or equipment in which they will invest their time, hopes and money. Hopefully, these decisions will be made with wisdom when they have access to all the information available. The goal of this book has been to make the latest information accessible to those involved in producing optimal sports performances. If this has been achieved, then we will have achieved our targets. We feel strongly that this will ultimately lead to peak performance.

Part V

LOOKING INTO THE FUTURE

18

The limits to human performance: Where to from here?

'Athletic records are still far below human physiological limits. The restraints on performance are psychological. Athletes do not work as hard once they have set a record or won a medal.'

Article in *Scientific American*, 1976

THE LIMITS TO HUMAN PERFORMANCE

The excitement of many sporting events is the rivalry between two teams or individual athletes competing for the same goal. But ever since records for human performance have been kept, there has always been something magical about setting a world best. Those few athletes who have broken a world record belong to a 'super-elite' group. They stand at the head of a short but distinguished line of former greats. But just how fast can men and women run, swim, cycle or row? How far and high can they jump? How much can they lift? Will women ever be able to compete with men over *any* distance in *any* sport? What are the physiological limits to human performance? An analysis of the factors limiting all athletic events is beyond the scope of this book. So the most famous of all athletic records, the mile, has been chosen to discuss some of these questions.

The progress of human performance

'The man who has made this [world mile] record is W.G. George. His time, 4 minutes 12 seconds. The probability is that this record will never be broken.'

Harry Andrews, coach (1903)

391

'Was it possible for a man to run a mile in four minutes? Of course, as a result of more competition and better training, man would gradually run miles in faster and faster times.'

> Sir Roger Bannister, first man to break four minutes for the mile

'The barrier to be overcome by the runner who wants to be a champion is psychological. The last record set and the willingness of athletes to try to break it are the determining factors for the next record.'

> Article in *Scientific American*, 1976

Almost 100 years after Walter George established the world best mark for the men's one mile, the record is some 30 seconds faster. If they raced together, the current record holder, Algeria's Noureddine Morceli, would finish more than half a lap of the track (215 m) ahead of George. However, the current women's record holder, Svetlana Masterkova of Russia, would still be soundly beaten by George. So why is the men's world mark for one mile still so far ahead of the women's? Can the differences in improvement seen in the men's and women's records be explained on a physiological basis?

When considering the progress of human sporting performance, a number of factors need to be considered. First, men have participated in organised competitions, in a large number of sports for more than a century. Only during the past 20–30 years have similar opportunities been afforded to women. For example, the International Amateur Athletic Federation (IAAF) did not sanction races for women that were longer than 1000 m until 1967. At this time the metric mile (1500 m) and the mile were 'officially' recognised. The 10,000 m for women was not added until as recently as 1981. It is somewhat unclear when the IAAF began to acknowledge the women's marathon (42.2 km), but this event was not contested in Olympic competition until the Los Angeles Games in 1984.

Second, analysis of recent race times for women shows that their world records and best performances are not as consistent as those for men, particularly over longer distances. Of course, one might reasonably argue that in most events this is a result of the shorter history of women's sport and the corresponding lack of competitive opportunities.

Thirdly, it is only during the past two decades that several countries, most notably China and some of the African nations, have acknowledged and belatedly encouraged women's participation in high-level sport. Thus, when pre-IAAF times are considered, the time span available to critically and objectively analyse women's performances should probably be limited to the last quarter-century because of insufficient opportunities for women to compete at almost every level open to males. Given this position of historical disadvantage, it is perhaps not surprising to find that since 1954, the rate of improvement of the women's world mile record is more than double that of the men's mark (15% versus 6.3%; Table 18.1).

Finally, a closer examination of Tables 18.1 and 18.2 reveals that of the eighteen men's mile world records since 1954 (achieved by thirteen runners), and the eighteen women's best performances (set by just twelve runners), only two records have been attained by African athletes. Considering the athletic dominance of the East African nations, most notably Kenya, over a wide range of distances (3000 m to

—— TABLE 18.1 ——————————————————————————————

The evolution of the men's one mile (1609 metre) world record since the first sub-four-minute mile in 1954

Athlete	Nationality	Performance (min:sec)	Date of record
Roger G. Bannister	Great Britain	3:59.4	06/05/54
John M. Landy	Australia	3:58.0	21/06/54
Derek Ibbotson	Great Britain	3:57.2	19/07/57
Herbert J. Elliot	Australia	3:54.5	06/08/58
Peter G. Snell	New Zealand	3:54.4	27/01/62
Peter G. Snell	New Zealand	3:54.1	17/11/64
Michael Jazy	France	3:53.6	09/06/65
James R. Ryun	USA	3:51.3	17/07/66
James R. Ryun	USA	3:51.1	23/06/67
Filbert Bayi	Tanzania	3:51.0	17/05/75
John G. Walker	New Zealand	3:49.4	12/08/75
Sebastian N. Coe	Great Britain	3:49.0	17/07/79
Steven M. Ovett	Great Britain	3:48.8	01/07/80
Sebastian N. Coe	Great Britain	3:48.53	19/08/81
Steven M. Ovett	Great Britain	3:48.40	26/08/81
Sebastian N. Coe	Great Britain	3:47.33	28/08/81
Stephen Cram	Great Britain	3:46.32	27/07/85
Noureddine Morceli	Algeria	3:44.39	12/09/93

Source: Adapted from Hawley, J.A. and Schabort, E.J. 'The limits to human performance. A physiological perspective' *South African Journal of Sports Medicine*, 3:7–12, 1996.

TABLE 18.2

The evolution of the women's one mile (1609 metre) world record since the first sub-five-minute mile in 1954

Athlete	Nationality	Performance (min:sec)	Date of record
Diane Leather	Great Britain	4:59.6	29/05/54
Diane Leather	Great Britain	4:50.8	24/05/55
Diane Leather	Great Britain	4:45.0	21/09/55
Marise Chamberlain	New Zealand	4:41.4	08/12/62
Anne Smith	Great Britain	4:39.2	13/05/67
Anne Smith	Great Britain	4:37.0	03/06/67
Maria Gommers	Holland	4:36.8	14/06/69
Ellen Tittel	East Germany	4:35.3	20/08/71
Paola Cacchi-Pigni	Italy	4:29.5	08/08/73
Natalia Marasescu	Romania	4:23.8	21/05/77
Natalia Marasescu	Romania	4:22.1	27/01/79
Mary Decker	USA	4:21.7	26/01/80
Lyudmila Veselkova	USSR	4:20.89	12/09/81
Mary Decker-Tabb	USA	4:18.08	09/07/82
Maricica Puica	Romania	4:17.44	16/09/82
Mary Slaney-Decker	USA	4:16.71	21/08/85
Paula Ivan	Romania	4:15.61	10/07/89
Svetlana Masterkova	Russia	4:12.56	14/08/96

Source: Adapted from Hawley, J.A. and Schabort, E.J. 'The limits to human performance. A physiological perspective', *South African Journal of Sports Medicine* 3:7–12, 1996.

the marathon) and events (road races, track and cross-country), this is somewhat surprising. These factors suggest that improvements from some relative newcomers might be expected in the not too distant future.

Can improvements in physiology explain improvements in performance?

'The main reason for the steady improvement (in the mile record) lies in the training—more than two hours each day, often in two sessions, instead of my daily 30 minutes!'

> Sir Roger Bannister, first man to break four minutes for the mile

'Clearly there is a limit determined by the structure of the human body.'

> Sir Roger Bannister

There are a number of key physiological factors related to successful endurance performance. These have been described in Chapter 6. The current issue is whether improvements in any one or more of these factors can explain the large improvements in human performance over the past century.

With regard to a runner's maximal aerobic power (VO_{2max}), values in excess of 80 ml/kg/min were measured for male middle-distance runners over 60 years ago. As the highest reported VO_{2max} for a runner recorded in the modern era in a reputable laboratory is 85 ml/kg/min for Dave Bedford, ex-world-record holder for 10,000 metres, it seems unlikely that increases in VO_{2max} are responsible for the large improvements in the world records for varying athletic events.

Instead, it may be that the gradual improvements in performance by elite athletes are more related to their improved ability to sustain a higher fraction of VO_{2max} in competition, and to better economy of motion and technique. This view is consistent with the evolution of training practices this past century (see Chapter 1). For example, from the early 1900s to the late 1960s, there was a steady increase in the frequency, intensity and duration of training, so that by the early 1970s most endurance athletes were undertaking several hours of training a day. But since that time, the training regimens of top athletes have not really changed.

Finally, an analysis of world records at distances from one mile to the marathon reveals that it is mainly an increase in specific endurance (i.e. the ability to resist fatigue), rather than any enhancement in basic speed, that is responsible for the gradual improvements in many events over the past 50 years. This improvement in the ability to maintain a given speed is hidden by the tradition of timing a race at a constant distance, rather than measuring the distance a runner could cover in a specific time. For example, in 1969 Derek Clayton of Australia ran a marathon in 2:08:32, at an average speed of 328 m per minute. This was slightly faster than the average running speed for the men's *one mile* record set a century earlier. In other words, Clayton demonstrated a specific endurance 26 times greater than the mile record holder of the 1860s. In physiological terms, for the same power output, Clayton was able to perform more than 26 times as much work.

Apart from the physiological improvements associated with superior performance, there are, of course, other factors which may explain why world records have continued to fall in many sports. In running, the introduction of synthetic running tracks can improve competitive performance by 2–3% compared to older traditional surfaces like grass and cinders. In cycling, aerodynamic bike design and improvements in clothing have contributed to new record performances (see Chapter 9). Professionalism, commercialism, and more numerous competitive opportunities mean that today, more potential record setters have the chance to train and compete on an almost full-time basis. It is also possible that the use of banned substances may have contributed to the improved performances of some athletes.

The limits to human performance— where to from here?

Perhaps of greater interest and relevance to athletes and sports scientists are the projected improvements in running times for various distances. Drs François Péronnet and Guy Thibault from the University of Montreal, Quebec, have performed complex mathematical modelling in an attempt to predict world records and the limits to performance. Table 18.3 lists their projections of both the men's and women's world record for the mile, along with the 'ultimate performance' for that distance. A mile in 3 minutes 30 seconds is projected for men by the year 2040. Interestingly, in 1954 Roger Bannister forecast that this mark would have been accomplished by the year 1990.

In order to attain such a level of performance, the miler of the future will need a $\dot{V}O_{2max}$ of about 90 ml/kg/min while also possessing sufficient basic speed to run 400 metres in 44 seconds and the 800 metres in around 1 minute 42 seconds. Although these times may seem unrealistic at first sight, the current world records for the 400 metres and 800 metres already surpass them (43.29 for the 400 metres by Harry Reynolds; 1:41.24 for 800 metres by Wilson Kipketer). Sports scientists predict that future improvements in world records will come not from any increase in instantaneous speed or power derived from the anaerobic power systems, but rather from an increase in fatigue resistance or specific endurance of the aerobic power systems. This being the case, then one might reasonably argue that the current men's world mile mark is already overdue for revision. There are presently many runners with the speed over both 400 metres and 800 metres who, with the development of sufficient specific endurance,

TABLE 18.3

Projection of the men's and women's world mile records

	Year			Ultimate performance
	2000	2028	2040	
Men	3:41.96	3:33.29	3:29.84	3:18.87
Women	4:10.79	4:00.83	3:59.82	3:43.24

Source: Adapted from Péronnet, F. and Thibault, G. 'Mathematical analysis of running performance and world running records' *Journal of Applied Physiology*, 67:453–65, 1989.

should be capable of significantly reducing the present record. According to equations derived from performance tables comparing various running distances from 800 metres to the marathon, the men's world mile record ought to be around 3 minutes 42 seconds to be comparable with both the present 5000 metres (12:39.74) and 10,000 metres (26:27.85) world best times.

Finally, it has been recently proposed that for certain running distances such as the marathon, the performances of women may equal those of men by the year 2000. Although this seems unlikely, in ultra-marathon events it is possible that women may close the gap. David Speechly and colleagues from the University of Witwatersrand in South Africa have shown that when male and female ultra-marathon runners are matched for age, training history and race time over the standard marathon, the women consistently outperform males over 90 kilometres. The faster ultra-distance performances of the females were attributed to their being able to run at a higher percentage of their VO_{2max} for longer periods. The precise reason for this finding was not clear.

It seems likely that any future improvements in the current world records for distances from one mile to the marathon will be achieved by those athletes able to sustain high running speeds and to resist the onset of muscular fatigue, rather than by any increase in absolute running velocity *per se*. For this to happen, the runners must be in a highly competitive situation which will bring out the highest level of performance. Based on current scientific evidence, it seems unlikely that women will outrun men for any distance until they can run the shorter distances as fast as the males.

THE GENDER GAP: IS IT WIDENING?

A pre-Atlanta Olympic survey of 1000 American adults found that 66% believe the day is coming when top females will beat the top males at the highest competitive level. But two sports scientists, Dr Stephen Seiler from Norway and Dr Stephen Sailer from the University of Chicago, don't agree. In fact, they say that the world's fastest women are getting slower, while the world's fastest men are getting faster. Their conclusions are based on data collected from 182 championship finals (91 men's, 91 women's) from twelve Olympics and five IAAF World Championships held between 1952 and 1996. The absolute size of the difference in performance between genders for events from 100 metres to the marathon range from 9% to 13%, and increase as the event distance gets longer. If the marathon isn't included, the gap for track running events has actually increased from 10.8% in the mid-1980s to 11.9% in the mid-1990s. So what is the explanation for this anomaly? Seiler and Sailer propose that the reason for the growth of the gender gap, at least in running, is that the use of banned performance-enhancing drugs, particularly anabolic steroids, has been reduced substantially. They argue that steroid use benefited female performances, more than males, and that the improvement in women's performances in the 1970s and 1980s was not 'world-wide' but, instead, confined to the former communist bloc countries of East Germany and the Soviet Union. Indeed, in those two decades 70% of Olympic and World Championship races went to former communist bloc nations. Such dominance ended abruptly in the 1990s as more effective drug testing was implemented. These scientists correctly point out that compared to the females, male performers from the communist bloc never came close to dominating world track and field. And they say that it will be at least another decade before female performances catch up to the levels of the 1980s. Perhaps the drug-induced records of past years need to be removed from the record books altogether? Trouble is, there might not be many left!

THE LIMITS TO HUMAN PERFORMANCE: A FINAL WORD FROM THE COACHES

One hundred metres men's freestyle swimming: An interview with Coach Gennadi Touretski

The men's 100 metre freestyle race is considered the blue riband event of Olympic swimming. Many gold medallists in this event have gone on to become household names. Johnny Weissmuller stunned the world, not only by winning consecutive gold medals in this event in the 1924 and 1928 Olympics, but by being the first swimmer to break the magical minute. Weissmuller, however, is just as well remembered for his role as Tarzan, which brought him world-wide cinema fame.

Over the next two decades, the rate of improvement in swimming times progressed slowly. At the 1960 Rome Olympics, Australian John Devitt received a controversial gold medal for his victory in the 100 metres freestyle. Devitt swam the distance in 55.2 seconds. But this just happened to be the identical time credited to silver medallist Lance Larson.

By the Munich Games of 1972, an electronically timed 51.22 second swim was needed by Mark Spitz to add the 100 metres gold to his record-breaking seven gold medal collection. The first time the 50-second barrier was broken was by American Jim Montgomery at the 1976 Montreal Olympics. Montgomery won the 100 metres freestyle event in a time of 49.99 seconds! As with many records, it seems that once a barrier was overcome, it paved the way for others to follow soon after. Montgomery's world record time was surpassed just three weeks later by Jonty Skinner, who swam 49.44 for the distance.

The present world champion (Perth, 1998), Olympic champion (Atlanta, 1996) and world-record holder in the men's 100 metres freestyle is Alexandre Popov. Incredibly, he holds the double sprint crown (50 and 100 metres) from both the 1992 and 1996 Olympic Games, and the 1994 World Championships. Although Popov was born in Russia, and continues to compete for his homeland, he currently lives and trains at the Australian Institute of Sport in Canberra where his coach and mentor, Gennadi Touretski, is now based.

Popov set the current world record for the 100 metres freestyle in Monte Carlo on 4 June 1994. His time of 48.21 seconds broke the previous record set by American swimmer Matt Biondi at the 1988 Seoul Olympics. That the record should stand for six years speaks of the difficulty of surpassing it. In an event where the crowd can usually only judge the winner by turning to the scoreboard to see the official times, measured to hundredths of a second, it seems amazing that the number 1 should flash beside Alex Popov's name so frequently. However, Gennadi Touretski is renowned for the analytical preparation of his swimmer, and there is nothing that is unplanned about Popov's success.

Touretski has analysed the 100 metres event into its individual components of the start, turn and free swimming. He says the starts and turns account for 20–25% of race success, and each should be achieved at a higher average speed than the clean swimming pace. For an optimal start, a swimmer must have his centre of gravity in line with the front edge of the starting block, and must push his hips forward to provide a triggering motion. The body must be outstretched in a straight line and must enter the water as a streamlined tube at the smallest possible angle to its surface. A streamlined and rigid body is also important in the drive and glide following a turn. The swimmer must approach the wall at maximum speed and achieve a minimum radius of rotation (head close to his knees). Then he must stay down under the following wave and break the surface of the water with a low angle of entry.

As for the swimming itself, even over a distance of 100 metres, swimmers begin to fatigue. Their speed is reduced by 10% over the final 15 metres. The winner of the race will be the swimmer who can sustain their technique over this final phase and resist fatigue. This is where Alex Popov has demonstrated his supremacy. He relies on both technique and racing experience to achieve his success. He swims over 2000 kilometres a year in training. But more importantly, he competes over 100 times each year to groove his race pattern. Before his Olympic medal-winning swims in 1992, his mean 100 metre race time, calculated from over a year of racing, was 50.3 seconds. Remarkably there was only a 3% variability in this time. In 1994, his mean race time from over 100 starts dropped to 49.87 seconds. Reliability of technique is a key issue, and Touretski is only partially joking when he suggests that his athlete is as reliable as the Swiss timing that measures his success. Constant racing is a matter of statistics and provides the opportunity to eliminate mistakes.

Alex Popov's technique raises an interesting point in the discussion of the limitations of the 100 metres freestyle record. A noted fish scientist, John Videler, has undertaken research on movement in an aquatic environment. According to his theory, the maximum speed that a man can achieve in water is a body length per second. Beyond this, any extra propulsive force is countered by extra drag. At 1.97 m tall, Alex Popov's current world record would appear to have reached this limit:

his current time equates to an average swimming speed of just over 2 m per second. Based on this, Videler suggests that the next man to break the world record for 100 m must be considerably taller than Popov.

One secret of the Popov swimming stroke is its efficiency. Biomechanical analysis has shown that it creates significantly less drag than is found in similar swimmers, so that his power output is up to 30% less for the same maximal velocity. The 'water feel' described by swimmers is the ability of the swimmer to balance the propulsion and resistance encountered throughout the stroke. Popov is able to minimise the intra-cycle differences in acceleration and deceleration that appear at different stages of the stroke. His technique looks effortless to an observer—using a perfect combination of the rhythm, range and relaxation principles developed by Touretski.

Can Alex Popov or another swimmer achieve a faster time? Touretski believes that the secret lies not in increasing power, but in decreasing the drag that works against it. Drag is increased by wave creation, body mass and surface area, and inefficient stroking. Other aquatic animals provide a clue to effortless movement. A seal of similar size can move seven times faster than a man at one-quarter of the energy cost. Touretski believes that the future of sprint swimming is in creating ways to take advantage of the elasticity of muscles, and to redevelop the swimming stroke so that the body is not a number of independently moving parts, but a single unit. An optimum level of rigidness of the whole body is needed to better transfer the power of the muscles into forward propulsion. There is a small margin for improvement in the present world record, simply by eliminating mistakes to produce a perfect combination of start, turn, clean swimming, and finish. However, greater leaps can be made by the swimmer who is brave enough to consider radical changes to the start and turn, and to swimming technique. In 'freestyle' swimming, such changes are theoretically allowable. Of course, different training patterns will be required to produce this New Age swimmer.

Touretski's prediction for the 100 metres freestyle record in the year 2008 is 47.5 seconds, with considerable streamlining of the present swimming style. However, if radical changes to technique are allowed by the governing bodies of world swimming, then 45 seconds is a possibility!

The one hour track cycling record

by Coach Peter Keen

'The hour record is everything.'

Graham Obree, professional cyclist and ex-one hour record holder

The hour is widely regarded as the most challenging of all cycling records. In this event cyclists attempt to cover the maximum distance possible in 60 minutes on a cycling track, without assistance. There are no other competitors, so tactics are very simple—cycle as fast as possible without inducing premature fatigue. Only two outcomes are possible: success or failure. Failure is guaranteed if the required speed is not attained in the early stages of the ride, as no cyclist in the 104-year history of the event has increased speed progressively throughout the hour. However, success is not certain until the previous record distance has been passed, usually with less than a minute remaining. The psychology of the hour record is thus as taxing as the physical strain!

Since Henri Desrange first established the record of 35.325 km in 1893 it has been held by such champions as Oscar Egg (42.360 km in 1912), Fausto Coppi (45.848 km in 1942) and Jacques Anquetil (46.159 km in 1956). In 1972, Eddy Merckx ventured to Mexico City to break the world record. A meticulous technician, Merckx had compressed bottles of Mexico City air sent to his home in Belgium, where he trained wearing rubber wet-suits to try and simulate the muggy conditions he would encounter. During his hour ride Merckx says he suffered as never before, and although he broke the record (49.431 km) he claimed he was never the same again.

The 50-kilometre barrier was first broken in the rarefied air of Mexico City when Francesco Moser rode the first modern disc wheel and aerodynamic bike (50.808 km). Britons Graham Obree (51.596 km) and Chris Boardman (52.27 km) traded the record early in 1993 before Obree snatched it back later that year (52.713 km). Five-time winner of the Tour de France, Miguel Indurain, covered 53.04 km in 1994 on the same track that Obree had used for the previous record. Tony Rominger was the first rider to cover more than 55 km in the hour (55.291 km in 1994), and the record is presently held by Chris Boardman at 56.375 km.

The relative simplicity of the task goes some way to explaining the enduring appeal of the hour record to both sports scientists and cyclists. Indeed, a number of mathematical models have been developed by scientists, based upon metabolic, environmental, mechanical and aerodynamic factors as the major determinants of cycling performance. The predictions of such models have inevitably encouraged speculation about the future progress of the record and its ultimate limits.

Dramatic improvements in the hour record between 1984 and 1996 demonstrate the key role that aerodynamics plays in high-speed cycling. A number of innovations in bicycle design and body position have enabled the energy cost of cycling to be dramatically reduced, without compromising the power output of the cyclist. In an attempt to ensure the supremacy of athleticism over equipment and technology, the world governing body of cycling (the Union Cycliste Internationale) has now reacted by introducing a series of rule changes aimed at standardising bicycle design and preventing further innovations. Although the wisdom of current legislation is questionable, it seems safe to conclude that large improvements in performance through bicycle design will not be permitted in the foreseeable future.

Only two options for improving performance in the hour record appear to remain: increase the sustainable mechanical power output of the athlete, or reduce power demand by modifying the environment. Air density, by far the greatest source of resistance, could be lowered by reducing air pressure, or increasing air temperature and humidity. The current record was set at a sea-level indoor velodrome under the following conditions: air pressure 765 mm; temperature 23°C, relative humidity 46%. It is possible to calculate the theoretical impact of modifying each of these variables, assuming that the mechanical power output of the athlete remains unchanged. However, this is a dangerous assumption. A moderate reduction in air pressure could induce marked arterial desaturation, and a high ambient temperature or humidity will present a serious thermoregulatory threat to the cyclist. An accurate cost/benefit analysis of these factors cannot be undertaken without first considering the precise physiological demands of the hour record.

Data gathered from a series of recent successful sea-level attempts provide an indication of the metabolic requirements of the record. An SRM power-meter system was used to measure power output during a number of rides at speeds of

50–60 km per hour. The purpose of these rides was to determine the effect of various riding positions and changes in equipment on speed. From this data it was possible to estimate that Chris Boardman's current record of 56.375 kilometres required an average power output of 442W. For Boardman, this equates to 6.4W per kilogram of body mass, or 238W per square metre of body surface area.

Laboratory assessment of Boardman's $\dot{V}O_2$ when riding at world record race pace at a cadence of 100 revolutions per minute indicates an oxygen uptake of 5.6 litres/minute, equivalent to 81 ml/kg/min (see Chapter 4). These figures assume that over the duration of the ride there is no cardiovascular drift and $\dot{V}O_2$ remains relatively stable. Given that the contribution of anaerobic metabolism in this event is negligible (see Chapter 3), Boardman must have sustained more than 90% of his $\dot{V}O_{2max}$ of 90 ml/kg/min for the entire hour! This extreme utilisation of aerobic power is confirmed by recordings of heart-rate on three different cyclists during recent hour record attempts. Heart-rate during these rides averaged 95% of maximum. Interestingly, heart-rate only rose by about ten beats per minute from the start of the race to the finish.

I have also conducted laboratory and field trials on Chris Boardman to quantify the likely thermoregulatory stress of the event. For practical reasons rectal temperature was not recorded immediately following completion of an hour record, but the available data indicate that in the climatic conditions described above, core temperature was likely to be slightly above 40°C.

Now that an accurate picture of the physiological and metabolic demands of the hour record has been described, it is possible to consider where improvements are most likely to occur.

There appears to be little evidence that it will be possible for cyclists to sustain a higher fractional utilisation of $\dot{V}O_{2max}$ than that currently observed (greater than 90%), or to increase a rider's $\dot{V}O_{2max}$ to much over 90 ml/kg/min. It is tempting to speculate that the lack of increase in $\dot{V}O_{2max}$ values of world-class endurance athletes over the last few decades might indicate that highly-trained humans are approaching the adaptive limits of their cardio-pulmonary apparatus. Support for this view comes from the observation that arterial desaturation of the blood during maximal exercise can be observed in some elite athletes at sea level and is triggered in most others with only minor adjustments to the partial pressure of oxygen. This fact alone raises doubts over the calculated advantage of using high-altitude locations to attack the hour record.

If the sustainable aerobic power is approaching an upper limit, then perhaps cycling economy offers more scope for performance improvements. The gross mechanical efficiency (a ratio of the power output of the rider to the energy input) of the current record holder riding at a workrate of 442W is 22.6%. This figure is considerably lower than the highest value (24.7%) I have observed in a world-class cyclist at a typical hour record cadence. If such an improvement was attainable through training and/or biomechanical adjustments without compromising sustainable aerobic power, a gain of nearly two km on the current record is possible.

The available data indicate that muscle fibre type and volume of training are the key determinants of cycling economy. This suggests that future training programs may focus on very high volume workouts in an attempt to induce further fast-to-slow fibre transformation in high threshold motor units. However, it is unclear what the consequences of such a training strategy will be for maximal aerobic power. Anecdotally, I have observed a negative relationship between cycling economy and VO_{2max} in highly trained racing cyclists—that is, cyclists with a high maximal aerobic power have poor efficiency. It seems that the expression of very high muscle contractile efficiency is in some way antagonistic to maximal oxygen conductance. If so, there is no guarantee that large gains in economy will be advantageous.

To conclude, it is not clear where large improvements in the hour record will be made if restrictions on technology are successful in preventing further aerodynamic innovations. The fact that fully enclosed recumbent cycles have covered over 70 kilometres in one hour demonstrates that there is clearly massive scope for improvement in this area! Theoretically there will be an optimal air pressure and temperature during which record rides should be attempted, but this is likely to vary widely depending on the specific physiological traits of the athlete. These and many other factors require much more research, as the bulk of available scientific literature has utilised non-elite subjects who are unlikely to demonstrate the same physiological responses to, say, a reduced air pressure or elevated air temperature, as those few individuals capable of exercising at extreme workrates.

Could the record be 60 kilometres by the year 2008? It seems unlikely if current regulations governing aerodynamic design remain in place. The relationship between a rider's speed and power output would mean that a dramatic increase in sustainable power output would be needed for a rider to cover close to 60 km in one hour. For the current world-record holder, a speed of 60 km an hour would require a power output of around 524W and an oxygen uptake of 96 ml/kg/min, a massive 18% increase from present values!

Comments on the Oxford versus Cambridge Boat Race

by Coach Daniel Topolski

The Oxford and Cambridge Boat Race is no ordinary race. It is as much a test of endurance, courage and the dogged street-fighting instincts reminiscent of the bare knuckle boxing matches of the Victorian age, as it is of the performance of today's finely-tuned athletes performing on the straight, side-by-side, six-lane 2000 metre 'fair' highways of the typical Olympic rowing course. This suggests that there must be some extra elements to consider when preparing the athletes for this great 178-year-old Varsity match. The most recent (1997) race, for instance, clearly showed that these unexpected and unique considerations are of utmost importance, and matter just as much as simply preparing the athletes to be the fastest crew on the day. In that race, Oxford, despite being arguably the faster crew, failed to capitalise on the tactical advantages available to them on the favourable bends and the fast-flowing stream and allowed Cambridge to get back into the race when they were struggling to find rhythm in the early stages of the race.

Furthermore, in their early winter training, they missed some vital elements in their preparations to help deal with those unexpected moments requiring sudden intense performance when the outcome of the race hung in the balance. You get only one chance, and if you fail to recognise it and delay your move, even by a second or two, you are doomed. Your training has to be geared, both mentally and physically, to recognise when to seize that moment.

What you do in the months leading up to the race will decide how mentally and physically you are able to respond to that critical moment in the race, because that moment will come usually at the most impossibly inappropriate and physically demanding time. Such unexpected moments come in every sport, of course, but what makes the Boat Race unique is the often turbulent nature of the course, the series of bends, the fast-flowing stream, the changing wind direction, and the very fact that it is a two-horse race with no heats or semi-finals, nor other crews to dilute the tension. Furthermore, it takes place five months before the usual World Championship or Olympic regattas, so the whole program has to be compressed into six months. Time is always short. All these elements make for constant unpredictability and a sense of shooting in the dark. Planning for situations becomes an art form.

So in the Boat Race the fastest crew does not necessarily win. Furthermore, in selecting the eight you do not always pick the eight individually strongest performers. The choice has to take into account all the test results from single sculling races, ergometer performances, physiological analyses, strength and endurance tests, seat-racing, side-by-side selection contests (usually done in fours and swapping two individuals at a time over a controlled series of timed and measured races) and pair matrix assessments. And once you have a detailed profile of all your athletes on an individual test basis, you try them out in different combinations in fours and in the eight. For much depends upon how they blend together.

In an eight, the whole must be greater than the sum of the parts, and as mentioned, the strongest eight individuals do not necessarily produce the fastest eight. Rhythm, lightness of touch, cohesion, timing, all contribute towards boat speed, while heavy-handedness or poor slide control produces an 'anchor' in the boat. A donkey in the mid-section 'engine room' of the boat blocks the rhythm, unsettles the run of the boat and becomes, in spite of himself, the classic boat stopper. No-one wants to row with him. The coach will make every effort to transform such a powerful and clumsy athlete into a boat mover. That is the challenge. But sometimes, no matter what you do, you cannot effect the change. He simply cannot find the coordination required and he gets left on the bank. To get eight athletes moving as one, in complete harmony, is daunting. It has been likened to tying a linking string to the legs of eight athletes and getting them to run a sub-four-minute mile in perfect step without breaking the link. So there are a host of disparate problems to be solved when putting together a rowing eight. And that task is made all the more complicated when that eight is a Boat Race crew because of all the physical imponderables associated with the race course I have mentioned above.

Let us look briefly at the sort of athlete we want in the sport of rowing. We need men and women with long levers, long arms and legs, so that the length of stroke can be achieved comfortably at full reach forward without having to over-compress the legs when the athlete, on his sliding seat, is in the forward position. For a heavyweight oarsman, 6 foot 2 inches (1.87 m) plus—but, ideally, 6 foot 5 inches (1.95 m) or so—is a good height, with a body weight of 14 stone or more (90 plus kg). Fifteen stone of man-muscle driving the oar through the water is clearly more effective than 11 stone—as long as he is fully fit.

Rowing, more than most sports, requires power, endurance and skill in equal measures. Rowers will have to work both aerobically and anaerobically during their races, so strength and muscle bulk is developed on the water and in the gym during weight training (heavy weights during the winter with low repetitions, progressing to medium weights and increasingly high repetitions closer to the racing season); and high-speed circuit work is used for speed endurance.

The aerobic training involves low-intensity work over long distance—between 16 and 24 km at a rating of 16 to 20 strokes a minute—and this forms the bulk (80%) of the winter work the rowers do on the water. Anaerobic threshold (AT) training at higher intensity but below the AT (with a pulse of approximately 170 beats per minute, although individuals vary a little) and speed work (pulse rate in excess of 175 beats per minute) form a small part of the training program in the winter period which increases in the pre-competition and competition periods. Some of the steady-state aerobic training at pulse rates of below 160 beats per minute can be done running, cycling or on the ergometer machines for greater convenience and to provide variety to the training, but in truth there is no better way of doing it than in the boat, where good technical coaching can be done at the same time on a regular basis. There is no better substitute for rowing than rowing—getting the rowing cycle perfectly grooved in.

The coach will also monitor the athletes' progress in terms of their fitness at regular intervals by testing lactate levels in the blood and charting the reduction in these measurements. This he can most easily do with the athletes on rowing ergometers. He will also use the ergometers for straight performance testing over 2 km or 5 km and for closely monitored training sessions over longer distances. Clearly, for a strength/endurance sport like rowing, we need athletes with a high $\dot{V}O_{2max}$. Furthermore, the higher the percentage of that maximum the athlete can use, the more effective he is in a long-distance event like the Boat Race.

The standard international distance in rowing is 2000 metres. But one of the main peculiarities of the Boat Race is that it is three times that distance, yet raced at pretty much the same intensity. So even the most experienced rower has to get to grips with the idea that once he has completed the usual 2000 metres, he still has another 2000 to go, possibly half a length down on the outside of the big Hammersmith bend and at a point where he has to raise the tempo; and then to finish off a third 2000, raced home with the same intensity as the first. This clearly requires some extra thought devoted to the training plan, to tactics, to motivation, and some alterations to the normal sort of preparation.

Because the Boat Race often involves young and inexperienced athletes, there is an important psychological battle to be fought. The athlete has to develop his confidence to perform at his best on the day in front of a huge audience. And to do that he needs to prove himself not only to his coaches, but to his team-mates and, ultimately, to himself. Therefore, much of the selection testing and racing is geared to building that confidence as much as it is to assessing the athlete physiologically. Once the eight individuals have proved themselves and won their seats, the crew confidence has to be built. That means taking on rival crews with hot pedigrees in regular fixtures. Crew confidence, self-belief and trust in crew-mates are essential for morale, for bonding, and for extracting performances over and above expectations.

I coached winning crews in the Boat Race during the 1970s and 1980s which, by rights, should have lost to better Cambridge eights. The book and film *True Blue* tell the story of one such crew. So the motivation and the psychological strength that each individual can bring to the joint effort is critical.

Unlike athletes training to race in the strictly organised context of a straight Olympic six-lane final, who must focus entirely upon their own perfect performances without being distracted by what their opponents are doing, the Boat Race participants have to be aware of their rivals. It is a two-horse race and part of the strategy requires them to know their enemy. The tactics they employ may depend on it.

So what can the sports scientist contribute to rowing, a sport which is constantly improving? Speed records are beaten year in, year out. One only has to chart the progress of four-time Olympic champion Steve Redgrave in the coxless pair since 1988 to see this phenomenon. The measuring of lactate levels and oxygen uptake during rowing becomes more sophisticated every year, but there are still improvements to be made in this area. What is clear is that the athletes who emerge from the Boat Race experience are of the highest calibre, mentally tough, physically outstanding and great team players. Their Olympic and World Championship medal tallies bear testimony to that.

Thoughts on the marathon

by Dick Telford, Australian National distance running coach

It is said that Pheidippides ran about 25 miles from Marathon to Athens in 490 BC to announce that the Persian invaders had been conquered. His immediate death did little to inspire the Greeks to include a 25 mile race in their Olympic Games program.

It was the daring, or some would say foolhardiness, of a Frenchman, one Michel Breal, to suggest that men should actually race over such a distance. It followed that a 'marathon' was included in the 1896 new Olympics in Athens and, as if to a script, Greek athlete Spiridon Louis did his home crowd proud by winning the inaugural event.

It was in 1908 that the current marathon distance of 26 miles and 385 yards was finally fixed at the London Olympics. The extension of the former distance to this uneven new distance was not the result of a more careful measurement of the Pheidippides run, but rather the result of a less scientific reason. Queen Alexandra was given the honour of starting the race outside her place of residence, Windsor Castle, and the distance from that location to the stadium was measured at the now famous distance of the modern marathon.

It is not all that surprising, in the light of the lack of specific training knowledge and the enduring pain of those who dared to run the distance, that the marathon was not a particularly popular event over the first few decades of this century. It was seen more as a superhuman performance, and one where races could result in grave circumstances. Jim Peters' performance in the 1954 Vancouver Empire Games epitomised this perception, as his remarkable albeit delirious determination had him rushed to hospital as he staggered toward the finish line. Peters was in fact the world best holder at the time, at 2:17:39. (We refer to a world best rather than world record in the marathon because of the variation in terrain, point-to-point or out and back loop courses, and, in the case of women, whether or not it is a mixed sex race, all factors which influence the completion time.)

However, I recall vividly, and indeed was caught up by the surge of interest in the 'fun-runs' and the new fascination with the marathon in the 60s and 70s with Abebe Bikila of Ethiopia capturing the imagination and hearts of people around the world. As a virtual unknown, he won the Olympic marathon in Rome in the world best time of 2:15:16.2. This time, slicing the barest of margins (0.4 sec), was not as remarkable as the fact that he ran the 26 miler in bare feet. Bikila won gold again in another world best in Tokyo in 1964 (2:12:11.2), this time in shoes. By the time of Bikila's premature death in 1969—the aftermath of a road accident four years previously—Australia's Derek Clayton had lowered the mark to 2:08:33.6 and a marathon 'boom' was in full swing. Now, mere mortals found that through systematic training and only a little inherited disposition to the event, they could achieve the new ultimate performance—they could conquer the marathon distance.

A decade later, in 1979, the emergence of the great Norwegian Grete Waitz resulted in the first women's performance under 2:30, after Australia's Adrienne Beames and Beth Bonner of the USA had broken the 3 hour barrier in 1971.

The world best for the men's marathon currently stands at 2:06:50, held by Belayneh Densimo of Ethiopia, created at Rotterdam in 1988. This was the same place Carlos Lopes of Portugal had taken 53 seconds from Steve Jones' (Great Britain) time to record 2:07:12. The women's WB is still held by another exceptionally talented Norwegian, Ingrid Kristensen, at 2:21:06, and was set in London in 1985.

It is interesting to note that, in the last decade, while the WB times for the marathon have not altered, the 10 km times certainly have. Mexican Arturo Barrios' 10 km WR in 1989 was 27:08.28 minutes and this now stands at 26:27.85 minutes after a scorching run by Kenya's Paul Tergat in 1997. The equivalent progression for the women is from 30:13.72 minutes in 1986 (Kristensen) to the outstanding run by Wang Yunxia of China in 1993 of 29:31.78 minutes that demoralised so many of the world's best women distance runners at the time (and probably continues to do so). Now when you look at the percentage improvements over the past ten years in the 10 km WR, it works out at around 2.5%. If one applies the same percentage improvement to the marathon over the same time frame, then the current WBs would be 2:03:40 and 2:18:46 for men and women respectively. Why has this not occurred?

FIGURE 18.1

Progression of the men's world-best time for the marathon

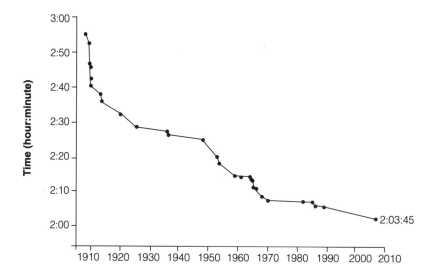

FIGURE 18.2

Progression of the women's world-best time for the marathon

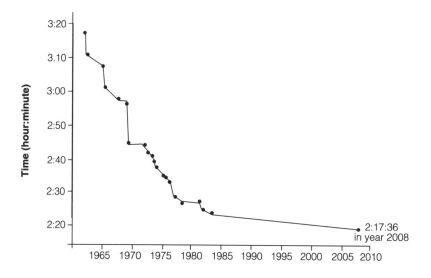

Perhaps runners are concentrating on championship events more than previously and running tactically usually in very warm conditions rather than attempting fast times. Perhaps the marathon hiaitus is just a 'glitch' and times will be lowered in due course. On the other hand, perhaps there is no reason to assume a correlation between the 10 km and the marathon over the last decade, just because there has been a corresponding improvement in times previously. Could it be that the marathon asymptote of ultimate performance is being approached sooner than we might imagine?

With all the money that is around for winning the big city marathons such as Boston, New York, London, Tokyo, Fukuoka, Berlin, Osaka, Rotterdam and others, and the big cash incentives for fast times, I think we can rule out the first reason. That we have already seen close to the best possible human marathon performance is also, in my book, highly unlikely, although the graphical representations in Figures 18.1 and 18.2 do illustrate the recent plateaus. To my mind, the 'glitch' theory is the most likely, and in discussion of this prospect let's review five significant factors that limit marathon performance. If it is possible that one or more of these factors is superior in a particular athlete (and all other factors influencing performance are at least equivalent to his/her predecessors) then it follows that a new WB is likely.

The five general factors most influential to marathon performance include three physiological, one anatomical and one psychological factor.

1. The pace a runner can sustain without significant perturbation in chemical equilibrium in a sustained effort. This is often referred to as the 'anaerobic threshold' or 'threshold' but we must include a time frame and the one I will nominate is 30 minutes. This pace is therefore closely related to the 10 km time because a large proportion of this race is run at 'threshold' pace. There is no doubt that human beings are breeding and/or being trained to higher thresholds, judging by the reduction in 10 km times. On this basis alone, we should expect faster marathons, provided other factors remain the same or are also improved. Could it be, though, that the modern runners of higher threshold speed are necessarily less well-equipped in these other factors?

2. The glycogen stores in the muscle and to a lesser extent, the liver, can differentiate runners in the marathon. It's no

value having a bigger motor (i.e. threshold) if the fuel tank (muscle glycogen) cannot sustain the journey of the marathon. Unfortunately, a runner with insufficient fuel storage cannot top up a depleted glycogen store in a muscle sufficiently by ingestion of glucose during the course of the race to sustain WB pace. The fastest 10 km runner is not necessarily the fastest marathon runner for this reason, but also for other reasons as well.

3. Economy of fuel utilisation is another factor. Obviously two runners with equal masses of stored glycogen will differ in their performances over a marathon if they use different amounts of glycogen at their initial race speed. Running efficiently has a say in this—the more inefficient a runner, the more energy is used at a given speed and the quicker the glycogen supply will diminish. It's likely not to be that simple in all cases however, because a less efficient runner may well have the ability to use a greater proportion of fat as a contribution to the power output and so possess the ability to conserve glycogen as well, if not better than his/her more efficient counterpart. This might be more likely to occur, for example, if the former runner had a higher threshold.

4. The marathoner's anatomy is a very important part of the fitness profile. A runner can be aerobically gifted, but if the body is not designed to withstand the stresses of the training required to develop the fuel storage and the efficiency, in particular the long runs and the threshold efforts week in and week out, year after year, then world-class performance will never be attained. No doubt a robust anatomy is in part inherited but it is probably developed as well. Unfortunately, overzealous training or prematurely long or intense work can cut a promising young runner's career short through injuries or ill-health.

5. Finally, the drive to continue to train for the years required to develop marathon greatness is an important charac-teristic and my feeling is that there are more African runners with this motivation than their more affluent counterparts in the developed nations (although I'm not suggesting that this is the only reason that the Africans are dominating distance running at the moment). But the drive to train hard is not the only psychological factor limiting performance. There is the ability to tolerate the signals sent at the 23-mile mark from the muscles, joints, cardiovascular–respiratory system and even the soles of the

feet to the runner's brain, all conveying the message that to continue to exert oneself at this intensity for longer could lead to dangerous consequences. Sometimes the runner who ignores these messages pays a heavy penalty—sometimes there is the glory of victory.

Having briefly reviewed the general limitations to performance, is it likely that any of these can be improved without any other detriment? I think the answer is 'yes' and the improvement in 10 km time is evidence that human beings are running around now with higher 'threshold' or 'maximal steady-state' speeds than they were ten years ago. Now, as I have alluded to above, all other factors being constant, the world-class runner with the higher threshold speed is likely to be able to run at world best marathon speed utilising a greater proportion of fat as fuel and so, most importantly, a lower proportion of glycogen. Given similar running economy (although a better economy could well be related to the higher threshold to start with), similar glycogen storage characteristics and similar psychological characteristics, our runner with more available glycogen is going to be able to maintain a faster overall speed.

We do not at this stage have evidence that the other major limiting factor to marathon performance—glycogen storage—can be improved, although it would be a brave person to suggest that we do not produce runners in future with bigger fuel tanks than previously. Human beings have a habit of continually outperforming predecessors as the genetic combination improves together with the training and other environmental influences. Science applied to sport has certainly improved the marathon performance in the past—the knowledge of how to manipulate training and nutrition to maximise glycogen storage has raised the general standard of marathons all over the world. A non-invasive method of assessing the glycogen stores would enable us to fine-tune this area before a marathon. Perhaps runners will be able to adapt to specialised diets to better utilise fats at marathon speeds and so reduce the impact of glycogen stores as a limiting factor. Perhaps science will offer us an advance in training methods to optimise the delicately balanced characteristics of aerobic capabilities, fuel storage and utilisation in the marathon runner.

It's interesting to remind ourselves that the half-marathon has been run a number of times in around or just less than one hour. Assuming an environment that provided no heat or cold stress, these runners should be able to continue at this pace (or slightly less when we account for the supra-threshold finish) for the full journey of the marathon if glycogen was no longer a limiting factor. This is, of course, a big 'if' but this would give us a two hour marathon or thereabouts and we have not yet seen how well the current best 10 km runners can run a half-marathon. One would expect the world-best time for a half-marathon to fall when top track runners do compete in the latter event in favourable conditions.

Finally, and it must be said, the use of erythropoetin (EPO) administration to increase the body's total haemoglobin mass and in turn enhance maximal oxygen uptake cannot be ruled out as its use is well known, at least at the time of writing, in the cycling world. Could it be that our world-class runners and their advisors are morally and ethically superior to our cyclists? Only the most naive would nod their heads, especially when in some cases the advisors are the same people. At this stage there is no reliable method of detecting EPO abuse, so it may well be that this hormone may influence world-best times in the future. It may well be asked why it has not done so already and that is a good question. Either it hasn't been used effectively on the right people, or it does not play as big a part in marathon running as it might in the shorter events or even the longer cycling events. Blood viscosity problems have been suggested as a reason EPO may not be as effective in the marathon as the blood tends to be more viscous when there are more circulating red cells. However, this is not likely to be a problem, at least not in cool marathons, for two reasons: first, marathoners have very large plasma volumes and are likely to accommodate more cells without compromising the window of optimal blood viscosity; and second, increases in blood viscosity at the raised core body temperature experienced during cool-weather marathons is buffered considerably in proportion to the increased core temperature.

So where might the marathon world-bests be in 2008, ten years on? The 10 km times are the only real support to the case that times will significantly improve, apart from the fact that we expect genetics and environmental influences to do their duty in the name of progress. The 10 km times have improved by about 2.5% over the past decade, but as I have pointed out, we should not expect a directly proportional improvement in the marathon. I don't think it is unreasonable however, to expect a 1.5% improvement in the marathon by the year 2000 and a further 1% improvement by the year

2008. Treating this in compound terms leaves me with the estimation of times of 2:05:00 and 2:19:00 for men and women respectively by the year 2000 and 2:03:45 and 2:17:36 by 2008. A lesser improvement would be consistent with the lack of progression over the last ten years and a greater one would represent a breakthrough in special training and energy supply techniques and/or the advent of a specially gifted person. What's your 'guesstimate'?

Selected reading list

General

Abt, Samuel, *A season in tumoil*, Velopress, Boulder, Colorado, 1995

Agnew, Ivan, *Kiwis can fly*, Marketforce Ltd, Auckland, 1976

Bannister, Roger, *The four minute mile*, Lyons & Burford, New York, 1981

Clarke, Ron and Harris, Norman, *The lonely breed*, Pelham Books, London, 1967

Coe, Sebastian and Miller, David, *Running free*, Sidgwick & Jackson, London, 1981

——*Born to run. A life in athletics*, Pavilion Books, London, 1992

Dale, Richard and Cameron, Colin, *The contenders*, Boxtree, London, 1994

Giller, Norman, *The golden milers*, Pelham Books, London, 1982

Johnson, Michael, *Slaying the dragon*, HarperCollins, New York, 1996

LeMond, Greg and Abt, Samuel, *The incredible comeback*, Stanley Paul, London, 1991

Lewis, Carl, with Marx, Jeffrey, *Inside track. My professional life in amateur track and field*, Simon and Schuster, New York, 1990

——*One more victory lap. My personal diary of an Olympic year*, Athletics International, Santa Monica, 1996

Louganis, Greg with Marcus, Eric, *Breaking the surface*, Random House, New York, 1995

Moneghetti, Steve and Howley, Peter, *In the long run. The making of a marathon runner*, Penguin Books, 1996

Sandrock, Michael, *Running with the legends*, Human Kinetics, Champaign, Illinois, 1996

Tanser, Toby, 'Train hard, win easy. The Kenyan way' *Track and Field News* Mountain View, California, 1997

Topolski, Daniel and Robinson, Patrick, *True blue. The Oxford Boat Race mutiny*, Bantam Books, London, 1989

Will-Weber, Mark, *The quotable runner*, Breakaway Books, New York, 1995

Chapter 1   Profiles of outstanding coaches

Coe, S. and Miller, D. *Coming back*, Sidgwick & Jackson, London, 1984

——*Born to run. A life in athletics*, Pavilion Books, London, 1992

Elliot, H. *The golden mile*, Cassell, London, 1961

Lydiard, A. and Gilmour, G. *Running. The Lydiard way*, World Publications, Mountain View, California, 1978

Nelson, C. 'Track's greatest champions' *Track and Field News* 1986

Sandrock, M. *Running with the legends. Training and racing insights from 21 great runners*, Human Kinetics, Champaign, Illinois, 1996

Chapter 2   Scientific principles of physical training

Bouchard, C. Dionne, F.T., Simoneau, J.A. and Boulay, M.R. 'Genetics of aerobic and anaerobic performances' *Exercise and Sports Sciences Reviews* 20: 27–58, 1992

Bowerman, W.J. and Freeman, W.H. *Coaching track and field*, Houghton Mifflin Company, Boston, 1974

Costill, D.L., Thomas, R., Robergs, R.A., Pascoe, D., Lambert C., Barr, S. and Fink, W.J. 'Adaptations to swimming training: influence of training volume' *Medicine and Science in Sports and Exercise* 23: 371–7, 1991

Graves J.E., Pollock, M.L., Leggett, S.H., Braith, R.W., Carpenter, D.M. and Bishop, L.E. 'Effect of reduced training frequency on muscular strength' *International Journal of Sports Medicine* 9: 316–19, 1988

Hawley, J.A. 'Cross-training: Fad or fiction?' *Runners World (South Africa)* 5(10): 14, 1997

Hortobagyi, T., Houmard, J.A., Stevenson, J.R., Fraser, D.D., Johns, R.A. and Israel, R.G. 'The effects of detraining on power athletes' *Medicine and Science in Sports and Exercise* 8: 929–35, 1993

Houmard, J.A. 'Impact of reduced training on performance in endurance athletes' *Sports Medicine* 12: 380–93, 1991

Houmard, J.A., Costill, D.L., Mitchell, J.B., Park, S.H., Hickner, R.C. and Roemmich, J.N. 'Reduced training maintains performance in distance runners' *International Journal of Sports Medicine* 11: 46–52, 1990

Houmard, J.A., Hortobagyi, T., Johns, R.A., Bruno, N.J., Nute, C.C., Shinebarger, M.H. and Welborn, J.W. 'Effect of short-term training cessation on performance measures in distance runners' *International Journal of Sports Medicine* 13: 572–6, 1992

Katch, V. 'The burden of disproof' *Medicine and Science in Sports and Exercise* 18: 593–5, 1986

Mujika, I., Chatard, J.C., Busso, T., Geyssant, A., Barale, F. and Lacoste, L. 'Effects of training on performance in competitive swimmers' *Canadian Journal of Applied Physiology* 20: 395–406, 1995

Mutton, D.L., Loy, S.F., Rogers, D.M., Holland, G.J., Vincent, W.J. and Heng, M. 'Effect of run vs combined cycle/run training on VO_{2max} and running performance' *Medicine and Science in Sports and Exercise* 25: 1393–7, 1993

Sandrock, M. *Running with the legends*, Human Kinetics, Champaign, Illinois, 1996

Tanaka, H. 'Effects of cross-training. Transfer of training effects on VO_{2max} between cycling, running and swimming' *Sports Medicine* 19: 330–9, 1994

Wenger, H.A. and Bell, G.J. 'The interactions of intensity, frequency and duration of exercise training in altering cardiorespiratory fitness' *Sports Medicine* 3: 346–56, 1986

Chapter 3 *Fuels for the fire: The body's power systems*

Bangsbo, J., Gollnick, P.D., Graham, T.E., Juel, C., Kiens, B., Mizuno, M. and Saltin, B. 'Anaerobic energy production and O_2 deficit–debt relationship during exhaustive exercise in humans' *Journal of Physiology* 422: 539–59, 1990

Brooks, G.A. and Fahey, T.D. *Exercise physiology. Human bioenergetics and its applications*, Macmillan, New York, 1985

Hawley, J.A. 'Power systems and swimming: Implications for high-intensity training' *Swim SA* 4: 6–7, November 1994

Hawley, J.A. and Hopkins, W.G. 'Aerobic glycolytic and aerobic lipolytic power systems. A new paradigm with implications for endurance and ultraendurance events' *Sports Medicine* 19: 240–50, 1995

Kyle, C.R. and Caiozzo, V.J. 'Experiments in human ergometry as applied to the design of human powered vehicles' *International Journal of Sports Biomechanics* 2: 6–19, 1986

Newsholme, E., Leech, T. and Duester, G. *Keep on running. The science of training and performance*, John Wiley and Sons, Chichester, 1994

Noakes, T.D. *Lore of running*, Oxford University Press, Cape Town, 1992

Chapter 4 Physiological testing for athletes: What the numbers mean

Costill, D.L. *Inside running. Basics of sports physiology*, Benchmark Press Inc., Indianapolis, 1986

Coyle, E.F., Feltner, M.E., Kautz, S.A., Hamilton, M.T., Montain, S.J., Baylor, A.M., Abraham, L.D. and Petrek, G.W. 'Physiological and biomechanical factors associated with elite endurance cycling performance' *Medicine and Science in Sports and Exercise* 23: 93–107, 1991

Davis, J.A., Brewer, J. and Atkin, D. 'Pre-season physiological characteristics of English first and second division soccer players' *Journal of Sports Sciences* 10: 541–7, 1992

Ekblom, B. and Bergh, U. 'Physiology and nutrition for cross-country skiers' in *Perspectives in exercise science and sports medicine*, vol. 7, *Physiology and nutrition for competitive sport*, eds D.R. Lamb, H.G. Knuttgen and R. Murray, Cooper Publishing Group, Carmel, Indiana, 1994, pp. 373–400

Faria, I.E. 'Applied physiology of cycling' *Sports Medicine* 1: 187–204, 1984

Hagerman, F.C. 'Physiology and nutrition for rowing' in *Perspectives in exercise science and sports medicine*, vol. 7, *Physiology and nutrition for competitive sport*, eds D.R. Lamb, H.G. Knuttgen and R. Murray, Cooper Publishing Group, Carmel, Indiana, 1994, pp. 221–302

Hahn, A. 'Identification of talent in Australian rowing' *Excel* 6: 5–11, 1990

Hawley, J.A. and Noakes, T.D. 'Peak power output predicts maximal oxygen uptake and performance time in trained cyclists' *European Journal of Applied Physiology* 65: 79–83, 1992

Jones, A.M. and Doust, J.H. 'A 1% treadmill grade most accurately reflects the energetic cost of outdoor running' *Journal of Sports Sciences* 14: 321–7, 1996

Leger, L.A., Mercier, D., Gadoury, C. and Lambert, J. 'The multistage 20 metre shuttle run test for aerobic fitness' *Journal of Sports Sciences* 6: 93–101, 1988

MacDougall, J.D., Wenger, H.A. and Green, H.J. (eds), *Physiological testing of the high-performance athlete*, 2nd edn, Human Kinetics, Champaign, Illinois, 1991, pp. 1–6

Maud, P.J. and Foster, C. (eds), *Physiological assessment of human fitness*, Human Kinetics, Champaign, Illinois, 1995

Noakes, T.D. 'Implications of exercise testing for prediction of athletic performance: A contemporary perspective' *Medicine and Science in Sports and Exercise* 20: 319–30, 1988

O'Toole, M.L. and Douglas, P.S. 'Applied physiology of triathlon' *Sports Medicine* 19: 251–67, 1995

Palmer, G.S., Dennis, S.C., Noakes, T.D. and Hawley, J.A. 'Assessment of the reproducibility of performance testing on an air-braked cycle ergometer' *International Journal of Sports Medicine* 17: 293–8, 1996

Pollock, M. 'Submaximal and maximal working capacity of elite distance runners. Part I. Cardiorespiratory aspects' in *The marathon: Physiological, medical, epidemiological and psychological studies*, ed. P. Milvy, Annals of the New York Academy of Sciences, 301: 310–22, 1977

Ramsbottom, R., Brewer, J. and Williams, C. 'A progressive shuttle run test to estimate maximal oxygen uptake' *British Journal of Sports Medicine* 22: 141–4, 1988

Schneider, D.A., Lacroix, K.A., Atkinson, G.R., Troped, P.J. and Pollack, J. 'Ventilatory threshold and maximal oxygen uptake during cycling and running in triathletes' *Medicine and Science in Sports and Exercise* 22: 257–64, 1990

Swain, D.P., Coast, J.R., Clifford, P.S., Milliken, M.C. and Stray-Gunderson, J. 'Influence of body size on oxygen consumption during bicycling' *Journal of Applied Physiology* 62: 668–72, 1987

Tanaka, H., Bassett, D.R., Swensen, T.C. and Sampedro, R.M. 'Aerobic and anaerobic power characteristics of competitive cyclists in the United States Cycling Federation' *International Journal of Sports Medicine* 14: 334–8, 1993

Telford, R.D., Hahn, A.G., Pyne, D.B. and Tumilty, D. 'Strength, anaerobic capacities and aerobic power of Australian track and road cyclists' *Excel* 6: 20–22, 1990

Chapter 5   Training for speed and power

Ae, M., Ito, A. and Suzuki, M. 'The men's 100 metres' *New Studies in Athletics* 7: 47–52, 1992

Allerheiligen, W.B. 'Speed development and plyometric training' in *Essentials of strength training and conditioning*, ed. T.R. Bacchle, Human Kinetics, Champaign, Illinois, 1994, pp. 314–26

Coetzer, P., Noakes, T.D., Sanders, B., Lambert, M.I., Bosch, A.N., Wiggins, T. and Dennis, S.C. 'Superior fatigue resistance of elite black South African distance runners' *Journal of Applied Physiology* 75: 1822–7, 1993

Cook, S.D., Schultz, G., Omey, M.L., Wolfe, M.W. and Brunet, M.F. 'Development of lower leg strength and flexibility with the strength shoe' *American Journal of Sports Medicine* 21: 445–8, 1993

Delecluse, C., Van Coppenolle, H., Willems, E., Van Leemputte, M., Diels, R. and Goris, M. 'Influence of high-resistance and high-velocity training on sprint performance' *Medicine and Science in Sports and Exercise* 27: 1203–9, 1995

de Koning, J.J., de Groot, G. and van Ingen Schenau, G.J. 'Mechanical aspects of the sprint start in Olympic speed skating' *International Journal of Sports Biomechanics* 5: 151–68, 1989

Dintiman, G., Ward, R. and Tellez, T. *Sports speed*, 2nd edn, Human Kinetics, Champaign, Illinois, 1987

Hatfield, F.C. 'Strength shoes: Pain, no gain' *Sportsscience news* (Training & Technology), March–April 1997, http://www.org/traintech/strengthshoes/fch.htm

'Meep-meep! Whoosh!' *Track and Field News*, 50: 57, April 1997

Mendoza, L. and Schollhorn, W. 'Training of the sprint start technique with biomechanical feedback' *Journal of Sports Sciences* 11: 25–29, 1993

Moravec, P., Ruzicka, J., Susanka, P., Dostal, M., Kodejs, M. and Norsek, M. 'The 1987 International Athletic Foundation/IAAF scientific project report: Time analysis of the 100 metres events at the II World Championships in Athletics' *New Studies in Athletics* 3: 61–96, 1988

Radford, P.F. 'Sprinting' in *Physiology of sports*, eds T. Reilly, N. Secher, P. Snell and   C. Williams, E & F Spon, London, 1990, pp. 71–99

Tabatschnik, B. 'Looking for 100-m speed' *Modern Athlete and Coach* 9: 14–16, 1983

van Ingen Schenau, G.J., de Koning, J.J. and de Groot, G. 'Optimisation of sprinting performance in running, cycling and speed skating' *Sports Medicine* 17: 259–75, 1994

Wilber, R.L., Zawadzki, K.M., Kearney, J.T., Shannon, M.P. and Disalvo, D. 'Physiological proiles of elite off-road and road cyclists' *Medicine and science in Sports and Exercise*, 29: 1090–4, 1997

Williams, C. and Gandy, G. 'Physiology and nutrition for sprinting' in *Perspectives in exercise science and sports medicine*, vol. 7, *Physiology and nutrition for competitive sport*, eds D.R. Lamb, H.G. Knuttgen and R. Murray, Cooper Publishing Group, Carmel, Indiana, 1994, pp. 55–98

Wilson, G.J., Newton, R.U., Murphy, A.J. and Humphries, B.J. 'The optimal training load for the development of dynamic athletic performance' *Medicine and Science in Sports and Exercise* 25: 1279–86, 1993

Chapter 6   Training techniques for successful endurance performance

Bale, J. and Sang, J. *Kenyan running*, Frank Cass, London, 1996

Bell, G.J., Petersen, S.R., Quinney, A.H. and Wenger, H.A. 'The effect of velocity-specific strength training on peak torque and anaerobic rowing power' *Journal of Sports Sciences* 7: 205–14, 1989

Coetzer, P., Noakes, T.D., Sanders, B., Lambert, M.I., Bosch, A.N., Wiggins, T. and Dennis, S.C. 'Superior fatigue resistance of elite black South African distance runners' *Journal of Applied Physiology* 75: 1822–27, 1993

Costill, D.L. *Inside running. Basics of sports physiology*, Benchmark Press Inc., Indianapolis, 1986

Costill, D.L., King, D.S., Thomas, R. and Hargreaves, M. 'Effects of reduced training on muscular power in swimmers' *The Physician and Sports Medicine* 13: 94–101, 1985

Costill, D.L., Thomas, R., Robergs, R.A., Pascoe, D., Lambert, C., Barr, S. and Fink, W.J. 'Adaptations to swimming training: Influence of training volume' *Medicine and Science in Sports and Exercise* 23: 371–7, 1991

Hagerman, F.C. 'Physiology and nutrition for rowing' in *Perspectives in exercise science and sports medicine*, vol. 7, *Physiology and nutrition for competitive sport*, eds D.R. Lamb, H.G. Knuttgen and R. Murray, Cooper Publishing Group, Carmel, Indiana, 1994, pp. 221–302

Hawley, J.A. 'The effects of tapering and reduced training on maximal strength and performance' *The New Zealand Coach* 3: 18–19, 1994

Hawley, J.A., Myburgh, K.H., Noakes, T.D. and Dennis, S.C. 'Training techniques to improve fatigue resistance and enhance endurance performance' *Journal of Sports Sciences* (Supplement) 15: 325–33, 1997

Hickson, R.C., Dvorak, B.A., Gorostiaga, E.M., Kurowski, T.T. and Foster, C. 'Potential for strength and endurance training to amplify endurance performance' *Journal of Applied Physiology* 65: 2285–90, 1988

Home, J., Hawley, J.A., Dennis, S.C. and Noakes, T.D. 'The effects of 6 weeks of resistance training on endurance cycling performance' *International Journal of Sports Medicine* (in review)

Hopkins, W.G. 'New guidelines for hard training' *The New Zealand Coach* 2: 16–20, 1993

Houmard, J.A. and Johns, A. 'Effects of taper on swim performance. Practical implications' *Sports Medicine* 17: 224–32, 1994

Korzeniowski, K. 'Training programs' *Stroke*, September 1991

LeMond, G. and Gordis, K. *Greg LeMond's complete book of bicycling*, Perigee Books, Putman Publishing Company, New York, 1990

Lindsay, F.H., Hawley, J.A., Myburgh, K.H., Schomer, H.H., Noakes, T.D. and Dennis, S.C. 'Improved athletic performance in highly trained cyclists after interval training' *Medicine and Science in Sports and Exercise* 28: 1427–34, 1996

Lydiard, A. and Gilmore, G. *Running. The Lydiard way*, World Publications, Mountain View, California, 1978

——*Running with Lydiard*, Hodder and Stoughton, Auckland, 1983

Marcinik, E.J., Potts, J., Schlabach, G., Will, S., Dawson, P. and Hurley, B.F. 'Effects of strength training on lactate threshold and endurance performance' *Medicine and Science in Sports and Exercise* 23: 739–43, 1991

Martin, D.E. and Coe, P.N. *Training distance runners*, Leisure Press, Champaign, Illinois, 1991

Morton, R.H. 'Modelling training and overtraining' *Journal of Sports Sciences* (Supplement) 15: 335–40, 1997

Paavolainen, L., Hakkinen, K. and Rusko, H. 'Effects of explosive type strength training on physical performance characteristics in cross-country skiers' *European Journal of Applied Physiology* 62: 251–5, 1991

Shepley, B. MacDougall, J.D., Cipriano, N., Sutton, J.R., Tarnopolsky, M.A. and Coates, G. 'Physiological effects of tapering in highly trained athletes' *Journal of Applied Physiology* 72: 706–11, 1992

Tanser, T. 'Train hard, win easy. The Kenyan way' *Track and Field News*, Mountain View, California, 1997

Wells, C.L. and Pate, R.R. 'Training for performance of prolonged exercise' in *Perspectives in exercise science and sports medicine*, vol. 1, *Prolonged exercise*, eds D.R. Lamb and R. Murray, Benchmark Press, Indianapolis, 1988, pp. 357–91

Westgarth-Taylor, C., Hawley, J.A., Rickard, S., Myburgh, K.H., Noakes, T.D. and Dennis, S.C. 'Metabolic and performance adaptations to interval training in endurance-trained cyclists' *European Journal of Applied Physiology* 75: 298–304, 1997

Weston, A., Myburgh, K.H., Lindsay, F.H., Dennis, S.C., Noakes, T.D. and Hawley, J.A. 'Skeletal muscle buffering capacity and endurance performance after high-intensity interval training by well-trained cyclists' *European Journal of Applied Physiology* 75: 7–13, 1997

Chapter 7 Training for team sports

Balsom, P.D., Seger, J.Y., Sjodin, B. and Ekblom, B. 'Maximal-intensity intermittent exercise: Effect of recovery duration' *International Journal of Sports Medicine* 13: 528–33, 1992

Bloomfield, J., Blanksby, B.A., Ackland, T.R. and Allison, G.T. 'The influence of strength training on overhead throwing velocity of elite water polo players' *Australian Journal of Science and Medicine in Sport* 22: 63–67, 1990

Brewer, J. and Davis, J. 'Applied physiology of rugby league' *Sports Medicine* 20: 129–35, 1995

Dintiman, G., Ward, R. and Tellez, T. *Sports speed*, 2nd edn, Human Kinetics, Champaign, Illinois, 1987

Ekblom, B. 'Applied physiology of soccer' *Sports Medicine* 3: 50–60, 1986

Gladwell, M. 'The sports taboo. Why blacks are like boys and whites are like girls' *The New Yorker*, 19 May 1997, pp. 50–55

Holmyard, D.J. and Hazeldine, R.J. 'Seasonal variations in the anthropometric and physiological characteristics of international rugby union players' in *Science and football II* eds T. Reilly, J. Clarys and A. Stibbe, E & F Spon, London, 1993, pp. 21–26

Jehue, R., Street, D. and Huizenga, R. 'Effect of time zone and game time changes on team performance: National Football League' *Medicine and Science in Sports and Exercise* 25: 127–31, 1993

Mei, R., Arthur, D. and Forrest, M. 'Time and motion analysis of professional rugby league: A case study' *Strength, Conditioning and Coaching* 3: 24–29, 1993

Monpetit, R.R. 'Applied physiology of squash' *Sports Medicine* 10: 31–41, 1990

Noakes, T.D. and Du Plessis, M. *Rugby without risk*, J.L. van Schaik, Pretoria, 1996

Reilly, T. 'Energetics of high-intensity exercise (soccer) with particular reference to fatigue' *Journal of Sports Sciences* (Supplement) 15: 257–63, 1997

——*Science and soccer*, E & F Spon, London, 1996

Reilly T. and Borie, A. 'Physiology applied to field hockey' *Sports Medicine* 14: 10–26, 1992

Reilly, T., Clarys, J. and Stibbe, A. *Science and football II*, E and F Spon, London, 1993

Reilly, T. and Thomas, V. 'A motion analysis of work-rate in different positional roles in professional football match-play' *Journal of Human Movement Studies* 2: 87–97, 1976

'Serving notice' *SA Sports Illustrated* 140: 15, 28 April 1977

Trolle, M., Aagaard, P., Simonsen, E.B., Bandsbo, J. and Klausen, K. 'Effects of strength training on kicking performance in soccer' in *Science and football II*, eds T. Reilly, J. Clarys and A. Stibbe, E & F Spon, London, 1993, pp. 95–97

Tumilty, D. 'Physiological characteristics of elite soccer players' *Sports Medicine* 16: 8–96, 1993

Wein, H. *The advanced science of hockey*, Pelham Books, London, 1981

Williams, M.H. *Beyond training. How athletes enhance performance legally and illegally*, Human Kinetics, Champaign, Illinois, 1989

Withers, R.T., Maricic, Z., Wasilewski, S. and Kelly, L. 'Match analysis of Australian professional soccer players' *Journal of Human Movement Studies* 8: 159–76, 1982

Chapter 8   Training aids and strategies: Do they help?

Aoyagi, Y., McLellan, T.M. and Shephard, R.J. 'Interactions of physical training and heat acclimation' *Sports Medicine* 23: 173–210, 1997

Daniels, J. and Oldridge, N. 'The effects of alternate exposure to altitude and sea level on world-class middle distance runners' *Medicine and Science in Sports* 2: 107–12, 1970

Dick, F.W. 'Training at altitude in practice' *International Journal of Sports Medicine* (Supplement) 13: S203–5, 1992

Freund, B.J., Allen, D. and Wilmore, J.H. 'Interaction of test protocol and inclined run training on maximal oxygen uptake' *Medicine and Science in Sports and Exercise* 18: 588–92, 1986

Gilman, M.B. 'The use of heart rate to monitor the intensity of endurance training' *Sports Medicine* 21: 73–79, 1996

Gore, C.J., Little, S.C., Hahn, A.G., Scroop, G.C., Norton, K.I., Bourdon, P.C., Woolford, S.M., Buckley, J.D., Stanef, T., Campbell, D.P., Watson, D.B. and Emonson, D.L. 'Reduced performance of male and female athletes at 580 m altitude' *European Journal of Applied Physiology* 75: 136–43, 1997

Hahn, A.G. 'The effect of altitude training on athletic performance at sea level. A review' *Excel* 7: 9–23, 1991

Hawley, J.A. 'The effects of tapering and reduced training on maximal strength and performance' *New Zealand Coach* 3: 18–19, 1994

Hopkins, W.G. 'Quantification of training in competitive sport. Methods and applications' *Sports Medicine* 12: 161–83, 1991

Karvonen, J. and Vuorimaa, T. 'Heart rate and exercise intensity during sports activities. Practical applications' *Sports Medicine* 5: 303–12, 1988

Levine, B.D. and Stray-Gundersen, J. 'A practical approach to altitude training: Where to live and train for optimal performance' *International Journal of Sports Medicine* 13: S209–12, 1992

Levine, B.D., Stray-Gundersen, J., Duhaime, G. and Snell, P.G. 'Living high—training low. The effect of acute altitude acclimatization/normoxic training in trained runners' *Medicine and Science in Sports and Exercise* (Supplement) 23: S25, 1991

Martin, D.E. 'The challenge of using altitude training to improve performance' in *Middle distances. Contemporary theory, technique and training*, ed. J. Jarver, 4th edn, *Track and Field News*, Mountain View, California, 1997, pp. 130–134

Martin, D.T., Ashenden, M., Parisotto, R., Pyne, D. and Hahn, A.G. 'Blood testing for professional cyclists. What's a fair hematocrit limit?' *Sportsscience news*, http://www.sportsci.org/news/news9703/AISblood.html

Rushall, B.S., Buono, M.J. and Sucec, A.A. 'Elite swimmers and altitude training' *Swimming Science Bulletin*, http://www-rohan.sdsu.edu/dept/coachsci/swimming/bullets /acclim14.html

Seiler, S. 'The new Dutch "slapskates": Will they revolutionise skating technique?' *Sportsscience news*, http://www.sportsci.org/news/news9703/slapskat.htm

Sparks, K. *The runner's book of training secrets*, Rodale Press Inc., Pennsylvania, 1996

Upton, P.A.H., Noakes, T.D. and Juritz, J.M. 'Thermal pants may reduce the risk of recurrent hamstring injuries in rugby players' *British Journal of Sports Medicine* 30: 57–60, 1996

White, M.D. and Cabanac, M. 'Physical dilation of the nostrils lowers the thermal strain of exercising humans' *European Journal of Applied Physiology* 70: 200–6, 1995

Wilber, R.L., Moffatt, R.J., Scott, B.E., Lee, D.T. and Cucuzzo, N.A. 'Influence of water run training on the maintenance of aerobic performance' *Medicine and Science in Sports and Exercise* 28: 1056–62, 1996

Wolski, L.A., McKenzie, D.C. and Wenger, H.A. 'Altitude training for improvements in sea level performance. Is there scientific evidence for benefit?' *Sports Medicine* 22: 251–63, 1996

Chapter 9   Competition: Getting it right on the day

Bassett, D.R., Flohr, J., Duey, W.J., Howley, E.T. and Pein, R.L. 'Metabolic responses to drafting during front crawl swimming' *Medicine and Science in Sports and Exercise* 23: 744–7, 1991

Booth, J., Marino, F. and Ward, J.J. 'Improved running performance in hot humid conditions following whole body pre-cooling' *Medicine and Science in Sports and Exercise* 29: 943–9, 1997

Brasher, C. *Munich 72*, Stanley Paul, London, 1972

Chatard, J.C., Senegas, X., Selles, M., Dreanot, P. and Geyssant, A. 'Wet suit effect: A comparison between competitive swimmers and triathletes' *Medicine and Science in Sports and Exercise* 27: 580–6, 1995

Cordain, L. and Kopriva, R. 'Wetsuits, body density and swimming performance' *British Journal of Sports Medicine* 25: 31–33, 1991

'Did Christie get hosed? False start rules questioned' *Track and Field News* 50: 62, February 1997

Foster, C., Schrager, M., Snyder, A.C. and Thompson, N.N. 'Pacing strategy and athletic performance' *Sports Medicine* 17: 77–85, 1994

Foster, C., Snyder, A.C., Thompson, N.N., Green, M.A., Foley, M. and Schrager, M. 'Effect of pacing strategy on cycle time trial performance' *Medicine and Science in Sports and Exercise* 25: 383–8, 1993

Hagerman, F.C. 'Physiology and nutrition for rowing' in *Perspectives in exercise science and sports medicine*, vol. 7, *Physiology and nutrition for competitive sport*, eds D.R. Lamb, N.G. Knuttgen and R. Murray, Cooper Publishing Group, 1994, pp. 221–302

Kyle, C.R. 'The mechanics and aerodynamics of cycling' in *Medical and scientific aspects of cycling*, eds E.R. Burke and M.M. Newsom, Human Kinetics, Champaign, Illinois, 1988, pp. 235–51

Martin, D.E. and Coe, P.N. *Training distance runners*, Leisure Press, Champaign, Illinois, 1991

Martin, D.T., Hahn, A.G., Ryan, R.K. and Smith, J.G. 'Why did members of the 1996 Olympic team pre-cool before competition? Research behind the "Aussie ice jacket"' AIS internal research report, 1996

McCole, S.D., Claney, K., Conte, J.C., Anderson, R. and Hagberg, J.M. 'Energy expenditure during bicycling' *Journal of Applied Physiology* 68: 748–53, 1990

Mitchell, J.B. and Huston, J.S. 'The effect of a high- and low-intensity warm-up on the physiological responses to a standardized swim and tethered swim performance' *Journal of Sports Sciences* 11: 159–65, 1993

Myler, G.R., Hahn, A.G. and Tumilty, D. 'The effect of preliminary skin cooling on performance of rowers in hot conditions' *Excel* 6: 17–20, 1989

Olds, T., Norton, K., Craig, N., Olive, S. and Lowe, E. 'The limits of the possible: Models of power supply and demand in cycling' *Australian Journal of Science and Medicine in Sport* 27: 29–33, 1995

Palmer, G.S., Hawley, J.A., Dennis, S.C. and Noakes, T.D. 'Heart rate response during a 4-d cycle stage race' *Medicine and Science in Sports and Exercise* 26: 1278–83, 1994

Palmer, G.A., Noakes, T.D. and Hawley, J.A. 'Effects of steady-state versus stochastic exercise on subsequent cycling performance' *Medicine and Science in Sports and Exercise* 25: 684–7, 1997

Parsons, L. and Day, S.J. 'Do wetsuits affect swimming speed?' *British Journal of Sports Medicine* 20: 129–31, 1986

Robinson, S., Robinson, D.L., Mountjoy, R.J. and Bullard, R.W. 'Influence of fatigue on the efficiency of men during exhausting runs' *Journal of Applied Physiology* 12: 197–201, 1958

Sharp, R.L. and Costill, D.L. 'Influence of body hair removal on physiological responses during breaststroke swimming' *Medicine and Science in Sports and Exercise* 21: 576–80, 1989

Starling, R.D., Costill, D.L., Trappe, T.A., Jozsi, A.C., Trappe, S.W. and Goodpaster, B.H. 'Effect of swimming suit design on the energy demands of swimming' *Medicine and Science in Sports and Exercise* 27: 1086–89, 1995

Tatterson, A., Martin, D.T., Marsh, S., Miller, K., Corbett, A., Boston, T., Hahn, A.G. and Febbraio, M.A. 'Effect of heat and humidity on laboratory time trial performance in elite road cyclists'. Sports Medicine Australia Conference Proceedings, October 1996

Chapter 10 The training diet

American Dietetic Association and Canadian Dietetic Association, 'Position stand on nutrition for physical fitness and athletic performance for adults' *Journal of the American Dietetic Association* 93: 691–6, 1993

Brand-Miller, J., Foster-Powell, K. and Colagiuri, S. *The G.I. factor*, Hodder & Stoughton, Sydney, 1996

Burke, L.M. 'Nutrition for the female athlete' in *Nutrition in women's health,* eds D. Krummel and P. Kris-Etherton, Aspen Publishers, Maryland, 1995, pp. 263–98

Burke, L.M. 'Dietary carbohydrates' in *IOC Encyclopedia of Sports Medicine*, ed. R.J. Maughan (in press)

Foster-Powell, K. and Brand-Miller, J. 'International tables of glycemic index' *American Journal of Clinical Nutrition* 62 (Supplement): 871–93, 1995

Hawley, J.A., Brouns, F. and Jeukendrup, A.E. 'Strategies to enhance fat utilisation during exercise' *Sports Medicine* 25:00-00 (in press)

Lambert, E.V., Speechly, D.S., Dennis, S.C. and Noakes, T.D. 'Enhanced endurance performance during moderate intensity exercise following 2 weeks adaptation to a high-fat diet in trained cyclists' *European Journal of Applied Physiology*, 69: 287–93, 1994

Muoio, D.M., Leddy, J.L., Horvath, P.J., Awad, A.B. and Pendergast, D.R. 'Effect of dietary fat on metabolic adjustments to maximal VO_{2max} and endurance in runners' *Medicine and Science in Sports and Exercise*, 26: 81–8, 1994

National Health and Medical Research Council, *Dietary guidelines for Australians*, Australian Government Publishing Service, Canberra, 1992

Phinney, S.D., Bistrian, B., Evans, W.J., Gervino, E. and Blackburn, G.L. 'The human metabolic response to chronic ketosis without caloric restriction: preservation of submaximal exercise capability with reduced carbohydrate oxidation' *Metabolism*, 32: 769–76, 1983

Sherman, W.M. and Leenders, N. 'Fat loading: the next magic bullet?' *International Journal of Sport Nutrition*, 5 (suppl): S1–S12, 1995

van Zyl, C., Lambert, E.V., Noakes, T.D., Hawley, J.A., Bosch, A.B. and Dennis, S.C. 'Effects of medium-chain triacylglycerol ingestion on carbohydrate metabolism and cycling performance' *Journal of Applied Physiology*, 80: 2217–25, 1996

Wolever, T.M.S. 'The glycemic index' *World Review of Nutrition and Dietetics* 62: 120–85, 1990

Chapter 11   Changing body size and shape

Brownell, K.D., Rodin, J. and Wilmore, J.H. *Eating, body weight and performance in athletes: Disorders of modern society*, Lea and Febiger, Philadelphia, 1992

Burke, L.M. 'Sport and body fatness' in *Exercise and obesity*, eds A.P. Hills and M.L. Wahlqvist, Gordon-Smith, London, 1994, pp. 213–28

Flynn, M.L., Costill, D.L., Kirwan, J.P., Mitchell, J.B., Houmard, J.A., Fink, W.J., Beltz, J.D. and D'Acquisto, L.J. 'Fat storage in athletes: Metabolic and hormonal responses to swimming and running' *International Journal of Sports Medicine* 11: 433–40, 1990

Jang, K.T., Flynn, M.G., Costill, D.L., Kirwan, J.P., Houmard, J.A., Mitchell, J.B. and D'Acquisto, L.J. 'Energy balance in competitive swimmers and runners' *Journal of Swimming Research* 3: 19–23, 1987

Kerr, D. 'Kinanthropometry' in *Clinical sports nutrition*, eds L.H.

Burke and V. Deakin, McGraw-Hill, Sydney, 1994, pp. 74–103

Lemon, P.W.R. 'Effect of exercise on protein requirements' *Journal of Sports Science* (special issue) 9: 53–70, 1990

Steen, S.N. and Brownell, K.D. 'Patterns of weight loss and regain in wrestlers: Has the tradition changed?' *Medicine and Science in Sports and Exercise* 22: 762–8, 1990

Chapter 12 Pre-event nutrition

Burke, L.M. 'Rehydration strategies before and after exercise' *Australian Journal of Nutrition and Dietetics* (Supplement 4), 53: S22–26, 1996

Febbraio, M.A. and Stewart, K.L. 'Carbohydrate feedings before prolonged exercise: Effect of glycemic index on muscle glycogenolysis and exercise performance' *Journal of Applied Physiology* 81: 1115–20, 1996

Foster, C., Costill, D.L. and Fink, W.J. 'Effects of preexercise feedings on endurance performance' *Medicine and Science in Sports* 11: 1–5, 1979

Hawley, J.A. and Burke, L.M. 'Effect of meal frequency and timing on physical performance' *British Journal of Nutrition* (Supplement 1), 77: S91–103, 1997

Hawley, J.A., Schabort, E.J., Noakes, T.D. and Dennis, S.C. 'Carbohydrate loading and exercise performance. An update' *Sports Medicine* 24: 73–81, 1997

Hitchins, S., Burke, L., Fallon, K., Yates, K., Tatterson, A., Dobson, G.P. and Martin, D.T. 'Hyperhydration with glycerol improves cycling time-trial performance in hot humid conditions.' Proceedings of Australian Conference of Science and Medicine in Sport, Canberra, 1996

Kristal-Boneh, E., Glusman, J.G., Shitrit, R., Chaemovitz, C. and Cassuto, Y. 'Physical performance and heat tolerance after chronic water loading and heat acclimation' *Aviation Space and Environmental Medicine* 66: 733–8, 1995

Sherman, W.M. 'Pre-event nutrition' *Gatorade Sports Science Exchange* 12(2), 1989

Sherman, W.M., Costill, D.L., Fink, W.J. and Miller J.M. 'Effect of diet-exercise manipulation on muscle glycogen and its subsequent utilisation during performance' *International Journal of Sports Medicine* 2: 114–18, 1981

Thomas, D.E., Brotherhood, J.R. and Brand, J.C. 'Carbohydrate feeding before exercise: Effect of glycemic index,' *International Journal of Sports Medicine* 12: 180–6, 1991

Chapter 13 Fluid and fuel intake for competition and training

American College of Sports Medicine 'Position stand on the prevention of thermal injuries during distance running' *Medicine and Science in Sports and Exercise*, 19: 529–33, 1987

American College of Sports Medicine 'Position stand on exercise and fluid replacement' *Medicine and Science in Sports and Exercise*, 28: i–vii, 1996

Below, P.R., Mora-Rodriguez, R., Gonzalez-Alonso, J. and Coyle, E.F, 'Fluid and carbohydrate ingestion independently improve performance during 1 h of intense exercise' *Medicine and Science in Sports and Exercise*, 27: 200–10, 1994

Burke, L.M. and Hawley, J.A. 'Fluid practices in team sports: guidelines for optimal practices' *Sports Medicine*, 24: 38–54, 1997

Coggan, A.R. 'Plasma glucose metabolism during exercise in humans' *Sports Medicine*, 11, 102–24, 1991

Coggan, A.R. and Coyle, E.F. 'Carbohydrate ingestion during prolonged exercise: effects on metabolism and performance', in J.O. Hollosy, (ed.) *Exercise and Sports Science Reviews*, 19: 1–40, 1991

Coyle, E.F., Coggan, A.R., Hemmert, M.K. and Ivy, J.L. 'Muscle glycogen utilisation during prolonged strenuous exercise when fed carbohydrate', *Journal of Applied Physiology*, 61: 165–72, 1986

Coyle, E.F. and Montain, S.J. 'Benefits of fluid replacement with carbohydrate during exercise' *Medicine and Science in Sports and Exercise*, 24 (9: Suppl): S324–S330, 1992

Hawley, J.A., Dennis, S.C. and Noakes, T.D. 'Carbohydrate, fluid and electrolyte requirements during prolonged exercise' in C.V. Kies and J.A. Driskell (eds) *Sports nutrition: minerals and electrolytes* Boca Raton: CRC Press, pp. 235–65, 1995

Jeukendrup, A.E., Brouns, F., Wagenmakers, A.J.M. and Saris, W.H.M. 'Carbohydrate-electrolyte feedings improve 1-H time trial cycling performance' *International Journal of Sports Medicine*, 18: 125–9, 1997

Maughan, R.J. and Noakes, T.D. 'Fluid replacement and exercise stress' *Sports Medicine*, 12: 16–31, 1991

Millard-Stafford, M., Rosskopf, L.B., Snow, T.K. and Hinson, B.T. 'Water versus carbohydrate-electrolyte ingestion before and during a 15-km run in the heat' *International Journal of Sport Nutrition*, 7: 26–38, 1997

Montain, S.J. and Coyle, E.F. 'The influence of graded dehydration on hyperthermia and cardiovascular drift during exercise' *Journal of Applied Physiology*, 73: 1340–50, 1992

Noakes, T.D. 'The hyponatremia of exercise' *International Journal of Sport Nutrition*, 2: 205–28, 1992

Noakes, T.D., Adams, B.A., Myburg, K.H., Greef, C., Lotz, T. and Nathan, H. 'The danger of inadequate water intake during prolonged exercise' *European Journal of Applied Physiology*, 57: 210–19, 1987

Noakes, T.D., Rehrer, N.J. and Maughan, R.J. 'The importance of volume in regulating gastric emptying' *Medicine and Science in Sports and Exercise*, 23: 307–13, 1991

Palmer, G.S. Clancy, M.C., Hawley, J.A., Rodger, I.M. and Burke, L.M. 'Carbohydrate ingestion does not improve 20 km time trial performance in well trained cyclists' *International Journal of Sports Medicine* (in press, 1988)

Sawka, M.N. and Pandolf, K.B. 'Effects of water loss on physiological function and exercise performance' in C.V. Gisolfi and D.R. Lamb *Perspectives in exercise science and sports medicine Volume 3: Fluid homeostasis during exercise.* Carmel, Indiana: Benchmark Press, 1990, pp. 1–38

Chapter 14 Eating for recovery

Burke, L.M., Collier, G.R. and Hargreaves, M. 'Muscle glycogen storage following prolonged exercise: Effect of the glycaemic index of carbohydrate feedings' *Journal of Applied Physiology* 75: 1019–23, 1993

Burke, L.M., Collier, G.R., Beasley, S.K., Davis, P.G., Fricker, P.A., Heeley, P., Walder, K. and Hargreaves, M. 'Effect of coingestion of fat and protein with carbohydrate feedings on muscle glycogen storage' *Journal of Applied Physiology* 78: 2187–92, 1995

Burke, L.M., Collier, G.R., Davis, P.G., Fricker, P.A., Sanigorski, A.J. and Hargreaves, M. 'Muscle glycogen storage following prolonged exercise: Effect of the frequency of carbohydrate feedings' *American Journal of Clinical Nutrition* 64: 115–19, 1996

Carter, J.E. and Gisolfi, C.V. 'Fluid replacement during and after exercise in the heat' *Medicine and Science in Sports and Exercise* 21: 532–9, 1989

Costill, D.L., Sherman, W.M., Fink, W.J., Maresh, C., Witten, M. and Miller, J.M. 'The role of dietary carbohydrates in muscle glycogen resynthesis after strenuous running' *American Journal of Clinical Nutrition* 34: 1831–6, 1981

Coyle, E.F., 'Timing and method of increased carbohydrate intake to cope with heavy training, competition and recovery' *Journal of Sports Sciences* (Special issue) 9: 29–52, 1991

Gonzalez-Alonso, J., Heaps, C.L. and Coyle, E. 'Rehydration after exercise with common beverages and water' *International Journal of Sports Medicine* 13: 399–406, 1992

Greenleaf, J.E., 'Problem: Thirst, drinking behaviour, and involuntary dehydration' *Medicine and Science in Sports and Exercise* 24: 645–56, 1992

Hubbard, R.W., Szlyk, P.C. and Armstrong, L.E. 'Influence of thirst and fluid palatability on fluid ingestion during exercise' in *Perspectives in exercise science and sports medicine*, vol. 3, *Fluid homeostasis during exercise*, eds C.V. Gisolfi and D.R. Lamb, Benchmark Press, Carmel, Indiana, 1990, pp. 39–96

Ivy, J.L. 'Muscle glycogen synthesis before and after exercise' *Sports Medicine* 11: 6–19, 1991

Ivy, J.L., Katz, A.L., Cutler, C.L., Sherman, W.M. and Coyle, E.F. 'Muscle glycogen synthesis after exercise: Effect of time of carbohydrate ingestion' *Journal of Applied Physiology* 64: 1480–85, 1988

Ivy, J.L., Lee, M.C., Bronzinick, J.T. and Reed, M.C. 'Muscle glycogen storage following different amounts of carbohydrate ingestion' *Journal of Applied Physiology* 65: 2018–23, 1988

Maughan, R.J. and Leiper, J.B. 'Sodium intake and post-exercise rehydration in man' *European Journal of Applied Physiology* 71: 311–19, 1995

Maughan, R.J., Leiper, J.B. and Shirreffs, S.M. 'Restoration of fluid balance after exercise-induced dehydration: Effects of food and fluid intake' *European Journal of Applied Physiology* 73: 317–25, 1996

Nadel, E.R., Mack, G.W. and Nose, H.N. 'Influence of fluid replacement beverages on body fluid homeostasis during exercise and recovery' in *Perspectives in exercise science and sports medicine*, vol. 3, *Fluid homeostasis during exercise*, eds C.V. Gisolfi and D.R. Lamb, Benchmark Press, Carmel, Indiana, 1990, pp. 181–205

O'Brien, C.P. 'Alcohol and sport: Impact of social drinking

on recreational and competitive sports performance' *Sports Medicine* 15: 71–77, 1993

Riebe, D., Maresh, C.M., Armstrong, L.E., Kenefick, R.W., Castellani, J.W., Echegaray, M.E., Clark, B.A. and Camaione, D.N. 'Effect of oral and intravenous rehydration on ratings of perceived exertion and thirst' *Medicine and Science in Sports and Exercise* 29: 117–24, 1997

Shirreffs, S.M. and Maughan, R.J. 'The effect of alcohol consumption on fluid retention following exercise-induced dehydration in man' *Journal of Physiology* 489: 33P–34P, 1995

Shirreffs, S.M., Taylor, A.J., Leiper, J.B. and Maughan, R.J. 'Post-exercise rehydration in man: Effects of volume consumed and sodium content of ingested fluids' *Medicine and Science in Sports and Exercise* 28: 1260–71, 1996

Zawadzki, K.M., Yaspelkis, B.B. and Ivy, J.L. 'Carbohydrate-protein complex increases the rate of muscle glycogen storage after exercise' *Journal of Applied Physiology* 72: 1854–9, 1992

Chapter 15 The tired athlete

Costill, D.L., Flynn, M.G., Kirwan, J.P., Houmard, J.A., Mitchell, J.B., Thomas, R.T and Park, S.H. 'Effects of repeated days of intensified training on muscle glycogen and swimming performance' *Medicine and Science in Sports and Exercise* 20: 249–54, 1988

Costill, D.L., Miller, J.M. 'Nutrition for endurance sport: Carbohydrate and fluid balance' *International Journal of Sports Medicine* 1: 2–14, 1980

Deakin, V. 'Iron deficiency in athletes: Identification, prevention and dietary treatment' in *Clinical sports nutrition*, eds L.M. Burke and V. Deakin, McGraw-Hill, Sydney, 1994, pp. 174–99

Haymes, E.M. and Lamanca, J.J. 'Iron loss in runners during exercise: Implications and recommendations' *Sports Medicine* 7: 277–85, 1989

Kirwan, J.P., Costill, D.L., Mitchell, J.B., Houmard, J.A., Flynn, M.G., Fink, W.J. and Beltz, J.D. 'Carbohydrate balance in competitive runners during successive days of intense training' *Journal of Applied Physiology* 65: 2601–6, 1988

Lamb, D.R., Rinehardt, K.R., Bartels, R.L., Sherman, W.M. and Snook, J.T. 'Dietary carbohydrate and intensity of interval swim training' *American Journal of Clinical Nutrition* 52: 1058–63, 1990

Sherman, W.M., Doyle, J.A., Lamb, D.R. and Strauss, H. 'Dietary carbohydrate, muscle glycogen, and exercise performance during 7 d of training' *American Journal of Clinical Nutrition* 57: 27–31, 1993

Sherman, W.M. and Wimer, GS. 'Insufficient dietary carbohydrate during training: Does it impair athletic performance?' *International Journal of Sport Nutrition* 1: 28–44, 1991

Simonsen, J.C., Sherman, W.M., Lamb, D.R., Dernbach, A.R., Doyle, J.A. and Strauss, R. 'Dietary carbohydrate, muscle glycogen and power output during rowing training' *Journal of Applied Physiology* 70: 1500–5, 1991

Chapter 16 Pills, potions and supplements

Burke, L.M. and Heeley, P. 'Dietary supplements and nutritional ergogenic aids in sport' in *Clinical sports nutrition*, eds L.M. Burke and V. Deakin, McGraw-Hill, Sydney, 1994, pp. 227–84

Greenhaff, P.L. 'Creatine and its application as an ergogenic aid' *International Journal of Sport Nutrition* 5: S100–10, 1995

Matson, L.G. and Tran, Z.T. 'Effects of sodium bicarbonate ingestion on anaerobic performance: A meta-analytic review' *International Journal of Sport Nutrition* 3: 2–28, 1993

Maughan, R.J. 'Creatine supplementation and exercise performance' *International Journal of Sport Nutrition* 5: 94–101, 1995

Sears, B. and Lawren, B. *Entering the Zone*, Harper Collins, New York, 1995

Spriet, L.L. 'Caffeine and performance' *International Journal of Sport Nutrition* 5: S84–99, 1995

Spriet, L.L. 'Ergogenic aids: Recent advances and retreats' in *Perspectives in exercise science and sports medicine*, vol. 10 *Optimising sports performance*, eds D.R. Lamb and R. Murray, Cooper Publishing Company, Carmel Indiana, 1997, pp. 185–234

Chapter 17 Where's the proof? Evaluating claims for new products or training interventions

Jeukendrup, A., Saris, W.H.M., Brouns, F. and Kester, A.D.M. 'A new validated endurance performance test' *Medicine and Science in Sports and Exercise* 27: 266–70, 1995

Palmer, G.S., Dennis, S.C., Noakes, T.D. and Hawley, J.A. 'Assessment of the reproducibility of performance testing on an air-braked cycle ergometer' *International Journal of Sports Medicine* 17: 293–8, 1996

Robertson, R.J. 'Introductory notes on validation and applications of ergogenics' in *Perspectives in exercise science and sports medicine*, vol. 4, *Ergogenics—enhancement of performance in exercise and sport*, eds R.D. Lamb and M.H. Williams, Cooper Publishing Company, Carmel, Indiana, 1991, pp. xvii–xxii

Schabort, E.J., Hawley, J.A. and Hopkins, W.G. 'Reliability of performance testing on the Concept II rowing ergometer' *Journal of Sports Sciences* (in press), 1998

Chapter 18 The limits to human performance: Where to from here?

Hawley, J.A. and Schabort, E.J. 'The limits to athletic performance: A physiological perspective' *South African Journal of Sports Medicine* 3: 7–12, 1996

Joyner, M.J. 'Physiological limiting factors and distance running: Influence of gender and age on record performances' in J.O. Holloszy (ed.), *Exercise and Sports Science Reviews* 21: 103–33, 1993

Morton, R.H. 'The supreme runner. What evidence now?' *Australian Journal of Sports Science* 3: 7–10, 1985

Péronnet, F. and Thibault, G. 'Mathematical analysis of running performance and world records' *Journal of Applied Physiology* 67: 453–65, 1989

Ryder, H.W., Carr, H.J. and Herget, P. 'Future performance in footracing' *Scientific American* 234: 109–19, 1976

Seiler, S. and Sailer, S. 'The gender gap in running performance—Shrinking, shrinking . . . now widening again!' *Sportsscience news* (Training & Technology), March–April 1997, http://www.org/traintech

Speechly, D.P., Taylor, S.R. and Rogers, G.G. 'Differences in ultra-endurance exercise in performance-matched male and female runners' *Medicine and Science in Sports and Exercise* 28: 359–65, 1996

zur Megede, E. and Hymans, R. *Progression of world best performances and official IAAF world records*, Multiprint, Monaco, 1996

Index